CONGREGATION B'NAI TORAH

ERU... P9-DHO-677

JEWISH
POWER

JEWISH POWER

Inside the
American Jewish
Establishment

J.J. GOLDBERG

ADDISON-WESLEY PUBLISHING COMPANY, INC.
Reading, Massachusetts   Menlo Park, California
New York   Don Mills, Ontario   Harlow, England
Amsterdam   Bonn   Sydney   Singapore   Tokyo   Madrid
San Juan   Paris   Seoul   Milan   Mexico City   Taipei

Many of the designations used by manufacturers and sellers to distinguish their
products are claimed as trademarks. Where those designations appear in this book
and Addison-Wesley was aware of a trademark claim, the designations have been
printed in initial capital letters.

Library of Congress Cataloging-in-Publication Data

Goldberg, J.J. (Jonathan Jeremy)
Jewish power : inside the American Jewish establishment / J.J. Goldberg.
p.   cm.
Includes bibliographical references and index.
ISBN 0-201-62242-4
1. Jews—United States—Politics and government.   2. Jews in
public life—United States.   3. Jews—United States—Attitudes toward Israel.
4. United States—Ethnic relations.   I. Title.
E184.J5G615   1996
305.892′4073—dc20   96-24541
                                                        CIP

Copyright © 1996 by J.J. Goldberg

All rights reserved. No part of this publication may be reproduced, stored in a retrieval
system, or transmitted, in any form or by any means, electronic, mechanical,
photocopying, recording, or otherwise, without the prior written permission of the
publisher. Printed in the United States of America. Published simultaneously in Canada.

Jacket design by Jean Seal
Text design by Helene Berinsky
Set in 11-point New Caledonia by Pagesetters

1   2   3   4   5   6   7   8   9-MA-0099989796
First printing, September 1996

TO SHIFRA,
who makes all things possible.

CONTENTS

ACKNOWLEDGMENTS

Many writers acknowledge a mentor who started them on their paths. Few, surely, have been given the kind of help that I have received from my friend and teacher, Joseph Telushkin. More than anyone, he has been responsible for turning this reporter into an author.

My agent, Richard Pine, offered invaluable support and counsel at each stage of this project, keeping me focused on the target and helping me to navigate the world of publishing. My editor at Addison-Wesley, Henning Gutmann, provided essential insights and a steady hand to steer the book to completion. Nicole Cormen, my copy editor, brought a searching eye for detail and a fine stylist's pen to my manuscript. Thanks are due, too, to the able staff of Addison-Wesley Publishing Company, particularly to Pat Jalbert, senior production supervisor, who was my guardian angel and became my friend.

Nessa Rapoport launched this project by suggesting the original concept to me. Adam Bellow helped me to develop the idea into a book proposal. Didi Goldenhar pointed me in the right direction at the outset.

Substantial portions of this book are derived from my work as a reporter. I am indebted to the editors who have worked with me and helped me to learn the journalist's craft: Phillip Ritzenberg, Sheldon Engelmayer, and Gary Rosenblatt at the New York *Jewish Week*; Joseph Millis at the London *Jewish Chronicle*; Seth Lipsky at the *Forward*; and Hirsh Goodman, David Horovitz, and Sharon Ashley at the *Jerusalem Report*. Thanks, too, to Howard Goldberg and Mitchel Levitas at the *New York Times*.

Many people contributed to this book by sharing their expertise with me, both on and off the record. I am especially grateful for their patience and kindness to Morris Amitay, Arnold Aronson, Phil Baum, Hyman Bookbinder, Marshall Breger, Eugene Byrd, Shoshana Cardin, Albert Chernin, Toby Dershowitz, Tom Dine, Abba Eban, Stuart Eizenstat, Eugene Fisher, Arnold Forster, Abraham Foxman, David Gelber, Dan Glickman, Jerry Goodman, David Harris, Arthur Hertzberg, Malcolm Hoenlein, Jess Hordes, Frances Horowitz, Stephen D. Isaacs, Mendel Kaplan, Frank Lautenberg, Irving Levine, Jacqueline Levine, Nita Lowey, David Luchins, Will Maslow, Israel

Miller, Aryeh Neier, Mohamed al-Orabi, Martin Peretz, Michael Perry, Gail Pressberg, William Quandt, Peter Rodman, A.M. Rosenthal, David Saperstein, Hideo Sato, Richard Schifter, Alexander Schindler, Henry Siegman, Howard Squadron, Jacob Stein, Marc Stern, Mark Talisman, Mike Wallace, and James Zogby.

My research was aided enormously by the capable staff of the Jacob Blaustein Library at the American Jewish Committee, Cyma Horowitz, Michele Anish, and Esther Eidensohn. My thanks, too, to Gerald Nagel at the United Jewish Appeal and to Frank Strauss, Jerry Rosen, and Norbert Fruehof at the Council of Jewish Federations, for helping to track down key bits of information.

I owe a deep debt of gratitude to the good friends who have watched Jewish politics with me over the years, traded theories with me, encouraged me when I was right and corrected me when I was wrong: Arlene Agus, Daniel Allen, David Arnow, Maggie Bar-Tura, Jacob Bender, Donna Bojarsky, Arik Carmon, Jerome Chanes, Steven M. Cohen, Larry Cohler, Sara Ehrman, Danny Goldberg, Bethamie Horowitz, Jonathan Jacoby, Gideon Mark, Moshe Nativ, Winston Pickett, Letty Cottin Pogrebin, David Pollock, William Rapfogel, M.J. Rosenberg, Menachem Rosensaft, Yuval Rotem, Uriel Savir, Stuart Schoffman, Myrna Shinbaum, Mark Sofer, David Twersky, Howard Weisband, and David Zwiebel.

Jerome Chanes, Nancy Hennessee, David Luchins, Mark Seal, Lawrence Sternberg, and David Szonyi generously read the manuscript and shared their insights with me. Dvorah Menashe Telushkin has been a muse and kindred spirit. Mark Seal has been my friend, colleague, and sounding board since our college days; his counsel and good humor have kept me going through many adventures.

My father, the late Arthur M. Goldberg, was my primary teacher and inspiration in all things political and moral. He would have loved to see this book, and I am sorry he could not. My mother, Lee Goldberg, has continued to swap ideas and tall tales with me over the years, and our conversations cheered me during many long writing days. My siblings, Maggie, Josh, and Deb, have all been tremendously supportive, in their own special ways, throughout this project.

Most of all I thank Shifra Bronznick, my best friend and partner in every sense of the word. She has stood by me and shared every step in this process, unstinting in her generosity, honesty, and encouragement. Our daughter, Emma, who entered our lives midway through the project, has made my life a constant delight; her zest for life helped me bring this work to completion. Without my two pies, Shifra and Emma, this book would not have been possible.

ACRONYMS OF JEWISH ORGANIZATIONS

AJC: May refer to American Jewish Committee or American Jewish Congress. "The two AJC's" means both AJCommittee and AJCongress. When no other context appears, AJC alone refers to the American Jewish Committee.

ADL: Anti-Defamation League

AIPAC: American Israel Public Affairs Committee

ARZA: Association of Reform Zionists of America

CAMERA: Committee for Accuracy in Middle East Reporting in America

CJF: Council of Jewish Federations

CRC: Community relations committee OR community relations council. The community-relations (or "defense") arm of a local Jewish welfare federation.

HIAS: Hebrew Immigrant Aid Society

JCRC: Jewish community relations council OR committee. Synonymous with CRC (see above).

JDC: American Jewish Joint Distribution Committee

NCRAC: Originally, National Community Relations Advisory Council. In 1971, its name was changed to National *Jewish* Community Relations Advisory Council, or NJCRAC. For simplicity's sake, I use the form NCRAC throughout this book.

NCSJ: National Conference on Soviet Jewry

ORT: *Obshtchesvo Rasprostranenia Truda* (society for rehabilitative labor), a Russian-Jewish trade-school network founded in 1880. Adopted the name Organization for Rehabilitation through Training after headquarters were relocated to U.S. in 1924; now operates trade schools worldwide, mainly in Israel.

OU: Orthodox Union (Union of Orthodox Jewish Congregations of America)

RAC: Religious Action Center of Reform Judaism

UAHC: Union of American Hebrew Congregations (the Reform synagogue union)

UJA: United Jewish Appeal for Overseas Relief

WZO: World Zionist Organization

ZOA: Zionist Organization of America

PROLOGUE

"Up Against Some Powerful Political Forces"

SHORTLY AFTER NOON on Thursday, September 12, 1991, President George Bush stepped up to the podium in the White House briefing room and addressed a special press conference on the Middle East. It would prove to be one of the turning points of his presidency: the day he locked horns with the American Jewish community.

The president had called the reporters together to discuss a delicate diplomatic maneuver in the Middle East peace process, the fragile centerpiece of his post–Cold War foreign policy. A week earlier, the government of Israel had asked Washington to guarantee $10 billion in Israeli commercial loans, to be drawn over the next five years. Bush planned to say no.

Israel, already America's largest foreign-aid recipient, wanted the huge new credit line in order to finance the resettlement of Jewish refugees streaming out of the collapsing Soviet Union. Bush had long championed the cause of Soviet Jewish emigration, but the timing of this latest request from Jerusalem was wrong, he told the reporters. He was hoping to convene an unprecedented Israel-Arab peace conference in Madrid in the coming weeks, after years of patiently nudging both sides toward the table. At this point, he was eager not to anger Arab leaders by showering sudden new largesse on Israel.

Accordingly, Bush announced that he was asking Congress to delay action on the loan guarantees for 120 days. However, he said, he was "up against some powerful political forces" bent on thwarting his will. Congress, in fact, appeared to be on the verge of approving the loan guarantees without him.

"I heard today there were something like a thousand lobbyists on the

Hill working the other side of the question," the president barked, pounding his fist on the podium with an anger usually reserved for foreign despots and congressional Democrats. "We've got one lonely little guy down here doing it."

The "political forces" confronting the president at that moment were about thirteen hundred leaders of local Jewish organizations from across the country. A gaggle of rabbis and schoolteachers, lawyers, social workers, and businesspeople, they had come to Washington for the day to discuss the loan guarantees with their elected representatives. Fanning out across Capitol Hill, the citizen-lobbyists were blanketing Congress with a single, passionate message: that the "humanitarian" cause of Soviet Jewish freedom should not be held hostage to the "political" vagaries of the Middle East peace process.

Bush's own Middle East experts, many of whom were Jews themselves, insisted that the goal of bringing peace to the war-torn Middle East was at least as humanitarian as resettling the Soviet refugees. But Congress seemed firmly aligned with the lobbyists. Today's blitz was the climax of a four-month lobbying campaign for the loan guarantees, which had garnered enough support to carry both houses of Congress—enough, in fact, not only to carry Congress, but to threaten Bush with the first veto override of his presidency, should he choose to press the point. Instead, Bush was going over the heads of Congress directly to the American public, complaining on television about the "powerful political forces" lined up against the "lonely little guy" in the White House.

His outburst had its desired effect. Congressional support for the loan guarantees dissolved overnight. The leadership in both houses agreed to Bush's four-month moratorium.

But the presidential victory did not come without a cost.

Shoshana Cardin was sitting in a Washington hotel room reviewing the day's lobbying when word came of Bush's remarks. A Baltimore civic leader and professional volunteer, she headed up the powerful forces that the president was complaining about. Her precise title was chairman of the Conference of Presidents of Major American Jewish Organizations. Known to its members as the Presidents Conference, the group is a loose coalition of four dozen Jewish religious associations, civil rights agencies, welfare funds, and fraternal societies. It includes most of the groups that make up the dizzying alphabet soup of American Jewish community life, ranging from household names like B'nai B'rith, Hadassah, and the United Jewish Appeal to obscure factions like the Jewish Labor Committee and the Jewish Institute for National Security Affairs.

Cardin herself had spent much of her adult life volunteering for Jewish charities. A tough, canny organizational infighter, she had held some of the most prestigious positions in national Jewish philanthropy before being chosen to head the National Conference on Soviet Jewry. No one had been surprised by her election the previous December as the first woman to chair the Presidents Conference.

Cardin had met with George Bush several times over the years, and found him to be an earnest, decent, likable man. The last thing she expected to hear from his mouth was a public attack on the rights of Jews as American citizens. And yet, that was what she believed she was hearing right now. Bush had just issued the first-ever public assault on the American Jewish community by a sitting president in the history of the Republic. What the president had said, as she heard it, was that when Jews advocated their beliefs as citizens, they were somehow engaging in unacceptable civic behavior. In fact, Cardin angrily decided, it was the president whose behavior was unacceptable.

For a "lonely little guy," George Herbert Walker Bush was riding high at the beginning of September 1991. Despite a sluggish economy, his approval rating in the polls was around 70 percent, higher than any president in memory at this three-quarter point (his predecessor, Ronald Reagan, had had an approval rating of just 42 percent at the same point in his first term). The opposition Democrats, out of power for more than a decade, were divided, dispirited, and helpless. Bush had used his veto more often than any president before him, twenty-two times to date, and had never once been overridden. Election to a second term in fourteen months' time was generally considered a sure thing.

On the world stage, the president's profile appeared nothing less than heroic. The collapse of the Soviet empire over the previous year and a half had left him the presumptive victor in the Cold War, head of the world's only remaining superpower. Just eight months earlier, he had led the combined forces of the United Nations in a triumphant war against the Iraqi dictator Saddam Hussein.

Now Bush was ready to secure his place in history by going after the brass ring of world diplomacy: solving the insoluble Israel-Arab conflict. The time was ripe for it. The Arabs were divided and confused by Saddam's adventurism. More important, they no longer had the Soviet Union backing them in their stubborn, forty-year rejection of Israel. Bush believed they could be induced to make peace, if Israel agreed to sweeten the deal by giving back the disputed buffer territories it had captured in the Six-Day War of June 1967.

Israel, unfortunately, was not playing by the script. Much to the president's annoyance, Prime Minister Yitzhak Shamir refused even to discuss a land-for-peace swap. A lifelong hardliner, mistrustful of Arabs and dedicated to the vision of a "Greater Land of Israel," Shamir was currently spending every available penny in his strapped budget to settle Israeli citizens in the disputed territories.

But in this autumn of 1991, Bush thought he had something that Shamir wanted even more than land. Israel was being deluged with Jewish refugees fleeing the chaos in the Soviet Union. By 1995, the influx was expected to top 1 million persons—one fifth of the tiny nation's entire population. The costs of resettling them over the next decade were projected at $70 billion—double the entire Israeli gross national product. At the moment, therefore, Israel was in no position to argue over Bush's terms for the loan guarantees. Surely settling the West Bank was not as important as resettling the Soviet refugees. Or so Bush reasoned.

Shoshana Cardin tuned in to CNN at two o'clock that Thursday afternoon to watch a replay of the president's press conference. It confirmed what she had been told earlier: his tone and body language seemed clearly intended to suggest that he was a helpless victim, facing some powerful conspiracy. Cardin was appalled.

The Presidents Conference was created by its members in the mid-1950s to express American Jewry's "consensus support for Israel." Together with its sister organization, the Washington-based American Israel Public Affairs Committee (AIPAC)—the famed "Israeli lobby"—it could pack a considerable punch when it chose to. But while AIPAC is a registered lobbying organization with a reputation for scrappiness, the

Presidents Conference traditionally has tried to avoid confrontation. Nearly all its member agencies are nonprofit, tax-exempt religious and charitable bodies, legally barred from engaging in partisan politics.

The same no-politics rule applied on the Israeli scene, though for different reasons. American Jewish organizations span a broad spectrum of views on Israel-Arab relations, Palestinian rights, and trading land for peace. But they share a long tradition of refusing to question Israeli government policy decisions. The Presidents Conference had agreed at birth to put its internal divisions aside, on the grounds that the duty of American Jews was purely and simply to support Israel. After all, the logic went, it was Israelis who put their lives on the line every day. Therefore, Israelis alone had the right to decide their own fate, through their democratically elected government.

This rule had been tested in fire in 1977, when Israel ended decades of Labor Party rule by electing the nationalist militant Menachem Begin as its prime minister. The man who chaired the Presidents Conference at the time was the arch-liberal Rabbi Alexander Schindler, leader of Reform Judaism. Yet he had embraced Begin without a moment's hesitation, thus ensuring an unbroken relationship between American Jews and Israel.

Shoshana Cardin was determined to do no less. A devoted liberal, she had little sympathy for Shamir's policies. But the American Jewish community was defending Israel, not its current policies. And she was not going to let the American Jewish community be pushed around.

Working with her top staff aide, Presidents Conference director Malcolm Hoenlein, Cardin quickly prepared a statement for the press, decrying the president's verbal assault on citizen advocacy, a building block of American democracy. They released it at three o'clock to a poorly attended press conference.

Early Thursday evening, they flew to New York, where Cardin convened the leadership of the Presidents Conference the next morning to discuss Bush's tirade and approve a personal reply. As the leader of America's organized Jewish community, Cardin wrote, she deeply appreciated Bush's many efforts to help Jews in danger from Russia to Ethiopia. Nonetheless, his televised remarks the day before were "disturbing and subject to misinterpretation."

Back in Washington, a small group of White House staff members was beginning to share Cardin's distress. Apparently it was not just the organized Jewish leadership that saw Bush's words as an attack on Jews. More than a few non-Jewish citizens had heard the president's press conference as a call to battle against the "powerful Jews," and they were ready to take up his banner. It seemed that Bush had touched an unforeseen chord in the American heartland. Beginning on Friday, the White House began receiving congratulatory telegrams and phone calls praising the president for putting the Jews in their place. By Monday morning's mail, the president had accumulated a small mound of Jew-bashing congratulations. This was not what he had had in mind, his aides concurred.

Looking back afterward, Cardin agreed that Bush's anti-Jewish tone was unintended. "I think," she would say a year later, "that he intended to intimidate Congress, to be certain that foreign policy would not be established by the Senate. For him it was a political issue." For the Jewish community, though, "it became more than a political issue." It was a matter of the basic right of an American citizen to petition the government.

On Tuesday, September 17, an embarrassed Bush wrote back to "Dear Shoshana." After thanking her for acknowledging his record on freeing Soviet Jews, the president wrote, "I am concerned that some of my comments at the Thursday press conference caused apprehension within the Jewish community." He continued abjectly, saying his "references to lobbyists and powerful political forces were never meant to be pejorative in any sense. As a veteran of many years in the governmental and political arena, I have a great respect for the exercise of free expression in the democratic process."

The Conference of Presidents of Major American Jewish Organizations released the exchange of letters to the nation's hundred-odd Jewish community newspapers for immediate publication. With that, the affair seemed to be over.

It did not end there, however. The national leadership of the organized Jewish community may have forgiven the president, but across the country, the American Jew had done no such thing. Most of the nation's 6 million-odd Jews belong to no major organizations, rarely attend synagogue, and do not read Jewish community newspapers. The vast majority probably had never even heard of Shoshana Cardin, nor of the Presidents Conference.

But they knew who George Bush was. He was the man that two-thirds of Jewish voters had voted against in 1988, the New England WASP–cum–Bible Belt oilman who represented many of the forces repugnant to the liberal, urban, intellectual American Jew. The rest of America's middle class may have been charmed rightward by a decade of trickle-down Reaganomics, but not the Jews. As the sociologist Milton Himmelfarb once observed, Jews earned like Episcopalians, but they still voted like Puerto Ricans.

In truth, the Jews' political breakdown was not that simple. The Republicans had been making inroads into the Jewish vote for twenty years.

Jews are a valued electoral prize. Despite their tiny numbers—less than 3 percent of the population—they are considered a key swing bloc. They are concentrated in a few big states that control nearly half the Electoral College. Perhaps more important, they are prodigious givers, providing between one fourth and one half of all Democratic campaign funds.

Also vital, they are energetic volunteers. "All you have in Democratic campaigns are Catholics and Jews," says Democratic political consultant James Carville. "I don't know why, but it's a standing joke. You show me twenty-five staffers in a Democratic campaign and you'll have maybe three Protestants."

It was Richard Nixon who had first sensed the opportunity to turn the Jewish vote away from the Democrats. His strategy was to appeal to widespread Jewish anxiety over embattled Israel, surrounded by a hostile Third World and dependent on American arms and diplomacy. That, plus the ever growing tensions between the Jewish and black communities, once twin pillars of the post–New Deal Democratic coalition, had helped the Republicans to drive their share of the Jewish vote up steadily from the miserable 10 percent garnered by Barry Goldwater in 1964 to the 40 percent won by Ronald Reagan in 1980.

Top positions within the organized Jewish leadership went to Republicans during the Nixon years, for the first time in generations. A group of wealthy Republican business executives, led by Detroit oil millionaire Max Fisher, one of the GOP's biggest fund-raisers, became the leading spokespersons for American Jewry during the early 1970s. Throughout the 1970s and 1980s, Jewish conservatives often spoke of a new era of "realism" dawning in Jewish political activism.

Those Republican hopes seemed to come crashing down on September 12, 1991, as George Bush appealed to the American people for support against the "powerful political forces" undermining his policies.

Jews follow public affairs closely, perhaps more than most other ethnic or religious groups in America. "I don't know of any group in American politics that picks up things as fast as the American Jewish community," says James Carville. "It's an involved, educated group, and they're tonally very sensitive to what people say. So if the president goes out and attacks the lobby, they're going to be very sensitive."

For a great many Jews, then, Bush's September 12 press conference was like a blinding flash in the night that would not go away. Even the most assimilated American Jews, even those who never attended synagogue— even those who had married Christians and were raising their children as Christians—even they, by and large, instinctively recoiled at phrases like "powerful political forces." In sermons and speeches, in letters to the editor, in private conversations, Jews across America discussed George Bush throughout the fall of 1991. Some younger Jews recalled stories they had heard from their grandmothers about anti-Semitic mobs attacking Jewish villagers in Poland and Russia, inflamed by lurid stereotypes of "powerful" Jewish bankers, well-poisoners, Christ-killers. Older Jews recalled from their own experiences the anti-Semitic propaganda of the 1930s, manufactured by German diplomats and repeated by radio preachers in the Depression-ridden American heartland, depicting America's economic woes as the result of crafty schemes by Jewish bankers and bolsheviks to undermine and control American society.

The result was anger. Jews who had never voted Republican—the majority—smugly reminded one another why not. Jews who had switched to the Republican column during the Nixon and Reagan years suddenly considered switching back. Most of all, Jews of every political stripe began writing letters of protest to their newspapers, to their representatives, and to the White House.

"September 12 will go down in Jewish history as the day of the great betrayal," said Jacqueline Levine, a senior American Jewish Congress leader. "His statement was a disgusting display of, if not anti-Semitism, then something very close to it."

"That bastard opened my eyes," said Ed Ames, a Los Angeles entertainer. Ames had never joined a Jewish organization before. In September 1991 he mailed in his first dues payment to AIPAC and became a volunteer lobbyist for Israel.

Another Jewish political activist, prominent in the Chicago business community, added, "It set off a lightbulb. People everywhere began to mobilize."

White House aides watched the groundswell with dismay. Shoshana Cardin and the Presidents Conference repeated the same message to them: if you want to fix things, approve the loan guarantees. Bush refused. The loan guarantees were firmly linked to the peace process, and to Yitzhak Shamir's policy of settling Israelis in the disputed territories. It was a standoff, as frustrated Jewish lobbyists in Washington put it, between settling the territories and resettling the Soviet refugees.

Within the Bush administration, reactions to the blowup were mixed. Some officials, including Bush himself, were anxious to find a way of making amends, so long as it did not undermine the Middle East peace process. Stung by the accusations of anti-Semitism, Bush made time during a November fund-raising trip to New York to meet at length with the Presidents Conference and make peace. Plans were laid for a string of pro-Jewish gestures, whose results would quickly prove dramatic, almost historic. In December, the U.N. General Assembly would meet to rescind its hated 1975 resolution equating Zionism with racism, crowning a two-decade struggle by Israel's friends in Congress. In the spring, Syria would be induced to permit its closely restricted community of four thousand Jews to depart the country after years under lock and key.

On the other hand, some administration figures were openly weary of trying to appease an angry interest group that numbered, after all, less than 3 percent of the population. As the loan guarantee standoff continued into the winter of 1992, Bush's alter ego, Secretary of State James A. Baker III, tersely brushed aside suggestions for a GOP-Jewish rapprochement. "Fuck 'em," he was reported to say (though he denied it). "They don't vote for us anyway."

Baker's assertion was true, whether or not he used those words. But things were more complicated, as he should have realized.

On November 5, 1991, seven weeks after Bush's fateful press conference, America went to the polls for an off-year election that should have held few surprises. The one interesting race was a shoo-in contest in Pennsylvania, where a U.S. Senate seat had been opened up the previous spring by the accidental death of John Heinz, an attractive, moderate young Republican.

The GOP's candidate was the popular ex-governor, Richard Thornburgh, another moderate and one of President Bush's closest political allies. Thornburgh had been Bush's attorney general before resigning in June to run for the seat. His Democratic opponent was a little-known college professor, Harris Wofford, who had once served in the Kennedy administration. As of September 17, Thornburgh was forty-four points ahead in the polls.

On September 27, the *Philadelphia Inquirer* published the stunning results of a new statewide poll. Thornburgh's lead had suddenly dropped to twenty-four points and was continuing to fall. Incredibly, the race was now Wofford's to lose. According to the *Inquirer*, Wofford strategists attributed their candidate's sudden surge to his "support for national health insurance." In the weeks to come, the health-care theme would be picked up by the national media as Wofford's inexplicable surge turned into an even more inexplicable victory on November 5.

However, insiders in both campaigns say there was an additional, more mundane reason for the upset: money. Within a week after President Bush's September 12 press conference, Republican and Democratic fundraisers alike began noticing a distinct shift in donations away from Thornburgh and toward Wofford. Filings with the Federal Elections Commission were more precise: while Thornburgh's October 16 filing showed that his year-to-date fund-raising was twice that of Wofford, the Democrat reversed the trend in the campaign's final weeks and raised cash at twice Thornburgh's pace.

Donors with Jewish surnames, who had made up nearly 10 percent of Thornburgh's October 16 filing, were almost totally absent from his final report.

To be sure, the new surge of money did not give Wofford a new message. But for the first time, Wofford had the means to tell his story to the voters. What had happened was that from all across the country, outraged Jews (and some passionately pro-Israel Christians) were focusing their anger at George Bush on his friend Dick Thornburgh. The accidental beneficiary was Professor—soon to be Senator—Harris Wofford.

Shortly after losing the election, a shaken Thornburgh went to see his friend in the White House and discuss what he believed might be a new trend as the nation entered a presidential election year. "I reminded the president," he recalled later, "that where I grew up in the Pennsylvania coal country, the miners used to put a canary in a cage at the mouth of a shaft. If there was a methane gas leak in the shaft, the canary would be the first to die, and that was your warning that there was trouble coming. I told him, 'Mr. President, I'm your canary. You've got a leak, and if you don't do something about it, it's going to get you, too.' "

Of course, Thornburgh hastens to point out, much more than Jewish support was leaking from Bush's reelection campaign hopes during that fall of 1991. The nation was growing tired of Republican rule after eleven straight years. The economy was mired in a seemingly endless recession. Middle-class Americans were feeling insecure about their jobs for the first time. Wofford capitalized on this insecurity by focusing on the symbolic, emotionally charged issue of health-care reform.

Bush had no answers on the economy. He was also vulnerable on other domestic issues, most of all on abortion. Many voters were broadly suspicious of his cozy relationship with the religious right. His main strength, foreign policy, seemed increasingly irrelevant now that the Soviet threat was gone. All these elements were building like vapors in a mine, waiting to bring Bush down. Thornburgh was the first to fall.

Bush's September 12 press conference, along with the broader Jewish disaffection that it symbolized, was just one part of the picture—not the biggest, not the smallest. But the press conference did indeed "hurt Thornburgh bad," said James Carville, who served as Harris Wofford's campaign manager and went on to run Bill Clinton's presidential campaign. "It hurt Republicans in Jewish fund-raising. And we started raising a lot more money."

Wofford himself would say the Jewish community was only "one of three or four major factors" in his victory. The others, he says, were the fundraising efforts of the AFL-CIO and the Democratic Senatorial Campaign Committee, and the general softness of Bush's popularity.

But the AFL-CIO had been active from the beginning of the campaign; it hadn't been enough to dent Thornburgh's popularity. As for the Democratic Senatorial Campaign Committee, it had been staying out of the Pennsylvania race. The senators sensed that Wofford couldn't win. They were planning to marshal their funds for the tough fights of 1992.

It wasn't until the Wofford campaign suddenly showed signs of life, with the infusion of cash in late September, that the national party lined up and lifted him to his upset victory in November.

And that upset, Wofford says, "helped Bush collapse."

No, the Jewish community, comprising just 4.7 percent of the population of Pennsylvania, was not the dominant political force in the state that fall. It was one of several.

But the Jews were indisputably a powerful political force. George Bush was not wrong in believing that when he convened his September 12 press conference.

Bush's mistake was saying it aloud.

Part I

THE MEANING OF JEWISH POWER

CHAPTER 1

Introduction:
American Jews and Their Politics

H ISTORY WILL RECORD that as the twentieth century drew to a close, American Jews were facing a political crisis unprecedented in its scope and nature. For the first time in their three and a half centuries as a community in America—and perhaps for the first time since the dawn of the Jewish Diaspora, two thousand years ago—the Jews had no greater enemy than themselves.

This is not to say that Jews no longer had enemies in the late twentieth century. There still were those who clamored for the destruction of the Jewish people, as there had been for thousands of years. Anti-Semitism, sometimes called the world's oldest bigotry, was still alive and threatening in dozens of countries around the globe. Indeed, many prominent Jews, from American rabbis to Israeli politicians, warned at the end of the twentieth century that anti-Semitism was making a disturbing comeback. This came as a shock; the venomous bigotry was thought to have flamed out just a few decades earlier, in the ashes of the Second World War. Yet somehow it thrived.

Enemies continued, too, to threaten the state of Israel, created at mid-century as a haven for survivors of the Nazi Holocaust and as a spiritual center for Jews everywhere. Some of Israel's bitterest enemies, led by Islamic Iran, were within reach of acquiring nuclear weaponry. That might enable them to destroy the Jewish state with the touch of a button.

No, the threats had not ended. Still, a detached, fair-minded observer of Jewish life might well have concluded that the Jewish people had achieved a historic reversal of fortune at the close of the twentieth century, in America and around the world.

After all, it was just a half-century earlier that one of the world's greatest industrial powers had set out on a mechanized campaign to murder every Jew on earth. American Jews could only stand by, helpless. It had taken a world war to stop Germany's campaign of genocide. Even then, the Jews' survival was only incidental; saving Jews had not been a principal Allied war goal.

And yet, fifty years after its greatest catastrophe, the Jewish people had dusted itself off and won a place at the table of international decision-making. Jews had achieved power.

There was, of course, the sovereign power of the state of Israel, a smallish emerging nation with an outsized military reputation. But that was not the half of it: when diplomats and journalists spoke of Jewish power in the late twentieth century, they were usually speaking of the American Jewish community. It was here that the Jews had truly emerged as a power in their own right, acknowledged and respected around the world.

From the Vatican to the Kremlin, from the White House to Capitol Hill, the world's movers and shakers view American Jewry as a force to be reckoned with. At home the Jewish community is sought out as an ally—or confronted as a worthy rival—by political parties, labor unions, churches, and interest groups as diverse as the civil rights movement and the Christian Coalition. The New York offices of the American Jewish Committee and the Anti-Defamation League have become obligatory stops for presidents and prime ministers visiting the United Nations or passing through en route to Washington. More than a dozen foreign embassies in Washington have diplomats assigned to a semi-official "Jewish desk," in charge of maintaining friendly ties with the Jewish community.

"Part of the new mythos of American Jews is that we're not a minority anymore—we've become part of the majority, and psychologically, that means something fantastically subtle," says political scientist David Luchins, a vice president of the Union of Orthodox Jewish Congregations of America and senior aide to New York's Senator Daniel Patrick Moynihan. "We are accepted now. We have access. The president of the United States meets regularly with the Jewish leadership. There's an incredible thing. You look back on the last twenty-five or thirty years and you have to stand in awe that this really has happened—in my lifetime, it really happened. We have arrived."

As for concrete evidence of the Jewish community's clout, it is not hard to find. There is, to begin with, the $3 billion foreign-aid package sent each year to Israel. Fully one fifth of America's foreign aid has gone to a nation of barely 5 million souls, one tenth of 1 percent of the world's population. Analysts commonly credited this imbalance to the power of the Jewish lobby.

Coupled with financial aid is the familiar fact of Washington's staunch support for Israel in the diplomatic arena, at what sometimes seemed like great cost to America's own interests. And there have been threats to those in Washington who opposed Israeli policy: the senators and representatives sent down to defeat, like Charles Percy and Paul Findley, for defying the Jewish lobby.

But American Jewish power does not begin and end with Israel. Even more dramatic than foreign aid, perhaps, was the Jackson-Vanik amendment. Passed by Congress in 1974, it made U.S.-Soviet trade relations conditional on the Soviets' treatment of their Jewish minority. The amendment remained on the books even after the Soviet Union collapsed in 1990, effectively giving the Jewish community a veto over America's commercial links with Moscow.

Jewish power is felt, too, in a wide variety of domestic spheres: immigration and refugee policy, civil rights and affirmative action, abortion rights, church-state separation issues, and much more. Local Jewish communities from New York to Los Angeles have become major players on their own turf, helping to make the rules and call the shots on matters from health care to zoning.

Yes, by the end of the twentieth century, American Jewry has come to be viewed around the globe as a serious player in the great game of politics, able to influence events, to define and achieve important goals, to reward its friends and punish its enemies.

"If you talk about power in Washington or in the United States, you should put a great emphasis on the American Jewish community," said Mohamed al-Orabi, an Egyptian diplomat who headed his embassy's Jewish desk in Washington in the early 1990s. "It is not bad thing. It is good to have people supporting you here in the United States. As an Arab country, we wish we could have the same groups supporting Egypt or Saudi Arabia."

In fact, just about everyone seems to take the Jewish community seriously. Everybody, that is, except the Jews.

To this day, American Jews remain largely oblivious to the sea change in the status of the Jewish community in the last half-century. Much of the world views American Jewry as a focused bloc of influential, determined believers, firmly entrenched in the American power structure. The average American Jew views his or her community as a scattered congregation of six million–odd individuals of similar origins and diverse beliefs, fortunate children and grandchildren of immigrant tailors and peddlers.

Politicians and diplomats point to the Jewish community as a model of success and assurance. American Jews—by a large and growing majority—consider themselves to be members of an isolated, vulnerable minority.

To the typical American Jew, the mere mention of "Jewish power" sounds like an anti-Semitic slur, as George Bush learned the hard way. "Even to remark on the relative political power of the American Jewish community—whether of the Israel lobby in Washington or of Jewish influence in domestic affairs—arouses fear in some quarters of giving ammunition to the anti-Semites," the historian David Biale wrote in his landmark 1985 study *Power and Powerlessness in Jewish History.*

So glaring is the contrast between how Jews are seen and how they see themselves, that Jewish social scientists speak almost casually of the "perception gap" between reality and Jewish sensibilities. The term (coined during the 1980s by intergroup affairs expert Jerome Chanes of the National Jewish Community Relations Advisory Council) refers to the gap between actual anti-Semitism in America, which has declined steadily over the last generation, and American Jews' fear of anti-Semitism, which has skyrocketed in the same period.

It is a fact that American anti-Semitism currently is at a historic low by most essential yardsticks. Hostility toward Jews, as measured in opinion polls, has dropped to what some social scientists consider a virtual zero point. Private discrimination against Jews in jobs, education, and housing has all but disappeared. Government action against Jews, the staple of European anti-Semitism for centuries, is almost inconceivable in this country. With a few important exceptions—the rise of some prominent anti-Jewish radicals in the black community, plus a troubling increase in anti-Jewish vandalism—anti-Semitism virtually has vanished from American public life.

By contrast, the percentage of Jews who tell pollsters that anti-Semitism is a "serious problem" in America nearly doubled during the course of the 1980s, from 45 percent in 1983 to almost 85 percent in 1990.

"The American Jewish community today is comfortable, secure, but lacking in self-confidence," the conservative social critic Irving Kristol wrote not long ago. "It shows frequent symptoms of hypochondria and neurasthenia. It is a community very vulnerable to its own repressed anxieties and self-doubt."

This hypochondria is emblematic of another, larger gap in current-day Jewish perception: the gap between the Jews' self-image of vulnerability and the reality of Jewish power.

Any serious description of American Jewish politics—the exercise of power by and within the Jewish community—must inevitably be colored by this perception gap. The gap runs like a crack through the base of the edifice called the Jewish community. Coursing up through the structure, it becomes a yawning chasm of ignorance and mutual incomprehension, dividing the Jewish community's leaders from their presumed followers.

The nature and workings of Jewish power politics are the major theme of this book. That chasm forms the minor theme: the fault line between the activists who conduct the Jewish community's business and represent its interests to the larger society, and the broader population of American Jews, who are almost entirely unaware of the work being done in their name.

Within this fault line lies the crisis of American Jewish politics. How long can leaders claim to lead when followers do not follow?

If American Jews bridle at the notion of "Jewish power," they have good reason. It is true that Jewish history for two thousand years has been told as a gloomy tale, replete with recurring themes of fear and persecution. And it is true that throughout these centuries, the image of the "powerful Jew" has figured prominently in anti-Jewish agitation.

For most of the last two millenia, Jews lived as a tiny, hated minority in Christian Europe. They were regularly restricted in their places of residence, in their work, and even in their rights of marriage and procreation. They were repeatedly accused of manipulating economies, poisoning wells, sacrificing children, and, of course, murdering God. On these pretexts they were subjected to recurring cycles of violence, mass expulsion, and mass murder.

The entire Jewish population of Germany was expelled from its native land in 1182; the same happened in England in 1290, in France in 1306 and again in 1394, in Austria in 1421, in Spain in 1492, and in Portugal in 1497. The Black Plague of 1348 touched off a continent-wide frenzy of murderous assaults on Jews. The Crusaders, en route to claim the Holy Land, slaughtered more Jews than Saracens. The Ukrainian Cossacks, rising up under Bogdan Chmielnicki in 1648 to throw off their Polish overlords, killed more Jews than Poles.

Even if Adolf Hitler had never been born, anti-Semitic violence still would be one of the greatest stains on the history of Christian Europe.

Always before the violence, there were fantastic, ludicrous tales told about the Jews. It was said, repeatedly, that Jews killed Christian children and baked their blood into the ritual Passover bread. It was said, repeatedly, that Jews sneaked into churches and stabbed the holy wafers in order to make Jesus bleed again. It was said, repeatedly, that Jews were engaged in a secret plot to dominate and enslave the entire world.

This last delusion—the myth of a secret, worldwide Jewish conspiracy—has survived and flourished in the modern age. Its bible is the *Protocols of the Learned Elders of Zion,* which surfaced in Russia around the turn of the twentieth century. Supposedly a secret draft of the Jews' master plan for conquest, in fact it was probably forged by a mad Russian monk at the behest of the czarist secret police. The truth about the *Protocols* has been widely known since its fraudulent origins were disclosed in 1921 by the London *Times.* Incredibly, the *Protocols* is still in print, still being hawked on streetcorners in Teheran, Caracas, and New York City.

Across the long sweep of Jewish history, it has been only a moment since Jewish communities first acquired the ability to turn world events in their own favor. Only in the last half-century have American Jews, the largest and most powerful Jewish community in history, been able to mobilize themselves effectively and become a cohesive institution with an acknowledged policy role in Washington and other capitals.

The change is too recent, perhaps, to have entered the consciousness of most American Jews.

At this point, the reader might be forgiven for thinking that something is wrong here. A quarter-century, let alone a half-century, seems more than enough time for a population as sophisticated as American Jewry to absorb so profound a transformation. Having narrowly survived utter extermination, a despised, persecuted minority becomes the toast of Pennsylvania Avenue within a generation. How could this go unnoticed by, of all people, the subjects themselves?

The answer is complicated. American Jewry's collective myopia results from a combination of historical factors. Any one of these factors might have skewed perceptions. Together, they have produced a massive failure to communicate.

First and most important among these factors is Jewish assimilation. During the same quarter-century in which the Jewish community was transformed from weakling into powerhouse, the individual American Jew underwent a metamorphosis no less sweeping. Fewer Jews were joining synagogues or donating to Jewish charities. Growing numbers were marrying outside the faith. Community leaders interpreted the statistics in cataclysmic terms, warning that Jews were on the verge of disappearing, of melting into the general American population.

As chapter 3 will demonstrate, this doomsday prediction is almost certainly wrong. It is based partly on false statistics, partly on preconceptions and misinterpretations. Year after year, the vast majority of American Jews—the ones who supposedly are disappearing—continue to attend synagogue once or twice annually, join their families for Passover and Hanukkah, and send their children for Bar and Bat Mitzvah training.

Jews are not disappearing. What they *are* doing is losing interest in the institutions of organized Judaism.

Until a generation ago, Jewish attachment was a complex bundle of intense family and community ties, shared culture, and religious taboos and rituals. No longer: for most American Jews, Judaism is becoming less a religion of laws and more a personal attribute. Like so much else in American culture, Judaism is turning into a free-floating set of feelings, interests, and occasional actions, which the individual Jew feels free to adopt or discard at will.

But—this is crucial—*it remains an attachment.* Jews remain Jews in their own minds. And they continue to insist that it matters to them.

The current transformation of the American Jewish religious identity is affecting the Jewish political process in many significant ways. One point is essential: the fundamental impact on Jewish myopia. Most American Jews are unaware of the changed public status of the American Jewish community because *they no longer pay attention to organized Jewish community life.* For most American Jews, Judaism has become a private matter.

No less important, a large minority of Jews is undergoing no such metamorphosis toward individualism. A sizable bloc—perhaps one fifth to one quarter of all American Jews, or 1 million to 1.5 million persons—is traveling in the *opposite* direction. They are becoming steadily "more Jewish" than before. More Jewish, in fact, than any large group of American Jews ever was: more traditionalist, more observant of Jewish ritual, more attentive to Jewish group interests, and steadily more alarmed over the backsliding ways of their 4 million "assimilated" brethren. And, not coincidentally, ever more suspicious of Gentile intentions toward Jews.

This "committed" minority provides much of the professional leadership for the broader Jewish community. Not surprisingly, then, the noncommunication between the Jewish leadership and the Jewish majority grows steadily more pronounced as the two subcommunities drift further apart.

There is another factor, much older than assimilation, that blinds American Jews to the reality of their own power. It is the enduring myth of Diaspora Jewish powerlessness, and the corollary myth of craven, ineffectual Jewish leadership. These myths work to make the reality of modern Jewish power invisible by rendering it simply incredible.

In traditional Jewish folklore, the Jews were helpless pawns, buffeted *me'evel leyom tov*—from mourning to celebration—by the vagaries of cruel despots, benign protectors, and Divine Providence itself. *"Bechol dor vador omdim aleinu lechaloteinu,"* reads the liturgy of the Passover festival: "In each generation they rise up against us to destroy us, but the Holy One, blessed be He, saves us from their hand."

There was little room in this cosmology for independent Jewish political action. At best, Jews could appeal to God for salvation by "repentance, prayer, and charity," as the Yom Kippur liturgy urged them to do. But as long as they were exiled from their ancient homeland, their fate was in the hands of others.

Reality did not quite match the myth. The centuries of Diaspora produced a long line of Jewish political figures: diplomats, power brokers, and even the occasional warrior-hero. Jewish communities throughout history were nearly always autonomous, self-governing enclaves. True, they had widely varying degrees of independence and security. Most lived under severe restrictions, but some dealt with their neighbors on a near-equal basis. The great Jewish community of Babylonia was governed for a thousand years by a descendant of King David known as the exilarch, who was a minister of the royal court. The Jewish communities of medieval Poland and Lithuania elected a *shtadlan,* or ambassador to the Polish court, who often dealt with the nobility on a near-equal basis. Many Renaissance princes appointed "court Jews" to manage their finances; some of these appointees wielded extraordinary power on the Jewish community's behalf.

These episodes of political success left few traces on the modern Jewish memory. Few Jews today have heard of the exilarchs. Those educated American Jews who know the terms *shtadlan* and "court Jew" usually associate them with groveling beggars or corrupt, self-serving parvenus.

The oblivion that has overtaken the political figures of the Jewish past is due partly to their ultimate failure. Jewish life in premodern Europe enjoyed many intervals of ease, but in the end it fell into a spiral of humiliation and persecution, descending through the century-long nightmare of czarist Russia to the horrors of the Second World War. Like politicians of every time and place, the political leaders of medieval Jewry came to be tarred, in retrospect, with the final failure of the system they served.

Equally important, the Jewish political tradition came out the loser in a long struggle for historical memory. The victor was a rival power-center in Jewish life: the rabbinate. Where the Jews' political leaders confronted Jewish minority status with pragmatism and compromise, the rabbis taught resignation and prayer. Unable to offer even partial comfort here and now, they promised a glorious messianic redemption in the end of days.

In some ways, then, the power politics of modern American Jewry represents the rebirth of a Jewish tradition that has lain dormant for three hundred years, since the collapse of the medieval Polish empire.

Between then and now, under a succession of Ukrainian Cossacks, Russian czars, and Nazi stormtroopers, a durable mythology has taken root. This mythology survives today in American Jewish folk memory. In it, Jews are utterly powerless and must live by their wits. Compromise is useless, or worse. Politics is made of messianic visions and apocalyptic goals. Some of these visions, like Zionism and socialism, may occasionally become reality.

In this mythology, those wealthy and powerful Jews who operate in the gray world of compromise and deal-making are only looking out for themselves. Formal spokespersons for the Jews—rabbis, *shtadlans*, community officials— are hapless buffoons, too dim to realize the futility of their task.

The American Jew's political myopia is rooted in an Old World tradition of dashed hopes and messianic dreams. But in the New World the Jews created mythologies of their own.

As Rabbi Arthur Hertzberg demonstrated in his illuminating 1988 historical essay, *The Jews in America: Four Centuries of an Uneasy Encounter,* the American Jewish community was founded and populated largely by the poorest and least educated Jews of Europe. Someone with a strong attachment to Jewish values did not travel halfway around the world to settle in an untamed wilderness without rules or boundaries. A good Jew stayed at home. Rebels, adventurers, and losers came to America.

Three main immigrant waves created American Jewry: Portuguese Marranos in the colonial era, German Jews in the mid-nineteenth century, and Russian Jews in the early twentieth. Each wave consisted of Jews who wanted to escape the world they knew. They were fleeing both from the Jewish community and from the Gentile society surrounding it, Hertzberg wrote. "[T]he immigrant Jews . . . felt betrayed by the societies, the governments, the rabbis, and the rich Jewish leaders who had cast them out, or, at the very least, had failed to find room for them. . . . They would not allow the very people who had betrayed them in Europe to exercise authority in America."

To be sure, these immigrants recreated a Jewish community in America. But it was a Jewish community with a difference. This was a new world, where religion was disestablished. Churches had no legal hold over believers; likewise, the Jewish community had no hold over Jews. It was defanged. Over time, Jews developed a new mythology of an organized American Jewish community led by well-meaning bumblers.

No one ever summed up the mythic image of inept Jewish leadership better than the late author-activist Paul Jacobs. In his 1965 memoir *Is Curly Jewish?* he offered an imaginary crisis that captured the layperson's picture of the three best-known Jewish agencies: the Anti-Defamation League of B'nai B'rith (ADL), American Jewish Committee (AJC), and the American Jewish Congress.

"A fanciful way of describing the work of these groups," Jacobs wrote, "is that some guy walks into the toilet of a ginmill on Third Avenue, New York, and while he's standing at the urinal, he notices that someone has written 'Screw the Jews' on the toilet wall." A quick phone call is made and "an ADL man rushes down to the bar" to dust the wall for fingerprints. The ADL checks the prints against its files of 2 million known anti-Semites, then publishes a photo of the wall in its next bulletin, saying it shows anti-Semitism is on the rise and "everyone should join B'nai B'rith." Next to arrive would be the representative of the American Jewish Committee, who would look around, then announce plans for a major academic study of "anti-Semitic wall-writing since Pompeii." AJC would also publish a booklet proving that a Jew had invented the martini, to be distributed in bars nationwide. Then the American Jewish Congress would arrive, throw up a picket line outside the bar, and petition the Supreme Court to bar the sale of liquor "to anyone making an anti-Semitic remark."

The most powerful myth surrounding American Jewish power is one shared by Jews and Gentiles alike. It is the mistaken equation of Jewish politics and Middle East policy: the notion that the Jewish political agenda begins and ends with Israel, and conversely, that Israel's support in Washington largely results from Jewish political power.

"Washington is a city of acronyms, and today one of the best-known in Congress is AIPAC," former Representative Paul Findley wrote in the opening of his 1985 book *They Dare to Speak Out: People and Institutions Confront Israel's Lobby.* "The mere mention of it brings a sober, if not furtive look, to the face of anyone on Capitol Hill who deals with Middle East policy. AIPAC—the American Israel Public Affairs Committee—is now the preeminent power in Washington lobbying."

Findley's book is the most famous of a host of studies that appeared in the 1980s and early 1990s, attempting to document the Israel lobby's stranglehold over American foreign policy. Others include *The Fateful Triangle,* by Noam Chomsky (1983); *Taking Sides,* by Stephen Green (1984); *The Lobby,* by Edward Tivnan (1987); and *The Passionate Attachment,* by George and Douglas Ball (1992).

What these books share is an underlying assumption that U.S. support for Israel is misguided and runs counter to American interests. By this reasoning, some force must exist that is powerful enough to subvert U.S. foreign policy according to its will. That force is the Jewish lobby; without it, the United States would not support Israel.

The Balls make their case with a summary of Jewish clout that is actually not far off the mark:

> The clout that Jewish Americans exercise in American politics is far incommensurate with their population. Their power derives primarily from an active interest in public affairs and a willingness to work hard for causes in which they believe. It derives also from their flair for understanding the

electoral process, their gift for efficient organization, and, most of all, from
their dedication to philanthropy, reinforced by supersensitive peer pressure
among members of a group forced together by a discrimination still apparent in far too many sectors of American society.

Israeli leaders have taken full advantage of these characteristics of
American Jewry. They have made it crystal clear that they expect Jewish
Americans to lobby for Israeli interests with members of both the executive
and legislative branches, and to present and defend Israel's case to major
American opinion makers.

Now, much of what the Balls say here is true. American Jews do exercise
political influence out of proportion to their numbers. Their clout does
derive in large part from their civic activism, their high level of philanthropic giving, and their group solidarity. And indeed Israel has tried for
years, often successfully, to use the Jewish community as a wedge in
Washington.

But the reality of Jewish power and its effect on America's Middle East
policy is much more complicated than the simple conspiracy theory laid out
by these overwrought critics. If the equation were as simple as the Balls
suggest—Jewish money and activism create Jewish clout, which creates
U.S. support for Israel—then U.S. support would be fairly consistent over
the five-decade period since Israel became a state.

That is not the case. Washington provided little aid and no weaponry to
Israel during the new nation's first and most vulnerable decade. America's
ties with Israel grew slowly during the 1960s, partly because of Jewish
involvement in the Kennedy and Johnson administrations, partly because of
Lyndon Johnson's admiration for Israel and its then-prime minister, Levi
Eshkol.

In fact, the strong U.S.-Israel alliance as we now know it, with its huge
arms sales and multibillion-dollar aid packages, commenced under Richard
M. Nixon, a Republican president elected with almost no Jewish backing.
Every president before him had attempted a posture of evenhandedness in
the Middle East, maintaining friendship with both Israel and its sworn enemies. Nixon dropped the attempt at balance and declared Israel for the first
time to be a "strategic asset" in the Cold War. On his watch, the United States
replaced France as Israel's main arms supplier. American aid to Israel skyrocketed from $300 million to $2.2 billion per year, making Israel the largest
recipient of U.S. foreign aid. U.S.-Israel relations became big business. That
made Israel's allies important players in Washington power politics.

In the years since Nixon first engineered America's massive commit-ment to Israel, the Jewish lobby has grown exponentially in reputation, access, and influence. AIPAC, the Jewish community's main foreign-policy lobbying organization, has grown from a three-person office into a well-oiled organization with a staff of 150 and a budget of $15 million. Jewish membership in the U.S. Congress has tripled.

Over the last two decades, the United States has established a govern-ment office to hunt down and expel Nazi war criminals, has made Jewish emigration from the Soviet Union a central foreign-policy goal, and has overseen the exodus to freedom of ancient Jewish communities in Syria and Ethiopia. In May 1991, Washington even brokered a one-day ceasefire in the bloody Ethiopian civil war, for the sole purpose of permitting Israeli airplanes to evacuate that nation's twenty thousand Jewish tribespeople in an unprecedented twenty-four-hour airlift. And, of course, America created a Holocaust museum, a $168 million memorial to Jewish suffering in Second World War Europe, built by congressional mandate (with private money on federal land) in the midst of the Smithsonian complex on the Mall.

Did American Jewish clout create the U.S.-Israel alliance? One could as plausibly argue the opposite: that the U.S.-Israel alliance created contem-porary American Jewish political power.

The real story of Jewish power is more complicated than either scenario. America under Richard Nixon moved toward Israel for its own reasons of Cold War politics and military strategy; domestic Jewish influence was only a secondary incentive.

The Jewish lobby was already in existence. It had been around for decades. Long before Nixon's presidency, it had played a leading role in reshaping the U.S. consensus on civil rights, church-state relations, immi-gration, and much more.

The forging of a U.S.-Israel alliance did not give birth to American Jewry's political establishment. But it thrust the Jewish establishment up-ward into a dizzying new political stratosphere. It transformed the Jewish community's political agenda. It forced America's most resolutely liberal constituency into an unfamiliar alliance with the mostly Gentile Cold War-riors of the national security establishment. And it made American Jewry a force on the international stage.

Other factors were working on the Jewish community at the same time, reinforcing the process of politicization and empowerment. Most important was the direct fallout of Israel's lightning victory in the Six-Day War of 1967. That victory touched off a wave of nationalist passion among Jews in America and around the world.

Across the ocean, the Six-Day War sparked an unexpected and dramatic rebirth of Jewish fervor among the 2 million Jews of the Soviet Union, who defied communist repression and broke a half-century of silence. In turn, the Soviet Jews' struggle for freedom inspired a broad-based popular movement among American Jews. And the American Jewish campaign for Soviet Jewry, in turn, reinforced the newfound coziness between the Jewish community's leaders and the American right.

The political reality of Jewish community life today is that a powerful machine has arisen in the last quarter-century to advance Jewish interests. It is far more powerful than most Jews realize, though not half so powerful as their enemies fantasize. Like any big bureaucracy, it operates within clear constraints and often makes mistakes; yet it has proved itself capable of making despots quake and halting armies in their tracks. A complex mechanism, it is incongruously made up of bodies whose very names bring a condescending smile to Jewish lips: B'nai B'rith, Hadassah, United Jewish Appeal, Anti-Defamation League. Groups like these are the engines— more precisely, the wheels in the engine—of Jewish power in America today.

If the average Jew finds all this hard to believe, so do many of the leaders who wield Jewish power. Senior officials of the organized Jewish community often seem dazed by the entire phenomenon. "The Jewish community has access today, at the local level, at the national level and the international level, to a point which my grandparents would never have imagined," says ADL national director Abraham Foxman. "They could never have imagined that their grandson would be this and can go there—and all that not because I'm a lord, not because I'm a millionaire, but because I am Abe Foxman, a Jewish official."

Many suggest that their clout, real as it seems, is based largely on an illusion. "A lot of what we're doing today," said the head of of one major Jewish agency, "is the invention of [the late German-born Zionist leader] Nahum Goldmann. He was the master illusionist. All the organizations he created—the World Jewish Congress, the Conference of Presidents—were designed to reinforce the myth of a powerful, mysterious body called world Jewry."

ADL's Foxman agrees: "The non-Jewish world to a large extent believes in the myth of the *Protocols of the Elders of Zion,* and to some extent we in the Jewish community have not disabused them."

"Look," Foxman says, "I know every time I meet with a world leader who comes to see me, he's not coming to see me because I'm Abe Foxman, the national director of the ADL. I know he's coming because he has been told, or someone sold him the concept, that the Jewish community is very strong and powerful. You know it because when you finish the conversation, they want to know what you can do for them in the media, what you can do for them in the Congress and so on."

"That's why the prime minister of Bosnia comes to see the Jewish community," Foxman continues. "That's why the prime minister of Albania comes, and the foreign minister of Bulgaria and El Salvador, Nicaragua, you name it. You've got to ask yourself, what is this about? The answer is, it's because they believe a little bit of that."

One could argue just as easily, and perhaps more plausibly, that the change is this: in the past generation, many non-Jews have come to take the Jews more seriously and give them more credit than the Jews give themselves. The result is a weird reversal of the age-old scourge of anti-Semitism. The Jewish community, after suffering countless centuries of malevolence and abuse that it did not seek and could not explain, now finds itself on the receiving end of favors that seem no less inexplicable.

And in a way, says congressional aide David Luchins, "That's political power.

"Political power is when you don't have to ask for it," Luchins says. "Political power is when your friends look out for you without you having to ask. We have an incredible amount of friends who do that—either because they believe in it, or because they think it's good politics, or because we're part of that Judeo-Christian mythos."

For example, he says, "the Congressional Black Caucus had a counter-budget that it proposed throughout the 70s and 80s, which cut spending to the bone on defense, which destroyed farm subsidies, and which kept in $3 billion for Israel. The reason was that a majority of the Black Caucus would not cut aid to Israel, despite occasional efforts by Gus Savage one year and John Conyers another year. They would not cut it because the Bill Grays and the Charlie Rangels weren't about to be tagged anti-Semites. They're not, and they wouldn't allow it.

"During the 1992 Democratic convention, the only speaker who devoted any time to the subject of Israel was poor Jesse Louis Jackson, who is doomed for the rest of his life to apologize to us every time he speaks because of some things he said against us back in the early 1980s. And why must he apologize? Because he loves us? No. It's because there's a sizable segment of the black community that insists on it. That's political power.

"Political power is that in this country, anti-Semitism is not something you're proud of. Pat Buchanan, who has offended the Jewish community on any number of issues, has to go out of his way to say he's not an anti-Semite. Even a David Duke, who used to dress up in a Nazi uniform, has to try and prove he's not an anti-Semite. They don't want to be seen as our enemies, because of who we are in America. That's political power."

The emergence of American Jewry as an independent power is not without its ironies. The basic idea of Zionism, the moving vision behind the creation of Israel, was that a Jewish state would give a voice to a voiceless people and return Jews to the stage of history after centuries of helplessness. American Jewish power has turned the Zionist idea on its head.

In August 1987, for example, when Israeli prime minister Yitzhak Shamir paid a state visit to Romania, his agenda included bilateral trade, tourism, Romanian assistance to Soviet Jewish émigrés, and Romanian mediation in the Israel-Arab dispute. In return, the *Jerusalem Post* reported, Romanian president Nicolae Ceauşescu planned to ask Shamir to use his influence with the American Jewish community to improve Romania's ties with Washington.

A month later Israeli foreign minister Shimon Peres, in New York for the U.N. General Assembly, met with the foreign minister of Turkey. Briefing the press afterward, Turkey's U.N. ambassador explained that Peres wanted Turkey to help Israel improve its ties in the Islamic world, and Turkey wanted Israel to put in a good word for it with the American Jewish community.

The purpose of this book is to explore the workings of Jewish power politics in contemporary America. We will examine the structure of the organized

Jewish community, the issues that drive the Jewish communal agenda, the internal politics of the major Jewish organizations, and the complicated relations between the Jewish community leadership and the masses of American Jews. We will look at various sources of Jewish clout, including fund-raising and media influence.

Readers looking for confirmation of their favorite myths will likely be disappointed. They will find no meaningful Jewish control of the media or high finance, numerous though Jews may be in those industries. They will find precious little clandestine Israeli action to subvert Congress or American public opinion.

For that matter, they will find little of the glitter that graces the daily gossip columns, and surprisingly few of the celebrity names that are most often associated with American Jewish power, such as Michael Milken, Michael Ovitz, Barbara Walters, and Barbra Streisand. These are powerful people, and they are Jews, but they do not represent Jewish power in America. The power of any group is the ability of its members to work together and change the world around them to suit their needs and purposes. That is what is meant by American power or black power, the power of the tobacco industry or of the Roman Catholic Church. Some Jewish celebrities will appear in this narrative because they participate in that process. Most do not.

On the other hand, readers accustomed to examining Jewish political activity will find surprisingly little evidence of hapless, bumbling, or corrupt Jewish leaders betraying their grassroots constituencies. Instead, readers will find a community bureaucracy that is reasonably efficient and fundamentally well-meaning, as big bureaucracies go.

However, readers also will find a Jewish political system that is in trouble, shaken by the sweeping changes in the world around it. These troubles partly are the aftermath of success: in a world where embattled Israel is signing peace treaties, where oppressed Jewish communities from Moscow to Damascus are stepping into the light of freedom, what battles remain? Without threats, what will rally Jews to the flag?

At the same time, the current malaise in the Jewish community reflects the dangerous uncertainties facing all political systems today, as the world enters the uncharted waters of the twenty-first century while clinging to the outdated maps of the twentieth.

The collapse of old dictatorships and the rise of new technologies has left societies across the globe plagued by starvation in the midst of plenty, and threatened by growing ignorance despite instant communication. Political leaders can only grope for answers to the riddles of future shock.

As they grope, they find their options restricted by the growing insecurity and mistrust of the public.

In a way, the American Jewish community is a vanguard of the new chaos. In a national political system that is increasingly balkanized, dominated by feuding interest groups that seem more concerned with their own agenda than with the common good, the Jewish community can fairly claim to be the pioneer. American Jews were the first ethnic or religious minority to win power and influence within the larger body politic by trumpeting their own weakness and victimhood. More recently, they have led the outcry against balkanization of American society—even as they have advanced the science by pioneering special-interest lobbying techniques that combine street protest with targeted political giving and backroom backscratching.

More important, American Jewry's current political struggles provide a microcosm of the political unease afflicting American society as a whole: the widespread mistrust of leaders and of public service and the discrediting of compromise as an honorable way to broker agreement.

Even the spread of Jewish assimilation—the growing abdication of Jewish community life by individual Jews—differs only in degree from Americans' declining participation in the broader political process.

In the end, the workings of the Jewish community are most important to the Jews themselves. A great deal of significant work is being done in the name of America's Jews by a small minority of them. Some of it is misguided; much more of it is useful and well-intentioned; all of it is underscrutinized. Like the American political system itself, the Jewish community's political system is threatened, more than anything, by the apathy of its constituents.

In the real world, political work goes on whether or not the public takes an interest. The only difference is whether the end result reflects the public's will or the will of a small minority. For this reason alone, Jews are invited to find out what is being done in their name. And other Americans are invited to read on and find out what their neighbors are up to.

CHAPTER 2

"Not for Myself":
Liberalism and the Jewish Agenda

Hillel the Elder said three things: If I am not for myself, who will be for me? But if I am only for myself, what am I? And if not now, when?
— Talmud, Tractate *Avot* ("The Ethics of the Fathers")

M ICHAEL LIEBERMAN, a staff lawyer with the Anti-Defamation League, spent the afternoon of July 27, 1994, in the reception room just outside the Senate chamber on Capitol Hill. He was watching nervously on closed-circuit television to see how the Senate voted on amendments to the massive Elementary and Secondary School Education Act of 1994.

The bill was a $12 billion showpiece of Bill Clinton's legislative agenda, mapping out a major overhaul of American education. Lieberman, deputy director of the ADL's Washington office, had spent most of the year worrying about one particular amendment, authored by North Carolina Republican Jesse Helms, that purported to defend a child's "constitutionally protected right" to pray in public school. Mike Lieberman was trying to block its passage.

Gathered with Lieberman around the television set, or a few feet away near the Senate elevators, were several dozen lobbyists who had toiled with him for months to stop the Helms amendment. When the votes were counted shortly before six o'clock that evening, the lobbyists cheered, hooted, and thrust their fists in the air, like football fans after a winning field goal. The Helms amendment had been defeated by a narrow 53 to 47 margin.

When the amendment first had come up back in February, seventy-five senators voted with Helms. Since then, thirty-one had been persuaded to switch sides, in a frenzied nationwide campaign of lobbying, letter-writing, and grassroots pressure.

"It was probably the biggest thing we've done since the loan guarantees," Lieberman later said.

As it often does in its biggest Washington battles, the ADL worked closely with the American Jewish Committee and the American Jewish Congress in the campaign to stop the Helms amendment. But the Jews did not fight alone. They were joined by a broad coalition of interest groups that opposed the amendment on political, philosophical, or economic grounds. Several were Christian groups that share the Jews' commitment to strict separation of church and state, including the Baptist Joint Committee for Public Affairs and the National Council of Churches of Christ.

Still others were educators' groups, such as the teachers' unions, the national school boards association, and the school administrators' association. They were fearful of the amendment's threat to strip federal aid from school districts that violated a child's "right to pray." The proposed legislation did not specify what that right consisted of. School administrators felt they were being led blindfolded toward a cliff.

Overseeing the coalition and coordinating its strategy were staffers from two nonsectarian liberal lobbies, the American Civil Liberties Union (ACLU) and People for the American Way.

"It was a high-stakes, nasty game," recalls Oliver "Buzz" Thomas, a legal strategist with the National Council of Churches. "I don't know any way to measure whose efforts convinced which senator. But the Jewish organizations were probably the most engaged of all the religious organizations. Without the organized effort of the Jewish community, we would have lost the issue."

The Christian groups, Thomas says, "sent out newsletters and contacted our leadership. But we didn't activate the telephone trees and do the kinds of things you do when you really want something to happen. My feeling is that nobody worked the grass roots like the Jewish community."

In general, Thomas says, the Jewish community is one of the most important players in the ongoing alliance to preserve the constitutional wall of separation between church and state. "I don't think anybody puts more effort into church-state issues than the Jewish community," he says.

Moreover, "if you talk about the broader Jewish involvement, and you weigh in Jews who are active in groups like ACLU and People for the American Way, the influence is just overwhelming."

To a lesser degree, the same thing can be said about Jewish participation in a host of other domestic policy arenas. In civil rights, immigration policy, abortion rights, labor organizing, and Democratic campaign financing, the Jewish community plays a crucial role in American liberalism, as it has through much of the twentieth century.

Indeed, the sturdy marriage of Jews and liberalism must be counted one of the great enigmas of American Jewish life, and perhaps of American politics in general. Why do Jews remain so persistently liberal? Why, despite their growing affluence and influence in America, do they continue to identify with underdogs and favor policies that hurt the rich?

The question has fascinated scholars for decades. "Most theorizing about Jewish political behaviour," writes Israeli political scientist Peter Medding, "has attempted to explain this supposedly universal phenomenon" of Jewish liberalism. According to "conventional wisdom," Medding writes, Jewish liberalism is "anomalous, given the class position of Jews in Western societies."

The statistics are impressive. One 1988 survey by the *Los Angeles Times* found that 41 percent of all American Jews called themselves liberals and 17 percent called themselves conservatives. Americans overall measured quite the reverse: 18 percent described themselves as liberals, compared to 30 percent who said they were conservatives. More recent surveys have shown much the same results.

Jews have been one of the most liberal segments of the American population for most of this century. They remain so today, despite repeated efforts by Jewish conservatives to woo them rightward. Jews have voted solidly Democratic in almost every presidential election of the twentieth century. (The only exceptions are 1920 and 1980; in both years, large blocs of Jews defected to third-party candidates on the left.) Even in the Republican congressional landslide of 1994, Jews gave nearly 80 percent of their votes to Democrats.

Jews are not just liberal; they are essential to American liberalism, and have been for a century. The first president of the American Federation of

Labor was a Jew, immigrant cigar-maker Samuel Gompers. The first president of the National Organization for Women was a Jew, author-activist
Betty Friedan. The first socialists ever elected to Congress were Jews,
Milwaukee journalist Victor Berger and New York attorney Meyer London.
(So is the only self-declared socialist in today's Congress, Vermont independent Bernard Sanders.) Close to half the young whites who went South as
civil rights workers during the 1960s were Jews, by most estimates. Two of
the most influential liberal activist groups of the post–Vietnam War era
were founded by Jews, Human Rights Watch/Helsinki Watch, founded by
New York publisher Robert Bernstein, and People for the American Way,
founded by Los Angeles television producer Norman Lear.

Even the National Association for the Advancement of Colored People
took shape in the home of a Jew, retired Columbia University literature
professor Joel Spingarn, who hosted the organization's pivotal 1915 Amenia
Conference at his estate outside New York City. An NAACP leader since its
founding in 1909, head of its militant faction, and the main ally of black
theorist W. E. B. Du Bois, Spingarn was elected NAACP board chairman in
1915, then served as president from 1929 until his death in 1939. He was
succeeded by his brother Arthur, who was in turn succeeded in 1966 by
Boston businessman Kivie Kaplan, who served until 1975, when the
NAACP elected its first black president.

The careers of individual Jewish liberals tell only part of the story. For at
least a half-century, the organized Jewish community has played a decisive
role in advancing America's evolving liberal agenda of tolerance and fair
play. A formal alliance of Jewish and black organizations orchestrated the
post–Second World War civil rights campaign that led to equal-rights laws
in dozens of states, and finally to the federal Civil Rights and Voting Rights
acts of the mid-1960s. The major Jewish organizations spearheaded the
long campaign for immigration reform, ending with the abolition of racial
quotas in 1965. Jewish organizations, working with a wide coalition of civic
groups and Christian churches, did much to create the current legal consensus on religious freedom and church-state separation.

Finally, in a nation where political campaigns are privately funded, an
estimated one fourth to one half of all Democratic Party campaign funds
are donated or raised by Jews.

Why? Partly it is because Jews have money, though that is only part of the truth. Jews are somewhat more affluent than other Americans. But they are not as affluent as popular stereotypes suggest. Median Jewish household income is between $40,000 and $50,000 per year, depending on the survey, compared to about $36,000 per year for Americans as a whole. More significant is the fact that Jews give more money to charity than do other Americans with comparable incomes.

But that is not why the Democratic Party is so dependent on Jewish money. The essential reason is this: Jews are the only major American demographic group whose liberalism does not decline as their income goes up. In effect, they provide the single biggest source of money for liberal political causes. Republicans have the entire world of American business to appeal to. Democrats have the Jews.

Richard Brookhiser, a conservative essayist, once suggested that the only difference between the Democratic Party and Reform Judaism was the holidays.

As if to test that hypothesis, the American Jewish Committee commissioned a survey in 1988 to see how Jews' political and social views differed from those of their neighbors. The survey questioned groups of Jewish and non-Jewish Americans separately and compared their answers.

In a few areas, notably support for the death penalty and attitudes toward the Soviet Union, Jewish and non-Jewish opinions were virtually indistinguishable. In several areas, mainly having to do with taxes and government spending, Jews were more liberal than non-Jews, but not dramatically so.

In one area, affirmative action for minorities, Jews were slightly more conservative than other whites: more supportive than non-Jews of government action to end discrimination, but more hostile to reverse discrimination, or race-based preference for minorities in hiring or schooling.

The most dramatic differences between Jews and non-Jews showed up in what are commonly called social issues. Asked about homosexual rights and opposition to censorship, for example, non-Jewish Americans were mildly supportive, but Jews strongly so. On abortion rights, the nation as a whole was mixed (45 percent favored unrestricted abortion, 44 percent favored some restrictions, 11 percent favored outlawing it altogether), while 87 percent of Jews favored free choice and almost none favored a total ban.

And then there was the issue of church-state separation. Here, Jewish and non-Jewish views were diametrically opposed. Jews were overwhelmingly against permitting public-school prayer or allowing religious symbols—*any* religious symbols—on government property. Other Americans were strongly in favor of both.

"We thus have the curious phenomenon," survey director Steven M. Cohen drily noted, "of far more gentiles than Jews expressing a readiness to accept the public display of a menorah."

The only other issue that divided Jews so starkly from their neighbors was the basic question of political self-identification. Americans as a whole are about evenly split between Democrats and Republicans, at roughly one third each, with the rest calling themselves independents. Jews identify themselves overwhelmingly as Democrats, by margins of 50 to 60 percent depending on the survey. No more than 15 percent call themselves Republicans.

Several popular theories attempt to explain the Jews' persistent attachment to liberalism. To many liberal activists, such as veteran human-rights crusader Aryeh Neier, famed ex-chief of the ACLU and cofounder of Helsinki Watch, Jewish liberalism stems from an awareness of a "shared history of persecution." For others, such as civil rights lawyer Jack Greenberg, former head of the NAACP Legal Defense Fund, it is little more than a residue of the radical politics that Russian Jewish refugees brought with them to America at the turn of the century and taught to their children.

Feminist author-activist Letty Cottin Pogrebin, a founder of *Ms.* magazine, sees Jewish liberalism as a natural outgrowth of Jewish tradition, passed on through rituals like the Passover recitation of the Exodus from Egypt. "Remembering our oppression helps us to identify with the oppressed," Pogrebin writes. Paradoxically, Pogrebin also credits Jewish liberalism to rebellion *against* tradition: she contends that oppressive, patriarchal customs have driven many Jews into movements for social change.

On the more conservative side of Jewish politics, many moderates, such as former Bush White House aide Jay Lefkowitz, argue that Jewish liberalism results from "old fears" of the anti-Semitism that was once rampant on the fundamentalist Christian right. Further to the right, hardliners often describe Jewish liberalism in psychological terms as a form of "Jewish self-hatred"—a sort of Stockholm syndrome that leads all too many Jews to identify with their enemies and disregard their own community's needs. "Jews are the only American minority whose members do not as a matter of course support the land of their people," writes Canadian-born Yiddish scholar Ruth Wisse, in her 1992 book-length essay *If I Am Not for Myself: The Liberal Betrayal of the Jews.*

Each of these theories sheds partial light on the truth. But all of them are at best partial explanations.

For example, the idea that Jewish liberalism is rooted in Jewish tradition rings true for many Jews. And indeed, some of the core values of American liberalism—such as taxing the rich to help the poor, or putting a mother's rights before those of a fetus—are firmly enshrined in Jewish religious doctrine.

However, as an explanation for the appeal of liberalism to American Jews, this theory falls short. The trouble is that American Jews' liberalism tends to decline as their traditionalism rises. Orthodox Jews, the most traditionalist in religious belief and behavior, appear consistently in surveys to be less liberal than Conservative Jews, who in turn are less liberal than Reform Jews. If Jewish traditionalism alone fostered liberalism, the trend should be just the reverse: the more traditional, the more liberal.

Many non-Jewish activists who come in contact with the organized Jewish community see Jewish liberalism in much more straightforward terms: as a simple matter of self-interest. For example, the Reverend Calvin Butts of Harlem's Abyssinian Baptist Church argues that, in their long-standing support for civil rights, "Jews have done what's best for them, because they too have historically been victims of exclusion and discrimination."

But Buzz Thomas of the National Council of Churches, a longtime ally of the Jewish community, suggests that the Jewish pursuit of self-interest is a subtle process. Unlike most liberal pressure groups, the Jewish lobby takes a consistently high-minded tone, which is more effective for not appearing self-interested. "Obviously the Jews have a lot at stake," Thomas says. "The United States has been the best place for them to be Jewish, to be on a level playing field, or at least as level as it can be when you're in a minority. But it doesn't seem to be as proprietary with the Jewish groups as with some organizations. The Jewish community has its own self-interest, but they function in a way that is based on a belief in principle. And that increases their effectiveness. Any time people on Capitol Hill feel you're working for a principle and not just self-interest, it's appealing to them."

To many liberals within the organized Jewish leadership, high-mindedness is smart politics. Working for broad principles allows one to join forces with other groups that have similar problems, expanding the reach of a small community. "We find that Jewish political clout necessarily includes the development of coalitions," says Hyman Bookbinder, former Washington representative of the American Jewish Committee. "Working with civil rights groups and labor groups widens our effectiveness, so we get them to be additional lobbyists. We show interest in their agendas and they help us in our agenda."

Japanese diplomat Hideo Sato agrees. The Tokyo foreign ministry's top expert on American Jewry, Sato believes that the Jewish community's willingness to fight for others is a major reason for its successes on its own behalf. "The Jewish organizations maintain their support for other minorities," Sato says. "They maintain their ties with blacks and Hispanics. It is very effective. What we appreciate about them is that they are unanimously against Japan-bashing. That is very much appreciated in the Ministry."

The payoff can be dramatic. According to Sato, Japan's diplomatic warming toward Israel during the late 1980s was due in good measure to Tokyo's blossoming ties with the organized American Jewish leadership. Contacts had begun in the early 1980s, when the American Jewish Committee sought a dialogue on the startling rise of anti-Semitic publications in Japan. The talks developed into an ongoing conversation between the Japanese government and several Jewish organizations. These discussions led directly, Sato says, to Tokyo's December 1992 decision to break with the Arab economic boycott of Israel. (Israel explained the breakthrough as having resulted from Foreign Minister Shimon Peres's visit to Japan the month before. Sato carefully explained that nothing happens that fast in Japan.)

As for the theory that American Jewish liberalism was imported by Russian Jewish immigrants in the early twentieth century, that misses the mark by a full century.

American Jewry's romance with the Democratic Party dates back to the presidential election of 1800, the first race fought on party lines. The reason is simple: Thomas Jefferson and his Democratic-Republicans (as they were then known) championed freedom of religion. The rival Federalists feared disorder unless the government were a force for morality, and that meant Christianity. "How then can a Jew but be a [Democratic] Republican?" wrote Benjamin Nones, president of the Philadelphia synagogue, during the 1800 campaign.

The 1800 campaign also saw the first public effort to woo Jewish voters *away* from the Democrats. A letter that fall in the *Philadelphia Gazette,* signed by Moses S. Solomons, urged Jews to help defeat Jefferson as a foe of "all religion." The strategy collapsed when Benjamin Nones exposed the letter as a fraud: "No such man as Moses S. Solomons has *ever been,* or is now a member of the Hebrew congregation of this city," the synagogue's board announced.

The bonds between Jews and Democrats grew over the next century. The Democrats continually expanded beyond Jefferson's base of small farmers and intellectuals to become the party of immigrants, Catholics, Jews, and urban workers. The New York Democratic organization, the Tammany Society, became America's first big-city political machine, virtually minting votes by organizing immigrants and delivering social services.

In 1860, the fledgling Republican party (as it is known today) tried again to win away the Jewish vote. Jews were voting Democratic by a two-to-one margin, wrote Illinois Republican strategist Abraham Jonas in a memo to a party leader, but they might be ripe for a switch. The Republicans reached out with several dramatic gestures, including the first-ever invitation to a rabbi to bless the U.S. House of Representatives. But these overtures fell flat. Jews remained in the Democratic column through the rest of the nineteenth century and most of the twentieth.

Appealing to a Jewish vote is the oldest and most broadly accepted practice in American Jewish politics. Still, Jews view this ritual with deeply mixed emotions. They often celebrate it as an affirmation of their full citizenship in the American body politic. Just as often they lament it as demeaning, pandering, and stereotypic.

It is all those things. For most of the twentieth century, wooing the Jewish vote meant walking through Jewish neighborhoods, donning a skullcap, and being photographed while eating a kosher knish. More recently, it has come to mean vowing eternal admiration for Israel and support for its every need, at least until Election Day.

Once in office, lawmakers commonly cite the Jewish vote as a key pragmatic consideration when they weigh a decision affecting Israel or church-state issues. Presidential candidates spend millions trying to woo the Jewish vote. Nearly every major presidential campaign since 1972 has set up a separate Jewish organization, with its own staff and budget, to stump among the Jews and appeal for their votes.

All this for a group of citizens that amounts to a statistically meaningless 2.5 percent of the American population. The effort seems strangely pointless.

In fact, numbers can be deceiving. Though they comprise just 2.5 percent or so of the overall population, Jews are estimated to make up more than 4 percent of the electorate. The reason is that they vote in greater numbers than other Americans. About 80 percent of Jews are registered to vote, compared to about 50 percent of all voting age adults. On top of that, registered Jews are more likely to vote than non-Jews. Jews are older, too. In the end, Jews are nearly twice as likely to vote as non-Jews.

And that's only half of the story. Most of America's Jews are concentrated in a handful of states, where they make up a relatively larger share of the population. In fact, 71 percent of all American Jews live in just seven states, where they constitute at least 3 percent of the population (and 6 percent or more of the electorate): New York, New Jersey, Florida, Massachusetts, Maryland, Connecticut, and California. Adding Pennsylvania and Illinois, where Jews number 2.7 percent and 2.3 percent of the population, respectively, fully 81 percent of all American Jews live in just nine states (Table 1).

TABLE 1: PERCENTAGE OF JEWS IN SELECTED STATES AND THEIR ELECTORATE

	Jews as % of population	Jews as % of electorate
New York	9.0	18.3
New Jersey	5.5	9.9
Florida	4.7	8.2
Massachusetts	4.5	8.3
Maryland	4.3	8.1
Connecticut	3.0	6.2
California	3.0	5.8
Pennsylvania	2.7	4.9
Illinois	2.3	3.9

These nine states cast 202 of the 535 votes in the Electoral College, or 37 percent of the total.

In presidential politics, numbers like these are extremely tempting, particularly in a close election. They mean, in theory at least, that a well-targeted appeal to a group of just a few hundred thousand people can swing whole segments of the Electoral College. That, of course, is where the American presidency is won or lost.

An illustration of the Jewish vote at its most potent came in the 1992 presidential election. The winner, Democrat Bill Clinton, beat Republican incumbent George Bush and independent candidate H. Ross Perot in a three-way race, with a 43 to 38 to 19 percent breakdown of the 101 million votes cast.

Among Jewish voters, the breakdown was quite different. According to Election Day exit polls commissioned by the American Jewish Congress, Jews voted 85 percent for Clinton, 10 percent for Bush, and 5 percent for Perot. A separate study by the respected Voter Research and Surveys (VRS) organization estimated the Jewish vote at 78 to 12 to 10 percent.

The National Jewish Democratic Council, a Washington-based group with close ties to the Democratic National Committee, cited both polls to claim after Election Day that Jewish voters had made up between 50 and 56 percent of Clinton's 5.5-million-vote victory margin.

The Jewish Democrats' claim is slightly misleading, though not by much. Careful political analysts measure the impact of a minority voting bloc not simply by how it votes, but by *how differently it votes from everyone else*. To measure the real role of the Jewish vote in Clinton's victory, then, one needs to examine what might be called the *Jewish differential*—the margin of Jewish voters who voted differently from the general electorate.

In Clinton's case, the results are still pretty impressive: Jews voted for him at nearly twice the overall rate. About half of those Jews who voted for the Democrat might have been expected to do so in any case, since 43 percent of all voters did so. The other half—nearly 1.5 million voters—voted the way they did, in effect, *because they were Jews*. This group—the Jewish differential vote—made up about one fourth of Clinton's margin of victory. Put differently, some 1.5 million of the 5.5 million voters who edged Clinton into the White House did so because of his appeal to Jewish voters (or George Bush's lack thereof).

A state-by-state analysis prepared by the National Jewish Democratic Council was even more compelling. In five states with a total of 86 electoral votes (New York, New Jersey, Ohio, Georgia, and Nevada), Jews made up 75 percent or more of Clinton's victory margin (using the low-end VRS estimate of the Jewish vote). Even if that figure is cut in half, to isolate the Jewish differential vote—the Jews who voted differently because they were Jewish—there are still five states where Clinton got more than one third of his margin because of his unique appeal to Jews.

In two of those states, Georgia and New Jersey, with 28 electoral votes combined, Jews were entirely responsible for Clinton's victory, delivering respectively 210 and 353 percent of his winning margin.

One could just as easily argue, of course, that black voters won the election for Clinton, or women or Hispanics or any other group that voted more Democratic than the norm. Even unmarried voters helped him: at 35 percent of the general electorate, they went for Clinton over Bush by 49 to 33 percent. By our definition, 2.1 million voters chose Clinton because they were single.

"In a close election, everything is a swing vote, because everything is so up in the air," said political analyst William Schneider, of the conservative American Enterprise Institute, in an interview during the 1992 campaign.

In fact, Schneider said, "I've never heard of the Jewish vote swinging an election. To begin with, only about half the Jewish vote is connected to the organized Jewish community. Much of the Jewish vote is not particularly responsive to the Israel issue. The only thing we can say for certain about the Jewish vote is that it is, on the whole, more liberal than other voters and more Democratic."

In Schneider's view, the lopsided Jewish support for Clinton in 1992 was due to a unique set of circumstances. "You have two kinds of Jewish voters as a rule," he explained. "There are those strongly identified with Israel, and the secular Jews who are not particularly identified with Israel. Both kinds of Jewish voters don't like George Bush, but for different reasons. The more conservative Jewish voters don't like his criticisms of Israel, and that is the definitive issue for them. The more secular, liberal Jewish voters don't mind his criticisms of Israel, but they aren't going to vote for him anyway because he's too conservative, and that's the definitive issue for them. You put those two together and there's very little Jewish support for George Bush."

✣   ✣   ✣

Jewish Republicans tend to view the voting habits of their fellow Jews as nothing less than a stubborn refusal to face reality. "You're not going to tell me that the record that has been amassed is worth the 13 percent that George Bush got," says Republican lawyer Maxwell Rabb, who served as a ranking aide in the Eisenhower White House. "Our community thinks it deserves all the rewards, but it doesn't want to pay for them. It's just like the general electorate, which wants to cut taxes and reduce the deficit and maintain full spending. Our community wants the Republicans to be with them, and then they basically don't support them. Thank God for the few dumb fools who stay in the Republican Party and keep things going."

"I'm not saying they shouldn't vote their minds," Rabb says. "But you can't tell me there aren't an awful lot of Jewish people who don't share the basic principles of the Republican Party."

In the final analysis, it is the hardheaded realists who have it wrong: the plain truth is that the Jewish vote *does* exist and *does* shift enough to be worth fighting for. The surest evidence is in the marketplace, where politicians battle for the Jewish vote year after year. They would not bother if there were no prize to be had.

What the politicians understand instinctively is that the prize to be won is not the whole Jewish community, but a large enough chunk to make a difference in target regions.

An examination of presidential election returns throughout the twentieth century shows that while most Jews nearly always have voted Democratic, the percentage has risen and fallen enough to turn elections (as shown in Table 2).

Only two Democrats in this century, James Cox in 1920 and Jimmy Carter in 1980, won less than half of the Jewish vote. Both candidates ran in years when Jewish voters were extraordinarily angry at outgoing Democratic administrations. In both campaigns, Republicans got more than their usual share of Jewish votes, but still fell short of a majority; the balance went to liberal third-party candidates. Both elections ended as Republican landslides, so the Jews did not make a difference.

In every other presidential year, the Democratic candidate has taken a majority of the Jewish vote. But the size of that majority has varied,

TABLE 2: JEWISH VOTE, U.S. PRESIDENTIAL RACES, 1916–1992

Year	% of Jewish vote	% of total vote	Year	% of Jewish vote	% of total vote
1916			**1956**		
Wilson (D)	55	51	Stevenson (D)	60	42
Hughes (R)	45	48	Eisenhower (R)	40	57
1920			**1960**		
Cox (D)	19	35	Kennedy (D)	82	50
Harding (R)	43	61	Nixon (R)	18	49
Debs (S)	38	3.5	**1964**		
1924			Johnson (D)	90	61
Davis (D)	51	29	Goldwater (R)	10	38
Coolidge (R)	27	54	**1968**		
La Follette (P)	22	16	Humphrey (D)	81	42
1928			Nixon (R)	17	43
Smith (D)	72	41	Wallace, G. C. (AI)	2	13.5
Hoover (R)	28	58	**1972**		
1932			McGovern (D)	65	38
Roosevelt (D)	82	59	Nixon (R)	35	61
Hoover (R)	18	40	**1976**		
1936			Carter (D)	64	50
Roosevelt (D)	85	62	Ford (R)	34	48
Landon (R)	15	37	**1980**		
1940			Carter (D)	45	41
Roosevelt (D)	90	54	Reagan (R)	39	51
Willkie (R)	10	45	Anderson (I)	15	7
1944			**1984**		
Roosevelt (D)	90	53	Mondale (D)	67	40
Dewey (R)	10	46	Reagan (R)	33	59
1948			**1988**		
Truman (D)	75	49	Dukakis (D)	64	45
Dewey (R)	10	45	Bush (R)	35	53
Wallace, H. A. (P)	15	2	**1992**		
Thurmond (SD)	–	2	Clinton (D)	78	43
1952			Bush (R)	12	38
Stevenson (D)	64	44	Perot (I)	10	19
Eisenhower (R)	36	55			

Key: AI = American Independent   R = Republican
      D = Democrat   S = Socialist
      I = Independent   SD = Southern Democrat
      P = Progressive

depending on the popularity of the Democrat and the unpopularity of the Republican.

What the numbers show is this: about 55 to 60 percent of Jewish voters will vote Democratic *almost* regardless of who is running. Another 10 percent or so will vote Republican, no matter what. The remainder—close to one third of the Jewish vote—can be swayed by candidates and their positions.

That swing vote—some 1 million to 1.5 million votes nationwide—is what politicians strive for when they campaign for the Jewish vote. In a tight race, it can make a crucial difference. In 1992, as we have seen, the Jewish swing vote contributed about one fourth of Bill Clinton's 5.5-million-vote margin. In 1944, the overwhelming Jewish vote for Democratic incumbent Franklin D. Roosevelt contributed perhaps one third of his narrow, 3-million-vote margin.

Even more dramatic was the Jewish role in the tight 1960 race between John F. Kennedy and Richard Nixon. Kennedy, the victorious Democrat, won just over 80 percent of the Jewish vote—20 percent more than Democrat Adlai Stevenson had won four years earlier. Between 1956 and 1960, that is, some half-million Jews switched from the Republican column to the Democratic column. The Democrat won by 118,550 votes out of the 68 million votes cast, according to the official tally.

The Jewish margin does not work only for Democrats. In 1968, when Richard Nixon made his second run at the White House, Jewish Republicans were organized under Max Fisher to mount a serious, concerted effort at boosting the GOP's share of the Jewish vote from the 10 percent that Barry Goldwater won in 1964. Thanks partly to their diligence, enough Jews switched sides in 1968 to boost the Republican share to 17 percent. At first glance, this shift may not seem significant. But the shift of 200,000 Jewish votes to Richard Nixon made a significant dent in an election that Nixon won by only 510,000 votes.

When Senator Jesse Helms first introduced his "constitutionally protected school prayer" amendment in February 1994, he attached it to a wide-ranging education bill called Goals 2000. Once it reached the Senate floor, the Helms amendment won handily, 75 to 22. A similar measure was introduced in the House version of the bill by two Southern Republicans, John "Jimmy" Duncan of Tennessee and Sam Johnson of Texas. It passed by a margin of 239 to 171.

Formally, the Democratic leadership in both chambers opposed the Helms amendment. They viewed it as a deliberate assault on the constitutional separation of church and state. In practice, however, their minds were elsewhere during that spring of 1994. Individual lawmakers thus were left free to support the measure almost unhindered. Knowing that voters were worried about their children's values, members of Congress sprang at this opportunity to vote for school prayer, confident that they were only backing prayer that was "constitutionally protected." Opposition to the Helms amendment was limited to hardline liberal ideologues—and Jews.

During the House debate on the amendment, Democratic leaders complained that "almost everyone debating on our side was Jewish, which didn't help," recalls lobbyist Jim Halpert of People for the American Way.

The Democrats' complaint reflected a dilemma that often confronts liberals when an issue of religious freedom reaches the floor of Congress: when the most audible voices are Jewish, the Gentile majority is tempted to think it has no stake in the issue, Halpert says. "The other members, who don't have a lot of Jews in their own constituencies, look at these folks and think to themselves, 'they don't represent my constituents.' I'm not saying they're anti-Semitic, but it colors the way they look at it."

Actually, only two of the four anti-Helms speakers on the House floor were Jewish: freshmen Jerry Nadler of New York and Eric Fingerhut of Ohio. The other two were the sturdy liberal warhorses Don Edwards of California and Pat Williams of Montana. But impressions can be stronger than reality.

After a bill is passed by both the House and Senate, it goes to a conference committee. There representatives of the two chambers sit down to reconcile the differences between their versions. Where the two versions match, the conference committee must leave the language alone.

Conference committees are put together by the heads of the committees where the bill originated. The House version of Goals 2000 began in the House Education and Labor Committee, chaired by Michigan Democrat William Ford. The day after the House passed the bill containing the Helms amendment, Ford summoned the chief lobbyists for the two key liberal opposition groups, Robert Peck of the ACLU and Jim Halpert of People for the American Way. There was no way to remove the amendment in conference, Ford told them, since both houses had passed matching versions. Yet letting it become law would represent a historic step backwards in a generations-long process of protecting religious minorities.

Instead, Ford suggested a drastic measure: sending the entire Goals 2000 bill back to the drawing board by returning it to the two chambers, unreconciled, without a conference. The bill had been inching its way through Congress since the Bush administration, evoking little opposition and less enthusiasm. "Nobody liked it except school administrators," Halpert recalls. Ford promised to convince the Clinton administration and the Democratic congressional leadership to back away from the bill. The lobbyists' job was to drum up support among rank-and-file lawmakers—a majority of whom had just voted for it.

Peck and Halpert mobilized lobbyists from Jewish organizations and teachers' groups. Within a few days, sixty representatives had been convinced to reverse their votes. The bill was sent back to the drawing board.

By the time Goals 2000 returned to the Senate floor, it was March 23, 1994, a Wednesday. Congress was scheduled to recess for Easter and Passover on Friday. The Senate passed the new version of the bill on Wednesday, gutting Helms's school-prayer language. Helms, furious, counterattacked with what amounted to a mini-filibuster aimed squarely at the Senate's Jewish members. He introduced a series of procedural motions that forced the Senate to stay in session through Saturday morning. He knew that the ten Jewish senators were all due home for the Passover seder on Saturday evening, and that one, Joseph Lieberman of Connecticut, an Orthodox Jew, had to leave town by Friday afternoon or he would be stuck in Washington until Monday night and miss the holiday.

It was only minutes before Lieberman's Friday flight that the anti-Helms forces became confident that they could stop Helms without him. Lieberman made it home for the holiday.

Defeated again, Helms immediately reinserted his amendment in a new education bill, the Clinton administration's Elementary and Secondary School Education Act of 1994. This fight promised to be even tougher. By now a broad coalition had been assembled to stop Helms, made up of civil liberties groups, Jewish organizations, teachers' unions, school administrators' groups, and several Christian churches. Lawmakers were being swamped with letters and phone calls stressing that the Helms language was not as innocuous as it sounded, and asking them not to vote for it again.

At the same time, Helms was working the halls himself, together with various allies from the Christian right who favored school prayer. Their message: a flip-flop by senators who already had voted to protect a child's right to pray could be costly in November.

To give lawmakers some cover, the liberal coalition decided to formulate an alternative measure that upheld the right to pray without inviting wholesale surrender of the separation of church and state. To provide additional cover, they resolved to have this new language introduced by a Republican senator. Their first choice was John Danforth of Missouri, an ordained Protestant minister. But Danforth, a hardline purist on church-state separation, refused to sponsor any softening of the Helms amendment; he wanted it defeated outright. The coalition then turned to another moderate Republican, Nancy Kassebaum of Kansas. She was reluctant to go up against Helms, but she agreed under pressure from several of her campaign donors, who had been mobilized by the Kansas City regional director of the American Jewish Committee.

As for the text of the substitute amendment, Peck and Halpert were talking about a measure that endorsed school prayer if it was indeed "constitutionally protected," but that required the government first to prove in court that a child's rights had been violated before a school could lose federal funding. They drew up a first draft, then convened an ad hoc group at the ACLU offices to refine the language and ensure that it was acceptable to all of their various constituencies.

The group met in early June 1994 to finalize the language. Present, in addition to Peck and Halpert, were Elliot Mincberg, general counsel of People for the American Way; Richard Foltin, a lawyer with the American Jewish Committee; and Mark Pelavin, Washington representative of the American Jewish Congress. Also invited, to make sure that all viewpoints were represented, was an aide from the Republican side of the Senate, Jeff Balaban, a lawyer on Danforth's staff.

It was, all in all, a well-balanced group—although, it occurred to Halpert as he looked around the room, everyone present was Jewish.

As straightforward as the national politics of American Jews may seem, the politics within the Jewish community are something else again. The inner workings of the Jewish organizational world are arcane, byzantine, and convoluted, so much so that even seasoned insiders often feel lost without a compass. The authoritative *American Jewish Year Book* lists about three hundred national Jewish organizations and close to two hundred local

federations of Jewish charities. Their combined budget—counting synagogue dues, Sunday school tuition, and Medicare payments to Jewish
hospitals—totals somewhere upwards of $6 billion per year. That is more
than the gross national product of half the members of the United Nations.
Indeed, the precise total has never even been calculated.

The confusion is deceptive, however. "It appears that there are a great
many organizations," says Japanese diplomat Hideo Sato. "But there are
really only about ten main organizations which have political activities, and
each has its own style. The others are more or less religious or academic or
social."

The combined activities of these "political" groups—community activists call them "defense" or "community-relations" agencies—amount to
less than $100 million per year, or just one half of 1 percent of the total
budget of the organized Jewish community.

Trying to figure out where the key Jewish organizations stand on the
major issues of the day is much easier than sorting out their structures. The
main community-relations agencies maintain a central council through
which they coordinate their policies. The council publishes a yearly summary of the Jewish community's positions on the big issues, complete with
minority dissents.

The council, known by the jawbreaking title of the National Jewish
Community Relations Advisory Council, or NCRAC (pronounced "nac-
rac"; see Acronyms of Jewish Organizations, page xiii), is nothing less than
the central policy council of the organized American Jewish community. Its
membership includes a dozen of the most powerful and broadly representative groups on the national Jewish scene: the three main synagogue unions,
Reform, Conservative, and Orthodox; the three main "defense agencies,"
Anti-Defamation League, American Jewish Committee, and American
Jewish Congress; and the three largest Jewish women's groups, Hadassah,
the National Council of Jewish Women, and Women's American ORT. Also
included, along with a handful of other national bodies, are 117 local
community councils, representing the world of Jewish federated charities
and their donors.

NCRAC's policy positions are hammered out in intense, year-long negotiations among the agencies, then voted on at the council's annual assembly
and published each fall in a booklet, the *Joint Program Plan*. The result can
seem almost impossibly diverse, reading like a catalogue of the year's stylish
liberal causes. The eighty-four–page plan for 1992 included, along with ten

pages on Israel and eight pages on anti-Semitism in Russia and the Arab world, no less than six pages on public-school education, six pages on abortion rights and the status of women, four pages on poverty, three pages each on immigration policy, federal courts, and universal health care, and four pages on the environment. The 1994 plan added two pages titled "Gun Control and Violence," plus a four-page section titled "Constitutional Protections in a Pluralistic Democracy." These protections addressed issues ranging from the death penalty and homosexual rights to term limits, campaign-finance reform, and congressional redistricting.

The sheer breadth of the organizations' political agenda leaves many Jewish activists confused and irritated. "The Nacrac group gets involved in all sorts of issues, in housing, in homelessness, in AIDS, which are not Jewish issues," complains New York attorney Seymour Reich, a former chairman of the Conference of Presidents of Major American Jewish Organizations. (The Presidents Conference is NCRAC's chief rival as lead voice in the Jewish community).

"They may be issues of concern to members of the Jewish community," Reich says. "But they are not Jewish issues."

If Reich's assertion is true, the fault is not NCRAC's. The council is not much more than a toothless reflection of its fiercely independent member-agencies. With its tiny seven-member staff and $1 million budget, it can hardly be more.

In fact, the range of NCRAC's policies is a pragmatic reflection of the Jewish community's range of interests. "American Jews live in the United States, and they care about the society in which they live," says David Harris, executive vice president of the American Jewish Committee. "And with few exceptions, Jews have come to the correct perception that the health of the larger society has implications for us as Americans and as Jews."

Nonetheless, the NCRAC agenda provokes widespread resentment among Jewish activists at the grass roots. In some cities where black-Jewish tensions run high, such as New York, Philadelphia, and Chicago, it is common to hear complaints against the Jewish defense agencies for their continuing support of black rights. During the early 1990s, when NCRAC was lobbying actively to support the Muslim government of Bosnia, some outraged Zionists complained out loud that Islam was the enemy of Judaism.

Often lost in the debate is the fact that most of the issues taken up by the

Jewish agencies involve at least some element of narrow Jewish self-interest. U.S. immigration policy defines the ability of American Jews to rescue their fellow Jews from Russia, Iran, and Syria. Congressional redistricting affects the number of Jews elected to Congress (which dropped from thirty-two in 1993 to twenty-four in 1995, partly as a result of the reapportionment that followed the 1990 census). The budgeting of health-care and anti-poverty dollars affects the stability of Jewish federated charities, which form the backbone of the entire Jewish community structure.

Most of all, constitutional matters such as school prayer and abortion rights affect the ability of Jews to live as equals in America.

In the spring of 1990, Rabbi Robert Loewy of suburban New Orleans went before his state legislature to testify on behalf of abortion rights in the name of the New Orleans Jewish Federation, the central organization of the local Jewish community. The way some of his colleagues told it afterward, he nearly started a pogrom.

The Louisiana legislature was debating a bill to outlaw virtually all abortions. The only exceptions allowed were in doctor-certified cases of threat to the mother's life. Rabbi Loewy, president of the Greater New Orleans Rabbinical Board, appeared before the house criminal-justice committee on June 7 to testify that the bill violated the freedom of Louisiana Jews to practice their religion.

In rabbinic canon law, the rabbi explained, human life does not simply begin at conception. It develops gradually, acquiring greater legal protection by stages as the fetus gains viability. Development continues even after birth, he added parenthetically; an infant that dies before the eighth day does not even receive a Jewish funeral.

In any case, he said, Judaism rules that the mother's needs automatically take precedence until the moment of birth. "There is," he told the committee, "a moral and ethical basis for a woman to undergo an abortion. Do not impose the view of some on all of us."

It was a highly unusual presentation. The case for abortion as a matter of Jewish religious freedom is a powerful one. But it had never before been made in a public forum.

The rabbi's speech quickly became an object lesson in the wisdom of the usual approach.

When the committee broke for lunch, a pack of reporters pounced on the bill's house sponsor, Representative Louis "Woody" Jenkins, and asked him to evaluate the morning's testimony. "Well," Jenkins said, "we heard from one crazy religion that doesn't even think babies are people after they're born."

A few days later, Rabbi Loewy returned to Baton Rouge to testify before the state senate. This time the fireworks started up at once. As the rabbi began to explain that the Jewish religion often favors abortion, the bill's senate sponsor, Senator Mike Cross, interrupted to ask if the rabbi's religion also encouraged prostitution and drug use. Loewy replied by explaining that the rabbinic view of abortion is taken from a literal reading of the Bible, which explicitly rules that abortion is not homicide. "That's not in my Bible," Cross retorted.

When the rabbi tried to cite the chapter and verse (Exodus 21:22: "If two men strive and one strikes a woman with child, so that her fruit departs, *and yet no harm follow,* he shall surely be fined." [emphasis mine]), the chairman cut him off and dismissed him.

The legislative assault on Robert Loewy—one state senator later called it "the rabbi roast"—prompted careful soul-searching within the New Orleans Jewish leadership. Several community officials wanted to respond vigorously to the intolerant tone of the rabbi's inquisitors. But the majority "decided not to try to play it up as an issue of anti-Semitism," Loewy recalled. "It was our impression that this was not designed to be an anti-Semitic attack, but a virulent pro-life attack on a pro-choice position."

More to the point, a Jewish counterattack might well have backfired. The anti-abortion lawmakers might not have started from the assumption that the Jews were their enemy, but they could easily have been driven to that view. And if the Jewish community pushed for such a head-on confrontation, it would lose.

Louisiana is a state known for its bare-knuckled politics. The *Almanac of American Politics* calls it "America's Third World." The summer of the abortion debate was also the summer that David Duke, the neo-Nazi and Klansman–turned–state legislator, was running for governor; come October, he would rack up 45 percent of the vote, including 55 percent of the white vote. The right wing was angry, mobilized, and looking for blood. "Their position was to paint anyone who disagreed with them as a murderer," said Leslie Gerwin, an officer of the Jewish federation and leading pro-choice activist. The Christian right was such a strong force in Louisiana—with fundamentalists in the state's north and Catholics in the south—that the Jenkins-Cross anti-abortion bill eventually would sweep both houses and overcome a governor's veto to become law in 1991.

In the midst of this pitched battle, the Jewish position on the abortion bill was straightforward. The Jewish federation, the community's central body, had come out formally against the bill. So had the Greater New Orleans Rabbinical Board, representing all eleven rabbis in town from Reform to Hasidic. Jews were represented disproportionately in the leadership of major pro-choice groups like Planned Parenthood of Louisiana, the League of Women Voters, and People for the American Way. The ad hoc coalition against the bill, Citizens for Personal Freedom, was run by a board member of the Jewish federation. Among the thirty groups on the coalition's steering committee were the federation's community-relations committee; three synagogue sisterhoods; and the local chapters of the Anti-Defamation League, the National Council of Jewish Women, and Hadassah.

The Jews were not shy about their views. Almost no one suggested they should be. In framing the bill as an assault on their religious freedom, however, the Jewish community's leaders may have gone one step too far. They were holding up Jewish rights as a shield for a separate issue, on the assumption that their opponents had too much respect for religious freedom, and for Jews, to press the attack. As they found out, that was a mistake.

Conservatives argue that the Jewish voter's stubborn, lopsided devotion to liberal causes is actually self-defeating. Rooted in an instinct for self-protection, it ends up alienating the political right, effectively putting all the Jews' eggs in one flimsy liberal basket.

"Politics is quid pro quo," says Max Fisher, senior Jewish philanthropist and Republican fund-raiser. "In my opinion the Jewish community is not appreciative enough of what's been done for them.

"They think of the Democratic party as a haven for liberalism, which I can understand," Fisher says. "But when you think about it, during the life of the state of Israel, the twenty-eight years under Republican presidents were the best years for Israel. Kennedy wouldn't ship any arms. Johnson didn't either. The first time the Israelis ever got big money was under Nixon. And I lobbied very hard after 1973 to see that the three billion dollars would be as much in aid as in loans. Look at what Bush and Baker did—in forty-five years of history, the Madrid conference they set up in 1991 is the first time anybody got the Arabs to sit down with the Israelis for peace talks. Did anybody appreciate that? No.

"Now, why was the Republicans' support for Israel so strong? That's the paradox," Fisher continues. "It was strong and people didn't appreciate it. Today they talk with love and affection for Reagan and Nixon, but when it came to voting, the peak of the Jewish vote [for Republicans] was never more than 40 percent. People have a tendency to forget the things that happened that are good. Jews have a particularly hard time remembering good things."

The slight has not gone unnoticed. According to the Reverend Pat Robertson, the influential Christian broadcaster and founder of the Christian Coalition, Jewish liberalism has evoked widespread resentment in Christian America. Jews, Robertson prophesies, will suffer greatly for this in the coming Apocalypse. They will be punished not only for having rejected Jesus, as Christians have preached throughout the ages, but also for "the ongoing attempt of liberal Jews to undermine the public strength of Christianity" in modern-day America.

Like many conservatives, Robertson is convinced that the declining quality of American moral life is caused by the secularization of America's public square, and not, for example, by growing economic inequality, or by the disruptive impact of new technologies. He believes that American Christians eventually will turn against Jews and Israel, angered over the role of "cosmopolitan, liberal, secular Jews" in promoting "freedom for smut and pornography and the murder of the unborn."

"The part that Jewish intellectuals and media activists have played in the assault on Christianity may very possibly prove to be a grave mistake," Robertson writes in his 1990 book, *The New Millenium.*

Actually, the participation of Jews in Republican and conservative politics has risen sharply in recent years. When Max Rabb and Max Fisher started to make their mark in the GOP in the 1940s and 1950s, they represented a rare breed. Up until the 1970s, Jewish Republicans were visible only in isolated pockets: liberal political activists such as the late Senator Jacob

Javits of New York, or conservative economic theorists such as Milton Friedman and Arthur Burns.

Today, Jews have assumed a significant presence on the American right. They cover a broad spectrum, from moderates like Senator Arlen Specter of Pennsylvania and Republican activist (and former Bush White House aide) Bobbie Kilberg of Virginia, to staunch conservatives like William Kristol, the onetime chief of staff to Vice President Dan Quayle, and Arthur Finkelstein, the campaign consultant whose clients range from Jesse Helms to Israel's Benjamin Netanyahu. They have an important national voice in their flagship journal, *Commentary,* the archconservative monthly published by the American Jewish Committee.

Here and there, Jewish conservatives constitute significant voting blocs. Orthodox Jews in New York City, some two hundred thousand strong, played a pivotal role in the Republican takeovers of the New York City mayor's office in 1993 and of the state governor's mansion in 1994. New York Orthodoxy's most militant politico, state assembly member Dov Hikind of Brooklyn (a conservative Democrat and former lieutenant to the far-right militant, Meir Kahane), has made himself one of the most sought-after power brokers in New York state politics.

In 1984, New York City's Mayor Edward Koch issued an executive order banning discrimination against homosexuals by city contractors. The order prompted lawsuits against the city by religious bodies that receive city funding for their social services, but do not hire homosexuals on religious principle. The three plaintiffs were the Salvation Army, Catholic Charities of New York, and Agudath Israel of America, an advocacy group representing the most traditional Orthodox Jews.

The judge handling the three lawsuits decided to consolidate all of them into a single case, and summoned representatives of the three plaintiffs into his chambers for a settlement conference. Also present were lawyers for the city and for the Lambda Legal Defense Fund, a gay rights group.

"It was a little bit uncomfortable," Agudath Israel's government affairs director, David Zwiebel, would recall later. "During the settlement conference, the lawyer for the Salvation Army laid out his position by saying, 'My clients regard homosexuals as sinners.' After we left the judge's chambers, the lawyer for the Lambda fund came up to me, a fellow named Feldman, and he said, 'You realize, don't you, that the words they use against gays are the same words they use against Jews when you're not around?' And the truth is, I know he's right. There's no question that the people we have been aligned with on a whole host of these social issues are not our friends."

Whatever gains Jewish conservatives may have made in recent years, the overall profile of the Jewish community—Jewish voters, Jewish of-ficeholders, most Jewish social activism, and majority opinion on the Jewish street—remains overwhelmingly Democratic and liberal. Of the nine Jews in the U.S. Senate in 1995, eight were Democrats; of the twenty-four Jews in the House of Representatives, twenty were Democrats.

Within the world of liberal organizations like the ACLU and People for the American Way, Jewish influence is so profound that non-Jews some-times blur the distinction between them and the formal Jewish community.

"You get this all the time in comments from congressional staff," says ACLU attorney Bob Peck. "They say, 'Next time you come, bring along members of other religious groups. Don't just bring more Jews.' They do it offhandedly, without a thought, and certainly without malice. It's simply clear to them that we have this background. Many of our leaders are recognizably Jewish. And it's clear there are things that we will understand more readily, because of who we are."

Indeed, Aryeh Neier, the dean of American human rights activism, says that over the course of his career—as director of the New York Civil Liberties Union, the ACLU, Human Rights Watch/Helsinki Watch, and now George Soros's Open Society Institutes—he has been allied with the main Jewish organizations "90 percent of the time."

"I don't have any magical belief in a genetic history or anything like that," Neier says. "But I do believe that identification as a Jew—both your self-identification and your identification by others as a Jew—makes a substantial imprint on someone."

CHAPTER 3

Vanishing Point:
The Struggle for the Jewish Soul

T HE MOOD ON THE SOUTH LAWN of the White House was festive but a bit surreal on the morning of September 13, 1993. Three thousand people, one of the largest crowds ever gathered at the White House, were assembled under a blazing late summer sun to watch as the prime minister of Israel and the chairman of the Palestine Liberation Organization shook hands under the benevolent gaze of the president of the United States. In signing their historic accord today, Yitzhak Rabin and Yasser Arafat were not ending the long dispute between their two peoples, but they were moving it to the negotiating table, and for the Middle East that was a sea change.

To most of the onlookers, an august assemblage of former presidents and secretaries of state, members of Congress, diplomats, and journalists from around the world, this was a day to be savored. It was one of those rare moments, like the signing of a disarmament pact or the creation of a new world body, when the things they do add up, when the profession of managing human events makes sense.

For those onlookers who were Jewish—something like a thousand lobbyists and community leaders, rabbis, politicians, journalists, and peace activists, perhaps one third of the crowd—the day's events raised a far more complex mix of emotions.

None could be unmoved at the sight of Israel's prime minister shaking hands with his sworn enemy. Most of the Jews present at the ceremony had spent a lifetime struggling to win security and peace for the Jewish state. But few had expected it to happen this way, in a negotiated compromise with the arch-terrorist Arafat. In fact, this was precisely what they had been fighting for years to protect Israel from.

It was two years and a day earlier that then-President Bush had stood just a few feet from that very spot and denounced the organized Jewish leadership as "powerful political forces" lobbying to undermine his diplomacy. They had responded furiously, rising like lions to battle. Now, as they and the deposed George Bush watched from the audience, Israel was giving away more than he had ever tried to take.

And so the Jewish leaders sat on the South Lawn and watched the ceremony in a swirl of exultation and foreboding, combined with a sort of vertigo, a sense of detachment, as though events had been snatched from their hands—as, indeed, they had been.

Shortly after the ceremony, a group of senior Jewish community leaders was invited to the White House for a briefing on the peace accords by Secretary of State Warren Christopher. When the leaders got there, they found they were in for a few surprises.

First, the Jews had not been the only ones invited; it was to be a joint session with leaders of the Arab-American community, their longtime enemies. Second, it was not really a briefing. Secretary Christopher immediately handed the microphone to Vice President Al Gore, who asked the participants to rise and share their feelings about the day's events. Then he asked them to participate in a joint Jewish-Arab effort to secure the peace accord by lending know-how and capital to their cousins in the Middle East.

At the end, President Clinton came on stage to reinforce Gore's message.

"You and I can help to strengthen the people who did this," the president said. "We have been given a millennial opportunity in the Middle East. I hope we will explore ways that this group can stay together, work together, and find common projects."

Clinton was handing the Jewish community a monumental challenge. For decades the institutions of American Jewry had been organized as a vast machinery of defense, a blunt weapon that sought out and punished the enemies of the Jewish state. Its lobbyists were primed to make friendship to Israel—and hostility to its enemies—a litmus test for Jewish support. Educators were trained to help young Jews recognize and fear threats to Jewish or Israeli security. Religious leaders ceaselessly invoked the pathos of historic Jewish suffering to promote loyalty and solidarity above all else. Fund-raisers used fears of destruction to raise the prodigious sums that fueled the entire machine.

Now the Jews were being asked point-blank, by their president no less, to turn the whole engine around on a dime. They were being asked to use their vast communal enterprise to lower walls, to reduce suspicions, to encourage openness and forgiveness. Nobody knew how to do that.

"You can always rally people *against*," Presidents Conference director Malcolm Hoenlein remarked later, in an interview. "It's very hard to rally people *for*."

And so the groups that had traditionally led the fight for Israel, such as AIPAC and the Presidents Conference, suddenly found themselves paralyzed with indecision. "I think people support the peace process, but they have a lot of concerns and questions," Hoenlein said. "There are times when it's better not to be in the middle of things but to step back."

There were some Jews, of course, who knew exactly how they felt and were ready to act. Some of Israel's most ardent American supporters concluded that the Rabin government was on a suicidal course, and they set out to derail it. Some introduced measures in Congress to prevent Washington from helping move the peace process forward. Others threatened to withhold donations from Jewish organizations that supported Israel. A handful had gone to a New York synagogue where Israel's ambassador to Washington, Itamar Rabinovitch, was speaking a day before the handshake, and pelted him with tomatoes.

The American Jewish community, alone among the world's major Jewish communities, has no officially recognized central representative body. In part this is due to American law: the government is flatly barred by the Constitution from recognizing any religious institution. Instead, America has spawned a seemingly endless array of Jewish organizations, ranging from synagogue unions and rabbinic associations to fraternal leagues, civil rights groups, and immigrant-aid societies. All are privately owned corporations. All clamor to make themselves heard as defenders of the Jews.

The organizations' popular image among Jews, to the extent that they have one, is of a bloated, redundant bureaucracy, staffed by interchangeable nonentities who serve no function except collecting paychecks. It does not help that so many of the names sound virtually identical: American Jewish Committee, American Jewish Congress, Union of American Hebrew Congregations, United Synagogue, United Jewish Appeal, United Israel Appeal, Council of Jewish Federations.

The officers and staff of the Jewish organizations encourage their image of disarray by competing frantically for the public's limited attention. In a universe of voluntary associations, each dependent on private fund-raising, no Jewish group can admit that it is merely a secondary support service. In order to catch the donor's eye, everyone has to be a star.

The donors themselves help to create the chaos. Many donors look on their favorite Jewish charity as a sort of surrogate synagogue, the main outlet for their Jewish identification. They take pride in their cause, and they want it noticed around town. When a crisis occurs somewhere on the globe, they want their organization to take a stand—no matter that their organization is a charitable fund for orphans or cancer research. "This is their Jewishness," says Anti-Defamation League director Abe Foxman.

In this fashion, for example, two of the largest Jewish women's volunteer groups have gradually become serious political forces. Hadassah is a women's Zionist organization originally created to support hospitals and children's shelters in Israel; Women's American ORT supports a network of trade schools serving poor Jews abroad. Both groups are now players in Washington on abortion rights and other issues.

Similarly, dozens of other organizations, from the American Jewish Congress to the Cantors' Assembly, have expanded their original mandates to become combination social clubs/cultural forums/public-policy agencies, all wrapped up in one.

"All these organizations provide points of access for Jews to become active participants in the culture of Jewish life," says NCRAC executive director Lawrence Rubin. "In effect, they *are* the culture."

To most outsiders, the forest of identical-sounding Jewish organizations is utterly bewildering. "The run-of-the-mill politician has no idea what all these Jewish organizations are," says Lou Borman, press secretary to former Pittsburgh mayor Sophie Maslow. "When they're deluged with invitations to speak at dinners, especially around election time, they don't know where to begin. In a city like Pittsburgh you've got dozens and dozens of Jewish organizations, and every one invites the mayor and council people to its dinner. The American Jewish Committee, the National Council of Jewish Women, the Jewish National Fund, Israel Bonds—they all make themselves heard."

To a degree, the chaos is more apparent than real. Of the three hundred–odd national Jewish organizations listed in the *American Jewish Year Book*, more than half are fraternal lodges, professional associations, fund-raising arms of an Israeli hospital or university, or agencies that provide a specific service such as aid to immigrants or to Jews in foreign lands.

Several dozen organizations represent the synagogue unions of Judaism's main theological wings (Reform, Conservative, Orthodox, and the smaller Reconstructionist) and their affiliated seminaries, rabbis' unions, and women's leagues.

At least three dozen other groups are divisions of the World Zionist Organization (WZO), the century-old body that created the state of Israel and now serves as its official link with the Jewish Diaspora. Of these WZO divisions, half are debating clubs linked to an Israeli political party: Labor Zionists, Likud Zionists, Religious Zionists, and so on. The other half are WZO operating departments that promote Israeli travel, publish books and magazines about Israel, supply Israeli teachers to Diaspora Jewish schools, or manage the flow of funds from the United Jewish Appeal to Israel. In theory, the WZO is a delicately structured network. In practice it looks and sounds like another jumble of redundant organizations.

There is another network of Jewish organizations, largely separate from the first, that blankets the American Jewish community with an integrated, nationwide system of social services. It operates nearly everywhere Jews live, and is supported by a single yearly fund-raising drive. Annual donations total close to $1 billion, more than the American Red Cross raises but less than the United Way. Insiders refer to it as the "federated system"; the average Jew knows it as the United Jewish Appeal, or UJA.

The basic unit of the federated system is the local Jewish welfare federation, a sort of Jewish community chest. There is one in almost every city or county where Jews live, operating family-counseling agencies, community centers, old-age homes, parochial schools, and other services. The New York federation, the nation's largest, supports more than 130 agencies including seven major hospitals, with a combined annual budget of some $2 billion (counting Medicare fees and anti-poverty grants; the federation itself raises just $200 million per year).

A small cluster of national agencies exists solely to service the local federations and their programs. The best known of these is the UJA itself, which helps the federations to design their fund-raising appeals, and then takes a share of each town's receipts for Jewish philanthropies in Israel and around the world.

Overseeing the entire federated system, or trying to, is the New York–based Council of Jewish Federations. The CJF provides federations with research, staff placement, and other services. Its annual general assembly is the biggest and best attended meeting on the American Jewish calendar, a sort of national market-day when everyone who needs money comes to find those who have it. The event is usually keynoted by the prime minister of Israel, and regularly hears reports from the heads of AIPAC, the Presidents Conference, the WZO, and anyone else who needs to pay rent.

Sitting atop a network that raises $1 billion and spends at least $2 billion more per year, the CJF theoretically is the most powerful body in the American Jewish community. But its power is largely illusory, for the council consists of 190 local federations—each a private corporation answerable to its own directors and jealous of its independence. If the CJF can ever win the right to govern its members, it indeed will be the most powerful body in American Jewish life; meanwhile, it is a sleeping giant.

Finally, there are the dozen-odd "community-relations" agencies. These are the bodies that manage the Jewish community's relations with non-Jewish communities. In popular jargon they are known as "defense" agencies. Outsiders sometimes call them the political side of the Jewish community.

Some of these agencies are independent corporations answerable only to their own boards, such as the American Jewish Committee and the American Jewish Congress (some thirty thousand members each), and Anti-Defamation League (no members, nominally a division of the B'nai B'rith fraternal order, in practice run by its own staff).

The others are known as "umbrella agencies," or groups of groups. Each umbrella brings together a set of Jewish organizations for joint action on a specific issue. These are the true nerve centers of the Jewish community.

For example, the National Jewish Community Relations Advisory Council (NCRAC) is essentially a traffic cop, coordinating the policies of the major organizations and serving as their liaison to local federations. The American Israel Public Affairs Committee (AIPAC) lobbies the U.S. Congress on issues that concern Israel and the Middle East. The World Jewish

Congress, an umbrella of Jewish groups from around the globe, responds to threats against Jewish communities worldwide. The Conference of Presidents, often called the highest body in organized American Jewry, expresses the community's views to the White House and the world at large.

Just outside the inner circle of Jewish defense agencies stands a gaggle of smaller advocacy groups whose apparent goal is to influence not the broader society, but the rest of the Jewish community. Most operate from the belief that the mainstream Jewish community is not representative of the average Jew, that the leadership is too liberal—or too conservative, depending on who is talking.

The best known of these protest groups are single-issue organizations that try to influence Middle East policy, such as the left-wing Americans for Peace Now and the right-wing Americans for a Safe Israel. Others focus mainly on domestic American affairs, like the conservative Toward Tradition group and the political circles around the left-wing *Tikkun* magazine.

The line between the center and the margins is not always firm. Americans for Peace Now, for example, was born as a loose string of protest groups during Israel's 1982 Lebanon incursion. Inside a decade it grew into a national organization with an affluent governing board and a Washington lobbying office. After the 1992 Israeli elections brought Rabin to power, the peace group decided to apply for membership in the Presidents Conference. The bid sparked furious opposition from Orthodox organizations and pro-Likud groups, which accused Peace Now leaders of supporting Arab terrorism. But with Israel's own government now speaking like a peace group itself, the membership was eventually approved, in a rare, secret ballot of organizational presidents.

The opposite path, from mainstream to fringe, was trod by the venerable Zionist Organization of America (ZOA). Founded in 1897 as the voice of Zionism in America, it eventually became a wing of Israel's Likud party. ZOA leaders tried for years to stay above Israel's partisan battles, but after the Rabin-Arafat handshake they were challenged from within their own ranks by right-wing militants. At a national convention in December 1993, hardline activist Morton Klein, a Philadelphia investment counselor who had led the anti-Peace Now campaign, was elected president of the ZOA.

✿   ✿   ✿

On July 29, 1994, ten months after the Rabin-Arafat handshake, two groups of Jewish lobbyists converged in a conference room on Capitol Hill and clashed in the night.

Afterwards, both sides would explain the tussle as a turf battle over who was entitled to lobby Congress on Israel's behalf. In fact, it was a historic moment in American Jewish lobbying: the first full-scale confrontation on Capitol Hill between Jewish supporters and opponents of the Israeli government. The pro-Israel side lost.

The two lobbying groups were AIPAC, the best-known pro-Israel lobby in Washington, and the ZOA, the oldest pro-Israel group in America. They had come to Capitol Hill that evening to watch as House and Senate negotiators sat down to reconcile the two chambers' versions of the foreign-aid bill.

Israel's $3 billion foreign-aid package was never in question that night; the problem was aid to the Arabs. Following Israel's historic peace accord with the Palestine Liberation Organization (PLO) the previous September, the Clinton administration had mounted an international effort to bolster the fledgling Palestinian authority with financial aid. The goal was to help the PLO become a good neighbor, and to strengthen it against Islamic militants. A combined U.S.-Israeli effort had led to the creation of an international fund, with forty-three nations pledging a total of $2 billion. One fourth of the money was to come from the United States. The first installment was in the foreign-aid bill.

The Senate version of the bill contained a time bomb, however. Pennsylvania Republican Arlen Specter and Alabama Democrat Richard Shelby had inserted an amendment that prevented any transfer of aid until the president certified that the PLO was complying fully with the agreements it had signed the previous fall.

The administration strongly opposed the Specter-Shelby amendment, arguing that it unnecessarily complicated the delicate peace process. More quietly, administration officials argued that Israel's leadership was not happy at the idea of holding Arafat to a standard he might not be able to meet, given the pressures on him from Palestinian radicals. In any case, the peace accord had left Israel all the weapons it needed to monitor Arafat's behavior, since he was to receive territory only when the Israeli army was ready to pull out. Adding extra hurdles in Washington amounted to second-guessing Israel's assessment on the ground. "We know how to monitor Arafat's behavior," sniffed one senior Israeli official. "We don't need anyone in America doing it for us."

But that was just the point. The Specter-Shelby amendment was the work of American Jewish conservatives who opposed the whole idea of an Israel-PLO peace accord. Since the handshake in September, a coalition of Orthodox rabbis, pro-Likud Zionists, and Republican hawks had come together to seek ways of blocking Palestinian aid and undermining the accord. Richard Shelby and Arlen Specter, the Senate's most conservative Democrat and its sole Jewish Republican, had agreed to introduce the coalition's handiwork on the Senate floor.

According to the rules of House-Senate conferences, lawmakers are expected to defend the version of a bill that has emerged from their chamber. But Democratic Senator Patrick Leahy of Vermont, who headed the Senate conferees on July 29, broke with tradition and disavowed the Specter-Shelby amendment. He and his House counterpart, Democrat David Obey of Wisconsin, had decided to kill the amendment, deferring to the administration's wishes.

Unexpectedly, one of the House conferees decided that this action left her free to break with tradition as well. Representative Nita Lowey, a Democrat from suburban Westchester, New York, announced that she was *supporting* the Senate amendment. She was one of the feistiest Jewish liberals in Congress, but the last congressional reapportionment had stretched her district into a corner of Queens, which happened to include the synagogue where Israeli Ambassador Rabinovitch had been pelted in September. Lowey did not want to meet the same fate. "If she doesn't go along, that rabbi will find a way to punish her," an aide explained. "And if she does go along, who's going to picket her house? Some liberal investment banker from Scarsdale? The president of the American Jewish Committee?"

Lowey also convinced two other House Democrats to join with her. They promptly received one more vote when a lobbyist, watching the proceedings from the side of the room, approached the conference table and swayed a Republican. With three House votes, the Specter-Shelby amendment passed. The conference leaders, Leahy and Obey, stormed out of the room, furiously protesting the breach of conference procedure. They were angry not just at Lowey for breaking with the House, but more important, at the lobbyist who had approached the conference table—an unheard-of procedural violation.

Leahy and Obey stayed away for close to an hour, returning at last after midnight to admit defeat. The foreign-aid bill became law, with the Specter-Shelby amendment intact.

The wayward lobbyist was Morton Klein, newly elected president of the ZOA. A close friend and supporter of Specter's, he had been working on the amendment for months.

A few days after Specter-Shelby became law, AIPAC president Steven Grossman wrote a letter to the Presidents Conference, complaining about Klein's activities on Capitol Hill and demanding disciplinary action against the ZOA. The Presidents Conference convened a group of senior community leaders in mid-August to consider the extraordinary circumstances— the oldest pro-Israel body in America lobbying against Israel at a crucial moment in the legislative process—and what to do. Klein refused to attend. AIPAC went ahead and presented its case, and the Presidents Conference sent a letter to Klein, regretting his undisciplined behavior.

In Klein's view, the Presidents Conference simply had no jurisdiction in this matter. True, it was accepted by virtually all Jewish organizational leaders as the highest decision-making body in the organized Jewish community. Yet, as nearly as Klein could recall, it was not making decisions, but merely reacting to diktats from Jerusalem. In the months since he had joined the Presidents Conference, there had not been a single vote on the peace accords, he said. Instead, the body simply had been issuing statements and expecting the rest of the Jewish community to follow.

"The Presidents Conference can't just walk in and decide for the community," said Klein. "The Jewish community is split fifty-fifty on the issue."

Klein's claim was a remarkable bit of mathematics. In fact, polls showed that American Jews supported the peace accords by overwhelming margins. A survey conducted by the American Jewish Committee two weeks after the handshake showed that American Jews supported the Israeli-PLO accords by a margin of more than nine to one. Fifty-seven percent were even prepared to see Israel take the next step and permit a Palestinian state to rise next door.

In another sense, however, Klein had his numbers exactly right. It was true that only one Jew in ten was opposed to the peace accord, but only one Jew in four or five participated regularly in the affairs of the organized Jewish community. And that one fourth included most of the peace accord's opponents.

No one knows exactly how many Jews live in America. A 1992 survey by the Anti-Defamation League asked a representative sample of Americans to guess how many of their fellow citizens were Jewish. Fully two fifths said the answer was 20 percent or more, meaning they believed that at least one American in five was a Jew. Another two fifths placed the figure between 5 and 20 percent.

The correct answer is about 2.5 percent, or one in forty.

But even that number is only approximate. The most scientific estimates of Jewish population vary widely from just over 5 million Jews to more than 6 million, or somewhere between 2 and 3 percent of the population. (By way of comparison, Catholics, at 60 million, are about ten times more numerous. Of the Protestant denominations, only Baptists at 28 million, Methodists at 12.5 million, and Lutherans at 8 million are more populous than Jews in the United States.)

Brown University demographer Sidney Goldstein, a leading expert on Jewish population, suggests that the population of the Jewish community could arguably be put as high as 8 million. He includes some 6 million Jews and an estimated 2 million non-Jews who live in the same household as Jews (mainly spouses and children of intermarried Jews) to make up what he calls the "Jewish political community." This refers to everyone whose lives and fates are intimately bound up with the Jewish community, and who might be expected to make political and voting decisions on that basis.

Why is the number of Jews so vague? For one thing, the U.S. Census Bureau is barred from asking Americans about their religion, because of constitutional rulings that separate church and state. Lacking government statistics, Jewish demographic information must be collected privately. The process is hugely expensive and imprecise. And many studies are flawed by the tendency of researchers to look for information that confirms their own beliefs. One figure that surfaces occasionally these days—that Jews are 1.8 percent of the population—is the result of conscious misinformation.

More problematic, there is no clear agreement in our modern age on just what is meant by "Jew." As a result, researchers are not sure whom to count.

Most Americans define Judaism as a religion and Jews as its believers. However, religion is only part of the answer. Jews usually consider themselves members of a worldwide ethnic group, usually called "the Jewish people," though it also has been called a nation, a tribe, and even a race. They are bound together by common ancestry, a shared history, and a common cultural heritage, along with religion. Most of all, Jews feel bound together by a sense of shared destiny: a legacy of persecution and a mutual duty to help one another, while seeking some moral meaning in it all.

In fact, religion itself plays an ambiguous role in the Judaism of most American Jews. In a comprehensive survey conducted in 1990 by the Council of Jewish Federations, more than three quarters of Jews chose "religion" to describe their Jewish identity, rather than "nationality" or "culture." Yet barely 40 percent said they belonged to a synagogue. (Synagogue membership may have been undercounted; all other recent surveys show it at around 50 percent.) In a 1989 survey by the American Jewish Committee, 82 percent of Jews said there "definitely" or "probably" is a God, but only 47 percent said God "answers your prayers." Just 41 percent said God "intervenes in the course of human events." Non-Jewish Americans are nearly twice as likely as Jews to say "yes" to these same questions.

Defining the boundaries of the Jewish community may sound to most ears like an arcane academic exercise. In fact it is a highly charged political question. Like the mapmakers who draw congressional districts, scholars who chart the religious contours of the American Jewish identity are defining its political contours as well.

Given the importance of the Jewish community's role in the national political process, the question of who wins the struggle to define the Jews should be of great interest to the American public at large.

As a group, Jews constitute one of the most liberal segments on the American political landscape. But not all Jews are equally liberal: studies show that their liberalism rises as their religious observance declines. Orthodox Jews are less liberal than Conservative Jews, who are in turn less liberal than Reform Jews, as noted in chapter 2.

Orthodox Jews make up less than one tenth of American Jewry overall. Most surveys find the rest divided roughly equally among Conservative Jews, Reform Jews, and those who choose no label (usually, researchers say, because they have not given it enough thought).

The influence of Orthodox Jews on the policies of the Jewish community is far out of proportion to their numbers, however.

The Jewish community of New York celebrates Israel's birthday each spring with a parade down Fifth Avenue, the popular Salute to Israel parade (New Yorkers call it the Israel Day parade). Part of the pantheon of ethnic New York pageantry that includes the St. Patrick's Day and Columbus Day parades, it features thousands of costumed Jewish schoolchildren, elaborate corporate floats, and marching bands from friendly non-Jewish high schools. Crowd estimates given out by the organizers routinely run from 150,000 to upwards of a half-million.

During the 1980s, however, the parade underwent a subtle, seldom noted change. As the secular Zionist youth groups that once led it dwindled in membership, the marchers' ranks were filled out with whole classes of students drafted from the Orthodox Jewish parochial schools of the region. Watchers on the sidelines were increasingly dominated by the children's parents and relatives. By 1990, police were quietly offering crowd estimates in the neighborhood of fifty thousand, one tenth the number trumpeted from the reviewing stand.

As the 1994 Israel Day parade approached, ads and posters began to appear around New York announcing a concert to follow the parade in nearby Central Park, sponsored by the National Council of Young Israel, a small Orthodox congregational group. A week before the parade, the concert ads were changed; now they announced that the concert would be a "special tribute to Jewish Communities of Greater Jerusalem, Judea, Samaria, Gaza, the Jordan Valley, and the Golan Heights"—the Jewish settlers of the occupied territories, the core of Israel's most militant domestic opposition.

At the appointed hour for the concert to begin, crowds began streaming off the parade route and into the park. More than twenty thousand people jammed the the concert grounds for what became a noisy anti-Israeli government rally, featuring ringing speeches by the hardline ex-general, Ariel Sharon, and a string of Orthodox militants.

The parade continued on Fifth Avenue, but only a thin line of onlookers remained to watch. The bulk of the crowd had joined the Orthodox anti-government rally.

Where were the rest of the Jews—the 90 percent who supported the peace process? "I think they're across town at the AIDS Walk," suggested one Orthodox Jewish journalist covering the event.

Orthodox Judaism is founded on the authority of rabbis to define religious law, which they hold to be binding on every Jew. Conservative rabbis give themselves wide latitude to reinterpret the law, particularly in modern contexts, making them deeply suspect in Orthodox eyes. Reform rabbis, who consider religious law a guideline for individuals, are viewed by the Orthodox as lacking any ritual standing at all.

For years, Orthodoxy has cooperated with other Jewish factions only on limited terms, joining to defend Jewish rights and protect Jews abroad, but refusing to discuss the substance of Jewish practice and belief. Even that limited cooperation is controversial within Orthodoxy; traditionalists, led by Agudath Israel, condemn the Orthodox Union for agreeing to sit under the same umbrella with the heretics at all.

But the election of Yitzhak Rabin in 1992 brought inter-Jewish acrimony into a new era.

Prior to that election, Jews across the religious and political spectrum customarily had united behind Israel, suppressing any disagreements they might have with its policies on the premise that Israelis had the right to make their own decisions democratically. American Jews, who did not put their lives on the line, were duty-bound to support the Israelis who did.

The Presidents Conference and its sister organization, AIPAC, both had been founded for the explicit purpose of supporting Israel's elected government, whatever its policies. But this principle only held as long as the Israeli government chose policies that the American Orthodox community was willing to support.

The Rabin government lost that support once it began actively seeking to end Israel's conflict with the Arabs on the basis of territorial compromise. Many Orthodox Jews, who believe that the entire land of Israel was promised to the Jews by God, concluded that Rabin was violating God's law. Others were not as quick to judge, but in a conflict with non-Orthodox Jews they instinctively closed ranks, making the Orthodox community seem for all the world like a monolith.

American Jewry's umbrella bodies rapidly found themselves paralyzed, hard pressed to find a middle ground for joint action. Moderates were waiting, hoping for calm to return so consensus might emerge. While they waited, right-wing militants scurried about Washington trying to undermine the Israel-P.L.O. peace accord. These rightists, a mixture of Orthodox Jews and non-Orthodox hawks, effectively disabled the organs of Jewish representation.

The disabling of the center was part of a larger trend. For two decades, elements of the Orthodox community had been undergoing a fundamentalist religious revival, not unlike those sweeping Christianity, Islam, and Hinduism. Militant pietists were driving the institutions of Orthodoxy rightward on a host of political and religious issues. The Orthodox institutions, in turn, were pressuring the umbrella bodies.

The Middle East was only one of the areas affected. Orthodox leaders were resisting compromise on a growing list of hot-button issues during the 1980s, from abortion rights to parochial school aid to shared use of Jewish ritual baths. The battles took place at the Presidents Conference and NCRAC, in local boards of rabbis, at gatherings of religious teachers, and on the allocations committees of Jewish federations.

Orthodox Jews were not solely responsible for the divisions within the Jewish community, though they often bore the blame in the popular mind. Just as often, obstructionist tactics came from smaller groups on the secular right, such as the ZOA or the Jewish War Veterans of America. Many disputes found the main bodies of Orthodoxy, the Orthodox Union and the Rabbinical Council of America, siding with the mainstream against the militants.

In the long run, however, the line between Orthodox and non-Orthodox was the most explosive. It was here that political, social, and religious resentments overlapped to create an alienation verging on schism. Minor disputes over specific issues blew up into major confrontations. NCRAC found itself increasingly unable during the 1980s to find a consensus stance to represent the Jewish community's view on abortion rights. Another umbrella, the American Zionist Movement, suffered a walkout by Orthodox groups in the 1990s when it voted to endorse equal rights for non-Orthodox Judaism in Israel.

The Synagogue Council of America, an umbrella body which since 1924 had united Judaism's three main religious wings for contact with other faiths, actually voted to disband in early 1995. Bickering between Orthodoxy and the other wings had increased to the point where "there was no reason to stay together anymore," said an official with one of the member groups.

And with collapse of the Synagogue Council came a potential crisis in relations between Judaism and the Roman Catholic Church. The Vatican had initiated a formal dialogue with Judaism in 1971, following the ecumenical call of the Second Vatican Council in 1965. The Jewish partner in the dialogue was an ungainly coordinating committee made up of the defense agencies, the World Jewish Congress, and the Synagogue Council. The defense agencies and the World Jewish Congress were there because Jewish leaders insisted that these were the most authoritative representatives of the Jewish people. The Synagogue Council was there because the Vatican demanded a dialogue not with civil rights agencies, but with "the faith community of Judaism."

Over the next two decades, the dialogue brought extensive changes in church teachings about Judaism. Oddly, there has been no reciprocation: to the frustration of Catholic participants, Jewish participants have never agreed to any examination of Jewish teaching, because of an Orthodox ban on interreligious "disputation." Non-Orthodox Jewish participants have repeatedly offered to set up a separate dialogue. In 1987, the Anti-Defamation League and the American Jewish Committee walked out of the Jewish coordinating committee, hoping to set up their own channel to the Vatican.

But the Vatican has consistently rejected any talk of a second channel or a dialogue without Orthodox participation. "We want to talk to the entire Jewish people," said Eugene Fisher, director of Catholic-Jewish relations at the National Conference of Catholic Bishops. Who they will talk to following the collapse of the Synagogue Council remains unclear.

Ralph Reed, executive director of the Christian Coalition, contends that decisions in a democracy are not necessarily made according to the beliefs of the majority, but more often according to who pushes hardest. "Politics is a matter of intensity," Reed says.

His is a common observation among political insiders in Washington.

Although democracy does mean that the majority rules, it also means that everyone is entitled to have a say before the vote. With enough passion and enough persistence, a minority can exert more influence than its numbers justify, as Ralph Reed knows better than most. At crucial moments, a minority can create a majority around itself by persuading some, cowing others, and wearing down the rest.

Whether this phenomenon is good or bad for democracy depends on whose ox is being gored. Standing against the crowd can be seen as either visionary or peevish, and there is no sure way to know which is which at the time. Today's thwarted majority may be tomorrow's profile in courage. Democratic leadership has always implied a dilemma, therefore: are leaders chosen to obey the public, or to lead it? Should they do the bidding of the majority, or follow their conscience?

The dilemma is even more complicated in a mass society like America's. When barely half the citizens bother to vote, it is difficult to find the public, much less discern what it wants. It is tempting for leaders to confuse the popular will with the voices of those who shout the loudest. As Reed suggests, the noisiest, most intense minorities can become a sort of visible public opinion.

In a community like the American Jewish community, whose approximately 6 million souls are scattered among some 250 million others—and a community in which three fourths of the public rarely shows its face—the disproportionate power of the minority is well nigh inevitable.

Since the moment the first Jews set foot in America, they have been pulled between two great gravitational forces: the inward pull of loyalty to Jewish tradition and the outward pull of integration with the larger society. Loyalists dating back to colonial days have urged their fellow Jews to stay close to the synagogue and obey the traditional rabbinic code, while freethinkers have mocked them for parochialism.

It was this tension that gave rise to the three great movements of American Judaism: Reform, Conservative, and Orthodox. Each was an attempt to define the respective limits of integration and loyalty.

Throughout the years, most Jews have tried to muddle their way down the middle with greater or lesser success—unable to accept the rules of traditional religion, yet terrified that their children, lacking any clear taboos, might simply marry out, abandon the fold, and raise their own children as non-Jews.

Today, even that anguished middle has begun to unravel. Instead of one community of largely conflicted individuals, American Jewry appears to be hardening into two communities, distant, uncomprehending, and vaguely hostile toward each other.

The essential dividing line is the one between those Jews who are affiliated to some form of Judaism and those who are not.

Affiliated or "committed" Jews, the mainspring of Jewish activism, are those—whether Orthodox, Conservative, or Reform—who attend synagogue, join Jewish organizations, donate to Jewish causes, and speak out on Jewish issues. Unaffiliated or "assimilated" Jews have little to do with the whole affair.

It's not easy to tell who is who, however, because affiliation is a relative matter. Studies consistently show that active Jewish community involvement rises along with traditionalism. Orthodox Jews are the most likely to attend synagogue weekly, give to Jewish charities, and observe daily ritual laws. Conservative Jews are radically less likely to observe ritual on a daily basis, though they are *more* likely to play an active role in what might be called Jewish civics: volunteering in community organizations such as the Jewish defense agencies and the UJA, which carry on the public life of American Jewry. Most of these civic groups are Conservative-dominated.

As for Reform Jews, they have been shown in repeated studies to be the most casual in their Jewish involvement. The late comedian Dennis Wolfberg captured a certain statistical truth when he joked that he and his wife had switched to a Reform synagogue "because we wanted the easy taste of Jew Lite."

To affiliated Jews, the unaffiliated are in the process of abandoning Judaism for reasons of apathy, ignorance, and self-hatred. To unaffiliated Jews, the affiliated are a dull, self-righteous clique whose Judaic message is irrelevant to modern life. Neither group is quite right, but neither group listens to the other to find out why.

The resulting hostility can be intense. But it is, in a sense, a one-way process. Committed Jews and assimilated Jews regularly call each other names, but only one group, the assimilated, has the liberty of walking away in disgust. The deeply committed Jews have nowhere else to go. Instead, they stay and fight.

With only one team on the field, the fights often tend to be a bit one-sided.

Most analyses divide the American Jewish community roughly in half, based on surveys of Jewish behavior. Studies show that about half of all Jewish households contribute to Jewish charities. Synagogue membership runs somewhere between 45 and 55 percent, depending on the survey. Somewhat fewer Jews (findings range from 28 to 45 percent) belong to Jewish voluntary organizations.

Community leaders, from the local synagogue president to the national officers of the UJA, regard the low rate of affiliation as the single most vexing issue in American Jewish life today. Low attachment to Jewish institutions is assumed to reflect a low interest in preserving Judaism. Jews who do not participate in Jewish public activities, it is assumed, will not pass along any feeling of Jewish attachment to their children. The children will not even bother marrying other Jews, and *their* children in turn will not even be raised as Jews at all. In short order, their stock will disappear into the mass of Gentile society.

In the commonly held Jewish view, eliminating the Jews as an identifiable group is precisely what their persecutors have tried to do through two cruel millenia in Europe. The thought that American Jews might now be doing this to themselves, voluntarily, is nothing short of terrifying to the committed Jew.

Anxiety over Jewish disappearance has simmered at the margins of community debate for decades, occasionally boiling over into a minor crisis. In the early 1960s, an Israeli official issued a study purporting to prove that American Jews were doomed to disappear altogether within a generation. *Look* magazine reported on the crisis in its 1963 cover story, "The Vanishing American Jew."

It was not the first such panic, nor the last. Reports of the Jews' imminent demise have been so commonplace that one eminent pre–Second World War Jewish historian, Simon Rawidowicz, wrote of the Jews as "the ever-dying people."

✤   ✤   ✤

For sheer hysteria, however, nothing in recent American Jewish history compares to the alarm touched off in November 1990 by the release of the National Jewish Population Survey. The survey, sponsored by the Council of Jewish Federations, was the biggest, most comprehensive study of American Jewish population patterns ever conducted.

Many of the survey's findings were, if intriguing, not quite earth-shattering: Jews had a lower rate of population growth than Americans as a whole. They were graying more rapidly and divorcing less often than other Americans. They were leaving New York and the Northeast and moving to the South and West. Those who moved were slow to join synagogues or give to Jewish charities in their new communities.

Of all the survey's numbers, however, there was one that electrified American Jewry from coast to coast. Within weeks it would spread by word of mouth and through newspaper headlines, impassioned sermons, and anguished editorials to become the best-known statistic in modern Jewish life.

The number was 52 percent. That, the survey found, was the number of Jews entering wedlock in the past five years who had married out of the faith.

The finding hit Jews across America like a bombshell. More than half of all American Jews, it suggested, were turning their backs on Judaism. Rabbis and community leaders predicted the imminent end of Jewish life in America. "The intermarriage process will take everything Jewish with it in its wake," warned Rabbi Pinchas Stolper, then executive vice president of the Orthodox Union. "It will grow and grow until it engulfs the entire community. It's another Holocaust."

"Let's face it, we Jews are an endangered species," said Boston philanthropist Phil Krupp, at a 1993 dinner in Palm Beach honoring his contributions to Israel's Ben-Gurion University.

In response to the CJF survey, Jewish organizations across the country assumed battle positions, scrambling for ways to ensure that American Judaism might continue into the next generation. Plans were made to shift millions of dollars from less urgent priorities—fighting anti-Semitism, defending Israel, helping the needy—to the all-important goal of Jewish religious education.

In Cleveland, Baltimore, and other cities, the local Jewish federations added millions to neighborhood religious school budgets. The national UJA proposed a $30 million program to fly every Jewish teenager to Israel for a summer, in order to impress youth with the drama of Jewish rebirth (Israel, asked to pay one third, torpedoed the proposal). Some of America's wealthiest Jewish families, including the Bronfmans, Wexners, Mandels, and Crowns, began setting aside millions of their own dollars to support these efforts or start their own.

Nationwide, a North American Commission on Jewish Continuity was formed under the aegis of the CJF. It brought together the top experts in Jewish religious education, the leaders of the major Jewish philanthropies, and the heads of the three main religious wings. All agreed to drop their usual hostility and join forces in the face of this unprecedented threat. Only the head of Agudath Israel, Rabbi Moshe Sherer, refused to join the commission, replying in a letter that enlisting the Reform movement in a campaign to stop assimilation was "like inviting the arsonist to help put out the fire."

Oddly enough, the number that started the panic—52 percent—was almost certainly wrong.

It now appears that the intermarriage figure was based on several obscure statistical errors, introduced into the population survey's results by researchers working on a tight schedule and a tighter budget. For several years the survey's designers denied that the errors existed; then they began admitting there were ambiguities in the survey, but insisted they were insignificant. There were some sharp exchanges as the survey's academic advisory council debated the errors, but ultimately the critics were voted down. The CJF stood by the survey's results.

The most important error was the use of weighting to tabulate survey responses. Most pollsters weight their results by giving added value to responses from groups that are statistically less likely to answer a poll, such as blacks, rural dwellers, Southerners, and the poor.

The CJF survey lacked funds to develop a Jewish weighting system. Instead the researchers simply used the standard weights. That is, they overcounted responses from black, poor, rural, and Southern Jews.

Critics charged that the survey's weighting system was flawed on several counts. In particular, other demographic evidence suggests that poor, rural, and Southern Jews do *not* avoid pollsters, unlike their Gentile neighbors. However, they *are* less likely to attend synagogue, observe kosher dietary laws, or marry Jews. Using the standard weighting, therefore, "tends to overestimate those Jews with weaker Jewish identities," said sociologist Steven M. Cohen of the Hebrew University in Jerusalem, a leading scholar of American Jewish demography and the survey's most persistent critic. As a result, the CJF survey painted a picture of America's Jews that was strikingly less "Jewish"—less observant of ritual, less attached to Israel, less affiliated to Jewish institutions—than any of the many surveys conducted in recent years. Remove the weights, on the other hand, and the CJF's survey "looks like all the other surveys," said Cohen.

"By my calculations, the intermarriage rate is more like 40 percent," Cohen stated. "That's still high, but it's not the 'Oh my God, it's more than half' figure that everyone is talking about."

Nor is it much higher than the intermarriage rate was in 1970, when the first National Jewish Population Survey found it to be 32 percent. Which is to say, intermarriage is not soaring. True, it has increased 25 percent in the last generation, but this is hardly the dramatic change commonly depicted. Indeed, many scholars have come to believe that the single-digit intermarriage rate cited before 1960, based on guesswork, was wildly wrong. This school argues that the rate has remained constant at about one third for a century or more.

In other words, *there is no crisis.*

Within the tiny world of Jewish population research, a surprising number of experts have said privately that they agree with Cohen's critique. Nevertheless, most refuse to endorse him publicly. Several fear losing access to the population survey's invaluable storehouse of raw data—a professional death sentence for any student of American Jewish behavior.

CJF research director Barry Kosmin, who directed the 1990 survey, brushed aside the entire flap as a tempest in a teapot. "If we'd spent two or three million dollars we could have developed our own weights and knocked the error down a bit," he says. "It isn't that crucial."

Besides, said Brown University sociologist Calvin Goldscheider, a survey adviser, "the precise numbers aren't that important if they force Jews to reexamine their values."

The current intermarriage scare is having a subtle effect on the balance of power within organized Jewish life. It is putting liberals on the defensive, by raising doubts about the very idea of full Jewish integration in an open society. Jewish institutions are devoting a growing share of their resources to shoring up the Jewish community from within, and are backing away from their traditional role of trying to better American society.

One of the most powerful weapons in the arsenal of Jewish political advocacy, the unbiased commitment to principle over self-interest, is fast becoming discredited in American Jewish leadership circles. Instead, leaders increasingly see it as their job to circle the wagons. Simply to say aloud that Jews should fight for the rights of all people—once a universal view—now invites public attack.

Movie actor Richard Dreyfuss, the Oscar-winning star of *The Goodbye Girl, Jaws,* and other hits, is a baby-boom liberal who was raised in an assimilated Jewish home in Los Angeles and was married for years to a non-Jew. In May 1992, he was invited to receive an award from a Jewish fund-raising organization, American Friends of the Israel Museum of the Diaspora.

Honoring celebrities is a common fund-raising ploy, meant to win media attention for the cause and to sell banquet tickets by attracting the honoree's well-heeled friends and starstruck fans. At Jewish fund-raisers, honorees traditionally accept their awards with passionate declarations of loyalty to Israel, Judaism, and whichever institution is sponsoring the dinner.

But on this particular evening at New York's Hotel Pierre, Dreyfuss broke with tradition. Instead of pablum, he served his black-tie audience a biting critique of mainstream Jewish politics and fund-raising. Jewish community life, he charged, is too narrowly focused on "the mythology of the Holocaust and the miracle of Israel." The result, he said, is an "inappropriate defensiveness," particularly in reaction to criticism of Israel and its policies. Dreyfuss spoke from personal experience; he had been physically assaulted in 1987 after addressing a rally for the Israeli peace movement.

The defensiveness of the Jewish community is understandable, Dreyfuss continued, considering the "unspeakable crimes" inflicted on Jews in living memory. But like every trauma victim, he said, Jews should be wary of "trusting all of our senses all of the time."

The danger, Dreyfuss warned, is that the "victim-warrior myth" might alienate Jews of the younger generation who are looking for personal meaning in their Judaism. "Our overriding, shared concern must be the maintenance and improvement of the Jewish character."

"I am a passionately secular Jewish agnostic who sincerely believes that Jews are the chosen people, so go figure," Dreyfuss said. "I believe we are chosen to illuminate the human condition. Our ethics are mankind's great-est victories."

Dreyfuss's speech touched off its very own storm of defensiveness. Publisher Mortimer Zuckerman, scheduled to follow Dreyfuss with a brief greeting, instead delivered an impromptu, thirty-five-minute jeremiad on the continuing dangers of anti-Jewish hostility around the world and in America. He cited Arab threats to Israel, anti-Semitism among American blacks, and an anti-Israel bias in the American news media. He offered no conclusion, but he did not have to. His target was obvious: Sunday soldiers like Richard Dreyfuss.

Elie Wiesel, the Nobel Prize–winning chronicler of the Holocaust, had spoken briefly to introduce Zuckerman. He gave only a mild sermon on the importance of close ties between Israel and the Diaspora. But a week later, at another fund-raising dinner (this one for the Religious Zionists of Amer-ica, who were honoring a real-estate developer), Wiesel blasted Dreyfuss with both barrels. "This actor," he said, "who had nothing to do with Israel and Judaism, gave us a lesson on what Jews should do. He said we needed a psychiatrist and then everything would be all right. He said Israel is not moral, and therefore we must interfere. The chutzpah! The arrogance!"

In fact, Wiesel elaborated, "the role of a Jew is to be with our people. *Ahavat Yisrael* [love of Israel] means when Israel needs us, we must be there. When Israel is attacked, we must defend her."

Wiesel is right that Jews care deeply about Israel. A wide variety of surveys has shown that three fourths affirm that "caring about Israel is a very important part of my being a Jew." Two thirds affirm that "if Israel were destroyed I would feel as if I had suffered one of the greatest personal tragedies in my life."

Less publicized, however, are the polls that ask Jews to rate Israel *in comparison* with other Jewish issues they care about. The results are telling.

One detailed poll, conducted by the American Jewish Committee in 1989, asked respondents to rank twelve selected Jewish symbols in order of importance to their "sense of being Jewish." Israel came in seventh—behind the Holocaust, the Day of Atonement, American anti-Semitism, God, the Torah, and Passover. Bringing up the rear were the Exodus from Egypt, the Sabbath, "Jewish law," the UJA, and "the Jewish radical tradition."

The same survey also asked respondents how important it was that their children engage in various Jewish activities. They were offered fourteen choices, from "feel good about being Jewish" and "learn about their Jewish heritage," to "support social justice causes" and "marry Jews."

"Care about Israel" came in twelfth. Only two choices ranked lower: "practice Jewish ritual" and "date only Jews."

Another survey, conducted in 1988 by the *Los Angeles Times,* asked a national sample of American Jews to name "the quality most important to their Jewish identity." Half chose "a commitment to social equality." The other half were divided evenly among Israel, religion, and "other."

The intermarriage scare is a warning flag in what promises to be an extended war for the Jewish soul. Increasingly, conservatives within the community are citing intermarriage statistics as an indictment of the fundamental premise of Jewish liberalism: the idea of the Jews' integration as equals in the larger society.

In a 1991 issue of *Commentary,* neoconservative essayist Irving Kristol declares that secular humanism, the ideology that has guided Western society for the last two centuries, is "brain dead," unable to respond to the "spiritual disarray that is at the root of moral chaos" in the West. In response, he predicts, America will turn increasingly toward religion. That will put minority religious groups at a disadvantage, of course. Kristol believes Jews should welcome the opportunity to turn back to their own religion.

But will this trend return Jews to the locked ghettos of pre-Enlightenment Europe? Kristol hopes not. "It is reasonable to believe that Jews will continue to be nervously 'at home' in America," he concludes wishfully. And well he might; Kristol himself is a lifelong secularist who joined a synagogue for the first time just before he wrote this article. ("I joined a Conservative synagogue," he said in an interview. "I couldn't find a neoconservative one.")

For many committed Jewish activists, circling the wagons has rapidly transcended its defensive posture to become an ideology and a rallying cry. One of the clearest calls comes from political scientist Daniel Elazar, an American-born Israeli with a broad following among the American Jewish leadership. Writing in the October 1995 issue of the monthly magazine *Moment,* Elazar argues that old "fissures" between Israel and Diaspora

Jews, or between religious and non-religious Jews, are obsolete. The important dividing line today, he writes, is between Jews who care about "the quality of Jewish civilization" and those "whose major desire is to achieve normal living." He appeals to all Jews who care about Judaism to "unite in struggle against those who want a world that is good for Jews but not necessarily for Jewishness or Judaism."

The effect of such a realignment would be to create a smaller, more cohesive Jewish community. It would also create a community in which the Orthodox were far more influential than they are today.

Those who want to close ranks in this fashion will find themselves very lonely, however. Very few Jews are candidates for a return to the ghetto.

The fact is that the American Jewish community is not divided in two between those who are in and those who are drifting out, as commonly perceived. In fact, it is divided in three.

Roughly 25 percent of all American Jews are committed to practicing Judaism all year, every year. Another 60 percent observe the Day of Atonement, Hanukkah, Passover, the Bar or Bat Mitzvah, and not much else; sociologist Steven M. Cohen calls this group "moderately affiliated." A third, alienated group of 10 or 15 percent does not even do that much.

Specifically, a wide variety of polls and studies shows that between 75 and 90 percent of all American Jews light candles on Hanukkah, attend a Passover seder, and observe the Jewish Day of Atonement. About 85 percent of all Jewish youngsters attend religious school between ages ten and thirteen in preparation for the Bar or Bat Mitzvah ceremony of confirmation (the majority of these drop out soon after the ceremony). Most telling, well over 90 percent of all American Jews say that being Jewish is a "very" or "fairly" important part of their lives. All of these figures have remained stable or risen slightly over the past generation. For most Jews, these five things—Atonement, Hanukkah, Passover, the Bar or Bat Mitzvah, and a general feeling of belonging—mark the extent of their involvement. When Jews are asked whether they observe any other Jewish holidays, such as the Sabbath, the Feast of Tabernacles, or Israel Independence Day, affirmative replies drop to between one quarter and one third of the population. Fewer still, just under 20 percent, say that they observe kosher dietary laws. Between 15 and 18 percent send their children to all-day Jewish parochial schools. These figures, too, have risen over the past generation.

True, synagogue membership and religious school enrollment both hover around 50 percent. But on closer examination, they reflect the 25–60–15 percent breakdown. Half the paid-up members—the community's committed one fourth—register year after year. The other half, drawn from the moderately affiliated majority, join when they need to prepare a child for Bar or Bat Mitzvah, then quit until the next child is ready.

The overwhelming majority of American Jews—including most of those who intermarry—continue to think of themselves as loyal to Judaism in their own way. Most say that their Jewish identity is a vital and important part of their sense of self. In one 1989 survey by the American Jewish Committee, 96 percent of Jews surveyed stated that they were "proud to be a Jew" and 86 percent said that "being Jewish is something special." Pointedly, 90 percent affirmed that "being Jewish so much a part of me that even if I stopped observing Jewish traditions and customs, I still couldn't stop being Jewish."

Pride in Judaism, then, is not changing. What *is* changing is the way Jews understand and experience Judaism. The intermarriage rate is only one symptom of that transformation.

Over the past generation, a sizable proportion of American Jews has come to regard Judaism as a fluid, highly personal aspect of their identity. Their ancestors' Judaism—the self-segregating, all-embracing world of European Judaism before the Holocaust—is becoming for most people a distant, fading memory. Today's American Jews tend to regard Judaism as an emotional complex of feelings, beliefs, associations, and occasional voluntary actions. "They're Jewish because they're not Christian," says Brown University sociologist Calvin Goldscheider.

Not surprisingly, most of the leadership of the organized Jewish community is drawn from the committed minority, which acts on behalf of—and in the name of—the less involved majority.

"Leadership" is a dubious word for it, though. The two groups of Jews are deeply estranged, and becoming more so. The minority-majority estrangement is nothing new, but it is snowballing in the wake of the intermarriage panic. The community of committed, traditional Jews is becoming ever more ingrown, ever more suspicious of outsiders, and ever more incomprehensible to the majority of their fellow Jews.

The estrangement works both ways. The very anxiety that committed Jews feel over the perceived decline in affiliation may well help fuel the disaffiliation process. In interviews with Jews around the country during the early 1990s, moderately or nonaffiliated Jews regularly reported that they would like to be closer to Judaism, but are repelled by the angry, hectoring tone of Jewish community life. "Every year or so I go back to synagogue hoping I'll feel something, but all they ever talk about is politics and Israel," says Tara Framer, a New York graphic designer in her thirties, in a comment typical of Jews of her generation. "If it were a more spiritual experience, I'd probably want to go back."

These turned-off Jews, in turn, abdicate the institutions of Jewish power to the traditionalists.

World Jewish Congress president Edgar Bronfman Sr. made his first major appearance before a domestic American audience at the 1994 General Assembly of the Council of Jewish Federations. Bronfman's own organization is best known for battling foreign dictators, but he had come before the welfare federations to discuss a very different sort of threat to the Jews: Jewish apathy.

Bronfman warned that the American Jewish community was on the verge of collapse because it was paying too much attention to defense from enemies and not enough to affairs of the soul. "We North American Jews are in grave danger of losing our Jewish identity," he declared.

"For a couple of generations our Jewishness has been expressed by our devotion to the State of Israel and our checks to the UJA," Bronfman told the huge crowd. But now that Israel was moving toward peace with its neighbors, it "will not command the same attention."

The great challenge facing Jews now, Bronfman declared, was to find a way to give their children the sense of spiritual mission that their immigrant grandparents had abandoned a century ago. How to do that? Through a massive increase in Jewish education; through lower parochial school tuition, high-tech teaching aids, big-budget campus programs, low-cost trips to Israel.

To pay for the big education push, Bronfman called for the formation of a "most prestigious commission" with the goal of "re-prioritizing how we spend the Jewish tax dollar."

"There are three defense agencies collecting money, as well as being funded by the federations: the ADL, the American Jewish Committee, and the American Jewish Congress," Bronfman said. "There is a plethora of all kinds of Jewish organizations, there are duplications, all with claims on that same dollar."

Bronfman speaks with a credibility almost unmatched among American Jewish leaders. One of the nation's wealthiest individuals, he gives generously to a wide variety of Jewish charities. As head of the World Jewish Congress since 1979, he has managed to create one of the most feared and effective Jewish organizations in the world.

Bronfman is also one of the very few Jewish multimillionaires who has been willing to use his economic clout to advance Jewish interests. He frequently ties international economic deals to concessions by foreign regimes on local Jewish rights or relations with Israel. In the spring of 1995, his Seagram Corporation used its controlling stock in Du Pont Chemicals to veto a controversial technology deal between a Du Pont subsidiary, Conoco Oil, and the radical Islamic regime in Iran, Israel's most implacable foe.

The Conoco deal was the sort of financial arm-twisting that many non-Jews—and perhaps many Jews—imagine to be a common form of Jewish power politics. In fact, it is a rarity. "Most of those guys will write us a check, but they'll never stick out their necks where business is concerned," says a senior official with one Jewish agency.

As a rare billionaire who *does* put his money on the line for Jewish causes, Bronfman is one of the very few community leaders whose doings are regularly reported in the mass media. Not coincidentally, he is one of the only Jewish leaders that most Jews have ever heard of.

Most other leaders of the organized Jewish community are virtually unknown to the public, including their supposed followers. Nearly all are elected by their organizations, but few members ever pay attention to the election process.

The fact is that every member of every synagogue in America has a theoretical vote in choosing the leaders of the Presidents Conference and NCRAC. Yet almost none of the congregants ever asks the rabbis or synagogue presidents how they will be voting.

Instead, the Jewish leadership has acquired the popular image of a self-appointed elite that controls the Jewish institutional world through its money. Right-wing Jewish populists regularly skewer the major organizations for being too liberal, too conciliatory, and too cautious in responding to intergroup conflict. Left-wing populists savage them just as harshly for being too supportive of conservative regimes, whether in Washington or Jerusalem.

"The skewing of the 'organized Jewish community' toward the wealthy and toward talented fundraisers encourages a climate of organizational conservatism that is out of step with the thinking of most American Jews," argues Michael Lerner, editor of the left-wing monthly Jewish journal *Tikkun*.

It would be more accurate to describe the Jewish leadership as an earnest group of Jews of average talents, squeezed between a host of opposing forces that are not easily reconciled.

Like leaders in mass societies everywhere in the world today, the leaders of the Jewish community are caught between a militant minority that makes its opinions known at every opportunity, and a large, tolerant majority that rarely shows its face.

"The people who go to meetings are more inclined to selectively care about the community maintaining its united front," says Jacqueline Levine, an American Jewish Congress leader and former chair of NCRAC. "In the end it's hard to see how liberal the Jewish community is. I often get the studies that come out showing Jews as liberal. But I talk to people and when I speak in the way I do, I don't get that many people who agree with me."

Jewish leaders must walk delicately between those two groups, never quite sure whom they represent. "That's why we speak so often of the 'organized' Jewish community," says Rabbi Israel Miller, who chaired the Presidents Conference in the mid-1970s. "It's very difficult to represent anybody who's not organized, even though you know you're speaking on their behalf."

On Valentine's Day, 1994, Rabbi Haskell Lookstein, spiritual leader of Congregation Kehillath Jeshurun on Manhattan's fashionable Upper East

Side, rose to the pulpit to welcome a distinguished visitor, U.S. Attorney General Janet Reno. She was in New York for a community forum sponsored by the local congresswoman, Carolyn Maloney. Lookstein's synagogue was merely hosting the event.

Before handing Reno the podium, Lookstein unexpectedly suspended protocol to give his guest a dramatic reprimand.

American Jews, the rabbi told a scowling Reno, had learned from the horrors of the Second World War "the importance of speaking truth to power." He, naturally, felt that he could do no less. "No issue unites American Jews more," he said, than the unfair sentence meted out to confessed Israeli spy Jonathan Jay Pollard, serving a life sentence for giving American military secrets to an ally. "Nearly every national Jewish organization has spoken out on the topic," Lookstein said. "American Jews would remember it gratefully" if Reno would reopen Pollard's case and free him.

Pollard was a U.S. Navy intelligence analyst who was arrested in 1986 on charges of passing classified information to Israel. A pudgy thirty-one-year-old with Maccabean delusions—AIPAC had once turned him down for a job after finding him unstable—he volunteered his services to Israel as a spy in 1985 after deciding that the Navy was withholding vital information from the Jewish state. He was caught a year later, after delivering hundreds of pounds of documents, when his frantic spending habits aroused FBI suspicions. In a plea bargain with the U.S. Attorney's office, he agreed to plead guilty in return for a promise that the prosecution would recommend leniency. Instead, he was sentenced in 1987 to life in prison.

After the sentencing, Pollard was unanimously condemned by the top leadership of the organized Jewish community. Morris B. Abram, the renowned civil rights attorney who chaired the Presidents Conference, called the espionage "inexcusable" and voiced approval for Pollard's life sentence. Nathan Perlmutter, then national director of the ADL, criticized Israel's "stupidity" in betraying American trust.

"The Pollard case is a nightmare-come-true for American Jews," wrote Richard Cohen, the staunchly pro-Israel *Washington Post* columnist. "In Pollard, the Israelis created an anti-Semitic stereotype—an American Jew of confused loyalties who sold out his country. Indignation and shame are felt in equal measure."

The Israeli government disavowed Pollard, saying that his recruitment had been a "rogue operation" (run, incongruously, out of the prime minister's office). But a small group of Israeli right-wing radicals and their

American allies rallied to Pollard's cause. They termed him a Jewish hero who had sacrificed himself to save Israel. They accused the Israeli government and the American Jewish leadership of abandoning him like a wounded soldier left on the battlefield. They demanded that the major American Jewish organizations lobby for his release.

"Jonathan Pollard was desperately trying to alert Israel to the danger from Iraq," said Rabbi Avraham "Avi" Weiss, a militant Orthodox activist, at a Free Pollard rally in New York in June 1992 (at Lookstein's synagogue). And, Weiss added, now that Pollard's fears about Iraq had been proven true, "now, today, Jonathan Pollard has become a Jewish-American political prisoner."

In 1990, under relentless pressure from Pollard's family and supporters like Weiss, the Jewish agencies set up an ad hoc Pollard task force, under NCRAC auspices, to consider whether or not to take up his cause. After hearing extensive evidence from both prosecution and defense lawyers, the Pollard task force—the three defense agencies; the three religious unions; the three largest local federations; plus Hadassah, B'nai B'rith, and the Presidents Conference—decided unanimously to leave the case alone.

"If we did anything to send the government the message that the Jewish community believes this *mamzer* [bastard] did the right thing, we would be undermining our own community," said a senior official with one of the organizations.

He had a point; reports from within the Pentagon suggest that Pollard's life sentence—harsher than most Soviet spies receive—came at the secret urging of the Joint Chiefs of Staff.

The reason, sources said, was to send a warning. Thousands of American Jews now work in various federal government positions, including highly sensitive posts, that largely were closed to Jews just a generation ago. In the meantime, the canard of Jewish disloyalty has been banished from American life, along with other timeworn prejudices. Sources said that the Joint Chiefs wanted the judge to send a message to the Jews of America, via Pollard: don't throw the question back open.

Jewish public opinion—*visible* public opinion, that is—did not want to hear the message. Over the next few years, the leaders of the major Jewish organizations were confronted by pro-Pollard activists wherever they turned. One by one, the organizations cautiously began speaking up on the Pollard case. In the end, even NCRAC wrote the White House to ask for a review. One top leader, former Presidents Conference chairman Seymour

Reich, says he became an active Pollard advocate after becoming convinced that it was the overwhelming sentiment of grassroots American Jews. "It's the one thing I hear about everywhere I go," he says.

How widespread was this view? The one poll conducted on the topic, a 1991 survey by the American Jewish Committee, found only 27 percent of all Jews agreeing that Pollard had been sentenced too harshly. Even fewer, just 22 percent, agreed that Jewish organizations should press for his release. Fifty-seven percent said they had no opinion on either question.

But only one side was making itself heard.

Part II

THE ROOTS OF
JEWISH POWER

CHAPTER 4

"Our Eccentric Situation": The Disorganization of the Jews

T HE FIRST FORMAL CONTACT between the Jewish community and the American government came in 1790, a year after George Washington was inaugurated as the first president of the new Republic.

In August of 1790, during a visit to Newport, Rhode Island, President Washington wrote a letter to the members of the local synagogue. Memorable for its warmth and eloquence, Washington's letter is still studied today in Jewish religious schools as a sort of founding charter of American Jewish freedom.

"The government of the United States of America," he wrote, "which gives to bigotry no sanction, to persecution no assistance, requires only that they who live under its protection should demean themselves as good citizens in giving it on all occasions their effectual support."

Washington's correspondence with the Jews that summer set the tone for all future relations between the American government and the Jewish community. He was probably the first leader of any nation in seventeen hundred years of Jewish wandering to address the Jews as free and equal fellow-citizens. But he went further than that; he declared that America was different from other nations precisely because it had "given to the world examples of an enlarged and liberal policy—a policy worthy of imitation. All possess alike liberty of conscience and immunities of citizenship."

The incident stamped American Jewish life in more ways than one. Few remember it now, but the Newport letter was just one of three letters that President Washington wrote to the Jews that year.

The reason was classic Jewish politics. Shortly after Washington's inauguration in April 1789, the heads of America's five tiny synagogues decided to send the new president a letter of "felicitation." All the leading Christian churches were doing it. But the Jews spent a year and a half squabbling over who would sign. In the end, they sent three separate letters. Poor George had to answer all three.

The Jews' original plan was for the letter to go out from Congregation Shearith Israel in New York City, the nation's first capital. But the elders of the New York synagogue dawdled for months, blaming an unexplained "local situation." In January, Congress moved the capital to Philadelphia. Now the Philadelphia synagogue offered to write the letter. But other congregations objected to the Philadelphia synagogue's president, a local merchant named Manuel Josephson. Though devout and learned, he was an Ashkenazic Jew of East European origin. Many of the Portuguese Sephardic grandees who dominated colonial Jewry considered him unworthy to speak for them.

In May, the Jews of Savannah broke ranks and sent their own letter "in behalf of the Hebrew congregations." They apologized that "[o]ur eccentric situation, added to a diffidence founded on the most profound respect, has thus long prevented our address." Washington graciously replied that the "delay which has naturally intervened between my election and your address has afforded me an opportunity for appreciating the merits of the federal-government." In August, the Jews of Newport added their good wishes; during the president's visit they handed him a letter that praised "the God of Israel" for protecting Washington and creating a government "which to bigotry gives no sanction, to persecution no assistance." Washington cribbed the best phrases for his reply, as was his habit.

Finally, in December 1790, Josephson had a brief audience with the president and gave him a letter in the name of the remaining congregations. "We have hitherto been prevented by various circumstances peculiar to our situation from adding our congratulations to those which the rest of America have offered," Josephson wrote. Washington's reply to him was the briefest of the three, and showed signs of exasperation; fully half his text was spent noting how many good wishes he had already received (all of which, he hastened to add, "form the purest source of my temporal felicity"). Finally he praised "our late glorious revolution," a choice phrase cribbed from Josephson.

None of the Jewish leaders besieging President Washington in 1790 bothered to explain the "peculiar circumstances" that had kept them from writing a simple letter. Part of their problem, surely, was the truth embodied in the old Jewish joke: two Jews, three opinions. Whether Washington himself understood their "eccentric situation," we shall never know. We can guess from his reply to Josephson that he was a bit dazed by it all.

Behind the bumbling, however, there was a new force at work to inhibit Jewish unity. For the first time in history, Jews lived in a country that separated church from state, that refused to recognize or regulate any religious body. It was right there in the Constitution's First Amendment, nearing ratification even as the Jews wrote (and wrote and wrote): "Congress shall make no law respecting an establishment of religion, or prohibiting the free exercise thereof."

Now, that obviously meant that America could not legally bar Jews from practicing their religion. Jews had never had such a guarantee; this alone justified all their breathless prayers of thanksgiving. It also meant that Congress could not turn Jews into second-class citizens by establishing a national church. This prohibition would eventually apply to the individual states as well, though it would take close to a century of state-by-state battles. Indeed, efforts to declare America officially a "Christian nation" continue to this day.

Less obviously, the ban on "establishment of religion" also had a down side for Judaism. If Jews were free to observe the laws of their faith, they were also free not to. In America, there would be no state-appointed chief rabbi or court Jew, no state-sanctioned Jewish council. Judaism would have no power over Jews here, except the power that Jews gave it voluntarily. As an institution, America's Jewish community thus was born with one hand tied behind its back.

Finally, there was this mixed blessing: if the government was forbidden to recognize any Jewish body, then anyone could step forward at any time and claim to speak for the Jews, and the government would have to provide equal time. That has happened over and over since George Washington's day.

The history of American Jewry can be told as a history of the Jews' continuing effort to create a voice for their growing community. Over the centuries, their presence has grown from five congregations on the Eastern seaboard into a vast maze of some three thousand synagogues from Maine to Hawaii. Along the way, countless attempts have been made to bring Jews together for joint action. Many of these efforts were successful for a time. Each failed when a dispute arose and some group walked out of the union to set up shop down the block. In short order, a new union would arise to bring those two groups together, until it too split, and so on.

Today, there are at least three hundred national Jewish organizations and countless local ones. The endless sequence of union and schism is reflected in the redundant names of the major organizations, as we have seen in chapter 3.

To a degree, this cycle reflects the egos and jealousies of the individuals who have built the Jewish institutional world. Like players in any other power game, American Jewish leaders sign up in large part for the thrill of playing and the glory of winning. The biggest difference between American Jewry and any other political playing field is that it has no perimeter fence. Nothing prevents losers from walking off and starting their own game—nothing, that is, except their sense of responsibility to the Jewish community.

At the same time, many of these schisms reflect a simple division of labor in carrying on the duties of the community's business. Others stem from honest disagreements about how this business should be conducted.

Most Jewish organizations exist to perform—or to influence the performance of—the responsibilities that have preoccupied Jewish communities in every time and place through history: conducting their religious life; helping their poor, sick, elderly, and immigrants; representing Jews to their Gentile neighbors; and defending Jews from their enemies at home and in other lands.

The first Jewish community, of course, was the ancient kingdom of Judah (or Judea) on the eastern shore of the Mediterranean Sea. When the kingdom was conquered in 586 B.C.E. and the Holy Temple was destroyed by the armies of Babylonia (today's Iraq), much of the Judean population was carried off into exile. In Babylon, the exiles were permitted to create a self-governing enclave, living by their own Judean laws and ruled over by a regent of the Judean royal house. Thus the first Diaspora Jewish community was born.

The exiles were permitted to return home fifty years later. Only a few went back, however. Those who did return were able to rebuild the Holy Temple and briefly reestablish the Judean kingdom, but it fell to the Roman legions in 70 C.E. Jewish sovereignty was ended almost for good.

But most Jews had never left Babylonia. They stayed there and flourished for sixteen hundred years as a semi-autonomous community. Their hereditary leader was a descendant of King David who bore the title of exilarch. He was a member of the Babylonian royal court and ruled over the Jews with all the pomp of an Oriental potentate. One exilarch even raised an army and declared independence, holding out for seven years until he was caught and crucified in 502 C.E.

The law governing the Babylonian Jewish community was the Judean law of the Bible, with its countless "thou shalts" and "thou shalt nots," covering everything from murder to commercial contracts, sexual ethics, and the preparation of meat. Reinterpreting the laws of a sovereign kingdom for minority life in exile was the task of legal scholars known as rabbis (from the Hebrew word *rabh,* meaning "master").

The rabbis' legal code was recorded in the fifth century C.E. in a sixty-three–volume compendium called the Talmud. Along with it, the rabbis composed prayers for the exiles to recite daily, praising God and asking to be brought back home to Judea.

Over the centuries, groups of Jews wandered the trade routes from China to England, settling down along the way to create Jewish communities. Each of these was built along the Babylonian model, as a self-governing fragment of the fallen Judean kingdom. Each had a rabbi to make law, and a governing council to raise taxes, care for the poor, and represent the Jews to the local sovereign.

Relations with their Gentile neighbors varied from excellent to abysmal, depending largely on the stability of the local society and its attitude toward minority faiths. In medieval China, Jews were accepted so warmly that they eventually dissolved into the surrounding culture, leaving nothing except a few descendants distinguished by curly hair and a subculture of nostalgia.

In Christian Europe, by contrast, Jews were kept in a state of permanent degradation, ordained by the Catholic Church to suffer for their rejection of Jesus. Though conditions varied from city to city and century to century, Jews typically were barred from most occupations, forbidden to hire Christians, regularly subjected to humiliating spectacles such as the "disputation" (a religious debate, with the loser baptised or killed), and locked up at night in enclosed alleys known as ghettos. Periodically, Jews suffered mob violence and mass murder. All of them were expelled from Germany in 1182, from England in 1290, from France in 1306 and again in 1394, from Austria in 1421, from Spain in 1492, and from Portugal in 1497.

Looking back on this tragic legacy, it is easy to overlook a key fact: that Jews, still God's chosen people in the eyes of the church, were permitted to survive the triumph of Christianity. No other pre-Christian religion of Europe was so lucky. Moreover, because Jews usually were restricted to cities, they frequently were more affluent, healthier, and more secure from violence than the average Christian peasant, who lived in the countryside amid poverty, disease, and the constant fear of war.

At times, Jewish communities in Christian Europe enjoyed something resembling genuine power over their own lives. The Jews of medieval Poland and Lithuania elected a national congress, the Council of the Four Lands, which met annually to set their own tax rates, make laws, and choose their *shtadlan,* or ambassador to the Polish court. During the late Renaissance, many European rulers appointed a "court Jew" who oversaw royal finances and informally spoke for the Jewish community. Some court Jews became enormously wealthy themselves; more than a few used their wealth and clout to protect Jews in danger at home and abroad.

Between the extremes of tolerance and persecution was Jewish life in the Muslim world. Islam, like Christianity, regarded itself as the successor faith to Judaism and so held the Jews in contempt. Jewish communities were subjected to a special tax and occasionally suffered humiliating restrictions. Nothing in the Muslim world, however, even remotely approached the persecution visited on the Jews by Christendom.

The greatest of the Jewish communities in the Muslim world flourished in Spain—called *Sepharad* in Hebrew—during its golden age under the Omayyad dynasty (755–1031). Jews there were allowed to participate fully in Spanish life while still maintaining their communal autonomy. Sephardic Jewry produced a brilliant succession of poets, theologians, musicians, scientists, generals, and even a prime minister. By the end of the Middle Ages, about one fourth of the world's 2 million Jews lived in Spain.

But Islamic Spain was under steady pressure from the advancing armies of the Christian reconquest. In 1391, a Christian revival rally in Seville touched off a wave of anti-Jewish rioting that continued sporadically across the peninsula for decades. Within a century, perhaps 250,000, or half of Spain's Jews, had been forced by mobs or local governments to accept baptism. Many continued to practice Judaism in secret, even though exposure could mean death for heresy.

In January 1492, Spain's last Muslim stronghold fell to the allied Christian monarchs Ferdinand of Aragon and Isabella of Castille. The victors declared a holiday and gave all remaining non-Christians until August 1 to be baptised or leave. Jews had few options: most of Catholic Europe was closed to them already, and Muslim North Africa was ruled by an unfriendly fundamentalism. Some fled for distant Constantinople. Most waited until the deadline, then accepted baptism or fled across the border to neighboring Portugal. That shelter proved short-lived; in 1497, King Manoel I ordered all Jews in Portugal to be baptised. This time there was no option of escape.

The forced converts remained for centuries a vulnerable, embittered minority in Portugal, and to a lesser degree in Spain. Their neighbors called them Marranos, apparently from the Spanish word for "swine." Some say it was an ironic reference to their eating habits. Most undoubtedly became sincere Christians. But an important few remained secretly Jewish, after a fashion.

Over the next three centuries, a dwindling band of Marranos created a secret culture with its own distinct beliefs and customs. Transmitting their faith by word of mouth, fearing exposure even from their own children, their Judaism became a stunted mutation based on remembered habits, bits and phrases from old prayers, and theology inferred from hostile references in Christian books.

"Throughout their suffering," writes Israeli historian Yirmiyahu Yovel, the Marranos "knew that the true way to salvation was not through Christ but through the Law of Moses, which their forefathers had received in ancient times. . . . What this tenaciously guarded treasure consisted of, however, they knew only in a fragmentary and distorted manner."

According to Yovel, Marrano culture fostered a compartmentalized life of alienation and assimilation, remarkably similar to modern Judaism. Rejecting their neighbors' values, clinging to a heritage of which they knew almost nothing, "[r]eligious skepticism and secularism were frequent results. Conversos who lost their Jewish faith without acquiring a Christian one found their attention directed to the secular, earthly affairs of this world, either in the form of work, commerce, and everyday life, or else in subtler forms of secularism—developing tastes for art and learning, cherishing one's own life, exploits and career."

By no coincidence, it was Marrano refugees from Portugal who created the first Jewish communities of North America.

For centuries after the Spanish expulsion, groups of Marranos crisscrossed the Atlantic seeking a place to live without fear. It was not easy for them to hide; until 1768, Portugal kept lists of "New Christians" with Jewish roots. Their movements were observed and restricted. They lived under constant threat of exposure and extermination at the hands of the Inquisition, which monitored Christians' piety. Entire groups of "Judaizers" were burned at the stake in Peru in 1639 and in Mexico in 1649. The burnings continued in Lisbon until 1760.

A few groups of Marranos made their way to Protestant Amsterdam and London, where they began to practice Judaism openly in the early 1600s. But theirs was Judaism with a difference. These Jews had become accustomed to living as full members of the surrounding society. They made no attempt to recreate the self-governing cloister of Jewish tradition before the Inquisition. Judaism became a private, voluntary practice.

As the flow of Marrano refugees from Portugal continued, some found it hard to accept even the open-minded Judaism that they encountered in Amsterdam. Newcomers discovered to their shock that the Judaism passed to them in whispers—a legacy of reason and free thought—turned out to be in fact an endless series of petty intrusions on their diet and behavior. A few, like the philosopher Baruch de Spinoza, simply refused to obey the rabbis and were excommunicated from Judaism.

The first Jewish community in North America was a boatload of Jews from Dutch Brazil who fled the conquering armies of Portugal and wound up in the Dutch port of Nieuw Amsterdam, today's New York City, in 1654. A boatload of destitute Marranos reaching London from Portugal in 1731 was shipped off the next year to the newly founded paupers' colony of Georgia. Another boatload escaping Lisbon in 1758 made its way directly to Rhode Island.

These first American Jews had no need or desire for a communal structure outside the synagogue. They had come from a world where Judaism was a private affair. Only rarely were they moved to speak as a group to the broader nation; then, it was usually to ask that they be treated as individuals.

Jewish community life began and ended with the synagogue, which held prayer services, paid a kosher butcher, and operated a school where children were taught arithmetic, English, Hebrew, and Spanish. Lay ministers led prayers, taught lessons, and circumcised infant boys; not a single rabbi lived in North America until 1840. From time to time, congregations tried to fine a member for violating the Sabbath, as was the custom in Europe, but they quickly gave that up. A Jew could simply walk away. Indeed, at the time of the Revolution, nearly half of the twenty-five hundred colonial Jews did not even belong to a synagogue.

The Jewish community generally had little to say to the larger Gentile society, as well. At less than one tenth of 1 percent of the population, the Jews simply were not a factor in American public life. Their one goal was to ensure that they be treated equally.

Equality was not assured by any means. Colonial Americans saw their new world as a Christian outpost. To most of them, religious freedom meant the freedom to build a community of the true faith; at best, it was a way to keep peace among competing Protestant sects. Judaism did not figure in anyone's vision. A Jew in Maryland was indicted in 1658 on a capital charge of blasphemy after telling an acquaintance that he did not believe in the Trinity (charges were dropped before trial). Not until 1740 were the colonies required, by act of Parliament in London, to let Jews be naturalized.

"There is no country in the world where the Christian religion retains a greater influence over the souls of men than America," French visitor Alexis de Tocqueville would write in 1848. ". . . The Americans combine the notions of Christianity and of liberty so intimately in their minds that it is impossible to make them conceive of the one without the other."

American Jewry came of age with Napoleon's defeat at Waterloo in 1815. A surge of autocratic reaction swept central Europe, sending thousands of frightened democrats fleeing across the Atlantic. This was America's first large immigration wave. In 1848, a failed democratic revolution in Germany sent even more refugees packing. Only a tiny percentage of these arrivals were Jews, but they were enough to swamp the existing community. American Jewry mushroomed from 4,000 in 1820 to 15,000 in 1840, to 50,000 in 1850, and 150,000 in 1860.

German immigrant Jews spread from the Atlantic coast to the interior and out to California. Synagogues sprang up in Cincinnati, St. Louis, New Orleans, and San Francisco. In the older Atlantic coastal communities, one synagogue was no longer enough; German Jews left the Sephardic congregations and built newer synagogues to follow their own Ashkenazic tradition.

The German immigrant tide overwhelmed the synagogues' alms chests. Independent Jewish charities sprang up. By 1860, New York alone had a Hebrew Assistance Society, a Hebrew Benevolent Society, a German Hebrew Benevolent Society, a Jews' Hospital, and two rival boys' shelters.

The Germans also brought American Jewry its first religious schism. Around the turn of the century, Jews in a few German cities had begun responding to the liberalizing tone of the Enlightenment—which called on Christians to open the ghetto gates and on Jews to embrace modernity—by "reforming" their synagogue worship. Prayers were shortened, sermons delivered in German instead of Hebrew, and reading was done in unison to replace the traditional free-for-all. In 1824, a group of congregants petitioned their synagogue in Charleston, South Carolina, urging the same reforms. They hoped that reform would stem "the apathy and neglect which have been manifested toward our holy religion" by growing numbers of young Jews. Outvoted, they left the congregation in 1825 and formed the Reformed Society of Israelites. Within two decades, more than half of the synagogues in America had adopted Reform Judaism. Traditionalists fought back in a war of words that continues to this day.

Beyond prayer and charity, Jews sought fellowship and mutual assistance. Barred from joining their local Elks and Odd Fellows, they formed their own fraternal lodges. The first was the Independent Order B'nai B'rith (Sons of the Covenant), formed in a New York saloon in 1843. Within a decade, there were dozens of imitators. B'nai B'rith itself formed lodges in nearly every city and town where Jews lived, becoming the most familiar Jewish voice in America. It was not set up, however, to provide a systematic program of nationwide Jewish defense.

Defense was essential. Despite the guarantees of the Constitution, Jews had to fight for their rights as Americans—state by state—by challenging laws, filing lawsuits, and building alliances. Much of the time, their champion was the Democratic Party. Now and then, they joined uneasily with Catholics, who suffered many of the same restrictions as Jews in Protestant America. In 1808, long before public schooling, Jews and Catholics together forced New York State to give their schools equal funding with Protestant schools. In 1825, Catholics led the fight for Maryland's "Jew Bill," permitting Jews to practice law and run for office.

At times, Jews were not even united among themselves. Rabbi Isaac Mayer Wise of Cincinnati, the leading advocate of Reform Judaism, argued for the abolition of Sunday-closing laws, calling them an affront to the Constitution. His nemesis, the Reverend Isaac Leeser of Philadelphia, the leading defender of Jewish Orthodoxy, approved the idea of state-imposed morality. He simply wanted Jews exempted, arguing that the Sunday-closing rule was unfair to Jews because they already closed their stores on Saturday.

Most often Jews followed Leeser's path, because it demanded less of the Christian majority. Some judges dismissed their appeals for exemption regardless, noting that most Jews in fact did *not* close on Saturday.

A few Jews went into politics themselves. Some ran for city councils, state legislatures, even Congress. Never, though, did they organize themselves as

Jews; they feared that this would reinforce the old Christian myths of Jewish conspiracy. "We wholly disclaim any wish or intention to be represented as a peculiar community," a group of Charleston Jews declared in an 1832 petition, when a Jew's race for city council touched off rumors that "the Jews" were planning to influence the election.

The first Jewish politician to make his religion a public issue was Mordecai Manuel Noah of New York. In the first decades of the Republic he was America's leading Jew, essentially because he made a career of advertising his Jewishness and daring the world to hold it against him.

Born in Philadelphia in 1785, Noah became a Democratic errand-boy in his teens, got commissioned as a major in the Pennsylvania militia, then applied to the State Department for a diplomatic post ("I wish to prove to foreign Powers that our Government is not regulated in the appointment of their officers by religious distinction," he wrote to Secretary of State Robert Smith in 1810). In 1813, Noah got his assignment: U.S. consul in Tunis. It was a diplomatic hot spot on the Barbary Coast, where America had just fought its first foreign war. As consul, Noah successfully won the release of some American hostages, but he was abruptly recalled in 1815 for reasons that are still unclear. Secretary of State James Monroe told him, implausibly, that he hadn't realized that "the faith which you profess would prove a diplomatic obstacle in a Moslem community." In fact, Noah's faith was the very reason he had been sent.

Called back home, Noah settled in New York; edited a few newspapers; wrote a few plays; and served as sheriff, port surveyor, judge, and Grand Sachem of the Tammany Democratic Club. His high point was a scheme to create a Jewish homeland on an island in Niagara Falls; he actually held a cornerstone-laying ceremony and parade in nearby Buffalo in 1825, decked out as "Governor and Judge of Israel" in an ermine robe he rented from a local Shakespeare troupe. But no one ever moved there.

Noah was considered something of a blowhard, even by his friends. And yet he became a symbol to American Jews. He spoke out constantly against bigotry and for restoration of the Jews to Palestine; he even persuaded the aging ex-presidents Adams and Jefferson to endorse his pre-Zionist idea. When European Jewish communities wanted to communicate with the Jews of America, they addressed their letters to Major Noah, New York. When Noah became president of the New York Hebrew Benevolent Society in 1842, donations shot up; even the governor sent $100. But after a year of his leadership the German Jews walked out and formed the German Hebrew Benevolent Society. Major Noah was hard to take.

Being loyal Democrats did not make American Jews liberals, exactly. In nineteenth-century America, Jews did not stick their necks out for social change. On the two great issues of pre–Civil War America—slavery and immigration—the Jewish community was all but silent.

Most Jews were immigrants, but America's immigration debate was basically a debate over Catholicism, which was becoming a mass phenomenon as a result of the immigration of German and Irish Catholics in the 1840s. Most Jews had deep misgivings about defending the church that had inflicted so many centuries of suffering on their forebears in Europe.

As to slavery, one abolitionist group actively sought ties with the Jewish community in 1853, assuming that their experiences in Egypt would make them sympathetic, but found no one to talk to. The Jews "have no organization of an ecclesiastical body to represent their general views," the group reported, and the Jewish community's two monthly newspapers "do not interfere in any subject which is not material to their religion." The editor of one of the newspapers, Orthodox leader Isaac Leeser, felt slavery was none of the Jewish community's business. The other editor, Reform leader Isaac Mayer Wise, was opposed to abolition.

A few individual Jews spoke out on the issues, such as the abolitionist guerrilla August Bondi, the feminist crusader Ernestine Rose, and Rabbi David Einhorn, whose anti-slavery sermons got him run out of Baltimore. But just as prominent in their day were Rabbi Morris Raphall of New York, whose pro-slavery sermonizing won him national renown; Representative Lewis Levin of Philadelphia, congressional leader of the anti-immigrant, anti-Catholic Native American Party; and Judah P. Benjamin of New Orleans, "the lion of the Confederacy," who left the U.S. Senate in 1861 to join Jefferson Davis's Confederate cabinet as attorney general, secretary of war, and finally, secretary of state.

The first national agency for Jewish defense arose in 1859, when delegates from twenty-four synagogues in fourteen cities convened in New York to form the Board of Delegates of American Israelites.

The board was a frank imitation of the century-old Board of Deputies of British Jews, headquartered in London. The British board had stunned the world in 1840 by forcing the rulers of far-off Syria to free a dozen Jews arrested in February on the dreary old "blood libel" charge: killing a Christian and baking his blood into bread. The British board's president, Sir Moses Montefiore, philanthropist and son-in-law of the banking Rothschilds, had orchestrated an international campaign to free the imprisoned Syrians. He mounted Jewish protest rallies across the continent, mobilized all his own contacts in British business and government, and brilliantly played European imperial rivalries against one another. By the time he was done, nearly every government in Europe had endorsed the Syrian Jews' cause. The prime minister of France, Syria's main patron, told his parliament that summer that the Jews "have more power than they know."

In America, by contrast, Jews spent long months bickering over whether and where to rally. They finally managed to mount a protest meeting in New York on August 17, 1840, calling on their government to help the imprisoned Syrians. As it happened, the State Department had already acted three days earlier, on August 14, at Montefiore's request.

The embarrassing fumble prompted demands for a national "synod" of American Jews. There were only a few dozen synagogues and fewer rabbis, yet the synod took two decades to convene. Its two main advocates were the bombastic Reform Rabbi Wise and his archrival, the dour Orthodox Isaac Leeser. Each suspected the other of seeking a sectarian platform, and each perpetually undermined the other.

While they argued, humiliation followed humiliation. In 1850, the United States and Switzerland initialed a mutual friendship treaty, guaranteeing each country's citizens full protection on the other's soil. The sole exception made was for Jews, who were legally barred from entering many Swiss cantons. American Jews protested that their own government was formally agreeing to deny them its protection. After four years of protests, the White House revised the treaty to drop the mention of Jews. Instead, it guaranteed equal protection to all—except where equality conflicted with state or canton laws. Now Zurich's anti-Jewish laws had the same force as South Carolina's antiblack laws. The Senate ratified the treaty in 1854.

In 1858, word came that an American Jew had been expelled from

Switzerland. Rabbi Wise called for nationwide protests. Rallies were mounted in a dozen cities. At each rally, delegates were chosen to attend a national Jewish assembly in Baltimore in October. Four delegations showed up. Undeterred, Wise led his delegates to Washington, brought them to meet Democratic President James Buchanan at the White House (a Jewish ex-Representative from Alabama set up the meeting), received a vague statement of presidential sympathy, and declared victory. The treaty remained unchanged.

In the interim, a new international storm had erupted in Italy during the summer of 1858. A Jewish child in Bologna, seven-year-old Edgardo Mortara, was removed from his parents' home by papal police and taken to a convent. The boy had been baptised secretly by his nurse. As a Christian, he could not legally be raised by Jews.

Again the British Board of Deputies organized worldwide protests. This time, American Jews moved quickly, staging rallies in eighteen cities. Support came from leading Protestant ministers, dozens of newspapers, the fledgling Republican Party, and the nativist, anti-Catholic Know Nothing Party. But President Buchanan refused to act. Jews represented some fifty thousand Democratic votes, Catholics close to a million. Besides, as Buchanan told Isaac Leeser at a White House meeting in 1859, if America could stay neutral in a moral issue as clear-cut as this, it might teach the rest of the world to stay out of America's affairs (meaning slavery).

As for young Mortara, he grew up to be a priest.

The Board of Delegates of American Israelites at last came into being when a younger generation shoved Wise and Leeser aside, tabled religious issues, and agreed to focus narrowly on Jewish civil rights. They succeeded brilliantly, thanks in large part to the board's Washington lobbyist, attorney Simon Wolf.

Wolf seemed to be everywhere at once. When the Union Army began recruiting Christian chaplains in 1861, Wolf got the order changed to include rabbis. When the wartime Congress prepared a constitutional amendment to declare America a Christian nation, Wolf wooed away a handful of senators and blocked it in committee. When General Ulysses Grant issued his infamous Order No. 11 in 1862—a clumsy attempt to halt

Confederate smuggling by expelling "Jews as a class" from the border states, forcing two thousand Jewish Kentuckians from their homes—Wolf brought a group of Kentuckians to meet President Lincoln. The order was reversed at once.

The board also mounted America's first national Jewish fund-raising drives for overseas relief: $20,000 for Jewish refugees in Morocco and $15,000 for cholera victims in Palestine. And in 1870, when state-sanctioned anti-Semitic riots broke out in Romania, the board pushed the matter onto the agenda of the U.S. Senate, then persuaded now-President Ulysses Grant to send a Jewish lawyer to Romania as its first American consul. (The consul's salary was paid by a group of wealthy New York Jews.) The diplomat, former B'nai B'rith president Benjamin Franklin Peixotto, arrived in Bucharest with a letter to the prince from President Grant, urging that Romania treat all its citizens equally, the way America did. The Romanian pogroms halted at once, at least for the five years that Peixotto was there.

Why did the Board of Delegates succeed where past organizing efforts had failed? In part, it was a matter of timing: the board came to Washington just as the new Republican Party was seeking its footing. The GOP was hungry for allies and eager to break the Democratic lock on Jewish votes. Republican President Ulysses Grant even offered a Jewish friend, New York bond-broker Joseph Seligman, the job of treasury secretary. Seligman declined, though he remained a faithful donor. GOP-Jewish cooperation remained fruitful through several administrations.

But the most important reason for the board's success was that American Jews were ready for a voice. They had been transformed in a generation from newcomers to insiders. The German Jewish immigrant peddlers of the 1840s had become American Jewish merchant princes of the 1870s. The wealthiest were connected by an intimate network of marriages, manners, clubs, schools, and elegant synagogues, recalled in lore as "Our Crowd." Jews like Joseph Seligman and his brothers, mining magnate Meyer Guggenheim, the retailers Nathan and Isidor Straus, and investment banker Jacob Schiff had become part of America's business elite. When they spoke, America listened.

Nothing illustrated the Jews' new status more clearly than the Senate response to the Romanian pogroms in 1870. The first news reports to reach the United States indicated that "thousands" had been killed in riots in late May. Protest rallies were held in Indianapolis, Louisville, and a half-dozen other cities. After some furious lobbying by Simon Wolf, the matter was brought to the Senate floor by Senator Oliver Morton of Indiana.

Morton read a statement from the Indianapolis Jewish rally and asked for action by the Senate Foreign Relations Committee. The committee chairman, Massachusetts GOP leader Charles Sumner, delicately told the chamber he was "disposed to believe that there is at least some gross exaggeration in the report" of mass murder. In reply, Senator Morton assured his colleagues that his statement had come from "gentlemen of the highest respectability and position, and they represent a very large and numerous class of people in Indianapolis and in Indiana." That was enough, it seems; the Senate ordered the Foreign Relations Committee to take up the matter with the State Department. (Sumner turned out to be correct. The riots' death toll had been zero.)

For all its successes, the Board of Delegates was short-lived. In 1878, after nineteen years, the board voted to merge with the newly formed Union of American Hebrew Congregations (UAHC), brainchild of the irrepressible Rabbi Isaac Mayer Wise.

Wise was still dreaming of his national Jewish "synod." After his old foe Leeser died in 1868, Wise began wooing traditionalist rabbis to join his Reformers in a grand congregational union. The union convened in 1873 in Cincinnati and quickly grew to encompass one hundred synagogues, half the national total. It annexed the Board of Delegates, opened a Hebrew Union College to train clergy, and laid plans for a central conference of American rabbis.

Wise's UAHC reigned as the supreme governing body of American Judaism for all of ten years. Its run ended when growing Reform influence led to an 1883 walkout by the traditionalists. The break came at the first Hebrew Union College graduation dinner, during the appetizer course, which featured the biblically banned shrimp. Two years later, Reform rabbis met in Pittsburgh and defiantly announced that the Bible's laws on diet and Sabbath were no longer to be taken literally, that Jews were now a "universal faith" rather than a nation in exile, and that restoring Jerusalem was merely a metaphor—symbolized by the Reformers' scandalous use of the word "temple" for their synagogues. The rupture with the traditionalists was final.

A few months later, the traditionalists regrouped in New York and founded the Jewish Theological Seminary, teaching a more conservative form of Judaism than the Reformers. Within several years, the Conservative rabbis organized their own Rabbinical Assembly and United Synagogue of America. American Judaism now had two formal branches.

In the interim, a third movement emerged, made up of fundamentalist Russian immigrants for whom even Conservative Judaism was too Americanized. Orthodox Judaism became the third leg of the splintered shambles that had once been Isaac Mayer Wise's Jewish synod.

American Jewry lost its central governing body just as it faced its greatest crisis ever: the mass immigration of Russian Jews. It began in 1881, when the assassination of Czar Alexander II by an anarchist prompted anti-Jewish riots across Russia. The Jewish exodus from Russia snowballed through four decades of mounting czarist persecution. By the time the flood ended, shut down by a hostile Congress in 1924, more than 2 million Jews had crossed the Atlantic. It was the largest single population movement in all of Jewish history.

Russia's 5 million Jews were a vast historical accident. The fanatically Christian Romanov monarchy had never permitted Jews on Russian soil. But in 1793 and again in 1795, Russia annexed parts of Poland, inadvertently inheriting the world's largest Jewish community. Over the next century, a succession of czars tried to digest the Jews variously through segregation, forced integration, and violent persecution. Czar Alexander III, who took the throne in 1881, adopted a three-pronged program to eliminate the Jews by forced conversion, forced emigration, and starvation. The Jews stampeded for the borders.

The Russian immigration terrified America's well-established quarter-million German Jews. They had spent a half-century building a sober, middle-class image as good neighbors. The Russian Jews were desperately poor, alien in dress, language, and smell. They were politically radicalized by their hatred of the czarist regime. Their most prominent leaders were either socialist revolutionaries or Zionist nationalists, romantic schemers who wanted to remove all the Jews bodily to ancient Palestine.

If the Russians kept pouring in, Rabbi Wise warned, "the good reputation of Judaism must naturally suffer."

This was already happening. In 1882, the *New York Tribune* reported that the immigrant Jews' "filthy condition" had made the city's parks unusable. In 1908, the New York City police commissioner, Theodore Bingham, wrote in America's leading literary magazine that "Hebrews" accounted for one quarter of the city's population but one half of its growing crime rate—"not astonishing," he added, given the character of "that race."

The collision of old-line German Jews and raucous Russian newcomers gave birth to the institutions—and the rivalries—that shape American Jewish politics to this day.

There were, to begin with, the charities. They were springing up everywhere as German Jews built institutions to help the ghetto poor and then fought with one another for the same donors. The rush of German Jewish society ladies to volunteer in the ghettos led to the formation of the National Council of Jewish Women in 1893. In Boston, community leaders decided in 1895 to force the competing local charities into a single "federated" fund-raising campaign. Within a decade, nearly every major Jewish community had a federation to coordinate its myriad soup kitchens, settlement houses, and tubercular clinics.

In the immigrant ghettos, radical ferment gave rise to dozens of tiny political parties that voiced the newcomers' grievances and plotted their salvation. Each had its own impossible plan for a perfect world, usually either socialist or Zionist. By the eve of the First World War, the main voices of the ghetto were the Zionists, led by Boston attorney Louis D. Brandeis, and the socialists, whose effective house organ was a daily Yiddish newspaper in New York, the *Forward*.

Politically, the most significant institutions to emerge from the Russian immigration—and the American backlash—were the "Big Three" Jewish civil rights organizations: the American Jewish Committee, the American Jewish Congress, and the Anti-Defamation League of B'nai B'rith.

The American Jewish Committee was the first. It was convened in 1906 by leaders of the German-Jewish social elite. Seeking ways to pressure

Russia for reforms and to combat growing anti-Semitism at home, the brahmins invited a hand-picked group of lawyers, businessmen, rabbis, and academics to confer in New York. They also invited a few selected Russians, as well as the heads of B'nai B'rith and the UAHC, including the aging Simon Wolf. The group briefly considered the idea of holding democratic elections among Jews around the country, but rejected it, fearing radicals would win. Instead they deputized themselves as "the American Jewish Committee." They laid out an ambitious program of lobbying, research, and diplomacy to improve Jewish conditions in Europe and combat the threats at home.

The Committee won instant acceptance in Washington and European capitals as the authoritative voice of American Jewry. This was not surprising, given its high-octane roster of judges, congressmen, and Wall Street barons. President Theodore Roosevelt plucked its best-known member, lawyer Oscar Straus, to serve as his secretary of labor and commerce, the first Jew to serve in a U.S. Cabinet. Roosevelt told Straus that he wanted "to show Russia and some other countries what we think of Jews in this country." The Labor Department, not coincidentally, ran the Bureau of Immigration.

Russia needed no reminders about Jewish influence in America. The wealthy Jews of New York had been trying to strong-arm the czarist regime for decades, seeking to ease Moscow's anti-Semitic policies (and slow the Russian Jewish immigration to America). In 1892, a group of New York Jews persuaded the *New York Times* (then owned by non-Jews) to send a special correspondent to Russia at the Jews' expense in order to expose czarist brutality. The articles aroused nationwide indignation in America, but the Russians only dug in their heels. In 1904, at the height of the Russo-Japanese War, investment banker Jacob Schiff of the Kuhn Loeb brokerage house volunteered to underwrite Japan's war bonds. The bond issue won Japan the war and earned Schiff a knighthood from the Japanese emperor. But Russia refused to bend.

In 1911, the American Jewish Committee gave its first full-dress demonstration of Jewish domestic clout: it persuaded the U.S. Senate to abrogate the eighty-year-old U.S.-Russian trade treaty of 1832.

Like the Swiss treaty fight back in the 1850s, the fight against the Russian trade treaty was presented as an American domestic issue. Russia's anti-Semitic laws extended not only to Russian Jews, but to American Jewish visitors as well. That violated the Russian treaty's equal protection clause, which required each country to respect the other's citizens. The Senate had been reluctant in the past to act against Russia's domestic policies, but rallied when it saw Americans discriminated against. Over the bitter objections of President William Howard Taft, the treaty was torn up. (The czarist regime remained unmoved.)

Not surprisingly, the American Jewish Committee was scorned in the immigrant ghettos as a self-appointed elite. The immigrants demanded an elected congress of American Jews.

The campaign for a Jewish congress was part of a wave of nationalist congress movements that were erupting across the globe as old empires tottered from Poland to India to South Africa. Spearheading the Jewish congress movement were the Zionists, who considered the Jews no less a captive nation than the Poles or the Serbs. The Zionists were joined by socialists, who wanted democratic Jewish elections for the same reason the brahmins feared them: the likelihood of a radical victory.

Yet the congress movement's immediate goal was a modest one: to send a Jewish delegation to the international peace conference that was expected to meet in Paris and redivide the world after the First World War.

The American Jewish Committee fought the congress movement bitterly, fearing the image of a Jewish "nation within a nation," as Jacob Schiff put it in a letter to Oscar Straus. But with the unstoppable Louis Brandeis leading the Zionist charge, the barons gave in. In a 1916 compromise brokered by the president of B'nai B'rith, the Committee agreed to participate in the American Jewish Congress on condition that it convene just once, choose an American Jewish delegation to Paris, then disband for good.

The American Jewish Congress was chosen in three days of unprecedented balloting in May 1917, at polling places set up in Jewish neighborhoods across America. It met in late 1918, chose a delegation to Paris, and disbanded. But in 1922, the congress was "reconvened" by Rabbi Stephen S. Wise, Brandeis's most charismatic disciple (and no relation to Isaac). Wise's new American Jewish Congress was actually no congress at all. It was a personal platform for his private blend of Jewish nationalism and militant liberalism.

The origin of the third defense agency was even more personal than Wise's "reconvened" Congress. The Anti-Defamation League of B'nai B'rith sprang from the imagination of one man, German-born lawyer Sigmund Livingston of Bloomington, Illinois.

Like most German-American Jews, Livingston was appalled at the flood of negative stereotypes filling the media during the immigrant years, from vaudeville "sheeny" jokes to sober analyses of "Hebrew crime." But where the big-city American Jewish Committee paladins tried to address the root causes of anti-Semitism, Livingston merely wanted to silence the anti-Semites. To him, bigotry was not a product of conditions, but simply an ugly mistake.

In 1908, Livingston persuaded his local B'nai B'rith lodge to let him chair a "Publicity Committee." From this perch he began writing letters. He urged newspapers not to identify criminals by religion. He hectored movie studios and vaudeville circuits not to feature comic stereotypes like the Jewish rag-peddler. He asked high schools not to stage Shakespeare's *Merchant of Venice*.

Livingston's campaign spread quickly to B'nai B'rith lodges across the country. In 1913, the order's top leadership invited him to preside over a nationwide bureau, dubbed the Anti-Defamation League of B'nai B'rith (ADL). The league progressed from writing letters to pamphlets and newspaper advertisements, all aiming to teach Americans that Jews were just like them. During the 1930s, as anti-Semitism became an organized mass-movement, the league diversified. It launched a fact-finding division to gather intelligence on the hate groups. It even hired agents to infiltrate fascist cells and collect information, which it passed along to the FBI or the media. Anti-Semites came to detest and fear the ADL.

Through the 1920s and 1930s, America's wave of immigrant-bashing and bigotry intensified. The U.S. Congress voted in 1921 and again in 1924 to limit immigration along ethnic lines, virtually ending Jewish immigration. In Europe, fascism was on the rise, drawing powerful followers in the United States.

The three Jewish defense agencies had their hands full. They added staff, opened regional offices, and begged for funds from local Jewish welfare federations.

Federation leaders were annoyed by the redundant demands, but could rarely refuse. The defense agencies had learned to recruit wealthy federation donors to their own boards. As each town's federation met to allocate its revenues, these donors became advocates for their favorite defense agencies. Federations could not turn down the big donors' requests, for fear of losing their gifts. The three agencies grew and grew.

In 1938, the federation heads finally took action to halt the blackmail. Working through their newly formed Council of Jewish Federations and Welfare Funds (CJF), they sat down the heads of the three major defense agencies—along with the Jewish Labor Committee, a project of the daily *Forward* and the big Jewish tailors' unions—and demanded that they all join forces. The result was a trifle disappointing: the General Jewish Council, a toothless body that met regularly to exchange views and insults.

In 1944, the federations again tried to stop the bickering. They abolished the General Jewish Council and reorganized the agencies into the National Community Relations Advisory Council, or NCRAC (pronounced "nac-rac," even after a "J" for "Jewish" was added in 1971). This body was more solidly designed than the General Jewish Council. It had its own staff and budget. More important, its base was expanded. Along with the national agencies, NCRAC included representatives of the federations themselves—at least the fourteen federations that had lately set up "community-relations committees" to direct their local efforts at fighting anti-Semitism. Federation membership meant steady input to NCRAC from the people out on the firing line. It also meant direct feedback from the people who paid the bills.

The 1944 CJF assembly voted to instruct all federations to set up their own community-relations committees and join NCRAC. In short order, NCRAC came to resemble the United Nations, with its two-tiered membership of local councils and national agencies. As in the U.N., the national agencies held veto power, giving them a privileged status befitting their clout and status. And, as in the U.N., the tension between the veto-holders and the others would prove well-nigh intractable.

All the efforts to create a central representative body of American Jews on the eve of the First World War had ended in disarray, just like all the attempts before. But another wartime cooperative effort had more lasting results: the campaign to provide material aid to the Jews of war-torn Europe.

The outbreak of hostilities in August 1914 caused incalculable misery to the already suffering Jews of Eastern Europe. Millions of them, still the world's largest Jewish community, lived directly in the path of the heaviest fighting on the war's Eastern Front, in Poland, western Russia and eastern Austria. Those whose homes were not destroyed by clashing armies often suffered in the chaos from marauding bands of civilians. Thousands more were dying of disease and starvation.

In October 1914, as reports flooded into New York, a group of Orthodox Jews met to form the Central Committee for the Relief of Jews Suffering Through the War. Three weeks later, they were invited to send a representative to a meeting convened by the American Jewish Committee. A new group was formed, dominated by the American Jewish Committee and chaired by its president, Louis Marshall. It was called the American Jewish Relief Committee.

The Orthodox agreed to cooperate, but balked at merging the two efforts. Instead, the two groups arranged to raise money separately and distribute the proceeds jointly in Europe. Another body was formed to carry out this distribution. Called simply the Joint Distribution Committee, it was chaired by Jacob Schiff's son-in-law, banker Felix Warburg.

"The Joint" was a phenomenal success from the start. It began raising funds (despite the original agreement) with a kickoff event at Carnegie Hall that brought in $1 million. Schiff alone gave $100,000; so did Sears Roebuck magnate Julius Rosenwald. A few months later, Rosenwald donated another $1 million, followed by another $1 million in 1917. Millions more came in tiny donations from Jewish garment workers, particularly after the socialists met to form the People's Relief Committee, which became the third partner in the Joint.

By the end of the First World War, the Joint had collected more than $16 million, nearly matching the mighty American Red Cross. It set up a network of distribution centers across Europe, some administered by German and Austrian Jewish agencies, others by the Joint's own staff. When the Ottoman Turks instituted a series of repressive measures against the Jews of Palestine, the Joint sent $1.5 million in cash and two boatloads of food.

The work continued after the war. One million Jews were homeless in Poland. In Russia and the Ukraine, revolution, civil war, and famine had left some 200,000 Jews dead. All told, the war and its aftermath were the worst disaster that had ever befallen the Jews (though worse was to come).

The Joint Distribution Committee became a permanent agency, with representatives on its board from every major faction of the Jewish community. It ran a national fund-raising campaign every year, working closely with the local Jewish federations to avoid competition.

In 1935, the federations forced the Zionists and the Joint Distribution Committee to combine their annual fund-raising campaigns into a single campaign, the Allied Jewish Appeal. It collapsed into squabbling before it even began. Three years later, alarmed by the growing menace of German Nazism, they tried again. This time the combined campaign was called the United Jewish Appeal for Overseas Relief, or UJA.

The UJA lasted just a year before collapsing again, this time because the Zionists, stung by their meager one-fifth share of the receipts, decided to go it alone. They came crawling back in 1940, having done even worse on their own, and the UJA was united for good.

After the Second World War, the Joint took the lead in feeding, sheltering, and rehabilitating the shattered Jewish survivors of the Nazi Holocaust. Today, it is still the principal American agency of worldwide Jewish relief, operating old-age homes in Romania, clinics in Ethiopia, schools in Morocco, and a network of social-service agencies in Israel. Its fund-raising arm, the United Jewish Appeal, has become a legend, one of the largest charitable operations in the United States.

The American Jewish institutions that grew out of the great Russian immigration and the First World War—the American Jewish Committee, the American Jewish Congress, the Anti-Defamation League, the National Council of Jewish Women, the federations, the Joint Distribution Committee, and the United Jewish Appeal—remain the central bodies of organized American Jewish life. Together with the synagogue unions, the Zionist movement, and the B'nai B'rith, they are the essential building blocks of American Jewry's vaunted political and financial machine. Almost every other Jewish organization is either a combination of these, or a minor player.

By the end of the First World War, then, the American Jewish community had created the structures it needed in order to exercise its full weight on the American scene. Jews soon would learn, to their shock, that one more factor was needed for Jewish success, and it was by no means guaranteed: the goodwill of the American people.

CHAPTER 5

From the Ashes:
Opening the Golden Door

R ALPH REED, executive director of Pat Robertson's Christian Coalition, came to address the annual policy conference of the American Israel Public Affairs Committee on May 8, 1995. The topic was the state of relations between Jews and the Christian right.

Those relations were poor in the spring of 1995, so poor that AIPAC had to take care that it not offend Jews by seeming too eager to offer Reed a platform. Instead, his appearance was set up as a panel debate, titled "Evangelical Christians and American Jews: Is Partnership Possible on the Pro-Israel Agenda?" His copanelists were two leading Jewish political activists, one from the left—Rabbi David Saperstein, head of the Washington office of Reform Judaism—and one from the right, Elliot Abrams, former Reagan administration official and now a leading neoconservative theorist.

Abrams spoke first and set a somber tone for the session. He issued a dire warning: the American Jewish community was in no position to pick and choose its friends, because it was a community on the brink of decline.

"For any of us to allow our own political views to interfere with our cooperation with a group that is valiantly pro-Israel, it seems to me, is nuts," Abrams said. "The American Jewish community was once under 4 percent of the population. It is now under 3 percent, and it is clearly heading for 2 percent. So the ability of the American Jewish community to protect Israel in the next generation is inevitably going to decline."

Indeed, he added, given the apparent eclipse of the Democratic Party, organized labor, and other traditional allies of the Jewish community, "[We] may be in for an era when the influence of the American Jewish community is in decline. For that reason I say to you, I don't know whether Ralph Reed needs us, but we need Ralph Reed."

Abrams's message seemed well received by the crowd, which had turned out in force for the early-morning session. The applause was no surprise: AIPAC's membership is known for its hardheaded pragmatism and its openness to wide-ranging alliances. Certainly, the two AIPAC officers who cochaired the session—ex-president Ed Levy and vice president Bob Mazer, both Midwestern businessmen identified with conservative causes—were beaming as Abrams spoke.

On the other hand, there was Ralph Reed, sitting right next to Abrams on the dais. Reed had come to AIPAC this morning to curry favor with the political leadership of American Jewry, not the other way around. One of the busiest people in America, he was making his third appearance in the space of a month before a major Jewish group.

"Many Jews have a stereotyped view of evangelical Christians," Reed told his audience, insisting in almost pleading tones that the widespread images of gun-toting anti-Semites in pickup trucks were unfair.

"Just because we don't share the same political agenda as liberal Jews, it should not mean we can't cooperate," he said. He concluded, "I hope you will count on us as a friend."

If the Jews were indeed facing a radical decline in influence, someone forgot to tell Ralph Reed.

Elliot Abrams had his numbers right but his facts wrong. It is not numbers that create Jewish influence, and it never was.

If Abrams had examined history a bit more carefully, he would have noticed that American Jews reached their highest share of the American population around 1924, when they peaked at just under 3.8 percent, after four decades of massive immigration from Russia. That was the year in which Jewish influence in America arguably touched bottom.

It was in 1924 that Congress shut off the growth of the Jewish community by adopting the Johnson-Reed Immigration Reform Act, slashing overall immigration and setting up ethnic quotas for future newcomers. The measure came after fifteen years of congressional debates, hearings, and scientific testimony had convinced lawmakers that Jews (along with Italians, Greeks, Slavs, and other non-Aryans) were corrupting America's racial stock. Earlier bills along the way had been stopped only by presidential veto, until a milder version of the Johnson act became law in 1921.

In January 1924, as the sweeping immigration measure awaited presidential signature, American Jewish Committee leader Louis Marshall asked to meet with President Calvin Coolidge to urge a veto. Coolidge refused to see him. The president's views were summed up in an article he had written a few years earlier in *Good Housekeeping* magazine, titled "Whose Country Is This?" "[B]iological laws show us that Nordics deteriorate when mixed with other races," Coolidge wrote.

A decade later, in the late 1930s, with Jews holding steady at around 3.7 percent of the U.S. population, the ethnic quotas would serve to block virtually every effort by the American Jewish community to save European Jews from the Nazi Holocaust. All attempts to ease the quotas ran into a brick wall of congressional opposition from a coalition of Southern Democrats and Republican isolationists.

One measure, submitted to the Senate in 1939 by New York Democrat Robert Wagner Sr., a Catholic, would have brought 20,000 German Jewish children to stay in American foster homes under Quaker sponsorship. The bill met a torrent of opposition and died in committee. "Strictly speaking, it is not a refugee bill at all," one witness testified, "for by the nature of the case most of those to be admitted would be of the Jewish race." The witness, Francis H. Kinnicutt of the Allied Patriotic Societies, was speaking on behalf of the American Legion, the Veterans of Foreign Wars, the Daughters of the American Revolution, and several dozen other groups. Scores of equally distinguished witnesses gave similar testimony.

At the time that Wagner's bill died, some sixty other bills were pending before Congress to *restrict* immigration even further.

During the Second World War itself, despite repeated Jewish pleas, President Franklin Roosevelt met with the leadership of the American Jewish community only once to discuss the Nazi atrocities. The meeting came one month after the State Department confirmed Germany's genocidal intentions, in December 1942. Roosevelt did almost all of the talking. After that, the president stonewalled the issue for fourteen murderous months, until he was embarrassed into taking action in January 1944 by a desperate Treasury Secretary Henry Morgenthau Jr., son of a German-Jewish merchant prince of "Our Crowd."

A *Fortune* magazine poll in April 1939 found that 94 percent of Americans disapproved of the way Germany was treating the Jews, but 83 percent opposed lowering the immigration quotas to admit more refugees. Only 8.7 percent favored admitting refugees.

The tide of anti-Jewish and anti-immigrant sentiment in America seemed unstoppable in the 1920s and 1930s. The Ku Klux Klan, anti-Jewish and anti-Catholic as well as anti-black, claimed 4 million members nationwide in 1924. Auto magnate Henry Ford, sometimes called America's most admired man, launched his own weekly magazine in 1920, the *Dearborn Independent*, to spread his ideas about an international Jewish bolshevik-banker-Hollywood conspiracy against Christian America. In 1925, the weekly reached a peak circulation of seven hundred thousand. (Ford discontinued it in 1927, under threat of a Jewish-sponsored consumer boycott. Nevertheless, he continued to espouse the same views in private.)

Anti-Jewish sentiment continued to grow in popularity and respectability, right up to the eve of the Second World War. Powerful radio preachers like Gerald Winrod and Father Charles Coughlin, forerunners of today's televangelists, filled the nation's airwaves with warnings of a Jewish conspiracy against Christian America. Imitators harangued crowds from streetcorners in every city in the nation.

Many of the nation's best universities, including Harvard and Columbia, adopted formal quotas to limit the number of Jewish students. Medical schools were so restrictive that young Jews who wanted to study medicine were usually forced to go abroad. Jews graduating from law school had to start their own law firms; no major Gentile firm would hire them. The same was true in accounting. Nearly every major industry—steel, oil, automobiles, chemicals—erected barriers to Jewish employment.

There was no legal recourse, because none of this discrimination was illegal. In many cities, Jewish federations set up specialized agencies known as Jewish vocational services, simply to match Jews with employers who would hire them. "If you go back to the want ads at that point, 'Gentile-only' was as common as 'whites only,' " recalls Arnold Aronson, who was a staffer with the Chicago Jewish Vocational Service in the late 1930s.

A half-century later, virtually every field of endeavor was open to Jews in America. Discrimination against Jews in hiring, education, and housing was illegal. Barriers had disappeared in all the top universities, the major law firms, and most industries. Major corporations that had once refused to hire Jews were now sporting Jewish chief executives, from E. I. Du Pont to the Walt Disney Company. By the last quarter of the twentieth century, Jews were commonly estimated to make up as much as 20 percent of the faculty at America's most prestigious universities and 20 percent of the lawyers at the top firms. And the idea that a president might refuse to meet with the Jewish community's leadership was no longer conceivable.

"Presentism," writes Jeffersonian scholar Douglas Wilson, "is the term that historians use for applying contemporary or otherwise inappropriate standards to the past. An awkward term at best, it nevertheless names a malaise that currently plagues American discussions of anything and everything concerning the past; the widespread inability to make appropriate allowances for prevailing historical conditions."

The accusation of "presentism" is most commonly leveled by conservative historians against liberal iconoclasts. The conservative goal, usually, is to rehabilitate the reputations of tarnished icons, such as Jefferson the slave-owner or, for that matter, America's pioneers, who exterminated aboriginal Americans to create the new nation.

Among Jewish community activists in current day America, it has become fashionable to suppose that if American Jews had spoken out forcefully during the Second World War, they could have convinced President Roosevelt to take direct action to save Jewish lives. "Instead of countering President Roosevelt's attempt to mask the problem, they surrendered to his policy of secrecy," Rabbi Haskell Lookstein charges in his 1985 study, *Were We Our Brothers' Keepers?* (Lookstein, not surprisingly, answers his own question with a resounding "no.")

Lookstein's book is part of a long chain of blame that began with the appearance in 1968 of Arthur D. Morse's *While Six Million Died*. Morse documents the existence within the wartime Roosevelt administration of extensive bureaucratic indifference—and, in many cases, opposition—to saving Jewish lives.

According to a revisionist history that has grown up since Morse's book, and is now widely accepted, America could have saved hundreds of thousands, if not millions, of European Jews—but chose not to. There were proposals during the war to bomb the rail lines to Auschwitz in order to slow the transport of Jews, or to bomb the crematoria themselves in order to stop the killing. There were appeals to relax American immigration restrictions and allow Jews in as refugees, in the event that they did escape.

In the current Jewish revision of history, Roosevelt could have saved Jews if he had wanted to, but he chose not to—either because, as Lookstein delicately puts it, he was "sensitive to public opinion" which opposed rescuing Jews, or because Roosevelt "in private" had a "disinterest in saving Jews qua Jews."

The established leadership of the Jewish community, in turn, could have pressured Roosevelt to do the right thing, but chose not to—being either frightened, dazzled by the president's charm, or simply indifferent to the slaughter.

The one dramatic step that was taken, the creation of the War Refugee Board in February 1944, saved about two hundred thousand Jewish lives during the last fifteen months of the war, according to historian David Wyman, the most authoritative of the revisionist scholars. It seems fair to assume that if Roosevelt had established the board in late November 1942, when he first received confirmation of the Nazis' Final Solution, rather than waiting fourteen months until his hand was forced by Treasury Secretary Henry Morgenthau, the number of Jewish lives saved might well have been at least twice that.

The theory of abandonment has become so universally accepted in Jewish activist circles that speakers at Jewish events now refer routinely to the "complicity" of wartime Jewish leaders who continued to support Roosevelt despite the president's obvious (to today's Jewish militants, at least) callousness and anti-Semitism. "Give us strength to lead our people like Joseph and Esther, and not like Henry Morgenthau and Felix Frankfurter," one Ohio lawyer intoned in a lunchtime invocation at a UJA Young Leadership Cabinet retreat in Illinois in the summer of 1993. "They could have influenced Roosevelt, but they chose not to." Nobody raised an eyebrow.

The fact is, of course, that if Hitler had won the Second World War, he would have tried to kill every Jew in the world. The only power that could stop him was the United States. Americans did not want to enter the war, neither the isolationist lawmakers who barred Jewish orphans in 1939, nor the voters who had elected them. Roosevelt's successful manipulation of

Congress and public opinion—first to support embattled England, then to take America to war and win it—is still remembered as one of the greatest displays of presidential leadership in American history.

Morse himself quotes Roosevelt's wife Eleanor, who often urged him to do more for the Jews, as having admitted that the master politician was afraid of voter backlash. "When I would protest," the First Lady said, "he would simply say, 'First things come first, and I can't alienate certain votes I need for measures that are more important at the moment by pushing any measure that would entail a fight.' "

At the time of the 1939 Wagner Child Refugee Bill, for example, "Roosevelt feared the antagonism of Congress," Morse notes, "for at that very moment he was seeking half a billion dollars from an isolationist Congress to expand the Air Corps and to construct naval bases. The President's priority clearly went to defense."

The new historians see these facts, but then reject them. They cannot accept the truth, because it is too horrible. In effect, they say: it could be that helping the Jews was impossible, but it should have been done anyway.

Wyman, in his introductory chapter, catalogues some of the vast evidence showing that American public opinion was hostile to Jewish rescue, and admits, "These attitudes raised formidable barriers to the development of an American initiative to save European Jews. Yet the need was critical."

Besides, he adds, "Other important factors in American society created the potential for a positive response. America was a generous nation, a land of immigrants, led by a national administration known for its humanitarian sympathies."

After all, Wyman points out, "Most Americans embraced Christianity, a faith committed to helping the helpless."

Indeed.

If revisionists mean to say that not all Americans were anti-Semites, this is true. Many Americans, perhaps most, were not anti-Semites who hoped for Jews to die in Germany. Even though majorities in Congress and public opinion were actively opposed to rescue efforts, it could be that, by extraordinary acts of political and moral leadership, a majority could have been persuaded to open the gates and help save Jews.

But to say that most Americans were against saving Jews in 1939 or 1944 is to understate the problem. Opposition to helping Jews was not merely widespread, it was *intense*. A sizable faction on the American political scene was so set against helping Jews that it was willing to pay a price, even inhibit the war effort, in order to *avoid* helping Jews.

In November 1942, for example, Roosevelt asked Congress for emergency powers to suspend immigration rules in *individual* cases. His goal was to ease the movement of spies, war prisoners, and the like. Congress refused, in large part because it suspected that these powers would be used to save Jewish refugees. "The ugly truth is that anti-Semitism was a definite factor in the bitter opposition to the President's request," *Newsweek* reported at the time.

Similarly, the obstructionist activities of administration officials—from U.S. consuls abroad who blocked Jewish visas, right up to the assistant secretary of state in charge of refugee affairs, Breckenridge Long—are frequently cited by revisionists as evidence that Roosevelt was apathetic or hostile toward saving Jewish lives. The argument is that the president should have fired such administrators.

But in America in 1942, hostility toward Jews was not grounds for firing a public official. If anything, some officials reveled in anti-Semitic behavior. John Rankin, a representative from Mississippi, referred regularly in public to "little kikes." His voters loved him.

In one important sense, the situation of Jews in America at that time was so dismal that it is now difficult to recapture. Anti-Jewish hostility was so widespread, and so *respectable*, that even a president who was sympathetic toward Jews had to weigh the formidable risks of helping them.

In a sense, the Jews' plight was much like that of American blacks. In 1941, Roosevelt created the federal government's first twentieth-century civil rights agency, the President's Committee on Fair Employment Practices. It was charged with finding and ending racial discrimination in war industries under government contract.

Revisionist critics point out that Roosevelt created the committee only under protest, after black labor leader A. Philip Randolph threatened to mount a march on Washington. This is true. It required an organized act by the black community to make the price of *not* creating the committee higher than the price of creating it. This also is true: no black leaders took such action until there was a president in the White House who was likely to agree with them, even under duress. Once a sympathetic president was in office, the pressure could be brought.

By the same token, Roosevelt created the War Refugee Board in 1944, with the task of saving Jews from the Nazi ovens, only after Henry Mor-genthau confronted him with documented evidence that action could be taken and was not being taken. Once the report was in writing, the price of not taking action became higher than the price of taking action, and Roosevelt acted.

But in each case, there was a price to be paid for taking action. Impor-tant and respectable segments of the American body politic wanted Jews kept out, just as important and respectable segments—often the same segments—wanted blacks kept down.

This was the great difference between the American Jews' situations in 1940 and in 1990. After the Second World War, hating Jews was no longer a respectable political stance. One might oppose something that the Jews wanted, but one had to give other reasons. Before 1945, one could oppose something simply because it *might* help the Jews.

What created the change?

In mid-1944, long after the Nazis' persecution of Jews was common knowl-edge, a poll found that 24 percent of Americans believed Jews were "a menace to America." Another poll in early 1945 found that 67 percent believed Jews had "too much power in America."

Beginning in late 1945, American attitudes toward Jews underwent a sudden, still-unexplained reversal. The percentage of Americans agreeing that Jews represented a "menace" to America dropped from 24 percent in 1944 to 5 percent in 1950 and 1 percent in 1962. The percentage affirming that Jews had "too much power" dropped from 67 percent in 1945 to 17 percent in 1962. The percentage who said that they would think twice about hiring a Jewish employee dropped from 43 percent in 1940 to 6 percent in 1962.

Most significant was the change in responses to the question that experts say is the most honest yardstick of prejudice: how one thinks one's neigh-bors feel. The percentage of Americans answering "yes" to that one—"Do you think anti-Jewish feeling is rising?"—dropped from 58 percent in 1945 to just 16 percent in 1950.

America's new acceptance of Jews was visible in many arenas, though one cannot always tell cause from effect: the election of Bess Myerson in 1945 as the first (and still the only) Jewish Miss America; the awarding of the 1947 Oscar for Best Picture to *Gentlemen's Agreement,* the film version

of Laura Z. Hobson's novel about anti-Semitism; the rise to the top of the
New York Times best-seller list of John Hersey's 1950 novel about the
Warsaw Ghetto, *The Wall*; the rise to the top of the hit parade that same
year of "Tzena Tzena," the Israeli folk song recorded by the Weavers (as
Side B to "Goodnight Irene").

Just as revealing was something that did *not* happen: the wave of popular
anti-Semitism that might well have followed the arrest of Julius and Ethel
Rosenberg for giving America's atomic bomb secrets to the Soviet Union.
The 1950 arrests of the Rosenbergs, along with Harry Gold, David Green-
glass, and British physicist Klaus Fuchs—all of them Jews with Communist
sympathies—sent shivers through American Jewry. As the trials dragged on
for three years, the organized Jewish leadership went on high alert nationwide. But nothing happened.

Fifteen years earlier, demagogues had been able to draw crowds by
denouncing an imaginary "Jewish Communist" threat. Now they had nothing to say in the face of a real one. One poll during the Rosenberg trial
found that only 5 percent of the public identified Jews with Communism.

Jews had been a major target when the House Committee on Un-
American Activities began its probe of Communist influence in Hollywood
in 1944. Led by the "kike"-bashing John Rankin and others, the three-year
witch-hunt embarrassed or ruined dozens of entertainment figures, most of
them Jews. A few defense groups, led by the Anti-Defamation League and
the Los Angeles Jewish Community Relations Committee, responded by
cooperating with the investigators to help prove that most Jews were not
Communists. Many more Jews were left with the vague sense, still visible in
Jewish liberalism, that an anti-Communist crusader is a thinly disguised
anti-Semite.

And yet, when Wisconsin Senator Joseph McCarthy began his own hunt
for Communists in Washington just two years later, the Jewish issue suddenly was off the table. McCarthy was a demagogue and witch-hunter who
ruined innocent lives and poisoned American political debate for a generation, but he bent over backwards to avoid anti-Semitism. He placed a Jew at
his right hand, New York lawyer Roy Cohn, both for effect and to help keep
anti-Semitism out of his hearings. He even met with the Anti-Defamation
League to try and clear the air of misunderstandings.

The ADL's then-deputy director Arnold Forster, who attended the
meeting, insists that McCarthy simply "used us" to dodge charges of bigotry. (If so, McCarthy would not be the last.) But if this is true, it points to a

remarkable change in the status of American Jews. Quite suddenly, they had gained the power to *confer* respectability.

A decade earlier, no reputable politician wanted to be seen as the Jews' friend. Now, the danger was to be seen as the Jews' enemy.

Why such a change? We can only guess. Sympathy for Jewish suffering must have played a role, once news coverage of the Nazis' crimes reached a wide audience. Partly, too, Jews must have benefited from widespread postwar revulsion against the evils of prejudice. This was coupled with a general mood of good-natured optimism that emerged from the victory over fascism and the booming economy of the 1950s. Surveys just after the war support each of these factors as partial reasons for the decline of anti-Semitism. However, the results fluctuate so wildly from survey to survey that not much can be concluded for certain. Many observers also suggest that the birth of Israel helped erase the old stereotype of the Jew as weakling.

Finally, there was this: in the first weeks and months after the end of the Second World War, the organized Jewish community launched a broad-ranging campaign to end prejudice and discrimination in America. It did so by challenging discriminatory laws, by winning passage of new legislation that outlawed discrimination, and by mobilizing the media and the academic community to discredit prejudice.

It was a huge, coordinated campaign, waged in the courts and the legislatures, in the media and in the streets.

No one directed the campaign from above. It rose up from below as a popular demand. "In winning the war against Nazism, people began to appreciate democracy," says ADL's Arnold Forster.

"Before the war," Forster said, "the attitude had been, 'Who're you going to sue—City Hall? That's the way it is. I can't get into medical school? I'll go to medical school in Europe. I can't buy a house in Scarsdale? I'll buy a house in Brooklyn.' That was the way it was.

"But after the war there was a sense in the air that we weren't going to take it anymore. Equality was in the air. We'd won a victory for human freedom. We wanted to continue that fight."

The effort began piecemeal. One Jewish organization sued a discriminatory employer, defending a returning GI. Another agency lobbied for immigration reform, to rescue the stranded victims of Hitler's death camps.

Slowly, taking one issue at a time, the major Jewish organizations began to work together. Committees were created to forge joint strategies, now among the Jewish organizations, now between these and the black organizations that were waging much the same fight. Eventually, the Jewish community forged coalitions with trade unions, liberal churches, and other groups, each around a distinct issue. Over two decades, they managed to reform America's race-based immigration laws and ban racial and religious discrimination in housing, schools, and the workplace. And finally, they helped to make Jews equal citizens by truly separating church and state: removing religious symbols from public spaces and making American civic culture a neutral zone where all could approach on the same footing.

In short order, the campaign for equality became a popular Jewish crusade. It started with a few Jewish organizations but soon involved hundreds of thousands of ordinary individual Jews. They poured en masse into the civil rights movement, the antiwar movement, the feminist movement, and other liberal causes from the 1950s through the 1970s.

Which was the cause and which the effect—the concerted Jewish campaign, or America's willingness to listen? It is impossible to say.

Only this is certain: the astounding drop in American anti-Jewish prejudice between 1945 and 1950 is probably the least studied aspect of Jewish political power in the modern era; yet it may be the most important. In the space of five years, America's image of the Jews changed from conspiratorial foreigners to good neighbors. As a consequence, the Jewish community at last was able to present its opinions on various issues and hope to be heard. The simple fact was that Americans for the first time were willing to listen to them.

And yet, the time and place where the Jewish equality campaign began are fairly easy to pinpoint. In 1944, the aging Rabbi Stephen Wise decided to hire a full-time executive director for the American Jewish Congress. He chose a young Canadian Jew named David Petegorsky. Petegorsky inherited a tiny infrastructure with little behind it except Rabbi Wise's outsized image. In the spring of 1945, he decided to create a legal department and start suing bigots.

The following August, Petegorsky hired his first lawyer: Will Maslow, thirty-eight-year-old general counsel of the President's Committee on Fair Employment Practices. Maslow's federal job was about to end; the President's Committee had been created to fight discrimination in war industries, and the war was over. The Southern-run Congress had cut off its funds.

The committee staff, mainly blacks and Jews, operated by locating discriminatory employers, collecting facts, then moving in with a combination of litigation and aggressive jawboning. It was a legal strategy that the American Civil Liberties Union had pioneered in the 1920s and the National Association for the Advancement of Colored People had begun to perfect in the 1930s.

Now Petegorsky wanted the Kiev-born, Chicago-reared Maslow to bring his law books to New York and launch a full-scale assault on American anti-Semitism. The battle plan was a document drafted by legal scholar Alexander Pekelis, a wartime Jewish refugee from Italy.

Pekelis's paper, "Full Equality in a Free Society," argued that decades of Jewish efforts to win equal rights had failed because Jews, a tiny minority, were trying to change the thinking of bigots whose minds were already made up. The proper approach, he argued, was to ignore bigots' opinions and attack their actions.

"The American Jewish Committee and the ADL used to argue that you can't attack discrimination without attacking its underlying cause, which is prejudice," Maslow recalled. "We said nonsense. We're going to attack discrimination wherever we find it."

Using the law as a weapon, Pekelis argued, the Jewish community should fight discrimination whenever it occurred—and whoever were its victims. Only a society that guaranteed the rights of all could ensure the rights of anyone.

If the goal was grand, the initial results were modest, sometimes laughably so. Maslow's first case was against the *New York Daily News,* a tabloid with a huge readership among working-class Catholics. The *Daily News* had been openly pro-fascist during the 1930s and aggressively neutral during the war, which some of its columnists frankly blamed on "the Jews." Now its radio station, WPIX, was applying to the Federal Communications Commission for a license to broadcast on the newly opened FM band. Maslow decided to challenge the application. His argument was that the bigotry of the *News* violated the FCC doctrine of using the airwaves to serve the public interest.

"It was a difficult thing to attack the largest-circulation newspaper in America," Maslow recalls. "Pekelis prepared a content analysis of the *Daily*

News to demonstrate its pattern of bias, and we submitted it to the FCC. During the hearings Pekelis testified very effectively. In addition to being very bright, he was very witty. And the license was denied, though not on the grounds we cited, because our argument raised constitutional issues. They simply preferred another applicant."

Years would pass before Maslow realized his blunder: "They were also applying for a television license at the same time. But we didn't file an objection to that, because we didn't know what the hell television was."

In the meantime, other cases were taken up. Maslow's department, dubbed the Commission on Law and Social Action, was growing and expanding its mission. He hired seven lawyers, "at a time when the Department of Justice didn't have a single lawyer in civil rights and the NAACP had one or two." He and his staff lobbied President Truman to create a national commission on civil rights. They sued the Metropolitan Life Insurance Company over racial segregation at its Stuyvesant Town housing project in New York City. They drafted fair-housing and fair-employment statutes for dozens of cities and states. One by one, states and cities began to outlaw the practices that kept minorities from entering certain colleges, living in certain neighborhoods, or working in certain businesses. Through it all, Maslow and his lawyers were in daily contact with the NAACP, planning strategies, trading ideas, and helping each other on briefs.

In short order, Maslow's chief deputy, the brilliant and irascible Leo Pfeffer, opened up a second front: developing the legal strategy for a direct Jewish assault on state-supported religion. At the time, most public as well as private schools nationwide had compulsory daily prayers. Many public schools also provided "released" class time for children to learn Bible and religion, on or off campus. These practices were regularly challenged in court, usually by minority Christians or atheists. Jews held back in fear of sparking an anti-Semitic backlash.

Pfeffer's revolutionary proposal was simply to join the ongoing fight by filing friend-of-the-court briefs in the name of the Jewish community. In 1947, he filed briefs in two historic cases before the U.S. Supreme Court: *Everson v. Board of Education*, which limited a New Jersey school district's right to aid parochial schools, and *McCollum v. Board of Education*, which overruled an Illinois released-time program.

During the 1950s, Pfeffer was a veritable steamroller, filing suits or joining them throughout the country. His watchword was absolute equality for Jews, which meant absolute separation of church and state. "Even assuming that no aid for parochial education means no aid for public education," he told NCRAC in 1963, his preference "would be rather no federal funds for public schools than inclusion of parochial schools."

Frequently, Pfeffer was invited to join in a local dispute by Jewish parents or community leaders distressed at the overtly Christian tone in their public schools. At other times, he was less than welcome. In 1959, he sided with the ACLU in a Florida case that challenged Bible readings and recitation of the Lord's Prayer in Miami classrooms. The case sparked intense Christian-Jewish tension throughout Florida, including a petition-and-bumper-sticker campaign by Presbyterians insisting that "the very fabric of American life is founded upon Christianity."

Local Jews were terrified. "The American Jewish Congress is going it alone in Dade County with the Jewish community at large having to pay the price," wrote a columnist in the weekly *Jewish Floridian*. The Anti-Defamation League and American Jewish Committee agreed. They launched a protest campaign against the American Jewish Congress in local Jewish communities around the country. In 1960, the Council of Jewish Federations formally rebuked Pfeffer, forcing the American Jewish Congress to promise in writing that it would "receive prior consent from the local Jewish community" before taking on a local case—or lose all its grants from local Jewish federations.

As for the Florida case, the court issued a mixed decision in 1961, barring some practices, upholding others, and urging all concerned to use some common sense. "[T]he Golden Rule should be observed," the judge wrote.

Before either side could appeal the ruling, the U.S. Supreme Court issued a decision in a New York case on school prayer that touched off a national uproar, through no doing of Pfeffer's. The case, *Engel v. Vitale*, involved the reading in a Long Island school district of the Regents' Prayer, a nonsectarian trifle composed by the state Board of Regents. The ACLU had brought the case, seeing it as an opportunity to strike down any and all school prayer. Pfeffer had been against it, arguing that the Regents' Prayer was too "innocuous" a vehicle to challenge the system. The *Engel* case also violated the Jewish defense agencies' practice of avoiding high-profile test cases with Jewish plaintiffs, so as to minimize anti-Jewish hostility.

When the high court accepted *Engel* anyway, all three defense agencies filed briefs opposing the prayer as an "establishment of religion" that violated the First Amendment. The Supreme Court agreed. In a six-to-one decision in June 1962, the court ruled that "a union of government and religion tends to destroy government and to degrade religion."

The *Engel* decision sparked a nationwide furor. Former presidents Eisenhower and Hoover objected; so did Protestant churchmen from liberal Reinhold Niebuhr to conservative Billy Graham, along with most of the nation's Catholic cardinals. The nation's governors voted to back a constitutional amendment to permit school prayer. "They put Negroes in the school, and now they've driven God out," said a congressman from Alabama.

A year later, the Supreme Court issued yet another decision, this one outlawing Bible readings in public schools. It came in a Pennsylvania case called *Abington Township School District v. Schempp*. The plaintiffs, the Schempps, were Unitarians, but their case had been directed from the beginning by the Philadelphia Jewish Community Relations Council. The American Jewish Congress joined in an amicus brief, as did the other Jewish agencies.

The *Schempp* decision marked a triumph for Pfeffer and his long campaign. The court had formally accepted his argument that Jews were equal partners in the American enterprise and that America could no longer conduct itself—formally or informally, nationally or locally—as a Christian nation. "Today the Nation is far more heterogeneous religiously," wrote Justice William Brennan in a concurring opinion, "including as it does substantial minorities not only of Catholics and Jews but as well of those who worship according to no version of the Bible and those who worship no God at all."

It was, as the American Jewish Congress reported to its members, a "social revolution" for religious equality.

Not everyone in organized Jewry welcomed this revolution. The much larger and wealthier American Jewish Committee and Anti-Defamation League, voices of the old German-Jewish middle and upper classes, continued to urge caution. During the 1930s, these two big agencies had fiercely resisted a boycott of German imports led by the American Jewish Congress. Now they opposed its sue-the-bastards legal strategy. Meetings of the National Community Relations Advisory Council sometimes turned into shouting matches. At NCRAC conferences in 1944 and 1946 to discuss the school-prayer controversy in the courts, the American Jewish Committee and the Anti-Defamation League stubbornly refused to endorse any campaign that risked offending America's Christian majority. The 1947 NCRAC conference saw a testy debate between the heads of the ADL and the American Jewish Congress over the question of prejudice versus discrimination: when Petegorsky outlined his plans for legal challenges, ADL chief Benjamin Epstein replied that anti-Semitic attitudes had to be changed first.

In 1949, the defense agencies were joined by a new player, the Reform movement, which finally decided to back up its liberal words by forming its Commission on Social Action.

The Reform commission soon became the most militant of all the defense agencies. Run on a shoestring from the New York offices of the Reform synagogue union, it could mobilize an army of congregants through the social-action committees of hundreds of Reform temples nationwide. Welding them into a national force was its Washington lobbying office, the Religious Action Center of Reform Judaism, opened in 1962; led since 1975 by the savvy, charismatic Rabbi David Saperstein, the RAC has become one of the most powerful Jewish bodies in Washington, second only to AIPAC.

At the municipal level, local Jewish community-relations councils were springing up in growing numbers. Each one served as a miniboard of deputies, uniting all the active Jewish defense groups in town, from B'nai B'rith lodges to American Jewish Committee chapters and synagogue social-action committees. Usually sponsored by the local Jewish federation, these councils forced all the players to speak with one voice, or at least share notes, while bolstering them with the not-inconsiderable clout of the federated philanthropies. There were fourteen community-relations councils in 1944 and thirty-one in 1954. By 1964, there were seventy-five.

The institution that brought together all these disparate forces and welded them into a single Jewish political machine was the National Community Relations Advisory Council, formed in 1944 as an umbrella group for the national agencies and local councils.

NCRAC nearly died just after its birth. In 1949, several member-federations hired a non-Jewish academic, Robert MacIver of Columbia University, to examine the council and suggest ways of reducing waste. The

MacIver Report, submitted to NCRAC in 1951, suggested that the member-agencies reduce duplication of their efforts and let NCRAC play a strong coordinating role. The two most powerful members, ADL and the American Jewish Committee, promptly walked out.

Instead of dying, however, NCRAC expanded, bringing in the three major synagogue unions and several smaller bodies to make up for the missing agencies.

NCRAC's survival was largely the work of one man, executive director Isaiah Minkoff, who headed the council from its formation until his death in 1975. A Polish-born former yeshiva student and labor organizer, he was a skilled orator who moved comfortably from talmudic law to socialist economics. He was organized Jewry's ultimate inside man, the one who could coax dozens of preening organizational chieftains under a single tent. He did it with bulldog determination and the negotiating skills of a carpet salesman. "He could con you by being the foxy grandfather and making you do things he wanted," says Irving Levine, a former national-affairs director at the American Jewish Committee.

"If you wanted to know who the organization man was in the American Jewish community, it was Isaiah Minkoff," says Rabbi Israel Miller, a senior Orthodox leader. "I called him my rebbe."

Minkoff's most crucial decision was to ignore the ADL–American Jewish Committee walkout. NCRAC's sole power was its ability to speak for the entire spectrum of Jewish opinion. That was impossible without the two most respected agencies. Minkoff stayed in constant contact with the renegade directors, ADL's Benjamin Epstein and the American Jewish Committee's John Slawson. He solicited their views on policy. He wheedled, cajoled, and bullied them into sending representatives to NCRAC strategy meetings. At the local level, he made sure that their members continued to participate in community-relations committees, the heart of NCRAC. When ADL and the American Jewish Committee formally rejoined NCRAC in 1965, it was a mere technicality.

"During the 1950s an amazing network grew up in the Jewish community," elaborates Levine. "You had the organizational base of the federations and CRCs [community-relations committees]. You had the national agencies, which were doing extraordinary work in terms of getting out published material and training the local people. The CRCs were much larger in terms of active leadership, but depended on the national agencies for guidance and material. And you had NCRAC coordinating it all with a staff of six people. NCRAC created a miracle."

Typical of Minkoff's methods was his response to the passage of the Immigration and Nationality Act of 1952. Popularly known as the McCarran act, it grew out of a three-year Senate study of the immigration quota system, launched in 1947. The American Jewish Committee had been pressing the lawmakers to scrap the system as racist. Instead, Congress did the reverse: as drafted by isolationist Nevada Democrat Pat McCarran, the act tightened ethnic restrictions, lowered total immigration, and added new restrictions—including ones that allowed Communists and subversives to be expelled from the United States even *after* they had been naturalized as citizens.

NCRAC convened a meeting of Jewish defense agencies to review the McCarran act and consider what to do next. Everyone agreed that the Jewish community must undertake a massive effort to repeal the quota system, but the ADL and the American Jewish Committee refused to join an operation under NCRAC auspices. Instead, Minkoff put NCRAC immigration specialist Jules Cohen in charge of a "non-auspices committee," operated by NCRAC under its "non-auspices." In 1955, this committee spearheaded the formation of a broad coalition for immigration reform, made up of civic associations, labor groups, and Protestant and Catholic groups. For a decade the coalition lobbied, leafleted, planted articles in magazines, and held public meetings on the racist nature of the immigration quota system. The entire operation was run by a steering committee of the "non-auspices committee," made up of four staffers from the three defense agencies and NCRAC.

The quotas were finally repealed by the Immigration Reform Act of 1965, passed by Congress during the civil rights surge of President Lyndon Johnson's early years.

Even more dramatic was the National Emergency Civil Rights Mobilization. Convened in 1950, it united thousands of civil rights activists—blacks and whites, church and synagogue leaders, union members, and civic activists—from across the country. Its primary goal was to demand a renewal of the fair employment practices committee, or FEPC, which Congress had disbanded as soon as the Second World War ended.

The mobilization was initiated by an ad hoc group called the National Council for a Permanent FEPC, created shortly after the war by the NAACP and NCRAC. Its president was Roy Wilkins, head of the NAACP; its secretary and sole staffer was Arnold Aronson, deputy director of NCRAC.

Their undertaking was a powerful show of force, and it created new momentum for civil rights in Washington and nationwide. In its aftermath, the FEPC council decided to broaden its mandate, bring in labor and church groups that had backed the mobilization, and dedicate itself to a long-term struggle for civil rights legislation. Renamed the Leadership Conference on Civil Rights, it continued to be run by Aronson out of the NCRAC offices until it rented its own space in Washington in the early 1960s. Shortly after moving to Washington, the leadership conference achieved its greatest victories: passage of the 1964 Civil Rights Act and the 1965 Voting Rights Act, which outlawed racial and religious discrimination nationwide for the first time since Reconstruction.

Within two decades after Will Maslow's 1945 move to New York, opposition to the American Jewish Congress's militant liberalism had nearly dissolved within the organized Jewish community. Quiet diplomacy was out; legal action was in. Discriminatory practices were challenged in state after state.

Donations poured into the Big Three defense agencies, and their budgets and staffs soared. The American Jewish Committee's annual budget quadrupled in the five years after the war, from $500,000 to more than $2 million. The ADL's budget was only slightly less. The American Jewish Congress, though running a poor third, was growing even faster: from about $50,000 during the war years to nearly $1.5 million in 1949. Even the Jewish Labor Committee reported an income of over $1 million in 1949.

The money was not always well spent. Jews had formidable enemies on the American right, and sometimes they underestimated the opposition's determination.

One of the Jewish community's most stunning miscalculations was the Displaced Persons Act, passed by Congress in 1948 and renewed in 1950. It was supposed to open America's doors to one hundred thousand homeless European war refugees.

The legislation had been dreamed up by the American Jewish Committee as a way to rescue some of the shattered Jewish Holocaust victims who were still languishing in the liberated concentration camps two years after the war's end. An impressive roster of allies was enlisted to help lobby the bill through Congress, including Catholic bishops, major Protestant churches, organized labor, and Eleanor Roosevelt.

But by the time the bill worked its way through the Republican-controlled Congress, it had been amended to exclude most Jews. For example, half of the visas were reserved for farmers, though the over-whelming majority of Jews were city dwellers. A follow-up bill passed in 1950 added similar restrictions after it was gutted by an isolationist Senate coalition of Republicans and Southern and Western Democrats, with Nevada's Pat McCarran in the lead.

In the end, only 16 percent of the 365,000 refugees brought to America under the Displaced Persons Act were Jews—some 65,000 in all. Most of the rest were Christians from Baltic nations, fleeing the advancing Soviet army. Of these, many were on the run because they were wanted as Nazi collaborators. Indeed, such a flood of Nazi collaborators entered the United States under the Displaced Persons Act that three decades later, Congress created a special investigative unit just to seek them out and send them back for prosecution.

In effect, a plan hatched by the American Jewish Committee to rescue Jewish Holocaust survivors ended up doing more for the Nazis' henchmen than for their victims.

Meanwhile, however, the ADL and the American Jewish Committee were undergoing revolutions of their own.

The ADL had from its founding in 1913 abhorred the very idea of offending Christian America. As noted in chapter 4, its action program originally was based on pamphleteering and letter-writing to persuade anti-Semites of their error. The ADL's longtime national director, Richard Gutstadt, believed in working behind the scenes and keeping disputes out of the news media. Shortly after taking over in 1931, he created a "fact-finding" department that quietly gathered intelligence on extremist organizations and fed the information to law enforcement agencies, avoiding the press so as not to fuel hostility. He even created a Bureau of Jewish Deportment, which taught Jews to avoid offensive behavior that might arouse anti-Semitism. One "deportment" bulletin advised Jews that it was in bad taste to wear furs in Florida during the summer.

But Gutstadt was dying of cancer at the end of the Second World War; the 1946 NCRAC conference would be his last. His successor, Benjamin Epstein, a young attorney, and Epstein's deputy, Arnold Forster, had been sniping at Gutstadt's cautious approach since before the war. Where Gutstadt called for "fact-finding," Forster and Epstein favored infiltrating pro-Nazi groups and stealing their files. Where Gutstadt avoided the media, Forster befriended the Jewish gossip columnist Walter Winchell and secretly fed him information to embarrass anti-Semites. In 1945, Epstein and Forster actually called their first press conference, to announce that they planned to seek indictments against an anti-Semitic street gang in New York City. The press conference infuriated Gutstadt and "nearly got us fired," Forster would recall. A year later Gutstadt was dead, and Epstein and Forster were in charge.

The deportment department was one of the first things to go.

The revolution at the American Jewish Committee was slower and more subtle, but ultimately more profound. Proudly elitist, still run by the descendants of "Our Crowd," the Committee was the wealthiest and most influential of the agencies. Its staff of one hundred engaged in a broad program of research, quiet lobbying, and diplomacy under the firm charge of the lay officers and members.

The American Jewish Committee could not resist the times, however. During the 1930s, it began helping local Jewish welfare federations to create their own community-relations committees (CRCs), each intended as a local American Jewish Committee in miniature. The Committee did not control the CRCs; each answered only to its members or to its parent federation. Like the federations, the CRCs were staffed largely by social workers, America's growing army of trained agents for social change.

In 1944, the American Jewish Committee's longtime executive vice president, the impeccably proper Morris Waldman, retired. His successor was John Slawson, a diminutive, strong-willed social worker of Russian-Jewish origin. Slawson outlined his credo in his first address to the Committee: "One cannot do things *for* the Jewish people; one must do it *with* the Jewish people."

Under Slawson, the Committee's board decided for the first time to create local chapters, opening its exclusive membership to a broader cross-section of American Jews. Slawson helped push the Committee toward open support for Jewish statehood, a once-radical notion. He also founded *Commentary* magazine, for years the most prestigious voice of American Jewish liberalism (until its late-1960s transformation into a voice of neoconservatism).

Perhaps most significant, Slawson expanded the Committee's research department. He began a passionate romance with the social sciences, which were then entering an avant-garde phase. During the late 1940s and into the 1950s, the American Jewish Committee became one of the nation's most important nonacademic sponsors of social-science research on the roots and meaning of prejudice. The Committee helped raise the funds to support the so-called Frankfurt school, a mostly Jewish group of sociologists who had fled Germany in 1934 and settled in New York—among them Bruno Bettelheim, Theodor Adorno, Herbert Marcuse, and Max Horkheimer.

The group's most important achievement was the publication during the 1950s of the five-volume *Studies in Prejudice*, commissioned by the American Jewish Committee. The series includes such standard works as *The Authoritarian Personality* by Theodor Adorno, *The Dynamics of Personality* by Bruno Bettelheim and Morris Janowitz, and *Anti-Semitism and Emotional Disorder* by Marie Jahoda and Nathan Ackerman.

The Committee's sponsorship of this research fostered a revolution in the way Americans looked at prejudice. One Committee-sponsored study by black psychologist Kenneth Clark, on the psychological impact of school segregation, became the basis of the 1954 Supreme Court decision outlawing segregated schools, *Brown v. Board of Education*.

Ultimately, the American Jewish Committee's work helped promote enormous changes in the way Jews looked at themselves and at prejudice. During the 1950s and 1960s, the Committee and the ADL schooled an entire generation of American Jews in the idea that prejudice was an emotional disorder. The Nazi Holocaust became a paradigm for all intergroup conflict, the logical conclusion of the slippery slope of prejudice. Intergroup conflict became a simple matter of ignorance or malice, as the ADL had argued since its founding. To seek explanations in the relationship between the conflicting groups—to find and resolve the *causes* of conflict, as the American Jewish Committee routinely had done in its early days—was now to blame the victim.

The new militance of the American Jew was well suited to fighting for the disenfranchised and winning a place at the table. Painting the world in black and white energized American Jews, made them uncompromising in defense of their rights—and the rights of others.

Once seated at the table, however, this newly energized Jew was ill-suited to coping with genuine conflict.

Conservative social theorist Thomas Sowell maintains that the essential difference between liberals and conservatives is optimism about the human condition. Liberals, Sowell claims, share a belief that people can improve their lives through collective effort. Conservatives think not; they tend to insist that human nature is too flawed, and too ingrained, to permit much improvement.

American Jews had every reason for pessimism as they entered the 1950s. They had just received a grand lesson in the evils of human nature, and 6 million of their kin had been slaughtered in the process. Three million more were trapped behind the Iron Curtain in a Stalinist nightmare. America itself seemed to many to be clinging to democracy only precariously.

And yet, the community entered the 1950s in a mood of almost giddy optimism. Here is how distinguished historians Oscar and Mary Handlin described the collective emotion, in a 1954 essay marking the three hundredth anniversary of Jewish community life in America: "At mid-twentieth century, American Jews could look back with satisfaction at their recent past. . . . The triumph of the healthier forces in American life offered a release from the tensions of the period that had passed. Jews now acquired a sense of integration in American life and displayed a fresh confidence in dealing with its problems."

CHAPTER 6

Six Days in June:
The Triumph of Jewish Insecurity

O N JUNE 5, 1967, Israeli fighter jets took off on a predawn raid that changed the face of the Middle East and altered the course of Jewish history.

The Israeli planes flew southwest toward Egypt, locked in on that Arab nation's main military airfields, and unleashed a torrent of bombs. Within an hour, nearly the entire Egyptian air force had been knocked out on the ground. Over the next six days, Israeli ground troops and tanks advanced against Egypt and its main allies, Syria to the north and Jordan to the east. By the time the fighting ended on June 10, Israeli troops had occupied neighboring territory two and a half times the size of Israel itself.

The crisis had been deliberately provoked three weeks earlier, by Egypt. Egyptian President Gamal Abdel Nasser, claiming that Israel was threatening his Syrian allies, ordered Egyptian troops on May 14 to enter the demilitarized Sinai desert that separated Egypt from Israel. In the following days, he dismissed the U.N. peacekeeping troops that had patrolled Sinai since 1957, closed off the narrow Straits of Tiran to blockade Israel's Red Sea port at Eilat, announced a joint military command with Syria and issued a stream of bloodcurdling threats about a "general battle" whose "goal will be to destroy Israel."

Israel responded by putting its army on full alert, and then waiting. While the citizenry fretfully anticipated apocalypse, Israeli diplomats tried fruitlessly to lift the siege. The waiting was economically and psychologically devastating: economically, because so much of Israel's labor force was mobilized in the citizen-reserves; psychologically, because so many Israelis were traumatized survivors of the Nazi Holocaust, terrified that history was about to repeat itself. "Nasser's strategy is the same as Hitler's," warned a leading columnist in the country's main newspaper.

In the end, Israel struck first. To the world's shock, its troops met only the flimsiest Arab resistance. Only a U.N.-imposed cease-fire six days later, on June 10, stopped the Israelis' advance. By that time they had captured the entire Sinai desert from Egypt, virtually unopposed. From Syria they took the strategic Golan Heights, which Syrian gunners had used for a decade to shell northern Israel. From Jordan they took the populous West Bank district, the hilly biblical heartland where the Hebrew patriarchs once walked. And they took the Old City of Jerusalem with its Wailing Wall, last vestige of the Holy Temple, Judaism's most sacred shrine, closed to Jews since the founding of Israel in 1948.

Those six days thoroughly changed the world's image of the young Jewish state. For nineteen years, Israel had seemed a tiny, helpless outpost, surrounded by powerful enemies that might destroy it at any moment. Now, in less than a week, it had been transformed into a conquering superpower.

For Jews, the change was utterly disorienting. A mere six days had catapulted them from looming disaster to a great victory, one of the most remarkable in military history. "Alone, unaided, neither seeking nor receiving help, our nation rose in self-defense," Israel's Oxford-educated foreign minister, Abba Eban, told the U.N. General Assembly in a dramatic speech on June 19, 1967. "So long as men cherish freedom, so long as small states strive for the dignity of existence, the exploits of Israel's armies will be told from one generation to another with the deepest pride."

Nowhere did Eban's words ring more true than among American Jews. The Israeli victory was told and retold in the coming years in synagogues, at Jewish gatherings, and in the Jewish ethnic press. Over a quarter-century, it acquired mythic stature, becoming a moment that a generation of American Jews would look back to as a personal watershed.

The victory marked the end of one era and the beginning of another in the life of the American Jewish community, the moment, it is often said, when American Jews gained pride in being Jewish. "Israel made us all stand a little taller in 1967," says longtime American Jewish Congress leader Jacqueline Levine, then a young community activist in Newark, New Jersey.

Even though it was fought between foreign states half a world away, the Six-Day War assumed immediate, personal significance for many American

Jews, even more so than the birth of the Jewish state. For the first time, many felt a powerful sense of identification with Israel, as though its fate were literally their own.

Reactions took many forms. In New York, a May 28 rally for Israel drew upwards of 150,000 people, more than any American Jewish gathering ever had. In Washington, Paul Berger, a young attorney known for his involvement in Jewish community affairs, began receiving late-night phone calls from government officials who had never acknowledged being Jewish; now they wanted to know how they could help.

Nationwide, the United Jewish Appeal conducted an "emergency campaign" to help Israel pay for the war and the punishing mobilization that had preceded it. In six months, an unprecedented $307 million was collected, more than double the UJA's total for the entire year before.

In Baltimore, Shoshana Cardin, then a young volunteer in several local Jewish women's organizations, was assigned to staff a table that the UJA had set up in a local bank lobby, for the convenience of Jews who were liquidating their accounts for Israeli relief. Those short of cash were donating jewelry. A few even mortgaged their homes, she recalls.

From around the country, several hundred Jewish college students volunteered to leave school early and go to Israel in order to help bring in the spring harvest, replacing mobilized Israeli reservists. When classes ended in June, thousands more volunteered. By the end of 1967, ten thousand young Americans had gone to Israel as volunteers. Nothing like it had ever happened before.

Countless more Jews who stayed home were transformed by the vicarious experience of the war. Michael J. ("M. J.") Rosenberg, a sophomore at the State University of New York at Albany in the spring of 1967, was a leader of the campus anti–Vietnam War movement and a left-wing columnist for the campus newspaper. But that May, he recalls, "I was consumed by the threat to Israel. I went from interested to worried to obsessed with what was happening." He quickly became involved in pro-Israel activism on campus. By the following winter, he was a nationally known figure in campus Jewish activism. After graduation, he moved to Washington and got a job with the American Israel Public Affairs Committee. From AIPAC, he went on to work on the staff of a militantly pro-Israel member of Congress, Jonathan Bingham of New York. Defending Israel became his career.

"Before the Six-Day War, being Jewish was never a major part of my life," Rosenberg says. "But the thought that Israel might be destroyed consumed me. It changed my life."

Across America there were thousands of M. J. Rosenbergs. "There was a real awakening of Jews across America and worldwide in the wake of the Six-Day War," says Richard Schifter, then a young Washington lawyer, later a ranking State Department official under Reagan and Bush. On the fourth day of the Six-Day War, Schifter went to Lafayette Park, opposite the White House, for a somber "save Israel" rally that turned into a victory celebration. "There was a huge crowd there. When the rally had first been called it looked like, God knows, Israel might be destroyed. And it turned out the war was going to be over in a very short time. And then there was this outpouring. From then on, there was just a new life in the community."

Shoshana Cardin confirms the watershed status of the war in American Jewish history: "Nineteen sixty-seven was a critical point in the psyche of the American Jewish community. It was at that point that the American Jewish community came together at its own initiative, with the recognition that there was a terrible challenge to the Jewish people. That their only state, the Jewish homeland, was under the threat of destruction, of annihilation, and that as a part of the Jewish people, we had to respond. It required little assistance on the part of the organized Jewish community for individual Jews to become involved."

Like most mythic events, the Six-Day War actually happened, but not quite the way people remember it. The tale has grown with the telling. Along the way it has obscured some realities that don't fit the myth.

To begin at the beginning, it was *not* the Six-Day War that transformed American Jewish life. If anything, it was the waiting period *before* the war. During those three tense weeks in May, countless American Jews experienced a shattering anxiety that Israel might be destroyed. It was an anxiety so consuming that it overshadowed what actually happened once the war came.

What happened, of course, was that Israel won the war handily. Though the public was astounded by the speed and decisiveness of the Israeli victory, intelligence analysts in Israel and America were not. They knew Israel's strength, and its enemies' weakness.

Still, once the extent of Arab incompetence became apparent—once it became clear that Israel was in no danger, and probably never had been—the reality might have given Jews a new dose of confidence.

The reaction was just the opposite. The events of May and June 1967 shattered the nerves of the American Jewish community. Amid their exhilaration, Jewish leaders and activists were left with an overwhelming feeling of vulnerability and isolation.

Objectively, the Six-Day War demonstrated that Israel was more secure than anyone had dreamed. Many things might happen to Israel, but destruction by Arab armies was not likely to be one of them. Over the next two decades, a series of renewed Arab-Israeli confrontations would prove that fact again and again.

What the American Jewish community learned from the war was the reverse: that Israel might be destroyed at any moment. It learned, too, that the world would permit this to happen, that the world was a hostile and dangerous place, that nobody cared about the Jews, and the Jews should care about nobody.

Jews had "a sudden realization that genocide, antisemitism [sic], a desire to murder Jews—all those things were not merely what one had been taught about a bad, stupid past. . . . Those things were real and present," American Jewish Committee research director Milton Himmelfarb wrote in *Commentary* in October 1967. As a result, he wrote, Jews were now reconsidering who were their friends and enemies. They were more suspicious of the left and less suspicious of the right; they had more faith in states and armies and less trust in talk and diplomacy. Jews were becoming, if not quite conservative, at least "Whiggish."

"How then shall we describe the change that seems to be taking place among us?" Himmelfarb asked. "What has been happening is a slow bringing into consciousness of a disillusionment that has been going on for a long time now with the characteristic outlook of modern, Enlightened Jews. It is a shift from the general to the particular, from the abstract to the concrete." Jews had now "relearned the old truth that you can depend only on yourself," he wrote. "We relearned the old, hard truth that only you can feel your own pain."

It was a curious moment in the history of ideas. Twenty years earlier, Jews had responded to the Nazi Holocaust by plunging headlong into a politics of trust and optimism. Their answer to the Second World War was a vow to create a world where such terrible things could not happen to anyone.

Now, wrote the American Jewish Committee's research director—and countless others who would echo him in the coming months and years—Jews were responding to Israel's great victory by retreating into a politics of fear and suspicion.

What could account for this extraordinary reversal of the spirit? Fear for Israel's military safety was part of the story, but only one part. Through the summer and fall of 1967, and continuing into 1968, American Jews were drawn into an extraordinary cycle of events, some related to the Six-Day War, some unrelated. Together, these events conspired to reinforce the bitterness of the siege and erase the joy of victory.

The first of these events was a direct consequence of the war. Israel's new status as a military heavyweight aroused deep misgivings among American liberals. It was the height of the Vietnam conflict. War and the military had become unpopular in academic and intellectual circles. These were the very circles that had been American Jewry's bastion of support for generations. Now they became centers of hostility. The spirit of the 1960s was hospitable to Israelis in sandals, it seemed, but not to Israelis in helmets. In short order, Jewish supporters of Israel found their views, and themselves, unwelcome in their familiar haunts.

Compounding the intellectuals' discomfort with Israel was the seizure of new territories, particularly the densely populated West Bank. Israel was more than a winner; it was a conqueror. Overnight, Israel's image on the American campus and in parts of the news media changed from threatened underdog to conquering bully.

The truth was that many Israelis, too, were uncomfortable with their new role as an occupying power. Within months after the war, Israel experienced something like a popular wave of troubled introspection, expressed in best-selling books such as *Siah Lohamim* ("Soldiers' Talk," published in English as *The Seventh Day: Soldiers Talk about the Six-Day War*) and popular hit songs such as "Song for Peace." Indeed, the Israeli government itself offered on June 19, just days after the war, to return nearly all its new acquisitions in exchange for negotiated peace treaties.

But the Arab states unanimously refused to negotiate. Instead, the League of Arab States demanded unilateral Israeli withdrawal. The league embarked on a furious effort to make Israel a pariah in the world diplomatic community. Within weeks, the league had created at the United Nations a solid anti-Israel bloc made up of Arab and Muslim states, most of the Communist bloc, and many of the so-called Third World states. The anti-Israel bloc formed a majority in the U.N. General Assembly. U.N. debates began to feature regular doses of crude anti-Semitic rhetoric. The worst offender, Ambassador Jamil Baroody of Saudi Arabia, took to reminding his audience that these same Jews had killed Jesus.

To see the United Nations transformed into a platform for unending attacks on Israel and Jews in general was emotionally devastating to Jewish liberals. Most Jews had looked on the world body as a cornerstone of their post–Second World War ideology of optimism. It was the living embodiment of their faith in humanity's better nature. A 1962 NCRAC resolution had called the United Nations "a major force for peace with dignity in a world of cold war tensions, suspicion and distrust." Now its spirit was captured in the lyrics of a postwar Israeli pop tune: "The whole world is against us."

The anti-Israel shift in the Third World, though further away, was scarcely less troubling. Israel considered itself the embodiment of Jewish national self-determination. It had worked hard over two decades to forge ties with other emerging nations in Africa and Asia. Now Israel found itself ostracized by erstwhile friends. It seemed the ancient poison of Jew-hatred was stronger than the solidarity of the oppressed.

Of all the reversals, though, the most destructive in the long run was the about-face of the Communist world. In 1948, the Soviet Union had supported Israeli independence diplomatically and militarily. During the 1950s, the Kremlin turned unfriendly, then hostile. By early 1967, Moscow had become a de facto military ally of the Arabs.

After the Six-Day War, Soviet hostility took a new and deadlier turn. The entire Communist world, except for Romania and Cuba, severed diplomatic relations with Israel. The Soviet Union itself became a bottomless well of anti-Israel and crudely anti-Semitic propaganda. The Soviets began arming and training Palestinian Arab guerrillas, who now launched a deadly war of terrorism against Israel, Jews, and the West.

The new Soviet stance was scarcely a disappointment to American Jews; most took a dim view of Communism in any case. But there was an indirect impact: Soviet positions were declaimed from the United Nations and duly reported in major newspapers, filling the air Jews breathed with virulent anti-Jewish propaganda of a sort not heard since the Nazis.

There was a broader, more serious spillover. Broad sectors of the

American left, though not Communist themselves, had come to put more faith in Moscow's foreign policy than in Washington's during the 1960s. The Vietnam War had decimated the credibility of anti-Communism among liberals. Anti-imperialism now held more sway. This was particularly the case on college campuses, where the young radicals of the New Left dominated public debate. In the late summer of 1967, the leading organization of the New Left, Students for a Democratic Society, held its national convention and adopted a militantly anti-Israel stance. A month later, a broad spectrum of New Left and radical groups met in Boston for the first National Convention on New Politics. They, too, voted to condemn Israel for its "imperialist Zionist war." In the following months, criticism of Israel as an occupying bully spread into ever broader segments of the American left, from Marxist radicals to the mainstream liberals of the National Council of Churches of Christ.

In response, Jews began resigning in droves from liberal and left-wing groups—and attacking those who did not do so as traitors to their own kind. "From this point on, I will support no movement that does not accept my people's struggle," the born-again Jewish student leader M. J. Rosenberg wrote in the *Village Voice* in February 1969, in a much reprinted essay that was pointedly titled, "To Uncle Tom and Other Such Jews."

A second event that helped to fuel the new Jewish isolationism had nothing to do with Israel, but over the years it has merged with the Six-Day War to become an inseparable part of the mythos of 1967.

In New York City that spring, the board of education decided to try an experiment in decentralizing the city's million-student school system. With funding from the Ford Foundation, it created local school districts in three neighborhoods. Each was to be run by a local school board, elected from the neighborhood.

One of the three local boards was in an impoverished, mainly black section of Brooklyn called Ocean Hill-Brownsville. Many parents there looked to decentralization as an opportunity for the black community to take control of its children's schooling, often seen as tainted by the pervasive racism of white America.

Most New York City teachers, then as now, were Jews. Teaching, like civil service, had been a favored Jewish pathway out of the ghetto a generation before. It was still a popular career path for liberal, socially dedicated Jewish youngsters of the postwar baby-boom generation.

Over the course of the 1967–68 school year, the Ocean Hill-Brownsville local board tried to increase the percentage of black teachers in the district. They quickly ran into stiff opposition from the New York City teachers' union, which wanted to protect its members' existing jobs and seniority. Tensions in the neighborhood reached a boiling point. Board meetings deteriorated into black-white shouting matches.

Black militants came to Ocean Hill-Brownsville from around the city to help mobilize parents and press the racial agenda. Some were followers of the anti-white, anti-Jewish Black Muslim movement. Others brought the Third World Marxist rhetoric that was popular at that time among black nationalists. Anonymous leaflets began to appear in the neighborhood, comparing Jewish teachers to Israeli imperialists who were subjugating Third World people of color.

One leaflet, distributed to teachers in a junior high school, proclaimed:

It Is Impossible For The Middle East Murderers of Colored People to Possibly Bring To This Important Task [of teaching] The Insight, The Concern, The Exposing Of The Truth That is a Must If The Years Of Brainwashing And Self-Hatred That Has Been Taught To Our Black Children By Those Bloodsucking Exploiters and Murderers Is To Be Overcome. The Idea Behind This Program Is Beautiful, But When The Money Changers Heard About It, They Took It Over, As Is Their Custom In The Black Community.

In the fall of 1968, the teachers' union went on strike to demand job security. In a bid for public sympathy, union president Albert Shanker decided to reprint some of the militant leaflets that had surfaced and circulate them citywide. Some of his top lieutenants argued against this tactic; they said it would inject a false issue of anti-Semitism into a confrontation that actually revolved around black-white disputes. Shanker went ahead anyway.

As his aides had predicted, Shanker's decision radicalized the tone of discussion in the city. Even though the leaflets did not represent the Ocean Hill-Brownsville school board, not even its militants, they created a tidal wave of outrage against the local board. In November, the city stepped in and dissolved the board, ending community control.

By now, feelings in the Jewish community had reached a fever pitch. Black militancy and anti-Semitism had become all but inseparable in Jewish public discussion. Civil rights advocates found themselves getting heckled in synagogues. Mainstream Jewish civil rights groups, such as the American Jewish Congress and the Anti-Defamation League, began to focus for the first time on anti-Semitism among black militants as a major threat to Jews. One young rabbi named Meir Kahane, dismissing the mainstream groups as toothless apologists, organized a Jewish Defense League armed with chains and baseball bats.

During the twenty years before the Six-Day War, a formal alliance had existed between the organized black community and the organized Jewish community. Their bond had been one of the cornerstones of a triumphant American liberalism. The Ocean Hill-Brownsville dispute suddenly made it hard for Jewish community leaders to continue participating in the alliance. Every black leader became suspected of anti-Semitism—if not of fomenting it, then at least of tolerating it in colleagues. As journalist Jonathan Kaufman noted in his *Broken Alliance: The Turbulent Times Between Blacks and Jews in America*, "The sound heard in New York in 1968 and 1969 was the sound of a coalition ripping itself apart."

The New York teachers' strike did not happen in a vacuum. Black nationalism had been splitting the civil rights movement for several years, dividing blacks who believed in interracial cooperation from blacks who opposed it. Whites in the civil rights movement, many of them Jewish, were being driven out en masse. For Jewish civil rights activists, the rise of black separatism was doubly distressing, both because of the intrusion of what seemed like bigotry, and simply because they resented being banished from a movement that was so central to their self-image as liberals and as Jews.

The Ocean Hill-Brownsville dispute was the turning point, however. Before, most Jews had believed that most blacks shared a common commitment to brotherhood and social justice. Afterwards, Jews who still believed this were on the defensive, as suspicion of black intentions moved to the center of the Jewish agenda.

A third aftershock of the Six-Day War took place half a world away, in the Soviet Union. Nevertheless, it deeply affected the way American Jews looked at politics—and the way American politics looked at the Jews. That event was the reemergence of the Soviet Jewish community from a half-century of terrified silence.

The suppression of Jewish life in the Soviet Union had been a slow process, building over decades. Like so many other evils of Communism, it at first was invisible to Western liberals, masked by the aura of goodwill that initially surrounded the Russian revolution. When the truth about Soviet anti-Semitism finally hit home to Jews in America, the fate of their first cousins in the old country became the most passionate cause in modern Jewish political activism.

Jews in Russia had overwhelmingly welcomed the 1917 revolution at the outset. The overthrow of the hated, murderous regime of the Romanov czars was cause for worldwide Jewish rejoicing. The revolution initially gave Russian Jews a freedom they had never known. Throughout the 1920s, there was an explosion of Yiddish publishing, theater, and film; of Jewish literature and scholarship in both Yiddish and Russian; and of Jewish political activity. The Soviet government even sponsored Jewish agricultural colonies, with help from the American Jewish Joint Distribution Committee.

The freedoms were abruptly curtailed in the late 1920s, when Joseph Stalin consolidated his hold as the Kremlin's strongman. Theaters and publishing houses were closed, organizations dissolved, synagogues boarded up. Contact with foreign Jewish communities was cut off. During the purges of the 1930s, the country's leading Jewish writers and artists were murdered, leaving the Jewish community virtually without a voice. There was a brief respite during the Second World War, when Stalin used Soviet Jews to curry support in the West. Immediately afterward, the last lights of Russian Jewish culture were extinguished.

The birth of Israel in 1948 touched off an explosive outpouring of Jewish fervor across Russia. Tens of thousands of Jews took to the streets when the first Israeli diplomatic team arrived in Moscow that September under Ambassador Golda Meir. The Kremlin's reply was swift and brutal: Jews, even the most loyal Communists among them, were purged from nearly all party and government positions. In 1952, the last two dozen Yiddish writers and poets in the Soviet Union were murdered on a single August morning in the basement of Moscow's Lubyanka prison. Nothing remained of Russian Jewish life except a half-dozen decrepit synagogues, two Yiddish-language Communist propaganda organs, and an underground whispering network, poignantly described by the young French-Jewish writer Elie Wiesel in his 1966 journal, *The Jews of Silence*.

Wiesel's book appeared in English in November 1967 and became a national best-seller in the United States. Things already were changing by then, however. The silence of Soviet Jewry was ending. Israel's June victory had stunned Jews in Russia, even more than in America. Moscow radio had predicted that Israel would be destroyed. When this did not happen, Soviet Jews experienced what many would later describe as an "awakening." Secret Hebrew classes sprang up in major cities. Jews wrote letters to newspapers, openly protesting anti-Semitic propaganda. Huge crowds gathered on Jewish holidays outside of the remaining synagogues to sing and dance. Thousands of Jews applied for visas to leave the Soviet Union and move to Israel, even though the very act of applying meant ostracism and unemployment.

The Kremlin cracked down again, but hesitantly this time. Key activists were arrested for encouraging emigration or teaching Hebrew. In December 1970, two Jewish activists from Leningrad were sentenced to death after trying to hijack a plane out of the Soviet Union. At the same time, several dozen applicants per month actually got permission to emigrate.

American Jews had been organizing protests against Soviet anti-Semitism since the early 1960s. But the post-1967 reawakening of Jews inside Russia transformed the scattered American protests into a mass movement. By 1972, the Soviet Jewry freedom struggle had become a national American Jewish crusade. Rallies across the country regularly brought hundreds of thousands of protesters into the streets.

Soviet Jewry forced its way onto the agenda of U.S.-Soviet relations, disrupting Richard Nixon's efforts at detente. The final result was the 1973 passage of the Jackson-Vanik Amendment. The rights of Jews in the Soviet Union had become the precondition for U.S.-Soviet economic dealings.

The fourth event that transformed American Jewry in the wake of 1967 was not actually an event, but a new way of seeing the world. It filtered into the consciousness of American Jews slowly, over the months and years that followed the Six-Day War. It was more subtle than the other outcomes, turning on no single moment, person, or place. Yet it was the deepest change, and the most influential, because it shaped Jewish responses to all other events: the rise of Holocaust awareness.

Much has been written about the Holocaust in the last half-century—too much, perhaps, to allow any longer for clear thinking or comprehension of the event. However, one crucial turning point in American Jewry's under-standing of the Holocaust clearly was the April 1968 publication of *While Six Million Died: A Chronicle of American Apathy*, by Arthur D. Morse.

Morse put together a withering indictment of the Roosevelt administra-tion on the charge—then startling, now familiar—of having neglected opportunities to save Jews from the Nazis. Since Morse's book appeared, the charge of abandonment has spawned a cottage industry all its own. Several best-selling books have appeared on this topic, along with an acclaimed documentary film and even an international "tribunal," chaired by former Supreme Court Justice Arthur J. Goldberg, which tried the Second World War–era American Jewish leadership for colluding with Roosevelt.

When it first appeared, Morse's book struck a deep chord in the Ameri-can Jewish community. For months, public discussion among Jews had been dominated by Israel's near-death experience the previous June and by its subsequent diplomatic isolation. Now began a snowballing fascination with Jewish aloneness and Gentile hostility, using the Holocaust as its symbol. Remembering the Holocaust became a central driving theme in Jewish community activity, a third pillar of Jewish life alongside defending Israel and saving Soviet Jewry. In some respects it was the most important pillar of all, for the Holocaust was the subtext that underlay and fueled the other two. Learning the lessons of the Holocaust, ensuring that it would never again happen, ending the decades of silence that had followed the events themselves—these became the watchwords of the American Jewish community.

It should be noted here that the decades-long silence enveloping the Holocaust prior to 1968 was, in fact, just one more myth. The Nazi genocide had been amply aired during the first two decades after the Second World War: the unprecedented Nuremberg war-crimes trials in 1945–1946; the internationally televised Eichmann trial in 1961; the publication of several best-selling books on the Holocaust, including John Hersey's *The Wall* in 1950, *The Diary of Anne Frank* in 1952, and Elie Wiesel's *Night* in 1960 and *Dawn* in 1961; as well as several much noticed Hollywood films that dealt searingly with the subject and deeply influenced viewers, from the critically acclaimed *The Juggler* in 1952 to the powerful documentary *Let My People Go*, nationally televised in 1965.

Yet all of this activity pales in comparison to the outpouring of the American Jewish Holocaust awareness movement since 1968. Multimillion-dollar Holocaust museums have opened in Washington and Los Angeles, with another planned in New York City, plus smaller ones in a hundred other communities. A U.S. government agency has been created to hunt down and punish Nazi war criminals. Public school curricula have been adopted nationwide to teach about the Holocaust, at the state and local level, in scores of colleges, and even in the U.S. military. And there has been an endless stream of scholarly and popular books, blockbuster film and television presentations, and much, much more.

The rise of the Holocaust awareness movement after 1968 did not break any shroud of silence muffling public awareness of the Nazis' war against the Jews. There had been no such silence.

What the new wave did accomplish was to change the "lesson of the Holocaust," so that it matched the new mood of anger and isolationism that had come to dominate the American Jewish community.

Before 1968, the Holocaust taught Jews that people could do one another great wrong when they lost sight of their common humanity in a world that could and should be better. After 1968, the message was that Jews should never let their guard down in a world that couldn't be much worse.

Of all the myths surrounding the Six-Day War and its aftermath, perhaps the most remarkable is the idea that it transformed the thinking of most American Jews. The truth is slightly different: although the war and its aftershocks probably affected most Jews, only a minority were utterly transformed in the manner retold in myth.

This difference is crucial. A great many American Jews found themselves sorely rattled during the year and a half from May 1967 through the autumn of 1968. They were alarmed by Israel's isolation at the United Nations, outraged by black anti-Semitism in New York, and haunted throughout by the specter of the Holocaust. Nevertheless, the stark disillusionment described by Milton Himmelfarb in *Commentary* in October 1967—the relearning of the "old, hard truth that only you can feel your own pain"—was limited to a minority.

It was a minority with an edge, however. The new Jewish particularists presumed, like Himmelfarb, to speak for the entire Jewish community. Driven by fear of anti-Semitism, by guilt over past Jewish timidity, and by suspicion of Gentiles, liberalism, and coalition politics, the new particularists simply took over the machinery of American Jewish politics. Hardly anyone tried to stop them. The opinions of the majority of American Jews became largely irrelevant to the process of policy-making. The Jewish community became the preserve of a passionate minority, driven by a terrible vision. This was the real revolution of 1967.

A few months after the Six-Day War, America's most respected student of Jewish behavior went to an affluent Chicago suburb to explore the war's impact on Jews. His investigations, published in October 1968, left him stunned.

The scholar was sociologist Marshall Sklare of Yeshiva University, an Orthodox-run institution in New York City. In 1965, he had published a pioneering, multilayered study of religious and social patterns among Jews in the pseudonymous "Lakeville," a Chicago suburb that he took to be representative of American Jewish life at large. He had found a surprisingly high level of Jewish attachment, contradicting the gloomy images then popular. Returning to "Lakeville" after the crisis of 1967, he expected to find a community transformed.

Instead, he found most Jews largely unchanged by the events. "Our respondents were shaken by the threat posed by the Crisis, were unambiguously pro-Israel, were tremendously stirred by the victory . . . ," Sklare wrote. "[Yet, they] have not shifted in their level of pro-Israel support, and have not evinced any extraordinary eagerness to visit Israel." In fact, the local rabbis and community leaders told Sklare that they "expected 'the change to be sharper than it actually has been.' "

How, he asked, could one explain "the absence of a revolutionary change in Jewish life?"

The answer, Sklare speculated, was that American Jews respond more readily to bad news than to good news. American Jews care deeply about Israel, he wrote, so deeply that its survival is essential in order "to preserve a feeling of our worth as human beings." If Israel had been destroyed, it would have been like a second Holocaust: "Hitler, whom we thought to be dead and conquered, would be alive again; the final victory would be his. By upsetting our sense of meaning, a new holocaust would have plunged American Jewry into a total anomie."

But because Israel had *won* the war, the Jews felt free to go about their business.

Sklare was half right in his explanation. It was true that most Jews were not transformed by the crisis. But that should have been clear from the outset. For all of Sklare's soaring rhetoric, most American Jews did not view Israel as an existential fount of meaning to the extent that he proclaimed. Israel was important to them, but not *that* important.

Sklare himself had proved this, just two years before the war. In his 1965 "Lakeville" studies, he had found a Jewish community that professed deep concern for Israel's welfare, but did not see Israel as central to its identity. American Judaism revolved around local and personal concerns: the Jews' families, their communities, their synagogues, and their social values.

Sklare found 65 percent of his respondents affirming that if Israel were to be destroyed, they would feel "a deep sense of loss" (another 25 percent said they would feel a sense of loss, but not a "deep" sense).

On the other hand, when he asked them what practices were "essential" to being a good Jew, "support Israel" came in only fourteenth out of twenty-two choices. Topping the list were "lead an ethical and moral life" (deemed essential by 93 percent), "accept being a Jew and not try to hide it" (85 percent) and "support all humanitarian causes" (67 percent). Other high-scoring essentials included "help the underprivileged improve their lot" (58 percent), "know the fundamentals of Judaism" (48 percent), and "work for the equality of Negroes" (44 percent). "Support Israel" was named as essential by only 21 percent, slightly behind "marry within the faith" (23 percent) and "attend services on High Holidays" (24 percent), though well ahead of "observe the dietary laws" and "have mostly Jewish friends" (1 percent each).

Strikingly similar results turned up a quarter-century later, in a survey of American Jewish attitudes by sociologist Steven M. Cohen. Cohen asked a national sample of American Jews whether or not the destruction of Israel would be "one of the greatest personal tragedies of my life"—certainly a deep sense of loss—and got the same 65 percent affirmative response.

And when Cohen asked his respondents what was "essential" to being a good Jew, his findings were much like Sklare's. Like the "Lakeville" Jews in 1965, Cohen's Jews in 1989 topped their list of essential Jewish acts with "lead an ethical and moral life," while dietary laws and Jewish friendships ranked near the bottom. Similarly, "support Israel" appeared halfway down the list (eighth of twenty choices, with 19 percent calling it "essential"), close to attending High Holiday services and marrying other Jews.

In one key respect, however, Cohen's 1989 list was strikingly different from Sklare's 1965 list. Choices that suggested political liberalism, either directly or implicitly—"work for social justice causes," "contribute to non-sectarian charities," or simply "be a liberal on political issues"—had moved from the top of the list to the bottom.

Had the Jews become less liberal? Voting patterns, survey responses, and countless other signs showed that they had not. What Jews had done, or been taught to do, was to dissociate liberalism and Judaism. Over the quarter-century that followed the Six-Day War, they had come to understand that the job of the Jewish community was not to represent them, their views, their needs, or their values.

Instead, a small minority of Jews had been allowed to take over the Jewish organizational infrastructure and turn it into an instrument of defensive nationalism. *These* were the Jews whose motives Sklare so eloquently described in his 1968 return to "Lakeville"—those whose fears of a "Hitler . . . alive again," and determination not to give him a "final victory," now formed the core of their "sense of being."

Most other Jews, awed by the passion of these born-again particularists, drew back a respectful distance. The battle for Israel was not their highest priority, yet no one wanted to give Hitler a posthumous victory. As their organizations became increasingly an engine of geopolitics, most American Jews looked elsewhere for expression of their own values. They left the community structures to the New Jews.

There were three distinct groups among these New Jews. And none of them was new. All three were existing factions on the Jewish landscape, but each was thrust into new prominence in the turbulent aftermath of 1967.

One group represented one of the most ancient forces in Jewish community life, Orthodox Judaism. A second incorporated one of the newest streams in Jewish thought, the secular nationalist movement known as

Zionism. The third group was hardly a force at all, just a tiny circle of intellectuals who called themselves neoconservatives.

The basic idea of Zionism, Jewish statehood in the land of Israel, is central to Jewish tradition. Throughout their two thousand years of dispersion, Jews everywhere have prayed three times a day for the rebuilding of Jerusalem and the ingathering of Jewish exiles. Poems and prayers for Jerusalem and its holy Mount Zion fill Jewish liturgy. Jews worldwide pray with their faces toward Jerusalem, and the Jewish religious calendar revolves around the agricultural cycles of the Middle East.

But if Zion is an ancient Jewish tradition, Zionism is not. Zionism began as a movement among secular intellectuals who were rebelling *against* traditional Judaism. The rabbinic legacy taught that the Jews had been exiled from Jerusalem as divine punishment for their sins. Only God could restore Zion, the rabbis taught, by sending the anointed Messiah to usher in the End of Days. The first Zionists were late-nineteenth-century modernists who insisted that history was shaped by human will, and that Jews need no longer accept the cruel fate God had chosen for them. The Zionists urged Jews to take their own destiny in their hands and strive for "normalization."

By the eve of the First World War, despite the near-unanimous opposition of the rabbinate, Zionism had become a mass movement among the Jews of Eastern Europe, driven to despair by czarist persecutions. As Zionism grew, it lost its rebellious tone. The World Zionist Organization (WZO), originally a small band of dreamers, became a sophisticated political machine led by professional technocrats at the helm of a large bureaucracy.

Their followers quickly divided into competing parties, each with its own notion of what kind of Jewish state should be built. Socialist Labor Zionists favored a Jewish workers' republic. General Zionists favored a free-market democracy, little different from London or New York. Religious Zionists, who braved the rabbis' disapproval to support the nationalists, hoped nonetheless to create an Orthodox theocracy in Israel. Every four years, elections were held noisily in Jewish neighborhoods around the world to determine which party would control the World Zionist Congress when it met to choose the WZO executive committee.

In America, Zionism began as a tiny fringe group. Its main appeal, as a solution to the crisis of anti-Semitism, meant little to American Jews; they had solved their problems by coming here. The established voices of America's old-line German Jewish community—the Reform rabbinate and the American Jewish Committee—flatly opposed the dangerous nationalism.

After the First World War, however, American Zionism soared in popularity, thanks in large measure to its new leader, Louis D. Brandeis. A liberal Boston attorney, raised in an assimilated home in Kentucky, Brandeis was recruited in 1914 by the European Zionist leadership to unite the squabbling American grouplets. Under Brandeis, dues-paying membership grew in a decade from 12,000 to 150,000. Zionist fund-raising campaigns were set up in every city where Jews lived. He served as formal head of the American Zionist executive committee for only two years, resigning in 1916 when he was appointed to the U.S. Supreme Court. But he remained active behind the scenes for years.

Brandeis had been drawn to Zionism not as a nationalist rebellion but as a philanthropic gesture. To him, Zionism meant helping suffering Jews abroad to better themselves. Unlike Zionists in other countries, he argued that supporting Zionism did not require a Jew to emigrate or take up a foreign loyalty. "[T]o be good Americans we must become better Jews, and to be better Jews we must become Zionists," he told a cheering Boston crowd in 1914.

Brandeis's corn-fed, all-American Zionism evoked derision among the WZO's European leaders. During the 1920s, they worked furiously to force him out of movement leadership. Yet his philanthropic version of Zionism captured the imaginations of the broader Jewish community. Early in the 1920s, the leaders of the American Jewish Committee accepted his ideology and agreed to support the Zionists' nation-building work in Palestine. The Reform rabbinate and the Jewish Socialists followed suit in the 1930s. By the end of the Second World War, every significant faction of the American Jewish community had united behind Jewish statehood. When Israel won independence in 1948, all but a handful of synagogues and Jewish organizations pitched in to support the fledgling state with money and political muscle.

During the 1950s and early 1960s, support for Israel was so widespread among American Jews that actual Zionists—members of the WZO—began to wonder out loud whether Zionism was needed any longer. Israelis said the Zionists' task was to persuade American Jews to pack up and move to

Israel, but most American Zionists had never accepted that job to begin
with.

As for the other great task of the Zionist movement—offering Jews a
vehicle for robust debate on how to shape their future—this no longer
appealed to the leadership of the WZO. With the establishment of Israel in
1948, the WZO had become an arm of government. Its primary duty,
enshrined in Israel's "Basic Law: National Institutions" of 1952, was to
manage Israel's relations with the Jewish Diaspora.

And what Israel wanted from the Diaspora was support, not arguments.

One day in late 1953, during one of their regular working meetings at the
State Department, America's top Middle East expert posed a sharp question to the president of the World Zionist Organization. Was there no way,
the diplomat asked the visiting Zionist, for the American Jews to create a
single mouthpiece?

The American was Henry Byroade, assistant secretary of state for Near
East and African affairs. A career diplomat, he enjoyed the drama of the
Middle East conflict, but he heartily detested the part of his job that forced
him to receive an endless stream of argumentative Jewish delegations from
New York. His boss, Secretary of State John Foster Dulles, felt the same
way in spades. Dulles had lost a close New York Senate race in 1948 to a
Jewish Democrat, ex-Governor Herbert Lehman, and he blamed the
noisily clannish Jewish vote.

The president of the WZO was Nahum Goldmann, a charming, peri-
patetic raconteur of German birth and multiple citizenship. While living in
Geneva during the 1930s, he had emerged as the WZO's most effective
diplomat, one of the few ranking Zionists who could meet with European
leaders and keep his sense of humor. After the Second World War, when
most of the top WZO leadership gathered in the new Jewish state, Goldmann set up shop in New York. From there he continued his globe-trotting.
He was welcomed in boardrooms and presidential palaces everywhere as
the spokesman of worldwide Diaspora Jewry. Besides the WZO he headed
the World Jewish Congress, the Conference on Jewish Material Claims
Against Nazi Germany, and a few other organizations.

Goldmann told Byroade that he would try to bring the American Jews
under a single roof. Working with Abba Eban, the Israeli ambassador in
Washington, Goldmann persuaded the heads of a dozen groups to come

together for an informal conference. The groups agreed to create an ongoing body, the Conference of Presidents of Major American Jewish Organizations. Goldmann chaired. Its purpose was a limited one: to express American Jewry's consensus of support for Israel.

For a few months, Goldmann ran the Presidents Conference out of his back pocket as one more title. But he soon decided that more structure was needed, and persuaded Chicago real-estate developer Philip Klutznick, international president of the B'nai B'rith order, to take over. A staff director was hired, Yehuda Hellman, a young Goldmann protégé recently arrived from Israel. With Goldmann and Eban watching over Hellman's shoulder, the Presidents Conference quickly won quasi-official recognition from the White House and the State Department as the voice of the Jewish community.

This new development did not stop the other organizations from banging on doors in Washington, however. The Presidents Conference "simply became one more voice they had to listen to," Eban recalled with a laugh, years later.

The American Jewish community now had two central voices: NCRAC (see chapter 5) and the Presidents Conference. And a third voice slowly was emerging: the American Israel Public Affairs Committee, which originally had been created in 1944 as the Washington office of the Zionist movement. After Israel won independence in 1948, the office was renamed and registered with the U.S. government as a lobby. In the mid-1950s, the Zionist lobby was reorganized again, this time to avoid allegations that it was an agent for a foreign government. A formal relationship was established with the Presidents Conference: AIPAC lobbied Congress while the Presidents Conference addressed the executive branch. Each organization was represented on the other's governing board.

Formally, AIPAC was now the homegrown lobbying arm of the organized American Jewish community. In practice, it was a one-man office run by its tireless founder-director, Canadian-born journalist Isaiah L. Kenen.

Affable and understated, Kenen genuinely liked and respected the lawmakers he worked with. The affection was largely mutual, a rare achievement for a lobbyist. Kenen had a widely acknowledged genius for timing and political judgment; as a result, a few phone calls to top congressional leaders usually sufficed to secure whatever it was that Israel needed.

It did not hurt that Israel was widely admired as a young democracy fighting for its life against fanatics and dictators. And when a phone call wasn't enough, Kenen kept a list of a few hundred "key contacts" around the country, local rabbis and community leaders who could get their elected representatives on the phone.

Kenen worked closely with Yehuda Hellman and NCRAC's Isaiah Minkoff in New York. Together they formed a sort of three-person directorate of organized Jewish influence, with Israel's Ambassador Eban an invisible fourth partner.

Over time, Kenen became something of a legend. "I would call him one of the great figures of American Jewish politics, along with Minkoff and Arnie Aronson," declares longtime American Jewish Committee staffer Irving Levine. "All of these guys were influenced by the emergence of social-work training. They understood process. They had moved beyond ideology and were the supreme pragmatists. Low-key was not the Jewish style. Most of the Jews were loud and aggressive and offended people. These three knew how to get along with people."

Orthodox Judaism was commonly thought to be a spent force before 1967. For two centuries it had been pummeled by the Age of Reason, repudiated by secularist Zionism, and, for many Jews, simply rendered implausible by the existential horror of the Nazi Holocaust. The central claim of Orthodoxy—that it was the sole authentic version of Judaism—rendered it marginal in the two principal Jewish communities that survived the Second World War, Reform-minded American Jewry and the secular-led state of Israel. Orthodoxy's greatest stronghold, the massive Jewish communities of Eastern Europe, had been exterminated.

The Orthodox Judaism that did take root in America and Israel before the Second World War was not traditional Orthodoxy but a modern variant. Known in America as Modern Orthodoxy, and in Israel as Religious Zionism, it combined ritual observance and philosophical pragmatism. Its most important concession was its willingness to coexist peacefully with the heresies that dominated Jewish life in Israel and America: Zionism and non-Orthodox Judaism.

The traditionalist rabbinate viewed Modern Orthodoxy with a good deal of alarm. In 1912, the grand rabbis of Eastern Europe convened—for the first time ever—to form an organization to combat the new heresies. The new body, Agudath Israel ("The Union of Israel"), soon became the international voice of Orthodox opposition to Zionism and non-Orthodox Judaism. But it failed to stem the growth of Modern Orthodoxy.

Modern Orthodox Jews rapidly developed a culture all their own. They held the line on dietary laws, Sabbath observance, and other rituals. However, they dropped many secondary customs, which traditionally had served to separate Jews from their neighbors. They embraced modern clothing fashions. They accepted once-scandalous deviations such as interfaith dialogue, political activism, concert-going, and coed dancing. For the most part, they offered no particular theology; the slogan of Modern Orthodoxy was "Torah and Science." That is, theology and modernism were to coexist peacefully, not try to explain one another.

One of the few Orthodox scholars to offer a deliberate theology of modernism was the chief rabbi of Palestine during the 1920s and 1930s, the Polish-born Rabbi Abraham Isaac Hacohen Kook. Writing in an impenetrably mystical Hebrew, Kook tried to disprove the traditionalists' view of Zionism as heresy. Zionism could not be a rebellion against God, Kook argued, since its main leaders were secularized liberals who did not even believe in God. God must have sent these unbelievers, he reasoned, to carry out His work by paving the way for the End of Days and the final restoration of Jerusalem.

The building of the Jewish state was not the long-awaited messianic era of redemption, Kook argued (thus sidestepping any hint of heresy). But it did look suspiciously like "the dawn of redemption," as he put it.

Kook's theology remained for decades a curiosity, even among Religious Zionists. However, the creation of Israel in 1948 made his "dawn of redemption" sound plausible for the first time. Orthodox Zionist youth groups adopted Kook's thought. The seminary he had founded in Jerusalem (now headed by his son, Rabbi Zvi Yehuda Kook), became a major Israeli religious center. Israel's state rabbinate prepared a Kookian prayer for weekly use in synagogues around the world, praying for the safety of the state of Israel, "the first flowering of our redemption."

With the stunning Israeli victory of 1967, the elder Rabbi Kook's ideas resounded throughout the Orthodox world. For Orthodox Jews, the against-the-odds triumph in the Six-Day War was a miracle that defied natural explanation. More than that, it represented a giant step toward redemption: the entire Holy Land now was under Israeli control for the first time since biblical days. The Temple Mount in East Jerusalem, the crypt of the Patriarchs in Hebron—all of the holiest sites in Judaism were in Jewish hands. It seemed to be the final confirmation of Kook's teachings.

In his Jerusalem seminary, the younger Rabbi Kook taught that the End of Days was fast approaching. Nothing remained except for the Messiah to reveal himself and build the Third Temple. That, and preventing Israel's secular government from undoing God's work by giving away parts of the Holy Land in what the ruling Labor Party called "territorial compromise."

In April 1968, a group of the younger Kook's students, led by a German-born firebrand named Rabbi Moshe Levinger, went to the occupied city of Hebron and checked into a hotel for Passover. When the holiday was over a group refused to leave, declaring that they had "returned to the City of the Patriarchs." The Israeli government was confused and divided by this partisan action, fearing to leave the militants in the center of a devoutly Muslim city of fifty thousand, but unable to muster the political will to dislodge them. After a weeks-long standoff, Levinger's group agreed to leave the hotel in return for government permission to set up house on a hill just outside Hebron.

The new Jewish township, Kiryat Arba, became the first of a network of Jewish settlements set up throughout the occupied territories by the disciples of Rabbi Kook. Led by Levinger and the aging Zvi Yehuda, they created a new organization to promote the settlements, called Gush Emunim ("The Bloc of the Faithful"). Its central premise: filling the territories with Jewish settlements would bring about the messianic era of final redemption. Giving away the territories would invite God's wrath, perhaps even cause the destruction of Israel and a third Jewish exile.

Within a decade, the Gush dominated much of the public debate in Orthodox Jewish communities from Hebron to Honolulu. Its influence stretched even beyond the Orthodox community. Jewish activists from left to right spoke of the young Gush settlers as the best and brightest of contemporary Judaism, spiritual heirs of the idealistic young Socialist-Zionist pioneers who had founded Israel. To many minds, the settlers transformed Orthodoxy's image from a doomed relic into the vanguard of the Jewish people.

Zionist influence on American policy was much greater in public perception than in reality. The Jews' new organizational prowess echoed ancient Christian myths of Jewish conspiracy. In the late 1940s, British Foreign Minister Ernest Bevin had been given to complaining bitterly about the power of "New York Jews" who had the Truman administration "in their pocket" and interfered with British foreign policy. During the 1950s, Secretary of State Dulles openly asserted the difficulty of making foreign-policy decisions that displeased the organized Jewish community.

Their concerns were greatly overstated. Jewish influence did not prevent Bevin's government from working to hinder Zionism at every turn, barring Zionist land acquisition and blocking Jewish immigration to Palestine from Nazi-ruled Europe, or indeed from giving military backing to the Arab side during Israel's 1948 war of independence. Nor did Jewish influence prevent the Eisenhower administration from aligning itself with Egypt during the Suez crisis in 1956.

Eisenhower, in fact, eventually would regret his decision to force a unilateral Israeli withdrawal from Sinai in 1957, in the face of vocal Jewish protests and strong congressional opposition. By facing down the Israelis, it would later appear, Eisenhower helped to build up Egypt's Nasser as a hero to anticolonialists throughout the Third World. Nasser's victory over the joint Israeli-British-French invasion forces in 1956 provided a rallying point for anti-Western revolutionaries for decades. Greater Jewish influence in Washington in the 1950s, Eisenhower told friends before his death, might have helped him avoid that mistake.

This is not to say that Kenen and the organized Jewish lobby had no influence on American foreign policy. But their power had severe limits. Zionist lobbyists were only occasionally successful when they tried to influence the details of U.S. policy. Just as often, they alienated policy-makers with their table-pounding single-mindedness. America's top Zionist leader in the 1940s, Rabbi Abba Hillel Silver of Cleveland, got himself banned from the White House altogether after President Truman tired of his bombast. David Niles, the White House liaison to ethnic minorities under Roosevelt and Truman, was so persistent in pressing for the Zionist cause that Truman is said to have stopped listening to him.

Congress frequently was willing to pass toothless statements of support for Israel. But the words rarely translated into concrete U.S. action on behalf of the embattled state. American financial aid for Israel never amounted to more than a tiny fraction of the total U.S. foreign-aid budget: grants of $63.7 million in economic aid in 1952 and $73.6 million in 1953, slashed by the Eisenhower administration to $41 million in 1954 (half of it in loans), then halved it again to $24 million in 1955—barely one tenth the amount sent that year to Vietnam, Laos, and Cambodia, and less than 1 percent of the year's total foreign-aid budget of $3.3 billion. As for military assistance, it was nonexistent.

For all the declarations of friendship, America and Israel simply were not allies during the 1940s and 1950s. Washington was bound to Iraq, Turkey, and Iran in a formal alliance, the Baghdad Pact. Israel was kept out for fear of offending America's Muslim allies. As the U.S.-Soviet competition for influence in the Middle East heated up in the late 1950s, America began sending weaponry to Jordan to keep it in the Western camp. Israel's sole arms supplier was France.

Zionist influence increased exponentially during the Kennedy and Johnson administrations, because the affluence and influence of Jews in American society had increased. Jews had become vital donors to the Democratic Party; they were key figures in the organized labor movement, which was essential to the Democratic Party; they were major figures in liberal intellectual, cultural, and academic circles. More than any of their predecessors in the Oval Office, John Kennedy and Lyndon Johnson counted numerous Jews among their close advisers, donors, and personal friends.

Kennedy initiated the first U.S. arms sales to Israel, approving a transfer of Hawk missiles that took place after his death in 1964. Johnson continued and intensified Kennedy's policy of warmth toward Israel. He was the first U.S. president to receive an Israeli prime minister on a state visit, welcoming Levi Eshkol to the White House in 1964. In 1966, Johnson approved the first sale of American warplanes to Israel.

Nonetheless, it remained for Richard Nixon, a Republican elected with little Jewish support, to create the now familiar U.S.-Israel alliance of more recent decades. It was Nixon who made Israel the largest single recipient of U.S. foreign aid; Nixon who initiated the policy of virtually limitless U.S. weapons sales to Israel. The notion of Israel as a strategic asset to the United States, not just as a moral commitment, was Nixon's innovation.

Yet Nixon was widely reviled in the Jewish community for his Red-bashing conservatism. And the dislike was mutual; only years later, with the publication of various tapes and diaries, would the full extent of his anti-Semitic views become known.

Paradoxically, Nixon kept close ties to several Jewish circles. Of these, the most important was the tiny group of writers and scholars known as the neoconservatives.

The Jewish neoconservatives were former liberals who began in the mid-1960s to voice a noisy disillusionment with liberalism. The "neo-" in "neoconservative" referred not to any startlingly new ideas they offered, but to their own newness in the ranks of conservatism.

There were common threads among these newcomers, remnants of their liberal roots. Unlike most traditional conservatives, they favored a strong American profile abroad, and they wanted to trim rather than eliminate government help for the poor. Some people on the Old Right saw them as no more than liberals in dress-up, a sort of Jewish Trojan Horse invading the American right.

Still, the neoconservative range of views was so broad that it could hardly be called a school of thought. What united them primarily was not a clear set of new ideas, but a shared revulsion for their old liberal ones.

The reasons for their journey rightward varied from one "neocon" to the next. Some, such as essayist Irving Kristol, the movement's intellectual godfather, were onetime Marxists whose hatred of Soviet Communism led them to a growing appreciation of American power—and hostility toward liberals who challenged it. Kristol launched the movement's flagship journal, *The Public Interest*, in 1965.

Others, such as editor Norman Podhoretz of *Commentary* magazine, arguably the best-known voice of neoconservatism, grew tired of the hypocrisy and excess they saw in middle-class liberalism, particularly as the 1960s proceeded. Podhoretz declared his personal independence from liberalism in a landmark 1963 essay, "My Negro Problem—and Ours." In it, he swore off liberal guilt toward blacks, claiming that in the part of Brooklyn where he had grown up, blacks were the oppressors, not the oppressed.

In addition to their shared hostility toward old comrades on the left, the neoconservatives were united by a lifetime of personal associations. "What is called 'neoconservatism' is a rather heterogeneous group," says Kristol. "What is true is that we all came out of the same pot, which is the New York socialist milieu."

The core group of neoconservatism was born during the 1930s in an alcove of the North Campus cafeteria at the City College of New York. The campus, populated mainly by children of working-class Jewish immigrants, was a hotbed of socialist factional feuding during the Depression years. The future neocons began as followers of a Trotskyite theoretician named Max Schachtman. Brilliant, witty, often accused of loving the argument more than the substance, the young Schachtmanites were revolutionary socialists who believed that Soviet Communism was worse than American capitalism. After college, they moved on to literary and academic careers and began a rightward march through the 1940s and 1950s. By the early 1960s, most had become defenders of the American system and enemies of its critics.

Not all the neoconservatives were Jewish, and those who were Jewish were ambivalent about it; they still clung to the secularism and anticlericalism of their old Marxist days. Nonetheless, they became known as a Jewish group, for several reasons. For one thing, most of them were Jews. More important, they were an anomaly: a school of thought dominated by Jews, on an American right which had always been alien territory to Jews. It was something like a Jewish village in a land where no Jews had lived before.

Most important, the neoconservatives proclaimed their existence through two magazines edited and published by Jews, Kristol's *The Public Interest* and Podhoretz's *Commentary*. Wags insisted that the difference between the magazines was that *Commentary* admitted it was Jewish. In fact, *The Public Interest* was an independent, nonsectarian journal, funded mainly by non-Jewish foundations. *Commentary* was sponsored by the American Jewish Committee, and proclaimed itself to be a journal of "thought and opinion on Jewish affairs and contemporary issues."

The American Jewish Committee had launched *Commentary* during the 1940s, with the idea of creating a prestigious forum for Jewish discourse. The experiment had been only partly successful; it had become a high-profile forum of general discourse, sponsored by the Jewish community, edited by Jews, and containing a monthly dollop of Judaic scholarship. *Commentary* offered readers an odd mix, combining Jewish scholarship of narrow appeal with contemporary issues of no Jewish content. Only occasionally did the magazine manage to bridge the two worlds, in articles dealing with foreign policy, the Middle East crisis, and the problem of Communism.

Then came 1967, and the Six-Day War, and the rebirth of Soviet Jewry, and the New York City teachers' strike. Suddenly, *Commentary* found itself at the center of the modern Jewish world. The events of 1967 and 1968, so unsettling to so many Jews, merely confirmed what the neoconservatives had been saying all along: that the world was a dangerous place; that the most dangerous force in it was Soviet Communism; that the conflict between Communism and democracy was not a negotiable spat but a war between good and evil; and, finally, that the anti-imperialist struggles of the Third World—including black radicalism in America—were just one more assault on democracy.

Hesitantly at first, but with growing confidence, Podhoretz and the band he assembled around *Commentary* began to articulate something approaching a consistent vision. It captured the imagination of the American political elite, which began to look to *Commentary* as the new voice of American Jews—in part because it offered a coherent explanation for the unease infecting American Jewry, in part because it was backed by the American Jewish Committee, and in part because of the brash self-confidence the neocons had exuded since their college days.

As time went on, the neocons began to predict confidently that American Jews were done with liberalism and would now switch their allegiance to the Republican column. In fact, that never happened. Every four years beginning in 1968, neoconservatives prophesized that the Jews were about to see the light and join their real friends on the right. Every four years, they were proven wrong again.

The rest of the country did switch in 1968, however. Richard Nixon's narrow victory over Hubert Humphrey in the that year's presidential election signaled the beginning of a new era in American politics, a quarter-century of nearly unbroken Republican rule in the White House.

Nixon saw in the neoconservatives more than just an explanation for Jewish unease. He saw them as a way into the hearts and minds—and the pocketbooks—of America's increasingly affluent and increasingly insecure Jewish community.

In the popular mind, the New Jews of 1967—the Zionists, the Orthodox, and the neoconservatives—quickly came to be identified as the leadership of the American Jewish community. Their defiance was so strident, and their anger so intense, that the rest of the Jewish community respectfully stood back and let the New Jews take the lead. The minority was permitted to speak for the mass and became the dominant voice of Jewish politics.

In this new mood, the cause of Jewish advocacy underwent a fundamental tranformation of values. The world after 1967 was regarded as a hostile place, divided between the Jews' friends and their enemies. The values that for so long had characterized American Judaism—equality, tolerance, and social justice—became suspect in New Jewish leadership circles. A new set of basic values came to replace them: loyalty to the Jewish people, commitment to its survival, and hostility toward its enemies.

The Jews who rose to the leadership of the Jewish community after 1967 were those who most embodied these new values. Jews now expected to be represented, not by those who best expressed their beliefs and aspirations, but by those who seemed to them to be "most Jewish": most loyal to the Jewish people and its traditions, or most hostile to its enemies.

CHAPTER 7

"Let My People Go!":
How the Jews Won the Cold War

T HE IDEA that the organized American Jewish community should step onto the world stage and flex its muscles as a power in international diplomacy was first raised formally on Sunday, September 25, 1972, during a meeting at the B'nai B'rith building in Washington, D.C.

The National Conference on Soviet Jewry (NCSJ) had convened its executive board that afternoon in an emergency session to consider the latest Kremlin assault on Jewish dignity. Six weeks earlier, responding to its snowballing Jewish exodus—Jews were leaving at a rate of over thirty thousand per year—the Soviet government had imposed a "diploma tax" on would-be emigrants. From now on, anyone wishing to leave the Soviet Union would first have to repay the state in full for his or her higher education. The tax came to more than $12,000 for a bachelor's degree and $20,000 for a Ph.D.

To American Jewish analysts, the new Soviet law looked like a naked ransom demand. The NCSJ was meeting to prepare the Jewish community's response. About 125 delegates were there, representing most of the three dozen national Jewish organizations and one hundred-odd local Jewish federations that formed the Soviet Jewry conference.

The delegates arrived in a fighting mood. Anger over Soviet anti-Semitism had been building in their communities for several years, and this latest Soviet escalation demanded a forceful reply. Most expected to hear some tough speeches, backed up by a unanimous resolution and some lobbying on Capitol Hill before they went home the next day. A strong congressional resolution seemed likely to follow, along with a nationwide grassroots campaign of demonstrations, letters, and petitions. Few attendees doubted that some fringe groups would respond violently.

What actually happened surprised almost everyone. A few hours after the meeting opened, NCSJ staff director Jerry Goodman received an urgent phone call from Richard Perle, an aide to Democratic Senator Henry Jackson of Washington State. Perle wanted to know whether his boss could come over and address the board meeting. Goodman did not know much about Jackson, but he knew that Perle was involved with some other Capitol Hill staffers in a quiet effort to draft a law linking U.S.-Soviet trade relations with Jewish emigration rights. The idea was controversial, and unlikely to pass, but Goodman thought that it would not hurt to have the board discuss the principle. After consulting with his own boss, NCSJ president Richard Maass, Goodman told Perle that the board would find time for the senator.

Jackson came over at once, armed with a fully prepared draft of a bill, which he read to the assembly. The measure was framed as an amendment to the proposed East-West Trade Reform Act, a key element in Richard Nixon's U.S.-Soviet detente policy. Among other things, the Nixon trade bill granted Moscow most-favored-nation status, the low-tariff preference normally given to America's trading partners but denied to most Communist states. Jackson's amendment would deny the trade benefit to any "non-market" (meaning Communist) country that prevented its citizens from emigrating.

Jackson told the NCSJ delegates that he seriously intended to see his measure through Congress, but he needed the backing of the Jewish community. This was not about politics, he added, joking about the lack of Jewish voters in his home state; it was a simple matter of right and wrong. A dour Lutheran of Norwegian ancestry, Jackson was one of the most unbending anti-Communists on Capitol Hill, though his domestic views were quite liberal. If the Soviets wanted U.S. help in resuscitating their economy, he wanted to make them pay in the coin of human rights. His was also a personal cause, Jackson added. As a young soldier during the Second World War, he had met Jewish death-camp survivors, "and I vowed I would do whatever I could to make sure this could never again happen to these people."

The NCSJ board debated the Jackson amendment late into the night. Repeated references were made to the failure of American Jews during the Second World War to save their European brethren from the Nazi ovens. Jackson's bill seemed an opportunity to avoid repeating the same mistake. It was a forceful measure, stronger than any weapon that the Jewish community now possessed. Already, impatience with the Soviets was fueling militant groups within the community, which were challenging the NCSJ's moderate, mainstream leadership. Here and there, some were turning to violence: just last January, a bombing by the radical Jewish Defense League had killed a secretary in the office of New York impresario Sol Hurok, a Jew who booked visiting Soviet artists. The growing extremism at the fringes worried the NCSJ leadership. It also put pressure on them to show their constituents some real action.

On the other hand, the Jackson amendment seemed highly unlikely to pass Congress, and the attempt could be costly politically. It might threaten some of the concessions wrung from the Soviets in the past year, including the modest but growing legal emigration rate. It was certain to anger the Nixon administration, which was proving to be more pro-Israel than any previous administration. Insulting the White House could hurt Israel, and that prospect made the Israeli foreign ministry extremely unhappy.

In the end, a divided NCSJ voted to break with the Israeli embassy and the advice of experienced community leaders, and endorsed the Jackson amendment. This would prove to be a decisive turning point, not only for the NCSJ and the Soviet Jewry movement, but for American Jewish politics in general.

The campaign for the Jackson amendment was the first of a series of American Jewish legislative initiatives that transformed the Jewish lobby into a Washington powerhouse during the 1970s.

The National Conference on Soviet Jewry began as an Israeli initiative in the early 1960s. Israel had been maintaining clandestine ties with Russia's "Jews of silence" since the early 1950s, via a secret unit run out of the Israeli prime minister's office. The unit, known as the Liaison Bureau, worked through Israeli diplomatic missions to supply Russian Jews with Bibles and prayer books, Hebrew calendars, textbooks, and simple contact with other Jews. In the late 1950s, operating through a diplomat in Israel's New York consulate, the Liaison Bureau began recruiting American Jews to help publicize the plight of Jews behind the Iron Curtain.

In early 1962, the Liaison Bureau stepped up its activities in America under the polished, urbane lawyer-diplomat Meir Rosenne. Rosenne enlisted the cooperation of the two Jewish members of President Kennedy's cabinet, Labor Secretary Arthur J. Goldberg and Health, Education, and Welfare Secretary Abraham Ribicoff. Then, setting up shop in New York City, he began working with Presidents Conference director Yehuda Hellman to develop a broad strategy to mobilize the American Jewish public. The Israeli role was kept strictly confidential; even the existence of the Liaison Bureau remained a state secret until well into the 1990s.

Rosenne and Hellman organized a protest rally in New York in 1963, then a two-day conference in Washington, D.C. in 1964. The Washington conference drew hundreds of delegates representing dozens of Jewish organizations from across the country. It was chaired by the president of the American Jewish Committee, famed civil rights attorney Morris B. Abram. The keynote speaker was Arthur Goldberg, now a Supreme Court justice.

When the conference was over, the delegates voted not to adjourn, but to constitute themselves as a permanent body. The American Jewish Conference on Soviet Jewry was set up as a coalition of national Jewish organizations, essentially a shadow Presidents Conference, but without a staff. The body was run from the offices of its member groups on a six-month rotation, beginning with the American Jewish Committee, then moving to the American Zionist Youth Foundation (an arm of the World Zionist Organization). Six months later, it moved to the National Community Relations Advisory Council, where its affairs were taken on by NCRAC's international-affairs specialist, Abraham Bayer.

Bayer was a passionate, excitable activist with boundless energy and a huge grassroots network of local contacts at his disposal. The operation stayed in Bayer's office for a full year, and then another. By 1970, the other national organizations had begun to cool toward the Soviet Jewry conference, viewing it as a NCRAC project. Only perpetual nagging from the Presidents Conference and the Liaison Bureau kept the other partners in the coalition.

In 1971, the American Jewish Conference on Soviet Jewry voted to move out of NCRAC headquarters and set up its own office. The NCRAC experience had proved the value of working through local Jewish community-relations councils, but it was also undermining the conference's status as a project of the entire community. Under the watchful eye of the Liaison Bureau's Washington agent, Nehemia Levanon, the conference was now renamed and reorganized. Its governing board tripled as delegates from the local Jewish councils and federations joined heads of the national organizations. A staff director was hired, Jerry Goodman, a young foreign-policy expert from the American Jewish Committee staff and a protégé of Levanon's. At Goodman's insistence, Richard Maass, a wealthy New York businessman and president of the American Jewish Committee, agreed to become chairman.

Tied to Israel, umbilically linked to the Presidents Conference and the federations—indeed, with a board controlled by those very organizations— the National Conference on Soviet Jewry was in no position to adopt its own independent policies. But that is just what it did on September 26, 1972, when the executive board voted to endorse the Jackson amendment.

The Jackson amendment was not originally the senator's idea. The concept was cooked up across Capitol Hill in the office of Representative Bertram Podell, a brash, wisecracking two-term Jewish Democrat from Brooklyn. Working on a suggestion from a student intern in his office, Podell drew up the first version of the Soviet trade-cutoff bill in the early summer of 1972. He showed his draft to lobbyist I. L. Kenen, the canny director of the American Israel Public Affairs Committee. Kenen, impressed, urged Podell to let him find a more prestigious sponsor for the measure, to improve its slim chances of passage. Podell agreed, and Kenen brought the draft to Richard Perle, Henry Jackson's chief of staff.

"And with that," one participant recalls, "Bert Podell promptly fell out of the history books." It didn't help that Podell fell out of Congress in 1974, indicted on an influence-peddling scheme that he still insists was a Nixon dirty trick.

Richard Perle was a brilliant, brooding defense expert with strongly neo-conservative leanings. His interest in Soviet Jews had been piqued during a recent trip to Israel arranged for him by Nehemia Levanon. Since then, he had drawn close to another Senate aide who shared many of his views, Morris Amitay, a former foreign-service officer, now chief of staff to Democratic Senator Abraham Ribicoff of Connecticut.

When the Soviet diploma tax was announced in August 1972, Perle and Amitay convened a group of friendly Senate staffers in the Old Senate Office Building to discuss the Podell amendment idea. Several of the Senate's top Democrats were represented, as well as one Republican: New York's Jacob Javits, a four-term liberal with a statesmanlike image, a long record of Jewish loyalty, and a keen eye for headlines. Also invited were AIPAC's Kenen and the Anti-Defamation League's Washington representative, David Brody. Jerry Goodman and Yehuda Hellman flew down from New York.

The meeting ended inconclusively. Goodman would recall leaving with the feeling that nothing much would come of it. A few weeks later, however, Senator Javits raised the idea in a speech before a Soviet Jewry protest rally in Manhattan's Garment District. The notion swept the crowd and spread rapidly by word of mouth among New York Jewish activists. "The minute Javits spoke, everyone knew something was going on," remembers rally organizer Malcolm Hoenlein, then director of the Greater New York Conference on Soviet Jewry.

In Washington, meanwhile, Perle and Amitay were working tirelessly. By the time the NCSJ gave its hesitant endorsement in late September, they already had lined up substantial support among Senate Democrats. A short time later, they found a House sponsor, Representative Charles Vanik, a Cleveland Democrat on the powerful Ways and Means Committee. A son of Czech immigrants, Vanik was a longtime battler for human rights in the Eastern bloc. His chief of staff, Mark Talisman, was a Jew with many ties to the Cleveland community. He was also a masterful legislative tactician.

In early October, Jackson met privately with Nixon at the White House to discuss the amendment. Nixon agreed to let Republican senators support it, in return for Jackson's pledge not to make it a partisan issue during the upcoming presidential election. The election pitted the pro-detente Nixon against the even more dovish George McGovern. It was a time of nationwide Vietnam fatigue. No one expected Jackson to succeed in such a blatant revival of the Cold War. Nixon and his aides, for their part, considered the whole project a bid by Jackson for early Jewish support in the 1976 presidential sweepstakes.

Within weeks, things were looking surprisingly different. Perle and Amitay had managed to round up 72 cosponsors in the Senate. In the House, Talisman was not far behind; by February, he had found 258 cosponsors. The three congressional aides identified wavering lawmakers, then worked with Goodman, Kenen, and Brody to find Jewish constituents who could call or visit them at home.

"One analysis showed that one third of those who signed on did so because they were importuned to do it," said Talisman. "One third were people close to organized labor, who were anti-Soviet no matter what. The other third just signed on spontaneously when we asked them to."

The Jackson-Vanik onslaught set off alarm bells at the White House. Nixon's program for detente was a complex, delicate system of interlocking deals, worked out over years of painful negotiations. It combined U.S. trade concessions with Soviet help in ending the Vietnam war, plus mutual arms reductions to reduce the threat of nuclear war for all sides. The Jackson-Vanik bill threatened to wreck the whole thing. Now began two years of tortuous, four-way bargaining to salvage detente, involving the White House, the Kremlin, Senator Jackson, and the American Jewish community leadership.

Nixon's initial strategy was to separate Jackson from his Jewish supporters. Although the NCSJ had endorsed the amendment, the Presidents Conference hadn't signed on. Nixon wanted to head that off. His point man was his national security adviser, Henry Kissinger. Besides being the administration's lead negotiator with the Russians, Kissinger's credentials—a Jewish immigrant who had lost most of his family to the Nazis—made him an impeccable choice to face the frightened Jewish leaders and ask them to lower their guard.

Nor did it hurt Nixon's cause that the two most senior leaders of the organized Jewish community were top Republican donors: Jacob Stein, chairman of the Presidents Conference, and Max Fisher, president of the Council of Jewish Federations.

Max Fisher was one of the wealthiest men in America and a beloved figure in Jewish leadership circles. Born in 1908 to a grocer in small-town Ohio, he had moved to Detroit after college and made a fortune on the spot oil market. He was a plainspoken, unreflective man, a college football player and lifelong Republican with a deep loyalty to his fellow Jews but not a shred of traditional Jewish learning. His willingness to write checks, and to squeeze them from friends, was legendary. That made him a central player in the world of federated Jewish philanthropy.

Fisher's generosity also made him a key GOP player. He stepped on the national stage as finance chairman of Michigan Governor George Romney's 1968 presidential race. When Romney lost to Richard Nixon, Fisher signed on with him. Over the next four years, Fisher became a White House regular, filling the Jewish-adviser role once played by Democratic donors like Abe Feinberg and Arthur Krim.

Fisher played his role with a difference, however. Unlike Jewish pleaders before him, Fisher always insisted that he did not speak for himself but for the American Jewish community and its elected leadership. Perhaps his unfamiliarity with Jewish community life made him overestimate the importance of Jewish organizations. Whatever the reason, his perception became reality.

Under the Nixon administration, the Presidents Conference became what it had always aspired to be: the official voice of American Jewry.

Jack Stein, chairman of the conference, was a decade younger than Fisher. Raised in Brooklyn, he had made his money developing shopping centers on New York's Long Island. He was introduced to Republican politics in 1960 by Fisher, and was often seen as his protégé. The two men could not have been more different. Stein, slight and balding, was a learned, religious Jew. He had entered the Presidents Conference not by writing checks but by winning the presidency of the United Synagogue of America, the congregational union of Conservative Judaism. Unlike Fisher, Stein drew his Republicanism, he says, from "personal relationships rather than philosophical or ideological relationships."

Kissinger approached Fisher and Stein with a few Soviet concessions already in hand: an end to the hated diploma tax and a hint that exit visas might soon rise to thirty-five thousand per year. Kissinger argued that more good could be obtained by keeping lines open to the Soviets than by closing them. Fisher was impressed. But Stein agonized, torn between a desire for results and a fear of selling out. In the end he agreed, reluctantly, to take Kissinger's message to the Presidents Conference.

"I take you back to a description by Maimonides of a leader as being an evil person," Stein says. "When you're taking a decision where only good is involved, you're not a leader. A leader makes decisions that balance opposing goods, or good and evil. And so he must participate in evil."

In April 1973, the Presidents Conference convened in New York for its much delayed vote on Jackson-Vanik. It was a long, ugly, acrimonious session, peppered with shouting and accusations of treason. Fisher, the revered senior statesman, remained largely above the fray, while "Jack Stein really got it. It got very personal," a participant recollects. In the end, the conference voted overwhelmingly to endorse the amendment.

Over the next two months, Kissinger arranged for Stein and Fisher to meet with top Soviet leaders, including Ambassador Anatoly Dobrynin, Foreign Minister Andrei Gromyko, and finally Communist Party boss Leonid Brezhnev. Their talks, and Kissinger's, produced a contradictory series of Soviet declarations, now hinting at forty thousand exit visas per year, now insisting that no restrictions existed in the first place, now protesting U.S. interference in Soviet domestic policy. Through it all, Kissinger continued pushing Jackson and the NCSJ to drop the amendment. Bitterness between Kissinger and the Jackson circle was becoming intensely personal.

In October 1973, with Nixon paralyzed by Watergate and Kissinger now secretary of state and chief steward of U.S. foreign policy, war broke out in the Middle East. Kissinger made one last attempt to head off the Jackson-Vanik amendment. During the third and most critical week of the Yom Kippur War, he met with Stein, Fisher, and Richard Maass. He argued that Moscow's help was needed to end the Middle East crisis and bring about a postwar peace. Stein and Fisher agreed to ask Jackson once more to back down. Jackson refused, retorting that Kissinger was "using you." Stein now decided to quit the fight, though Fisher continued to oppose the amendment.

For several more weeks, the besieged Nixon fought alone, begging lawmakers not to complicate U.S.-Soviet detente. But it was too late. On December 13, 1973, the House of Representatives approved the Jackson-Vanik amendment by an overwhelming vote of 388 to 44.

Seeing that the game was up, Kissinger switched his tactics from fighting Jackson to joining him. Over the next year, as Nixon sank ever deeper in the Watergate morass, Kissinger convinced the Soviets that Jewish emigration was a necessary price for winning the coveted trade benefits. At the same time, he convinced Jackson to accept a presidential waiver, giving the Soviets temporary trade benefits one year at a time, as long as they met a benchmark of minimum emigration. Jackson reluctantly agreed. He was no longer operating alone, but as part of a three-man negotiating team that included the Senate's two Jewish members, Ribicoff and Javits. Realism was the order of the day on all sides.

Finding a benchmark proved harder than Kissinger expected, however. The Soviets at first offered thirty-five thousand exit visas per year, then forty thousand. The senators started at one hundred thousand, but agreed to accept seventy-five thousand.

On August 9, 1974, Richard Nixon resigned. He was succeeded by his vice president, former Representative Gerald Ford of Michigan, who promised to govern in a "marriage" with Congress. Ambassador Dobrynin panicked, fearing that a strengthened Congress would kill the trade bill altogether. He cut short a vacation and rushed back to Washington to meet with Ford. The president quickly called in Javits and Ribicoff, and final agreement was reached on a sixty thousand–visa benchmark. After several more weeks of details, the deal was formalized. In an October 18 letter to Jackson, Kissinger outlined Soviet "assurances" on emigration. Soviet Jewish freedom was now a formal element of American foreign policy, and an integral part of the fabric of U.S.-Soviet detente.

Within days, the historic deal inexplicably fell apart. On October 26, Gromyko wrote to Kissinger protesting the use of the word "assurances." The Kremlin was offering no more than "elucidations" of its plans, he insisted. In any case, he added ominously, Moscow expected exit requests to decline in the future.

Kissinger kept the Gromyko letter secret from Congress, apparently hoping that he could fix things before the deal exploded. On December 13, the Senate passed the amended Trade Reform Act by 77 votes to 4. But five days later, the Soviets made their defection public. Tass, the government news agency, reported on December 18 that "leading circles" in Moscow considered it "unacceptable" to link trade with Soviet "internal affairs." Moscow had backed out of the deal. Emigration soon plummeted, and Soviet harassment of Jewish activists soared.

What caused the Kissinger-Jackson agreement to unravel? Kissinger reportedly blamed Richard Perle and Morris Amitay for embarrassing the Soviets by releasing to the press his October 18 letter to Jackson, thus flouting the Soviets' desire to keep the deal low-key. But most Jewish accounts of the collapse focus on a secondary incident: the passage in September of an unrelated piece of legislation that rendered Jackson-Vanik's trade benefits virtually worthless to the Soviets.

It came in a Senate amendment to a routine bill that renewed funding for the U.S. Export-Import Bank. The amendment, sponsored by Democrat Adlai Stevenson III of Illinois, limited Soviet import credits to $300 million over a five-year period—barely one fourth of what they were already getting, even without most-favored-nation status. Stevenson's amendment appeared so quietly and passed so quickly that neither Kissinger nor the Jewish organizations noticed it until it was law. Stevenson reportedly got the idea from organized labor supporters in Illinois. He never discussed it with Jewish lobbyists or Jackson-Vanik strategists on Capitol Hill.

"It just got sprung on us from nowhere," says Pete Lakeland, a former Javits aide. "It almost guaranteed that the Russians would lose interest in following through on the Jackson amendment. There was supposed to be not only a stick but also a carrot. The possibility of a much higher credit had been dangled. The Soviets were really hurting at the time in terms of economics and foreign exchange. There appeared to be a powerful group in the Soviet Union that was willing to lay off [of] the Jews, at least pragmatically. The Stevenson amendment really drove the nail into any possibility that the Soviets would consider a deal on the Jackson amendment."

Why wasn't Stevenson pressured to withdraw his amendment during the two months between its Senate adoption in September and its final passage into law in December? The question evokes stammering on all sides. "Kissinger should have been monitoring it," says Jerry Goodman. "He was just not on top of it. We were relying on the administration to watch these things."

As for the Jewish leadership, Goodman adds, "we felt we couldn't oppose it openly. We would have been seen as apologists."

Since the passage of the Jackson-Vanik amendment in 1974, Jewish activists in America and the Soviet Union alike have never stopped hailing it as the weapon that turned the tide in the freedom struggle of Soviet Jews. The truth is very nearly the opposite.

The amendment had an electrifying effect on the morale of Jewish activists inside the Soviet Union. It showed them they were not alone, that they had powerful friends halfway around the globe. But in its intended result, it backfired: emigration went down, not up.

Once the Soviets scrapped their deal with Kissinger, they never made any attempt to meet the emigration benchmark and win most-favored-nation rights. In Washington, no one tried to repeal the Stevenson amendment, which might have made a Jackson waiver more enticing to the Soviets. The two laws remained on the books throughout the remainder of the U.S.-Soviet Cold War, symbols of ideological purity turned brittle. They constituted an impossible hurdle to trade between the two superpowers.

Soviet Jewish emigration continued to rise and fall over the years, but solely as a matter of Soviet whim, reflecting Kremlin perceptions of U.S.-Soviet relations. Western bargaining power had been eliminated.

Was the entire exercise a mistake, then? Some observers insist that it was. "History has proven I was probably right when I opposed Jackson-Vanik," says Max Fisher. "Nixon was trying to work it out by personal diplomacy. Kissinger thought he could get out thirty or forty thousand a year if they'd worked that angle. When you think of it over twenty years, you could have gotten out quite a number of Jews."

But while the amendment may have done little to improve the lot of Jews in the Soviet Union, it brought about a sea change in the status of Jews in America. Jewish activists had taken on the Nixon administration and the Kremlin and won. Jews had proven to the world and to themselves that they could stand up and fight for themselves. The stain of Holocaust abandonment had finally been removed.

There was more than a little bit of self-delusion here, of course. The Jewish community had not led the struggle for the Jackson-Vanik amendment; it had been dragged into it, warming to the fight only gradually. Still, by the end, the amendment had to be considered a Jewish victory, if only because others saw it that way and perception became reality. Even if just one third of the lawmakers who voted in favor were responding directly to Jewish "importuning," as Talisman argues, many more responded to the continual agitation coming from the Jewish community. From op-ed articles to street demonstrations and violent protest, American Jews were making it clear to the broader public through the 1970s that Soviet Jewish freedom was a matter of deep concern to them. The country listened.

The world listened, too, even if the Soviet Union did not. "Jackson-Vanik is one of the best examples in legislative history of perception becoming reality," says Talisman. "It became a benchmark against which other countries had to measure themselves. The Czechs, the Hungarians, the Romanians—they all looked at Jackson-Vanik and realized they'd better improve their behavior. They all met with us over the next decade." As a result, the organized American Jewish community gained enormous bargaining power across the globe.

Perception became reality in the changed posture of Jewish political activity at home. The Jewish community saw that it could change laws, and in so doing change history. Attention and money shifted from New York to

Washington. The national headquarters of the main Jewish organizations remained in New York, still American Jewry's population center, but their Washington offices became major power centers.

The Jewish community's influence in Washington, particularly in Congress, had been a given in American politics for decades. Congress had taken numerous actions over the years to please Jewish voters and donors, from anti-czarist protest resolutions at the turn of the century to hearings on Jewish statehood after the Second World War. But with rare exceptions, they were all noise. Though Congress was often willing to say things that pleased Jews, it was rarely willing to take action, and almost never willing to challenge the White House. The American Jewish community before 1974 was hardly the all-powerful lobby imagined by politicians in London and Cairo. It was more like a gorilla in a cage: always able to get attention and a few sweets when it roared and rattled the bars, but helpless to control the broader flow of events outside.

The Jackson-Vanik amendment shattered that status quo. With a non-Jewish lawmaker leading the charge—backed up by scores of Jewish legislative aides, Jewish strategists, and Jewish community leaders around the country pressuring their own lawmakers to fall in line—Congress had rolled over administration resistance and passed a proactive law that changed the structure of U.S.-Soviet relations. Whether or not the legislation helped its intended beneficiaries, the Jews of Russia, it sent an unmistakable message around the world that the Jews of America were not to be trifled with.

Jackson-Vanik changed the status of the Jewish community in another, more subtle way. Jews became the poster children of a renewed Cold War. The credibility of American anti-Communism, crippled by the McCarthy excesses of the 1950s, had been utterly decimated by the Vietnam debacle. Jackson-Vanik gave it new life by giving it a new moral argument. The Jewish lobby, for years a central element in coalitions of the liberal left, now became an important factor on the national-security–minded right. In fact, the Jewish community now assumed a crucial role in Washington: it was one of the only major players with close ties to both the left and the right. Suddenly the Jews were power brokers.

Over the next decade, the Jewish community used its new power repeatedly, in a lightning series of legislative initiatives. Laws were passed to attack the Arab boycott of Israel, to regularize the entry of Soviet Jewish refugees to the United States, to hunt down Nazi war criminals admitted as displaced persons in the early 1950s. Each victory was easier than the last, as the organizations learned to cooperate.

One of the first people to recognize the Jews' new clout was Walter Stern, a New York investment manager active in several Jewish organizations. During the oil crisis that followed the Yom Kippur War, Stern brought together a group of like-minded Jewish business leaders to discuss the danger of Arab economic warfare and consider Jewish responses. As the group gelled, representatives were brought in from the Big Three defense agencies, ADL and the two AJCs. "I was on the boards of several groups, but since I was a lay person instead of staff, I had no loyalty to any one of them," Stern says. "And I wanted them to cooperate."

Staffing the project was Jess Hordes, a recent Johns Hopkins graduate with a Ph.D. in international relations. He set up shop in a borrowed office at AIPAC headquarters in Washington, and began monitoring the flow of petrodollars into the American economy. His salary was paid from a fund put together by the Big Three.

Hordes's initial assignment was to look for Arab investments entering the United States in the form of recycled petrodollars. "The initial fear was that the Arabs would try and buy up sensitive industries," Hordes says. "Within a year it became clear they were not going to buy anything like Chrysler. There were laws in place, and there were sensitivities they did not want to ruffle. They were buying more standard portfolios. On the other hand, they were being much more clever and hiring influential lawyers and lobbyists, [former Kennedy aide] Fred Dutton and others, Capitol Hill and State Department types who had good access."

It soon became evident that "one of the major impacts of the oil price increase and the petrodollar flow was the impact on American trade with Israel—and the more generally chilling effect of the Arab boycott," Hordes recalls. The problem was "the four-fold increase in the price of oil, which had a depressing effect on Western economies. Suddenly you had Arab economies appearing as an area where business slack could be picked up." In order to break into those markets, American companies began complying in growing numbers with the Arab economic boycott of Israel.

The boycott had been imposed by the Arab League in 1946. It was a complex operation designed to quarantine and cripple the Jewish state. It not only banned direct Arab-Israeli business dealings, but also barred firms that did business with Israel from doing business in Arab countries. It even banned products with parts and components made by boycotted firms. Firms seeking to do business in Arab countries had to file papers with the Arab Boycott Office in Damascus, certifying that their firm and its products were Israel-free. Companies applying to do contract work in the Middle East—construction, management, consulting—were required to list their employees' religions, so Jews could be kept out.

AIPAC had tried a few times during the 1950s and 1960s to get legislation through Congress outlawing boycott compliance by U.S. firms. The White House consistently opposed it, arguing that it would only anger the Arabs, slow down Middle East peace efforts, and lose business for American firms. One bill actually passed Congress in 1965, but was watered down under threat of a Lyndon Johnson veto. The final version merely required firms to report to the Commerce Department whenever they complied with the boycott. President Johnson feared that anything stronger might backfire against the American embargoes of Cuba, China, North Vietnam, and North Korea. Chastened, Israel and its Washington lobbyists backed away.

The New York–based Jewish defense agencies were not so shy. They saw the boycott as a civil rights issue because it involved discrimination against American Jews. Through NCRAC, they had been protesting the boycott since the mid-1950s. After the Six-Day War, their agitation intensified. The American Jewish Congress set up a special department to fight the boycott, headed by retiring executive director Will Maslow. Coca-Cola, which refused to market its products in Israel, found itself facing a nationwide Jewish protest campaign, featuring mass Coke-spilling at street rallies. ADL director Ben Epstein, dubbing anti-Zionism a "new anti-Semitism," sent a secret agent to penetrate Coke's European operations.

Israeli reactions to the protests ranged from apathetic to hostile. The Israeli finance ministry kept figures on the boycott's impact on the Israeli economy, but the foreign ministry viewed the issue as a sideshow, minor compared with the military threat to Israel's existence. Israeli leaders also resented the American Jews' focus on the boycott's civil rights dimension, which deflected attention from the real victim, Israel. In Washington, Ambassador Eban and his successor, Avraham Harman, repeatedly pressed the defense agencies to back away. Once, when the ADL mounted a boycott of Toyota for refusing to trade with Israel, Israeli finance minister Pinhas Sapir intervened and got the boycott cancelled. Confronted later by ADL officials, Sapir explained that a Toyota distributor in Chicago had threatened to withhold his $75,000-a-year UJA gift.

In 1974, as public furor raged over the Arab oil embargo, the Senate held public hearings on the Arab boycott and its impact on America. Stern's group worked closely with the lawmakers, feeding them information and witnesses. Revelations were shocking: Saudi blacklists of U.S. corporations; U.S. government funds invested in firms that boycotted Jewish-owned banks; and, most controversial of all, a secret policy by the Army Corps of Engineers to bar Jews from its multibillion-dollar Middle East construction projects. Each new revelation received extensive coverage in the news media, thanks to a few friendly editors at the *Wall Street Journal* and the *New York Times*.

In early 1975, Stern's group decided to push for a law outlawing U.S. business compliance with the boycott. In March, Representative Jonathan Bingham, a Bronx Democrat, introduced a strict antiboycott bill that his staff had drawn up with Jess Hordes. A rival measure, basically stiffening the 1965 reporting rule, was introduced in the Senate by Adlai Stevenson.

Throughout 1975, a public-relations war waged in the press, the airwaves, and the halls of Congress, pitting the Jewish agencies against the Ford administration, Arab lobbyists, and the business community. The bill's opponents were in an unenviable position: in the name of pragmatism and free trade, they seemed to be defending foreign powers that discriminated against Americans. Moreover, those foreign powers were among the most disliked groups in the American mind at the time.

And so big business kept a low profile, leaving the dirty work of fighting the bill to President Gerald Ford, Treasury Secretary William Simon, and Secretary of State Henry Kissinger. "We believe that peace in the Middle East is the only ultimate answer," said Simon, oddly echoing the Israeli foreign ministry's position.

In mid-1976, the House asked the Commerce Department for boycott statements filed by American firms under the 1965 reporting law. Commerce refused to release the information. The ADL then sued Commerce Secretary Rogers Morton. When the House finally got the Commerce documents in July, it found that boycotted-related U.S. trade was far more extensive than the administration had said: $4.5 billion rather than $10 million. In late September, the Bingham amendment passed the House by an overwhelming vote of 318 to 63. The Senate passed Stevenson's measure shortly afterward, 65 to 13.

That December, Minneapolis manufacturer and chairman of the ADL's lay board, Burton Joseph, was approached by Irving Shapiro, a childhood friend who was now chairman of E. I. Du Pont. Shapiro's rise to the top of Du Pont a few months earlier had been a minor earthquake; Jews were almost never named to head major American corporations, outside of a few traditionally Jewish fields like retailing and filmmaking. The *New York Times* had reported Shapiro's appointment in a front-page article in its business section. Shapiro was not just Jewish, but a "Jewish Jew"—a proudly identified, synagogue-going Jew who had not changed his name.

Shapiro told Joseph he wanted to find a compromise that could satisfy the Jewish community without damaging American business. He was speaking for the entire business community; besides heading Du Pont he chaired the Business Roundtable, a lobbying group representing 170 of the nation's biggest corporations. Joseph agreed to set up a meeting between the Roundtable and the Jewish defense agencies in late January.

When the two sides came together, the political atmosphere had changed dramatically. Gerald Ford had lost the White House to Jimmy Carter, the governor of Georgia. Carter had won the Democratic nomination by running as an outsider, unlinked to the traditional big-city, big-labor Democratic machines. Hoping to win over the suspicious Democratic voters (and donors) of the urban, liberal, and very tradition-minded Jewish community, Carter took on the Arab boycott during a televised debate, promising to work for passage of antiboycott legislation. The promise had been inserted in his briefing notes by a Jewish campaign aide, Atlanta attorney Stuart Eizenstat.

In January, talks began between the Big Three and the Business Roundtable. A compromise was found that outlawed active boycott compliance by U.S. firms, but made an exception when a firm had been passively chosen by an Arab partner in a "unilateral selection." The compromise quickly fell apart, however; while they were talking, a stricter bill was introduced in the House by Representative Benjamin Rosenthal, a Jewish Democrat from Queens, using language his staff had drawn up with Jess Hordes. As Roundtable members huffed about betrayal, the administration stepped in—in the person of Stuart Eizenstat, now White House domestic affairs chief. He insisted that the sides get back together.

With the White House looking on impatiently, a formal negotiating committee was put together. The Business Roundtable was represented by a group of lawyers headed by Citibank's Hans Angermueller. The Jewish community was represented by three Washington lawyers who were active lay members of the Big Three: Max Kampelman for the ADL, Alfred Moses for the American Jewish Committee, and Paul Berger for the American Jewish Congress. Jess Hordes provided staff support. Eizenstat oversaw the talks from the White House, to keep them moving. By May, they had found a new compromise text. It was introduced in the Senate by Pennsylvania Republican John Heinz and passed easily.

The passage of the antiboycott bill in May 1977 completed the process begun by Senator Henry Jackson five years earlier. The organized Jewish community had created a law from beginning to end. It had identified a problem, placed it in the public eye, created legislation, and moved it into law, overcoming the objections of the administration and the business community. The Jewish organizations had worked together more or less seamlessly, securing the cooperation of friendly Jews in the news media, business, the administration, and Congress. The result was a major change in U.S. policy.

"It's not uncommon in legislation generally for lobbying groups to stick in some language or formulation that gets incorporated in a larger bill," says Hordes, who went on to become director of the ADL's Washington office. "What was particular about this case, as against the experience of Jewish lobbyists like Kenen in the 1960s, was the level of the players and the central role the Jewish community played in creating this legislation."

After winding up the Jackson-Vanik campaign, Mark Talisman went to work as Washington representative of the Council of Jewish Federations. His first job was to deal with the happy results of a decade of Soviet Jewry protest: the stream of Jewish refugees who were leaving the Soviet Union and landing on the shores of the United States, where they threw themselves on the mercy of the organized Jewish community.

The first Soviet Jewry activists in the 1960s hardly intended their work to result in Jewish immigration to the United States. The movement was from the start a Zionist enterprise, conceived by Israelis and driven by activists who wanted the world's second-largest Jewish community "repatriated"— brought en masse "back" to Israel, their ancestral homeland. Nonetheless, from the moment the Soviets began permitting large-scale emigration after the Six-Day War, a percentage headed for America instead. That percentage grew steadily over time: from 19 percent in 1974 to 37 percent in 1975, almost 50 percent in 1976, and 65 percent in 1979 (Table 3).

In actual numbers, the flow of refugees to America was considerable. Despite the failure of the Kissinger-Jackson agreement and continuing Soviet harassment of Jewish activists, thousands were being let out. The Kremlin refused to discuss it, but the rise and fall of exit permits seemed closely related to Soviet optimism over ties with Washington: down after the collapse of the Jackson deal, slowly back up as detente warmed again during the Ford and Carter administrations, then down again after the Soviet invasion of Afghanistan and the subsequent freeze in U.S.-Soviet relations. During the Reagan years, emigration plummeted. It bottomed out at 896 in 1984, just before Mikhail Gorbachev rose to power.

TABLE 3: SOVIET JEWISH EMIGRATION, 1974–1980

Year	Emigration total	% to U.S.
1974	20,628	19%
1975	13,221	37%
1976	14,261	49%
1977	16,736	50%
1978	28,864	58%
1979	51,320	65%
1980	21,471	81%

Source: National Conference on Soviet Jewry.

By the mid-1970s, Soviet Jewish refugees were heading for America at a rate approaching ten thousand per year. Nearly all arrived destitute. They posed a complex challenge for the Jewish community: first getting them U.S. visas, then finding homes and jobs and teaching them English. Newcomers needed help navigating the unknown world of capitalism, from opening a checking account to writing a resume. They needed help, too, entering the bewildering world of Judaism, alien to them after three generations of enforced atheism. All told, it was a huge, expensive undertaking. Just bringing the émigrés across Europe, through the border bureaucracy, and into America, cost the United Jewish Appeal thousands of dollars per person. Once the refugees were here, the expense fell on the local Jewish federations in the half-dozen cities where nearly all the newcomers chose to settle: New York, Chicago, Miami, Boston, San Francisco, and Los Angeles.

To ease the burden, Talisman proposed getting the federal government to match the Jewish community's expenditures. Audacious as it seemed, it was not a hard sell. Congress had already shown overwhelming willingness to throw the power of the United States behind Soviet Jewish freedom. Now it was just a matter of asking the legislature to put its money where its mouth was. Indeed, there was a precedent already in the federal budget. Beginning in 1973, at the initiative of Bronx Democrat Jonathan Bingham, the House had been allocating $25 million per year to the United Israel Appeal, an arm of the UJA, to help underwrite the resettlement of Soviet immigrants in Israel. This was a continuation of that work here in America, the land of freedom.

It did not hurt the measure's prospects that Talisman was at the helm. "Mark initiated it, drafted the legislation and nursed it through Congress," said CJF executive vice president Philip Bernstein, Talisman's boss. "He was very skillful, not only in how legislation was drafted but in the entire process of how it became law. He used to run the Harvard program for newcomers in Congress, to introduce them to the legislative process. So he knew not only the entire process, but all the players."

Working with Stuart Eizenstat, Talisman enlisted the Carter White House to sponsor the bill in the Democratic Congress. On Capitol Hill, the bill's top supporter was Senator Daniel Inouye of Hawaii, the one-armed chairman of the intelligence committee, a leading figure in the Watergate investigation and a passionate devotee of Israel and Judaism (he had sold Israel Bonds as a young man and once considered converting to Judaism). The funding passed.

If winning federal assistance to resettle the refugees once they arrived was easy, getting them into the country in the first place was far trickier. Émigrés left the Soviet Union with visas for Israel, then took a train to Vienna, where they were met by representatives of the Jewish Agency for Israel, an offshoot of the World Zionist Organization. Those who did not want to go to Israel had to "drop out" of the process in Vienna. They then proceeded to the Hebrew Immigrant Aid Society (HIAS), an American agency housed in the offices of the Joint Distribution Committee, down the hall from the Jewish Agency. HIAS helped the would-be immigrants apply for U.S. visas. While they waited, the Joint put them up at a transit camp just outside Vienna.

Whether they received U.S. visas, and how fast, was up to individual

American immigration officers. Standard immigration was regulated by a series of laws that set an annual cap on the number of entrants. Applicants sometimes waited for years. HIAS arranged for most Soviet émigrés to be classified as refugees, putting them outside the normal quota system. Refugees had a special status, defined by a different immigration law, and they came under the responsibility of the State Department's bureau of refugee affairs. But in order to win refugee classification, migrants had to convince an immigration officer that they were actually fleeing from persecution.

Persons leaving a Communist country were normally presumed to be fleeing persecution. Still, officers frequently wanted proof, and refugees could not always provide documents. Many waited for months. The Joint's transit camp began to fill up. Pressure was applied by the White House on the Immigration and Naturalization Service (INS) to speed the process. But there was no way to supervise every INS agent in Europe.

In mid-1979, the Jewish community's refugee problem became a full-blown refugee crisis. The reason was the Islamic revolution in Iran. The rise of the fundamentalist Khomeini regime, with its militantly anti-Zionist rhetoric, spread terror among the eighty thousand Jews in Iran. Most were highly westernized in culture and outlook. Many were middle-class merchants, alarmed at the regime's economic populism. All were considered suspect because of their ties to Israel and the world Jewish community.

Within weeks, escape routes were set up to spirit Iranian Jews across the borders of Turkey and Afghanistan, where they were picked up by the Joint Distribution Committee and taken to Vienna. In Vienna, they ran into the INS bureaucracy. Some officers tended to view the escapees simply as Iranians, potential subversives seeking entry into the United States from a hostile country.

An even stickier problem arose at home in America, where colleges were host to tens of thousands of Iranian students. A few were openly pro-Khomeini. With anti-Iran feelings at fever pitch during the hostage crisis, public pressure ran strong to send all the students home. Several thousand of them were Jews.

To expel all Iranian students regardless of their views might have been unfair, but to send the Jews back to Iran "would have been disastrous," Talisman says.

The Jews were not the only ones at risk. Even greater peril faced

Iranians of the Baha'i faith, a tiny, pacifist offshoot of Islam that the mullahs considered heretical and had marked for persecution.

Talisman turned again to Eizenstat at the White House. The INS was ordered to exempt Jews and Baha'is from the harsh treatment being meted out to Iranians at the borders. Talisman then turned his attention to Congress. His aim was to revise U.S. immigration law, to regularize the admission of refugees.

Working with Eizenstat and New Jersey Representative Peter Rodino, chairman of the House Judiciary Committee and an old friend, Talisman created a system to standardize refugee policy. Talisman's draft bill brought the United States into compliance with international law for the first time by accepting the U.N. definition of a refugee as any person fleeing persecution at home for political, religious, or certain other reasons.

The new law required individuals applying for refugee status to be sponsored in the United States by one of a select group of nonprofit agencies, which would be responsible for their initial housing, medical care, and language training. The federal government would cover a share of the nonprofit agencies' costs. The number of refugees to be admitted each year would be fixed in annual discussions among the State Department, Congress, and the nonprofit agencies.

It was, for all practical purposes, a formalization in law of the informal relationship Talisman had set up to get government help for the Jewish federations resettling Soviet Jews. Now the process was open to any nonprofit agency that wanted to bring refugees into the United States.

The bill sailed through both houses of Congress in 1980. A working group of nonprofit agencies was set up to conduct the annual negotiations with the State Department. It included Lutheran, Catholic, and several smaller churches, along with the International Rescue Committee, a nonsectarian charity established by Albert Einstein and others in the 1930s to rescue Jews from Nazi Germany. Representing the Jewish community was the Hebrew Immigrant Aid Society, a national service agency funded by the local federations and closely tied to the CJF.

In addition to negotiating with the State Department, the working group also divided responsibility for refugees who did not have any obvious sponsor. Vietnamese Buddhists, for example, were handled mainly by the Catholic charities, which were already taking care of Vietnamese Catholics. HIAS dealt with the Tibetans, who already had a special relationship with the Jewish community; the Dalai Lama was intrigued by the

Jews' success in surviving through centuries of exile as a diaspora faith community.

The arrangement was highly satisfactory to all parties in Washington but one: the Israeli embassy.

Israel had been watching with mounting unhappiness during the 1970s as the percentage of Soviet émigrés dropping out in Vienna steadily rose. Although most American Jews had been fighting for their Soviet brethren out of a belief that human beings had a natural, God-given right to live wherever they chose, Israel had been fighting for a very different principle: the God-given right of Jews to live in Israel. Israeli officials continually pointed out that Jews were being allowed to leave the Soviet Union only on Israeli entry visas, proving that the Soviets accepted the Israeli view of the exodus as a "repatriation" (the Soviets themselves never said, either way). Israelis warned that if the Zionist motivation were removed, the Soviets might simply shut the gates. American Jews replied that if the émigrés lost their freedom of choice, America might back away from a crusade that it had endorsed under false pretenses.

When the American Jews' notion of free choice became enshrined in a federal law formalizing the flow of Soviet Jews to America, Israelis went on the warpath. The chairman of the Jewish Agency, the Mexican-born Israeli politician Aryeh Dulzin, issued thunderous warnings that the American Jewish community was joining the crusade against Zionism. HIAS was attacked as an anti-Israel agency; its staffers in Vienna were accused of enticing émigrés to drop out so as to weaken the Jewish state. The battle infected Jewish community activity in the United States, dividing federation leaders who identified with the Jewish Agency from those who identified with domestic Jewish welfare programs. Those whose main interest was Soviet Jewry were split down the middle.

In the end, a 1981 emergency meeting of Jewish Agency, HIAS, Joint, and CJF officials produced an American capitulation. HIAS agreed to accept refugees for American processing only if they had immediate family already in the United States. The rest would be housed in a Joint-run camp in Naples until they agreed to continue on to Israel.

But three months later, the HIAS backed out of the agreement, after finding that émigrés were choosing to stay in the Naples camp rather than go to Israel. The "freedom of choice" dispute between the Jewish Agency and the CJF remained unresolved for another decade. Israel was un-prepared to deal with the American Jewish community as an equal partner, much less as a rival.

By the end of the 1970s, American Jews had taken on the Nixon and Ford administrations, the Kremlin, big business, and even Israel, and beaten them all.

The final battle—and the toughest one, oddly enough—was against Nazi war criminals. Hundreds, perhaps thousands, of suspected war crimi-nals had slipped into the United States as refugees after the Second World War, under the botched terms of the Displaced Persons acts of 1948 and 1950. During the 1970s, the Jewish community and its allies in Congress started a campaign to deport them. It turned out that the Nazis had a few friends of their own.

The presence of war criminals in America first came to public attention in July 1964 with the publication of a *New York Times* exposé on Hermine Braunsteiner Ryan. A Nazi death-camp guard during the Second World War, she had been convicted of atrocities by a postwar tribunal, was de-tained briefly, then married a GI and settled down in a quiet New York neighborhood. The *Times* story attracted the attention of the Immigration and Naturalization Service, which accused her of lying about her war crimes when she became a U.S. citizen.

Proceedings were instituted to strip Ryan's citizenship and deport her. The case dragged through the federal bureaucracy for seven years, before she finally gave up her citizenship voluntarily in 1971. Two years later, she was sent back to West Germany, but only after Bonn asked for her extradi-tion. The INS had been unable to do a thing.

Ryan's extradition was only the beginning of the problem. As her case was winding down, the World Jewish Congress sent the INS a list of fifty-nine suspected war criminals who had been seen on American streets by their former victims. The INS assigned a special case officer to investigate the accusations and bring action. But as his colleagues had discovered in the Ryan case, there was nothing he could legally do.

The problem was one of those inane bureaucratic muddles that so often determine great events, leaving cynical outsiders convinced that malice or conspiracy must have played a role. In this case, the INS had to collect evidence from the Soviet bloc, find surviving witnesses in Europe and Israel, and locate documents in West Germany. As an agency of the Justice Department, the INS had no jurisdiction to approach foreign governments; all such approaches are supposed to go through the State Department. However, there was no mechanism for the Justice Department to get the State Department moving.

In April 1974, the issue of the bungled investigations was raised on the floor of Congress by a freshman representative from Brooklyn named Elizabeth Holtzman. She had entered the House a year before by defeating one of its most legendary members, Emanuel Celler, who represented the vast Jewish precincts of south Brooklyn for close to a half-century. First elected in 1924, Celler was for years Washington's most fearless defender of Zionism, Jewish immigration, civil rights, and organized labor. Holtzman brought him down in a fierce primary battle that focused on his age. The war criminals issue was her first chance to prove herself as his successor.

In June 1974, Holtzman's protests were reinforced by Representative Joshua Eilberg, a mild-mannered Jew from Philadelphia who chaired the House subcommittee on immigration. Under pressure from Holtzman, a member of his subcommittee, he wrote a series of strong letters to Secretary of State Kissinger protesting the department's "failure to cooperate" with the INS. A Kissinger aide replied that gathering evidence and testimony from the Soviet bloc was impractical, particularly since there was "no way to verify the credibility" of witnesses "provided us by the Soviet authorities."

The sniping continued back and forth for four years, while the fifty-nine World Jewish Congress files inched their way through the justice system with no results. In June 1976, Eilberg broadened his attack to include not only Kissinger's State Department but also the Justice Department, headed by Attorney General Edward Levi. The inaction continued into 1977, under the Democratic administration of Jimmy Carter, proving that the ineptitude was non-partisan. In August 1977, Carter's attorney general took the entire mess away from the INS and set up a special litigation unit, with five lawyers assigned to prosecuting Nazi war criminals. Over the next two years, they tried five cases and lost four.

In 1978, Holtzman introduced a measure in Congress to create a special unit with all the powers it needed to investigate, prosecute, and deport war criminals, plus an independent budget to get the job done. The Holtzman amendment was signed into law in March 1979, creating the Office of Special Investigations (OSI) in the Department of Justice. Symbolically, its first director was Walter Rockler, a prosecutor at the Nuremberg war-crimes tribunal that followed the Second World War.

As of January 1996, the Office of Special Investigations had investigated more than one thousand suspected Nazi war criminals, brought charges against ninety-eight, and deported forty-four. With a $3 million annual budget and a staff of eleven lawyers and eight historians (down from twice that strength at its peak in the late 1980s) it was "the most successful government Nazi-hunting organization on earth," as an ABC News report put it. No other country—not Israel, not Germany, not the former Soviet Union—pursues Nazi war criminals more vigorously than the United States.

But the unit walks a delicate line between its status as a government agency enforcing U.S. law and its unspoken mission to avenge Jewish suffering. The OSI was born as a result of years of Jewish political pressure. Two of its directors have been Jews: Neal Sher, who headed the unit from 1983 until he left to run AIPAC in 1994, and his successor, Eli Rosenbaum. Rosenbaum joined the OSI as a law intern in 1979 and spent his entire professional career there, except for one year in private practice and three years as general counsel of the World Jewish Congress.

Nonetheless, OSI staffers bristle at the suggestion that their work is a Jewish mission. "The OSI is not a Jewish agency but a federal government agency enforcing American law," says former director Sher.

The point about American law is crucial. The OSI does not prosecute war crimes as such, since Nazi war crimes took place far outside American jurisdiction. The unit simply investigates and sues naturalized U.S. citizens who are suspected of lying on their immigration papers—by hiding past war crimes that would have disqualified them from entering the United States in the first place. Those found guilty are not jailed as criminals, but merely stripped of their American citizenship and, in most cases, deported. Their trials for war crimes come, if at all, once they get home.

On the other hand, the unit's targets are not without power of their own. Many are prominent leaders in the world of East European émigrés, such as Ukrainian-Americans and Latvian-Americans, who are well-organized and vocal in many of the same ways as the Jewish community, and every bit as protective of their own. The prominence of onetime Nazi collaborators in these ethnic communities occasionally causes embarrassment to their allies; in 1988, eight accused war criminals turned up as officers in the ethnic outreach program of George Bush's presidential campaign. Bush quickly dismissed them from his campaign.

But other Republicans are less squeamish. Journalist Pat Buchanan, onetime White House aide and sometime presidential candidate, attacks the Office of Special Investigations as an agency "thoroughly corrupted by its own malice and spirit of revenge."

Opponents of the OSI argue that the Nazi-hunters' targets, mainly East European ethnics, are unfairly targeted because they performed menial tasks for Nazi occupation forces. They maintain that the captive nations of Eastern Europe were trapped between the opposing evils of German Nazism and Russian Communism. It is wrong, so the argument goes, for America to punish those who saw Communism as the greater evil.

In this atmosphere of moral neutrality between Nazism and Communism, it follows that pursuing Nazi war criminals a half-century after their crimes is not in society's interest. Rather, Nazi-hunting reflects the narrow interests of the Jews.

The most explicit accusation of Jewish influence came in a 1993 ruling by a federal appeals court in Cincinnati. The defendant was John Demjanjuk, a Ukrainian-born mechanic from Cleveland. The OSI had identified him as "Ivan the Terrible," a sadistic guard at the Treblinka concentration camp. Demjanjuk claimed that his was a case of mistaken identity, but the court ruled otherwise, stripped him of his citizenship, and extradited him in 1986 to Israel, where he was tried for war crimes.

Israel's top court acquitted him. It found that he probably had been a concentration camp guard, but not, amazingly, the one in the indictment. Demjanjuk now appealed his expulsion from the United States, charging that the OSI had deliberately withheld evidence that would have cleared him. His appeal claimed that the OSI acted under pressure from the Jewish community.

A special investigator named by the U.S. Court of Appeals found no evidence of Jewish pressure. The court dismissed the finding. "It is obvious that the prevailing mindset at OSI was that the office must try to please and maintain very close relationships with various interest groups because their continued existence depended on it," a three-judge panel wrote in an opinion authored by Judge Gilbert Merritt. As evidence of the alleged pressure, Merritt cited two incidents: a 1978 letter from Representative Joshua Eilberg to the attorney general, and a 1986 visit to Israel by OSI founding director Allan Ryan as a guest of the ADL.

The ADL called the ruling "fodder for anti-Semites." One scholarly critic called it an "ethnic slur" that "inescapably gives official recognition to anti-Jewish stereotypes in a way that has probably not been seen in this country since the last century." They both had a point; Eilberg's letter had been sent a year *before* the OSI was created, warning the Justice Department not to fumble the just-revealed Demjanjuk case as it had fumbled past war-criminal cases. This was precisely why Congress was creating the OSI to begin with.

As for Ryan's trip to Israel, it came three years *after* he left the OSI. The ADL pointed this out in a letter to Judge Merritt, but the court declined to admit that letter in evidence.

According to OSI director Rosenbaum, the OSI does not work closely with the ADL or any other Jewish organization in pursuing its work. "There's a certain myth that has developed that these cases originate with Nazi hunters or survivors who recognize their tormentors on the street," he says. Almost all the OSI's cases, he explains, begin with tips from foreign governments, or from the work of OSI staff researchers who cross-check U.S. immigration records against Nazi archives.

The debate begs a larger question: why is the pursuit of Nazi war criminals a "Jewish" interest? True, there is a natural difference in intensity between the Jewish and non-Jewish passion for hunting Nazis. To most Americans, the Holocaust is fast fading into history, however horrific. Jews have a greater emotional stake, not just because so many Jews are Holocaust survivors or their relatives, but because, as most Jews are keenly aware, the Nazis' goal was to kill every Jew. In that sense, every Jew is a survivor.

In a broader view, the Holocaust was like any other crime: an offense against society, not just against the victims. The American criminal justice system prosecutes crimes not in the name of the victim, but in the name of "the people." In that sense, special-interest groups that press for more vigorous prosecution—feminist groups demanding harsher rape laws, or black groups that demanded a retrial in the Rodney King case—are acting on behalf of society as a whole. They are doing the rest of us a favor.

Following this logic, Jewish groups that press for continued prosecution of Nazi war criminals, even a half-century later, are serving society's interest as much as the Jewish community's. Every time another Nazi war criminal is punished, society is reminded once more that genocide should not go unpunished. By continuing to pursue justice against Nazis, Jewish groups remind the world that the crimes of the Nazis were crimes against all of humanity, as the first war-crimes tribunal at Nuremberg ruled. Thus the OSI helps to bring home the lessons of the Holocaust again and again to America and the world.

Much of the credit for the rise of Holocaust awareness belongs to the survivors of the horror themselves. Perhaps a quarter-million settled in the United States after the war and quietly set about rebuilding their lives, putting the past behind them.

Israel's highly publicized kidnapping and trial in 1961 of Adolph Eichmann, the architect of the Nazis' Final Solution, forced survivors to confront the memories that most had tried to bury. During the 1960s, groups of survivors began to organize locally to tell their stories and demand recognition from the Jewish community. The Six-Day War gave the "survivors' movement" a gale-force burst of momentum, and by 1973, Holocaust memorial observances were being conducted yearly in more than one hundred communities. In 1974, NCRAC adopted formal guidelines for Holocaust commemoration, directing Jewish organizations to sponsor annual Holocaust Day observances in every city, to press for Holocaust education in the schools, and to put the Holocaust high on the agenda of all Jewish-Christian dialogue.

By 1978, Holocaust remembrance was becoming a national tidal wave. The broadcast that April of *Holocaust*, the blockbuster NBC-TV miniseries, drew some 120 million viewers, making it one of the most watched events in television history. The central problem in modern Jewish theology was now a fixture of American popular culture.

It was also, increasingly, a matter of smart politics.

The first to propose a national memorial to the Holocaust was Mark Siegel, a Jewish liaison on the staff of the Carter White House. He raised the idea in a 1977 memo, suggesting it as a way to press for Senate ratification of the International Convention on Genocide.

The genocide convention was adopted by the United Nations in 1949 in response to the Holocaust. It defined racial mass-murder as a crime against humanity. American ratification had been held up in the Senate for three decades by a small group of Southern Democrats and conservative Republicans, essentially the same group that had closed the gates in 1938 and gutted the Displaced Persons acts in 1948. They saw the genocide treaty as a Communist assault on U.S. sovereignty. Jesse Helms of North Carolina, elected to the Senate in 1974, was now the treaty's leading opponent.

In Siegel's view, a national Holocaust memorial might undercut Helms and his allies by focusing public attention on the evils of genocide and the need to defend human rights across borders. It seemed like an idea with guaranteed appeal to a human-rights advocate such as Jimmy Carter.

Siegel's boss, White House domestic-policy chief Stuart Eizenstat, liked the memorial idea for a related reason. He was distressed over the growing phenomenon of Holocaust denial. A small group of far-right ideologues, centered in California, had been winning headlines with their theory that the Nazi Holocaust was a hoax cooked up by Jews. The Jews' goal, supposedly, was to win world sympathy, to mask their own crimes in the banks and media they controlled, and to drum up support for Israel.

As a symbol of human rights, the Holocaust memorial idea sat around in the White House for nearly a year. In the spring of 1978, it was dusted off for a more compelling reason, namely domestic politics. Carter's standing among Jews was in disastrous shape as a result of his continuing clashes with Prime Minister Menachem Begin of Israel. It was sure to damage his reelection effort.

In March 1978, domestic-policy aide Ellen Goldstein sent a memo to Eizenstat reminding him of Siegel's memorial idea. She suggested that it might be linked to Israel's thirtieth anniversary, two months away. Democrats were looking to the date as a chance to throw a party for the Jews at the White House and patch things up. Reading Goldstein's memo, Eizenstat recalls, "it didn't escape my thought that it could help with political relations." And so Carter used the occasion of Israel's thirtieth birthday to announce the creation of the President's Commission on the Holocaust.

With the formation of the president's Holocaust commission, later renamed the U.S. Holocaust Memorial Council, the Jewish community's campaign to put Jewish suffering on the national agenda was essentially won. The commission convened under its chairman, the revered Holocaust survivor and chronicler Elie Wiesel, and voted to build a national museum. The lessons of the Holocaust were now the Jewish community's moral legacy to America.

But just what are those lessons?

The word "genocide" was first coined in 1943 by Polish-born refugee attorney Raphael Lemkin, using the Latin roots *geno-* (from *gens,* or "tribe") and *-cide* (as in "homicide" or "patricide"). It was meant to denote the Nazis' effort to kill an entire nation of people, the Jews. The U.N. genocide convention both broadened and weakened the term by including any atrocity intended to eliminate a group "in whole or in part." Over time, it came to be a catchphrase for just about any act of mass murder or ethnic repression, from American action in Vietnam to the Soviet suppression of Jewish culture. Menachem Begin compared PLO chief Yasser Arafat to Adolf Hitler in 1981, arguing that Arafat's goal of destroying the state of Israel amounted to the same thing as Hitler's goal of exterminating the Jews (disregarding whether Arafat was remotely *capable* of eliminating Israel). Broadcast executive Ted Turner, in a July 1995 speech, compared himself to a Jew in Nazi Germany after he lost a bid to buy a television network.

The members of the U.S. Holocaust Memorial Council had no such confusion. Their museum was to tell the story of the Nazi bid to exterminate the Jews, period. Other groups swept up in the Nazis' homicidal rampage against the Jews—Gypsies, homosexuals, Socialists—would be remembered as victims of Nazism, but not as targets of Holocaust. A few other groups that lobbied to be included among the victims, including Lithuanians and Ukrainians, were kept out because of their high rate of collaboration *with* the Nazis. At Wiesel's insistence, the killing of the Jews remained front and center.

One question was not so easily resolved: the Armenian Holocaust. Early in the deliberations, an Armenian-American entrepreneur offered to donate a substantial sum to the museum on condition that it commemorate the 1915–1916 Turkish campaign of mass murder against the Armenians. Jewish liberals often pointed to the Armenians as a kindred example of a diaspora people that had suffered horrible persecution but retained their identity. Hitler himself had cited the 1915 massacres as an inspiration.

The Turks were not the Germans, however. At worst, they had intended to erase the Armenian presence in Turkey, not to kill every Armenian alive. Furthermore, Turkey was now a close ally of the United States; also important, it was Israel's most important link to the Muslim world. And Turkey had never acknowledged any guilt for the 1916 horrors. Too, there was Turkey's ancient and prosperous Jewish community, which dated back to 1492 when Turkey offered a rare refuge to Jews fleeing Spain.

Turkey's efforts to keep the Armenians out of the museum were not subtle. In a White House meeting with Eizenstat, Turkey's ambassador to Washington threatened "not to be able to protect the security of the Turkish Jewish community and not to be able to guarantee Turkish-Israeli relations," Eizenstat remembers. Turkish Jewish leaders delivered the same message in a letter to the World Jewish Congress, pleading that their future was at stake. The Israeli embassy weighed in, arguing that an Armenian display would harm Israel's security.

The Holocaust memorial commission resolved its Armenian problem by caving in most of the way. Instead of mounting a full-scale display on the Armenian massacre, as planned, it settled for an oblique reference through a quote from Hitler—"Who remembers the Armenians?"—that mentioned the Armenians' fate as a source of inspiration for his own anti-Jewish plans.

The Armenian Holocaust debate did not end there. Prominent Jewish leaders carried the fight to Congress, where Armenian-American groups were trying to win passage of a resolution honoring their suffering. In a series of congressional confrontations through the 1980s, supporters of an Armenian resolution ran into opposition from some of Israel's leading supporters, notably Representative Stephen Solarz of Brooklyn and lawyer-lobbyist Paul Berger, a top lay figure in the UJA.

Berger continues to insist that the Holocaust should not be compared to other events. "Once you open the door to things that are not related to the Holocaust, where do you draw the line? People wanted to involve the Cambodians, the American Indians, even the Palestinians [in the Holocaust museum exhibit]. I say, where do you draw the line?

"I think the special historic experience of Jews as Jews is a different story, and reflects how the world has looked at the Jews in a special way. That is not to say there haven't been other kinds of sufferings. But to involve other kinds of suffering distracts from the experience of Jews as Jews."

To many minds, American Jewish advocacy reached the pinnacle of its success on Thursday morning, April 22, 1993, when President Bill Clinton dedicated the United States Holocaust Museum. Built by congressional mandate on federal land—though paid for with $168 million in private donations—it was America's four-story "living memorial" to the European Jews massacred by Nazi Germany.

The museum dedication capped a week of nonstop Holocaust commemoration in the capital. On Monday, the president and the first lady spent two and a half hours touring the museum. On Tuesday, congressional and Jewish community leaders gathered in the Capitol Rotunda for their annual Holocaust Remembrance Day observance. On Wednesday, the Clintons and Gores hosted five hundred Jewish community leaders at a formal White House reception. On Thursday, as ten thousand people watched under an unseasonably blustery sky, the president lit an eternal flame to dedicate the museum, flanked by the Nobel laureate Elie Wiesel and the chairman of the museum's board, Baltimore real-estate investor Harvey Meyerhoff.

"I've never been as proud of being a Jew and an American as I was this week," said the capital's best-known Jewish community spokesman, Hyman Bookbinder, emeritus director of the American Jewish Committee's Washington office. "This week we saw the effect of all our political work and our moral efforts, despite all the problems. Day after day there was action and expressions of understanding of our pain."

Indeed, the Jews had won recognition this week. Leaders of a dozen foreign nations came to Washington for the museum dedication. The street in front of the museum, Fifteenth Street Southwest, was renamed Raoul Wallenberg Place to honor a Swedish diplomat who gave his life saving Hungarian Jews from the German Nazis.

"Here on the town square of our national life," said President Clinton in his dedication speech, "on this fiftieth anniversary of the Warsaw Ghetto uprising, at Eisenhower Plaza on Raoul Wallenberg Place, we dedicate the United States Holocaust Museum and so bind one of the darkest lessons in history to the hopeful soul of America."

Within a few days after opening its doors, the museum would establish itself as the single most sought-after tourist attraction in Washington. Alongside the national museums of art, American history, natural science, and space travel, America now had a national museum of Jewish suffering.

CHAPTER 8

Jerusalem on the Potomac:
The Rise and Rise of the Israel Lobby

THE JEWISH LEGISLATIVE TRIUMPHS of the 1970s came to a climax in 1981, in a political battle that remains the most storied episode in the history of American Jewish politics: the battle over AWACS.

AWACS stands for "airborne warning and command system." It is the Pentagon's name for a line of C-5 cargo planes outfitted as flying spyships, with the most advanced electronic surveillance gear available. In the fall of 1980, the Saudi government decided to buy five of them from the outgoing Carter administration. Israel opposed the sale, arguing that the Saudis were still at war with Israel and committed to its destruction, to which end they might find the AWACS useful.

With a presidential election nearing, Republican challenger Ronald Reagan campaigned against the sale. Once in office, Reagan turned around and approved it.

Stopping the White House from selling weapons to a foreign country requires a majority vote in both houses of Congress. The AWACS sale touched off a bruising eleven-month battle between the Jewish community and the White House for a handful of Senate votes, closely monitored in the national and world press. When it was over, AIPAC, the pro-Israel lobbying organization, emerged as one of the preeminent forces in Washington power politics. "The result was the end of AIPAC's national obscurity, and the beginning of a revolution in Jewish politics," wrote journalist Edward Tivnan in his unsympathetic 1987 history of AIPAC, *The Lobby*. "The AWACS battle is a striking example of the current state of the art of Jewish political power."

In the years since, the story of AWACS has been told and retold as an arch-paradigm of ethnic lobbying clout, "a fascinating case study on the interaction of interest groups, the president, and Congress in foreign policy decision making," as political scientists John Spanier and Eric Uslaner put it in their text, *American Foreign Policy Making and the Democratic Dilemmas*.

Curiously enough, the Jews *lost* the AWACS battle.

The administration eventually found the votes it needed, the sale went through, and the Saudis got their spyplanes as promised. The Democratic-run House voted on October 1 to reject the sale by an impressive three-to-one margin. The Republican-led Senate was leaning against the sale, too, but when it voted three weeks later, the president won the day. Party loyalty had intervened, along with naked White House threats. There were also a few unforeseen developments, including the mid-October assassination of Egyptian President Anwar Sadat, which reminded lawmakers how fragile and precious were the moderates of the Arab world.

In other words, AIPAC's reputation for invincibility is built on a defeat.

More curious still, it was not even AIPAC's fight. AIPAC was only one of many Jewish groups involved in the AWACS struggle. Like the losing campaign for loan guarantees a decade later, the campaign against AWACS was waged by a broad consortium under the umbrella of NCRAC working with AIPAC and the Presidents Conference. The Presidents Conference oversaw the efforts of the national agencies to flood the media, forge interfaith coalitions, and create a national mood of urgency. NCRAC delivered its armies of local community leaders to call their representatives and talk tough. AIPAC did what it had always done: it lobbied. It supplied lawmakers with facts and figures, helped identify fence-sitters, and hand-delivered promises and threats in the name of the Jewish community. It was, in effect, the campaign's public face to Washington.

In many ways, the AWACS campaign reprised the earlier Jackson-Vanik and antiboycott bill campaigns. Like them it pitted the administration, big business, and the paid lobbyists of foreign embassies (once Soviet, now Arab) against a well-organized, fully mobilized Jewish community and its allies on Capitol Hill.

There were two big differences. One was that in the AWACS campaign, the Jews lost. The other was that the failed AWACS campaign ended up spawning a myth of Jewish invincibility.

More to the point, it created the myth of AIPAC.

A decade earlier, the Nixon administration had expanded America's ties with Israel, arguing that aid to the Jewish state was not just a donation but an investment. Israel after 1970 was not merely a worthy cause; it was a strategic Cold War asset. By implication, America needed Israel as much as Israel needed America.

Israel and its American supporters learned to mouth the new refrain, but they did not fully absorb its meaning at first. For a decade, Jerusalem continued approaching Washington with a measure of humility, careful not to wear out its welcome. AWACS was Israel's way of signaling that those days were over. From now on, there was no more Mr. Nice Guy in Jerusalem. Israel was henceforth willing to bite the hand that fed it.

Carefully nurtured, the myth of a swaggering Jewish superpower took quick root in Washington in the early 1980s. Israel's critics, dazzled by the display, published a rash of overwrought exposes: Noam Chomsky's *The Fateful Triangle* in 1983, Stephen Green's *Taking Sides* in 1984, Paul Findley's *They Dare to Speak Out* in 1985, Edward Tivnan's *The Lobby* in 1987, Andrew and Leslie Cockburn's *Dangerous Liaison* in 1991, and George and Douglas Ball's *The Passionate Attachment* in 1992.

The myth of AIPAC surfaced only several years later, after the myth of invincibility was entrenched. Chomsky's book does not mention AIPAC. Green's book mentions it only once. In Findley's book, published a year later, AIPAC is already a lead player. By the time of Tivnan's book, AIPAC is the whole show.

Tivnan was the first writer to cite AWACS as the maiden voyage of battleship AIPAC. It was not. To the contrary, AWACS was the *last* major performance by AIPAC in the role of disciplined cog in a well-oiled Jewish community machine. AWACS was the episode that taught AIPAC the value of going it alone. In the years ahead, as AIPAC retooled itself, it would cultivate the myth of AWACS as its own finest hour.

Why did AIPAC ascend so rapidly on the wings of so public a defeat? There were three reasons.

One was the change of regime in Washington. The presidency of Ronald Reagan ushered in a long-term shift in America's political mood, militantly anti-Communist abroad, deeply conservative at home. The new atmosphere was more hospitable than ever to Israel, archenemy of the Communist left. But it would prove increasingly hostile to Israel's traditional defenders in Washington, the established American Jewish leaders with their left-of-center domestic agenda.

A vacuum was created: a political space for a new Jewish leadership that could work comfortably with the new Washington establishment, a Jewish leadership with no agenda except Israel.

The second reason for AIPAC's paradoxical rise was a change of regime in Jerusalem. Four years earlier, in May 1977, just as the antiboycott bill was becoming U.S. law, Israeli voters went to the polls and ended two generations of rule by the left-of-center Israel Labor Party. In its place came the Likud, a conservative bloc of parties headed by the nationalist firebrand Menachem Begin.

American Jewry's top leaders embraced the new prime minister at once. Despite their long ties to Labor, they hailed the turnover as a tribute to Israeli democracy, and they pledged Israel their continuing loyalty. The Likud would soon learn that as good as it was to have American Jewish supporters who were loyal to Israel, it would be better to have friends who were loyal to the Likud.

The third factor was a change of regime at AIPAC itself. In October 1980, just weeks before the AWACS battle was joined, AIPAC took on a new staff director, Thomas Dine. He was a Capitol Hill veteran who had worked on the staffs of liberal senators Edward Kennedy and Frank Church, with time out as a research fellow at the Brookings Institution.

Dine came to AIPAC with a formidable background in the mechanics of U.S. foreign policy-making, but not the slightest knowledge of Judaism or the Jewish community. AWACS was his initiation by fire. When the fight was over, he set about engineering a revolution at AIPAC—its structure, its links to the organized Jewish community, its relationship to the political process, and most important, its public image. It was Dine who created battleship AIPAC.

"I wanted AIPAC to be a grassroots organization," Dine explained in a 1992 interview. "My basic assumption is that votes are won or lost at the grass roots, not in Washington. Number two, I wanted AIPAC to have a much broader reach into the policy-making processes of our own government. And that meant both the legislative and executive branches. Number three, I wanted AIPAC to be of the community. That meant expanding the number of people involved in the policy-making."

In fact, AIPAC had proven repeatedly that it could deliver grassroots pressure whenever it wanted to, through the Jewish agencies. That was how the AWACS battled had been waged. What AIPAC lacked was not grass roots, but its *own* grass roots, loyal only to AIPAC. Dine set about turning the organization from a small agency, run by the national Jewish organizations as their congressional lobbying arm, into an independent mass-membership powerhouse run by its wealthiest donors.

In the dozen years that Dine served as AIPAC's director, its membership grew fivefold, its budget tenfold. As the organization grew, it became increasingly visible, not just on Capitol Hill but throughout the federal government. Dine's AIPAC redefined lobbying, the traditional art of influencing Congress. It embarked on an oxymoronic campaign of "executive lobbying": working directly with officials in the executive branch to shape policy at the departments of State, Defense, Commerce, and anywhere else Israel had business.

AIPAC became an all-purpose pressure machine. Along the way, its reputation metamorphosed. Once a quiet, behind-the-scenes operator, it became a familiar, hulking presence in the press and the Washington rumor mill. This was no accident, either. Dine openly trumpeted AIPAC's clout, boasting about "Jewish political power" to mass audiences, in the obvious belief that an outsized reputation would intimidate the opposition.

Equally important, though less noticed, was the reform of AIPAC's governing structure. Under Dine, the ruling executive committee tripled in size. Formerly the committee had been controlled by the heads of the New York–based national Jewish organizations. Now the Jewish community leaders were a minority, outnumbered by AIPAC's own contributors.

Swelling the executive committee did not make AIPAC "of the community." To the contrary, it removed the lobby from the national Jewish communal structure, such as it was, and placed it firmly in the hands of a few big donors whose only loyalty was to AIPAC.

Ruling over the entire operation—above the executive committee, the membership, the staff, over Dine himself—was a tiny coterie of deeply conservative, publicity-shy multimillionaires known as the officers' group. Their leader was a Los Angeles real-estate developer named Larry Weinberg. He became president of AIPAC in 1976, oversaw the hiring of Tom Dine in 1980, chose his own successors after stepping down as president in 1982, molded the officers' group into a vehicle for his own leadership, and oversaw the firing of Dine in 1993. He remained the effective leader of AIPAC well into the 1990s, long after Dine was gone.

For its first three decades, from the time it was set up in 1944, AIPAC was essentially a one-man operation run by its founding director, the affable, understated I. L. Kenen. As modest as it was, nothing more was needed. Israel in Kenen's day was a popular humanitarian cause on Capitol Hill, but little more than that. American relations with Israel were not yet the high-stakes game they would be once the Middle East became a surrogate Cold War battleground. Kenen's style of friendly, collegial lobbying worked well for his limited agenda.

Kenen's instructions, such as they were, came from his governing board, originally made up of the heads of the Zionist organizations, then of the major Jewish organizations that rallied around Israel during the 1950s. When a lawmaker seemed to need extra pressure, Kenen turned to a list of key contacts, several hundred Jewish community leaders around the country who were able and willing to get their representatives on the phone.

Kenen retired in 1974, shortly before the final passage of the Jackson-Vanik amendment. His successor was Senate aide Morris Amitay, one of the amendment's architects.

It was a historic transition. Amitay had just shown the Jewish community a new style of sharp-elbowed, take-no-prisoners politics. It was a style more in tune than Kenen's with the confrontational world of post-Watergate Washington.

During his six years at the helm of AIPAC, Amitay computerized the lobby's offices, moved them to Capitol Hill, increased the staff from a handful to several dozen, and tripled the annual budget from $400,000 to $1.2 million. Kenen's key-contacts list was expanded from a few hundred names to eleven thousand.

Under Dine, AIPAC would grow to a staff of 150, a budget of $15 million, and a membership of more than fifty-five thousand.

If Amitay's AIPAC was transformed beyond recognition, so was the world around it. Israel's place in the world had changed enormously, both for worse and for better.

The years since 1967 had seen a marked improvement in Israel's strategic position. The capture of the Golan, Sinai, and West Bank moved Arab guns for the first time out of range of Israel's populous heartland. This "strategic depth," combined with a growing U.S. investment in arms and cash, changed the geometry of the Israeli-Arab conflict. The Arab states were still formally committed to destroying Israel, but it was more and more unlikely.

The subsequent growth in the American government's commitment to Israel was dramatic. In the two decades before 1967, U.S. aid to Israel had averaged just $66 million per year, most of it in Food for Peace loans. But in 1971, following a September 1970 Israeli action that saved the Jordanian monarchy from a PLO uprising, a deeply impressed Richard Nixon boosted U.S. assistance to $634 million, most of it in military aid. Following the Yom Kippur War of October 1973, U.S. aid skyrocketed yet again to $2.2 billion, making Israel the largest single recipient of American foreign assistance. Arms shipments to Israel, begun sporadically under Lyndon Johnson, flowed along a steady pipeline under Nixon. Israel became a virtual U.S. protectorate.

And yet Israelis felt less secure than ever in the mid-1970s. Israel's military rule in the occupied territories had given the Arabs a potent propaganda weapon. Opposition to Israel turned into something resembling a worldwide moral crusade for the displaced Palestinians—despite the ever-mounting violence of the Palestinian nationalist movement, which escalated during the early 1970s from attacking Israeli soldiers to murdering Israeli schoolchildren and blowing up Israel-bound civilian airliners. The world community responded by inviting Palestinian leader Yasser Arafat to address the U.N. General Assembly as a liberation leader in November 1974. A year later, the assembly voted to condemn Zionism, the basic doctrine of Jewish nationalism, as a form of "racism or racial discrimination." Israel was now officially a pariah according to international law.

Compounding Israel's sense of isolation, paradoxically, was the growing alliance with Washington. Secretary of State Henry Kissinger, hoping to capitalize on Israel's new strength and America's new leverage, set out in the mid-1970s to negotiate a series of agreements between Israel, Egypt, and Syria, aimed at reducing the likelihood of war. Closing the agreements meant winning concessions from both sides, often through blunt U.S. pressure. To many Israelis, the American pressure made it feel as though their only friend had turned against them.

Israel's senior leadership was not so panicked. Yitzhak Rabin, who succeeded Golda Meir as prime minister in 1974, was an Israeli-born career soldier who regarded existential fears of anti-Semitism as a Diaspora Jewish neurosis. To him the occupied territories were neither God-given patrimony nor a seawall against age-old hatreds; they were merely strategic positions to be kept or traded as circumstances required. "It doesn't matter to me if I need a visa to visit Bethlehem," he told Israel's *Yediot Aharonot* newspaper in an interview just before taking office.

Rabin and his aides entered the Kissinger negotiations as hard bargainers with a clear sense of their bottom line. They knew which hills they could part with and what they needed in return, and they used every weapon at their disposal to keep the upper hand.

And one of the most potent weapons at their disposal was the American Jewish community, primed for battle, terrified for Israel's future.

The first crucial step in the birth of the superlobby was taken by American Jews themselves, at the November 1973 General Assembly of the Council of Jewish Federations. It was three weeks after the end of the Yom Kippur War, and an Arab oil embargo was causing gasoline shortages and widespread resentment around the country. Assembly delegates, fearing a popular backlash against Israel and Jews, voted to launch an emergency public-relations campaign on Israel's behalf.

"There was anxiety, almost panic in the community," recalls one assembly participant, Albert Chernin, then head of the Philadelphia Jewish Community Relations Council (JCRC). "With the oil embargo, there were reports of bumper stickers in the Midwest reading 'Burn Jews—Not Oil,' although the ADL claims it never found the first one."

The assembly voted to set up a $3 million emergency public-relations fund, to be administered by a special task force on Israel. It was to be run out of NCRAC headquarters, combining the national clout and know-how of the major agencies with the local resources of the federations and community-relations councils.

The task force took a year and a half to get up and running, but once launched it took off at a gallop. "It was a very effective task force," says Rabbi Israel Miller, an Orthodox Zionist leader who chaired the Presidents Conference at the time. "We had the top professionals in the American Jewish community attending meetings. We were able to accomplish a great deal in mobilizing the American Jewish community."

Under NCRAC's guidance, member groups were urged to reach out to the press, academia, Christian clergy, and local politicians, emphasizing Israel's democratic character and the Arabs' refusal to make peace, explaining the benefits of Israeli occupation to West Bank Arabs, reminding their neighbors of "the complicity, if only by silence, of the western Gentile world in the disaster that befell Jewry in World War II."

The task force's work went well beyond atmospherics, however. When called on, it became a national alarm system mobilizing the Jews to battle. President Ford was the first to taste its power, when he declared his "reassessment" of U.S.-Israel relations in March 1976. The reassessment was meant to break a stalemate in the Kissinger negotiations by forcing a minor Israeli concession. Within six weeks, it was Ford who conceded, after seventy-six senators signed a letter demanding that he back off. Two years later Ford's successor, Jimmy Carter, felt the task force's sting when he decided to sell a squadron of F-15 fighter jets to Saudi Arabia. The F-15 fight was like a dress rehearsal for AWACS: it was prolonged, nasty, and ultimately unsuccessful, and—despite the failure of the task force—it was most unsettling to the Carter White House.

But the task force contained the seeds of its own destruction. Because it was run by NCRAC, it had a built-in feature that would prove incompatible with successful pro-Israel lobbying: Jewish public opinion.

NCRAC was structured as a consulting council where members came together, discussed their differences, and then voted. It even published the minority views of dissenters. Poles apart was the administrative style of the Presidents Conference, which avoided open discussion and almost never voted. It consisted of a single staffer, director Yehuda Hellman, who contacted member groups to line up endorsements for his steady stream of pro-Israel policy statements. When a rare disagreement arose, he tried to coax stragglers along or simply found a more acceptable phrasing.

The two agencies coexisted amicably for two decades, thanks in large part to their directors. Despite their different personalities, the phlegmatic Hellman and NCRAC's ebullient Isaiah Minkoff shared a common language. Both had learned their trade in the conspiratorial world of the pre-Holocaust Polish Jewish labor movement, where a folksy smile usually masked a hardheaded, manipulative stubbornness.

But in 1975, just as the Israel task force started operations, Minkoff retired. His successor was the brilliant, irascible Al Chernin, a former NCRAC staffer who had left to head the Philadelphia JCRC. Born and bred in Indianapolis, educated as a social worker, Chernin had an all-American, process-oriented working style that was worlds removed from Hellman's.

Process, in fact, would prove to be NCRAC's undoing. In Minkoff's time, the two umbrella agencies had adhered to an informal division of labor. NCRAC, while responsible for the full range of Jewish policy, deliberately kept a low profile on Middle East matters. "In domestic areas we made policy," Chernin says, "but in Israel affairs the policy was a given. Our job was to communicate it to the communities. We saw the Presidents Conference as the public voice of the Jewish community, especially to the president and the administration. And for the public record, at least, it represented the community's policy-making body on Israel. In reality, it was the vehicle through which Israel communicated its policy to the community."

With the creation of the Israel task force, the division of labor between the two groups collapsed. The Jewish community's Middle East policy was now housed in a body that debated, voted, and recorded dissents. A collision with Israel was inevitable.

The right of Jews to dissent from Israeli policy is the most sordidly painful issue to arise in Jewish community life in the last generation. Paradoxically, for a group that prides itself on feisty independence, the Jewish community came down solidly *against* its own members' freedom of expression during the mid-1970s. The full weight of community wrath was brought down firmly on a few who tried to speak their own minds.

The issue first arose in the late 1960s as a debate over the war in

Vietnam. In private meetings, Lyndon Johnson complained about the prominence of Jews in the antiwar movement, calling it hypocritical for Jews to demand that America support Israel but abandon South Vietnam. Community leaders argued bitterly over the implied White House threat, splitting along ideological lines that would soon become familiar: the Orthodox Union, Anti-Defamation League, and Jewish War Veterans on the right; the Reform union, American Jewish Congress, and National Council of Jewish Women on the left; the Conservative movement and American Jewish Committee trying forlornly to hold the center.

After Richard Nixon raised the stakes to Israel by increasing U.S. support, Prime Minister Golda Meir weighed into the debate with pro-war public statements and private appeals to Jewish leaders. Her ambassador in Washington, Yitzhak Rabin, actually flew to New York in 1970 to bully a small band of students who planned to carry antiwar placards in the annual Salute to Israel parade.

In the wake of the Yom Kippur War, the debate switched from Vietnam to the Middle East. In early 1974, Arafat began putting out feelers to Israel, suggesting that he might be ready to consider some sort of coexistence between Israel and the Palestinians. A few Jewish community activists called for a response. Israel came down hard on the wayward doves.

The test case was Breira (meaning "alternative"), a tiny group of intellectuals formed in the spring of 1973 to promote "open discussion of Israel-diaspora relations." After the October war, it became a vehicle for the Israeli left to promote its views of Israeli-Palestinian "mutual recognition" among American Jews.

With a budget of less than $50,000 and a membership that never topped fifteen hundred, Breira posed no threat to the major Jewish organizations. Most supporters were graduate students or junior rabbis, including a sizable number of staff rabbis from the B'nai B'rith Hillel Foundations, the Jewish campus chaplaincy service.

Yet Breira provoked a national furor, some of it clearly spontaneous, some manifestly coordinated. Leaders of virtually every major Jewish organization spoke out against it. The president of the Reform rabbinate, Rabbi Arthur Lelyveld, who had once marched with Martin Luther King Jr., announced that groups like Breira "give aid and comfort . . . to those who would cut aid to Israel and leave it defenseless before murderers and terrorists." The president of the American Jewish Congress, Rabbi Arthur

Hertzberg, refused to speak at meeting where a Breira member was to appear. B'nai B'rith was pressured to discipline Hillel rabbis who joined the dissenters. In some cities, Breira members were invited to visit the local Israeli consulate for tongue-lashings by ranking diplomats. By 1976, members were resigning Breira in droves. In 1977, the battered organization finally gave up and dissolved itself.

Dissent was not limited to Breira. Prominent Jews were writing newspaper columns and buying advertising space to criticize Israeli policy, and each new protest sparked a new wave of counterprotests. Literary critic Irving Howe, who in May 1976 signed an ad opposing Jewish settlement of the occupied territories, complained that the signers were "subjected to unseemly pressures in their communities and organizations." He called it "*heimishe* [homelike] witch hunting."

By mid-1976, the crackdown was sparking a backlash. NCRAC and the American Jewish Committee ordered up internal studies on the limits of dissent. The Presidents Conference and the Synagogue Council of America held public inquiries on the topic. All these organizations reached the same conclusion: American Jews had the right to discuss issues freely, but only within discreet forums, outside public view. "I am for an exchange of views between American Jews and Israel," Israeli ambassador Simcha Dinitz told one gathering, "but the *New York Times* and the *Washington Post* do not have to be the first channel of dispute between American Jews and Israel." Airing disputes in public, he said, conveyed weakness and division at a time when Israel was fighting for its survival.

Working closely with Dinitz and his staff, the Presidents Conference and NCRAC began to develop a set of baseline principles to govern behavior within the organized Jewish community. They boiled down to three basic tenets. One was that Israelis were the only ones entitled to decide Israeli policy, since they alone bore the risks. The second was that American Jews must stand publicly united with Israel, and air disagreements only in private. The third was that Israel could not negotiate with Palestinian terrorists, since talking to them would grant them legitimacy.

These rules were quickly taken up by the Jewish leadership as sacred writ from Jerusalem. Jews who disagreed found themselves unwelcome in community forums, asked to leave governing boards, shouted down at meetings. Even luminaries like Nahum Goldmann and Philip Klutznick, the founders of the Presidents Conference, began to find themselves ostracized after they endorsed Middle East compromise.

Though few knew it at the time, Jimmy Carter came to Washington in January 1977 determined to solve the Middle East conflict, even if it made him a one-term president. He was drawn to the region by his born-again Christian beliefs. He took it on faith that conflicts could be resolved through understanding and compromise. He leaned emotionally toward the dispossessed of the world, which in the Middle East now meant the Palestinians. His background in rural Georgia, far from the cities of the Northeast, may have blinded him to the firestorm of Jewish anxiety he was about to stir up.

Carter's troubles with the Jewish community began in March, just weeks after his inauguration. After receiving Prime Minister Rabin at the White House for a chilly round of talks, the president publicly spelled out his ideas about Middle East peace. One of these was to address the "political dimension" of the Palestinian problem. A week later, he openly called in a speech for a "Palestinian homeland." No president had ever come so close to recognizing Palestinian nationalism. Relations between the White House and the Jewish community quickly reached a crisis level.

Carter's top staff liaison to the Jewish community, Los Angeles attorney Ed Sanders, a former president of AIPAC, attempted to defuse the tensions by inviting Jewish leaders to the White House for small get-acquainted chats. Hoping to avoid the lockstep pro-Israel mentality of the Presidents Conference, he decided to reach out to local federation and JCRC leaders. NCRAC and the CJF quickly put an end to that. "The Jewish community had created an instrumentality in the Presidents Conference to be the liaison to the White House," Chernin says. "Now the president was trying to play by different rules and pick his own Jewish leaders. We couldn't allow ourselves to be seduced." Sanders backed off.

In September, the State Department tried the same thing, hoping to win Jewish support for a reconvened Geneva peace conference, which Israel strongly opposed. Leaders of the Presidents Conference were invited to meet with Secretary of State Cyrus Vance, but they learned in advance that others had been invited from outside the conference. Reform leader Alexander Schindler, who chaired the Presidents Conference, obtained a list of invitees and brought them to Washington a day early for a rehearsal.

Everyone was given a scripted role to play. When the group entered Vance's office the next day, Schindler was visibly in charge. "We took that meeting away from them," Schindler recollects with a chuckle.

Even Rabbi Moshe Sherer, president of the devoutly anti-Reform Agudath Israel, rose to inform Vance that everyone in the room stood behind Rabbi Schindler. "I nearly fell over," Schindler said. "In his own *shul* he never calls me 'rabbi.' But when we're fighting for Israel we're all one."

In fact, at that moment, the unity of the American Jewish community was facing its greatest challenge ever. Israeli voters had gone to the polls in May 1977 and ousted Yitzhak Rabin's Labor Party, ending fifty years of labor rule in the Jewish homeland. The new prime minister was Menachem Begin, Polish-born leader of the rightist Likud bloc. Deeply conservative on economic and social matters, he was the antithesis of American Jewish liberalism. As for Palestinian rights, he rejected the very idea of compromise. He opposed returning any territory, even to Jordan, even for peace. To him, the West Bank was the heart of the "Greater Land of Israel."

Begin's election sent shock waves throughout the American political system. In the news media, in academia, at the top levels of the Carter administration, Israel's new prime minister was viewed as an apparition of doom.

It was Schindler who stepped in at that moment to ease the transition to the right. Though he was president of the staunchly liberal Reform union, he believed his first responsibility was as chair of the Presidents Conference. And as the leader of American Jewry, he considered it his duty to ensure that Israel enjoyed unbroken support.

"When we learned the election results," Schindler recalls, "I immediately sent a message to all the organizations and local communities, saying Israel is a democracy and we have to support the democratically elected head of Israel." But the Begin-bashing just spread; in one memorable excess, *Time* magazine informed its readers that Begin "rhymes with Fagin," the crudely anti-Semitic caricature from Dickens's *Oliver Twist*. Schindler and Hellman flew to Washington for a grim meeting with White House domestic-affairs chief Stuart Eizenstat. "I came out feeling we needed to say something," Schindler says. The question was how to be heard.

Schindler decided to go to Israel and come back. "I said to Yehuda, we have no platform. Let's go to Israel, so we can come back and report on what we learned there." The two took a cab from the White House to National Airport, where they phoned Begin's office from a pay phone to say they were coming—Hellman at once, Schindler via Miami, where he had Reform union business.

"I knew in advance what we would say on return," Schindler says. "That Begin had come from the far right, but that in order to govern he has to occupy the center. That we shouldn't be afraid of people from the far right. After all, who made peace with China, if not Nixon?"

Once in Israel, Schindler discovered to his surprise that he actually liked Begin. Instead of a fire-breathing radical he found a courtly, soft-spoken European gentleman of the old school. More important, Schindler found a rare Israeli who was interested in the fate of the Diaspora. "I felt more understanding for world Jewry on Begin's part, certainly, than on Rabin's," Schindler observes. "Rabin had always struck me like a Canaanite who didn't give a damn about world Jewry, except as a pawn. Begin really cared."

Schindler flew home and informed the White House of his favorable impressions. As he expected, his endorsement got wide press coverage. The White House gave Begin a cordial reception when he made his first visit in July. Outside Washington, Jewish audiences received Begin with the same adulation they had once showered on Golda Meir and David Ben-Gurion.

Schindler's embrace of Begin could not undo the deep policy differences between Begin and the Carter administration. Begin rejected the very idea of conflict resolution through compromise; his entire life had been dedicated to the pursuit of Jewish strength and defiance in a hostile world. He and Carter were doomed to collide head-on.

Before Begin and Carter could destroy each other, they found a savior in Anwar Sadat. On November 9, 1977, Sadat told his parliament that he would travel "to the ends of the earth" to end the Middle East conflict. "Israel will be astonished when it hears me saying now before you that I am ready to go to their house, to the Knesset itself and to talk to them." Ten days later, Sadat arrived in Jerusalem on the historic visit that broke the Middle East logjam.

A year and a half of tortuous, on-again, off-again Israeli-Egyptian negotiations followed before Sadat and Begin could sign a peace treaty on the

White House lawn on March 26, 1979. The talks were ugly, acrimonious, and frequently threatened to break down entirely. Within Israel, Begin's reluctance to compromise sparked a national protest movement, led by military officers, demanding "Peace Now." Even his foreign minister, onetime war hero Moshe Dayan, eventually quit in disgust at Begin's intransigence.

The growing image of Israeli intransigence brought the American Jewish community to the verge of panic. Local leaders found themselves forced to defend Israeli positions that they could not understand. Contacts with non-Jewish dialogue partners—church leaders, civil rights leaders, labor leaders—were becoming testy. Synagogue rabbis reported distress among their congregants at what looked like Israeli reluctance to make peace.

In the spring of 1978, during tense negotiations over the future of the Sinai peninsula, the NCRAC Israel task force staged regional seminars across the country to help local activists understand and explain Israel's positions. What they found was profound unease.

"There was a clear sense being expressed that we had to communicate our concerns to the government of Israel," Chernin recalls. "We had always taken the position that our function was not to issue public pronunciamentos on Israeli government policy. We felt we had ample opportunities to express our differences through discreet channels. The grass-roots consensus we got from the CRCs was, if you have those channels, use them."

In early April, the Jewish leadership decided to act. The presidents and executive directors of NCRAC and the Big Three defense agencies flew to Israel together to confront Begin with the unpopularity of his policies.

The eight leaders stayed in Israel for three days. They were whisked from the airport to Jerusalem for a three-hour meeting with Begin. From there, they were taken to meet with Foreign Minister Dayan and Defense Minister Ezer Weizman. They received helicopter tours of the West Bank and Sinai, to learn why Israel could not give up its settlements. Then they were invited back to meet Begin again.

"What impressed me," Chernin says, "was that with all the criticism of Begin, I found him to be the first prime minister who was really open to dialogue. We got into a very civil exchange."

The eight flew home just in time for the Passover holiday, "convinced that the Israelis would not give up the settlements in the Sinai." After

Passover, they reconvened at the White House, where Vice President Walter Mondale had asked them to share their impressions. After ten minutes, they were unexpectedly joined by Carter, who stayed to talk for an hour. Carter surprised the group with his "openness," Chernin says.

The mission left the community leaders with a renewed sense of vigor and confidence. They reported to the field that Begin was listening, that their concerns mattered.

In fact, Israel began losing interest in NCRAC. It was too unpredictable. Slowly, almost imperceptibly, Jerusalem began reducing the level of attention it gave to the agency. Israeli diplomats began directing their main efforts elsewhere: to the member agencies, to the Presidents Conference, and most of all to AIPAC. By the mid-1980s, the Israel task force was dissolved and NCRAC had become a minor player in the great game of Jewish power, largely irrelevant to the Middle East diplomatic process, its declarations viewed with disdain in Jerusalem.

The Reagan administration's first contact with the Jewish lobby was the AWACS battle of 1981. The administration drew two lessons from the experience. One was that Jewish lobbyists could be a formidable opponent. The second was that they could be an equally formidable friend. Starting just days after the Senate vote on AWACS, administration officials began seeking out AIPAC officials and inviting them to join in the planning of government policy.

In part this was just smart politics. Involving AIPAC in shaping policy helped ensure that the lobby would not oppose policy later on.

Besides, AIPAC could be a useful ally. Given its awesome reputation among the lawmakers on Capitol Hill as the political voice of organized Jewry, and particularly given its close ties to the Democrats, the lobby could often sell administration policies that the White House itself could not sell. AIPAC was regularly enlisted to line up congressional support for the overall foreign-aid package, an unpopular program with little grass-roots backing outside the Jewish community. Even as hostile an observer as Paul Findley concedes that foreign aid "might have difficulty surviving at all" if not for AIPAC. In February 1983, AIPAC director Tom Dine was the only professional lobbyist named to a blue-ribbon citizens' commission assembled by Secretary of State George Shultz to review the U.S. foreign-aid program. The following October, President Reagan personally enlisted

AIPAC's help to fight a congressional resolution that would have forced him to pull U.S. Marines out of Beirut. The president won that one, after a handful of senators were turned around by AIPAC lobbyists.

Through the 1980s, AIPAC lobbyists regularly helped the Reagan administration line up Democratic congressional support on unlikely issues from Central America to sub-Saharan Africa. The lobbyists told the liberals that Israel needed its friends to compromise on other issues in order to maintain solid American support for Israel. Besides, the lobbyists argued, a strong U.S. defense posture was good for Israel, since a weakened America could not defend its small allies. Liberals grumbled, but they went along often enough to make a difference.

In return, the Reagan administration set about making itself into the most pro-Israel administration in history. In the fall of 1981, Israel was permitted for the first time to sign a formal military pact with Washington, becoming a partner, not a stepchild, of American policy. Israel and America embarked on a series of joint adventures, both overt and covert: aiding the Nicaraguan contras, training security forces in Zaire, sending arms secretly to Iran. Cooperation in weapons development, sharing of technology, and information and intelligence reached unprecedented proportions. Israel's annual U.S. aid package, already higher than any other country's, was edged ever higher. Loans were made into grants. Supplemental grants were added.

The alliance between the Reagan administration and AIPAC transcended politics, however.

Ronald Reagan himself had a deep, multilayered Jewish connection that was emotional and intellectual as much as it was political. Reagan was the first Republican president since Teddy Roosevelt to count Jews among his personal friends. Those close to the president said that his sense of kinship with Jews went back to his days as a young actor in Hollywood, where he came of age in what was in effect a small community led by Jews.

Later, during his emergence on the national stage in the 1970s, his thinking on foreign affairs was strongly influenced by the mostly Jewish neoconservative clique centered around the American Jewish Committee's *Commentary* magazine. Reagan and his advisers accepted the neoconservative doctrine that Israel was a surrogate for the Free World, threatened by an alliance of Communist dictatorships and Third World terrorists. Once in office, Reagan appointed large numbers of Jewish neoconservatives to administration posts, particularly in mid-level positions where broad policies are most often translated into action. That he did not appoint any Jews to his cabinet—for the first time in any presidency since the Truman administration—went unnoticed.

Forging a working alliance with the Jewish community was no easy task for a conservative Republican. The neoconservatives, for all their intellectual brilliance, remained a tiny band of generals with no troops. Jews were still overwhelmingly Democratic and liberal. The Jewish shift to the right that neocons had been predicting since 1968 never materialized.

Instead, the major Jewish organizations began fighting the Reagan administration tooth and nail on a broad range of emotional issues, from abortion rights to civil rights to school prayer. Whatever gratitude the Jews felt for Reagan's friendship to Israel, it did not translate into political support. Reagan actually lost Jewish votes in his 1984 reelection bid, dropping from 40 percent to 33 percent. Democrat Walter Mondale, who lost every state except his own Minnesota, won two thirds of the Jews' votes.

AIPAC was a different kind of Jewish organization, for the simple reason that it had only one issue: Israel. A friend of Israel was a friend of AIPAC, period.

In June 1982, the fault line between hawks and doves, which had been threatening to split American Jewry apart for a decade and a half, broke open. Following a Palestinian attack on Israel's ambassador in London, Israeli troops entered Lebanon to strike at PLO strongholds. The operation was announced as a quick strike at terrorist bases in southern Lebanon, just over the border. Instead, the Israelis continued north to Beirut, the Lebanese capital, which they proceeded to bombard and then occupy. In September, a Lebanese Christian militia group allied to Israel entered two Palestinian refugee camps on the outskirts of Beirut and massacred close to 800 civilians in cold blood.

The invasion of Lebanon, the shelling of Beirut, and the massacres in the camps had a devastating impact on American Jewish attitudes toward Israel. So did the response of Prime Minister Begin, who dismissed his critics wholesale as anti-Semites. Rabbi Arthur Hertzberg, who had once refused to share a panel with a Breira member, wrote an essay for the *New York Times* op-ed page, titled "Begin Must Go." Alexander Schindler called for the creation of an international "Jewish parliament," as a forum for Diaspora Jews to express their views to Israel, in a December 1982 speech to the Reform union.

A 1983 survey of American Jewish popular opinion, conducted by the American Jewish Committee, found Jews agreeing nearly two to one that they were "often troubled by the policies of the current Israeli government" (48 percent to 29 percent, with 23 percent "not sure"). A separate poll of community leaders—board members of the Big Three, B'nai B'rith, and the UJA—found even more distress, with fully 70 percent agreeing they were "often troubled" and only 21 percent disagreeing. By four to one, Jewish leaders agreed that Begin's policies "have hurt Israel in the United States."

In the fall of 1982, both the Presidents Conference and AIPAC sent private messages to Begin urging him to moderate his policies. The Presidents Conference dispatched Schindler to meet with Begin personally, to ask for a state commission of inquiry into the massacres.

In August 1983, Menachem Begin resigned abruptly as prime minister, nine months after the death of his wife and six months after a commission he had appointed found his government partly responsible for the Beirut massacres. He was succeeded by Yitzhak Shamir, leader of the Likud's hardline faction. A dour, taciturn ex-intelligence agent, he had once commanded an anti-British terrorist band in pre-1948 Palestine.

In July 1984, Shamir led his party into a general election and lost, winning only 41 seats in the 120-member parliament. The Labor Party, led by Shimon Peres, took 44 seats. But neither party was able to forge a ruling coalition out of the small, splintered religious and fringe parties that held the remaining seats. Instead, Shamir and Peres agreed to join forces in a government of national unity. Peres was named prime minister, his deputy Yitzhak Rabin became defense minister, and Shamir became foreign minister. It was agreed that Peres and Shamir would switch jobs in two years.

The result was four years of intrigue and backstabbing. Peres, during his two years in charge, engineered an Israeli troop pullback in Lebanon, reduced inflation from 800 percent annually to 40 percent, and held the first Israeli-Egyptian summit since 1978. He also began secret talks with Jordan's King Hussein, gradually expanding Jordan's role on the West Bank and moving toward a peace agreement in which Jordan would take over the territory altogether. Shamir, during his two years as prime minister, managed to scuttle the deal with Jordan and greatly expand the pace of Jewish settlement in the West Bank. By the end of the four-year term of the so-called unity government, Israelis were regularly describing it as a "two-headed monster" and "government of national paralysis."

In one arena, however, there was little competition between Peres and Shamir: relations with the American Jewish community. Shamir had that field to himself.

"I would say that ignoring American Jewry was one of the biggest mistakes we made," said one senior Peres adviser, in an interview shortly after Shamir took over. "We simply didn't think it was important, and we let Shamir's people do whatever they wanted."

Before Shamir, Israel's political relationship with the American Jewish leadership was an informal affair, based on personal contacts by Israel's ambassador in Washington and consul general in New York. Shamir developed it into a complex operation involving diplomats, Israeli civil servants, and Likud party officials, all answering directly to Shamir's chief of staff, a hardline rightist career diplomat named Yossi Ben-Aharon. Their collective assignment was to turn the American Jewish establishment into an organ of Likud policy.

This was not a simple task. The existence of the unity government gave a new twist to the old principle that Jews must publicly support the policies of the Israeli government. Many were now asking *which* government policy they were supposed to defend. As Shamir and Peres bickered and undercut each other, therefore, American Jews divided along the old left-right fault line. Some, like Reform leader Alexander Schindler and American Jewish Congress director Henry Siegman, became open critics of the settler movement and advocates of Peres's land-for-peace compromise plan. Others, led by ADL director Nathan Perlmutter and a brace of outspoken Orthodox rabbis, stood solidly with Shamir.

The genius of Shamir's strategy—or Ben-Aharon's—was to manipulate the central bodies of Jewish representation so that, without taking sides, they became voices for the Likud half of the government. The Presidents Conference and AIPAC, which lent themselves most readily to manipulation, were rewarded with access and public recognition; more than ever, they were recognized as the all but official voices of American Jewry.

NCRAC, which was not so easily controlled, was simply shoved to the margins, starved for access and attention. Gradually it was reduced to irrelevancy in Middle East policy.

One key tactic was seeing that the right leaders were chosen. During the Begin years, the Presidents Conference had been chaired in succession by the presidents of the Reform movement, NCRAC, and the American Jewish Congress. Each was dutifully pro-Israel, but all refused Begin's repeated demands to endorse his settlements policy or attack the idea of compromise. Under Shamir, the Presidents Conference was chaired by the head of the Orthodox Union, then by the head of the ADL, and then, beginning in 1986, by the head of the National Conference on Soviet Jewry, renowned civil rights attorney Morris B. Abram. The neoconservative Abram had directed President Reagan's civil rights commission, and his national prominence guaranteed enormous visibility for the Presidents Conference—and for Shamir's views.

In May 1986, just as Abram was about to take over, Presidents Conference executive director Yehuda Hellman suddenly died. His replacement was Malcolm Hoenlein, a onetime Soviet Jewry activist from Philadelphia who had spent the last decade running the Jewish Community Relations Council of New York. New York's vast, fractious Jewish community had never managed to unite in a JCRC until 1976; Hoenlein, the founding director, had built the council into a powerful force in New York and Washington politics.

Hoenlein was an Orthodox Jew, mildly rightist but deeply pragmatic. His nomination had Ben-Aharon's warm endorsement. Peres's advisers briefly debated vetoing the appointment, on the premise that the Presidents Conference job should be subject to the same bipartisan agreement as any top ambassadorial appointment or civil service job. "We decided not to bother," said a Peres aide. "At the time we didn't see the point."

Hoenlein quickly took firm control. Witty, engaging, passionately articulate, he established himself as an essential figure in U.S. Middle East policymaking, a key conduit between Washington and an increasingly testy Shamir. He cultivated New York's business and media elite, becoming a regular fixture at fashionable power breakfasts at the Regency Hotel, where the city's movers and shakers met each morning. With less publicity, he became an advocate for the Likud and for the West Bank settler movement, lending his name to their fund-raising events and inviting their American representatives to take an ever greater role in the work of the Presidents Conference. American supporters of the Labor Party were subjected to a steady barrage of public and private attacks.

In April 1987, Shimon Peres, now foreign minister, met with King Hussein in a London hotel to wrap up their long, secret negotiation over a peace deal. Israel would return most of the West Bank to Hussein, and Jordan would sign a peace treaty with Israel. Because Hussein would not get back everything he had lost in 1967, he insisted that the deal take place under the cover of an international peace conference, so that he did not have to face the rest of the Arabs alone. Peres agreed, on condition that the conference could not make decisions and impose them on Israel.

Peres sent an aide to meet with Secretary of State George Shultz and ask him to adopt the plan as his own, as a way of coaxing a reluctant Shamir on board. Shultz refused to play along, saying that Peres should convince his own prime minister. Peres brought the plan to Shamir, who flatly rejected it.

Now began an elaborate shadow dance. Peres and his aides, knowing that Shultz liked the London agreement, tried to persuade American Jews to persuade Shultz to persuade Shamir. Shamir tried to head them off. Peres enjoyed more support among American Jews. But Shamir understood American Jewish politics.

During the spring and summer, the American Jewish Committee and the American Jewish Congress both endorsed the London plan, the Committee in a dense analysis that was largely ignored, the Congress in a press conference that was reported on the front page of the *New York Times*. Peres, appearing before the Presidents Conference in late September, was challenged on the propriety of American Jewish organizations differing from Israeli government policy. He answered that it would be "un-Jewish" of him to demand that Jews muzzle their own views.

The *Jerusalem Post* reported the next day that Peres had made "an appeal to U.S. Jewry to become actively involved in Israel's internal debate." Shamir responded furiously, warning Morris Abram in an angry letter that American Jews had no business deciding Israel's future. As for Peres, Shamir wrote, any Israeli who tried to bypass the Israeli voters "by appealing to friends abroad who do not vote in Israel would deal a blow to our sovereignty and democratic traditions." Indeed, Shamir added, fear of outside pressure was "one of the main reasons we object to an international conference."

Abram, cowed, wrote back that whatever individual members might say, the Presidents Conference would not take a position on the international peace conference. Peres wrote to Shamir that he had never asked them to take a position in the first place.

Nobody took the time to notice that the Israeli government had not taken a position either. The unity government was deadlocked on the international conference. Shamir's "we object" referred to himself and his friends. But his bluster forced everyone else to back down.

Two months after the flap, an Israeli motorist in the occupied Gaza Strip lost control of his truck and rammed into two Arab vans, killing six people. The accident touched off a wave of rioting that spread throughout the occupied territories. Within days, it had become an organized Palestinian uprising. The *intifadah* would last five years and leave the PLO firmly in charge of the West Bank and Gaza. In the summer of 1988, King Hussein washed his hands of the territories.

On paper, at least, the job of the Presidents Conference was to forge a consensus on Israel from among the diverse views of organized American Jews. Translating those views into political clout in Washington was the job of AIPAC.

The two groups have closely interlocking directorates. AIPAC is one of the fifty organizations that make up the Presidents Conference. The members of the Presidents Conference each have one seat on AIPAC's executive committee, and whoever chairs the Presidents Conference is a member of AIPAC's inner ruling body, the officers' group.

After the Lebanon War, however, AIPAC doubled the size of its executive committee, so that the Jewish organizational leaders could be outvoted by a bloc of individuals chosen directly from among AIPAC's mass membership. As the executive committee became more and more unwieldy, the officers' group began to operate more freely.

In practice, decisions were now being taken by a small group headed by a past AIPAC president, Larry Weinberg of Los Angeles.

Weinberg is a contradictory character: an intellectual in the rough-and-tumble world of real estate, a registered Democrat who was largely responsible for the working alliance between the organized Jewish community and the Reagan administration. Longtime owner of basketball's Portland Trail Blazers—he bought into the team for $1 million in 1970 and sold it for $63 million in 1988—he was described by Portland sportswriters as "a kind and gentle man." AIPAC staffers and officers were in awe of him.

Associates say Weinberg was a McGovern Democrat who underwent a wrenching metamorphosis during the 1970s, amid the traumas that followed the Yom Kippur War. Elected president of AIPAC in 1976, he developed a close friendship with Menachem Begin, soured badly on Jimmy Carter, and became an ardent backer of Ronald Reagan's 1980 presidential bid.

His thinking was not easily characterized, however. It was Weinberg who led the AIPAC executive committee in its 1980 decision to hire Tom Dine, a veteran liberal who had worked as a foreign-policy aide to Senator Edward Kennedy. Weinberg also brought in, as Dine's research director and de facto number-two, a conservative foreign-policy expert from the Los Angeles–based RAND corporation named Steven Rosen. The hardline Rosen and the liberal Dine would balance each other, not always comfortably, over the next decade.

After stepping down as AIPAC president in 1982, Weinberg devoted himself to creating a new Washington think tank. His goal, he told friends, was to alter the intellectual atmosphere surrounding Middle East policy discussions in the capital. The Washington Institute for Near East Policy opened its doors in 1984 with Weinberg's wife Barbi, herself a formidable power in Jewish community circles, as president. The executive director was Martin Indyk, an Australian Jewish Middle East scholar who had worked with Steven Rosen in the AIPAC research department.

The Washington Institute was typical of Weinberg's unpredictable thinking. Even though it was established to help move Beltway thinking toward Israel, it became a stronghold of Labor thinking at the height of the Likud era. It brought established Israeli critics of the Likud, such as journalists Hirsh Goodman and Ze'ev Schiff, and set them up as visiting fellows. It published the writings of American theorists such as Dennis Ross and Richard Haass, whose work for the Bush administration would make them bêtes noires of the Shamir government. The institute's overall purpose was not to sell Israeli policies, but "to define the agenda in a way that's conducive to Israeli interests," said one outside observer, former National

Security Council staffer William Quandt. "When people just accept your assumptions, you're halfway there in a policy debate."

Weinberg's successors as AIPAC president were a series of conservative Republicans: Robert Asher, a Chicago lighting-fixtures dealer; Edward C. Levy Jr., a Detroit building-supplies dealer; and Mayer "Bubba" Mitchell, a scrap-metal dealer from Mobile, Alabama. Each was a prodigious GOP donor with good entrée to the White House. That made them useful spokespersons for AIPAC and Israel. However, none of them brought Weinberg's intellectual tools.

At times, the gap proved embarrassing. In one notorious incident, Ed Levy, who headed AIPAC from 1988 to 1990, went to the Pentagon to lobby for a Hawk missile that Israel was trying to acquire. But he forgot which version of the Hawk he was asking for, and ending up demanding the wrong one.

Weinberg and his successors—insiders called them "the Gang of Four"—were an unlikely but effective team. Asher, Levy, and Mitchell shared a delight in the hands-on work of pro-Israel lobbying, from visiting the White House to stalking the halls of Congress to micromanaging the AIPAC staff. While looking to Weinberg for intellectual guidance on the subtleties of Middle East diplomacy, they were the ones who oversaw the restructuring and expansion of AIPAC from the compact machine that Morris Amitay had built into the vast army it would become.

Leading the AIPAC army like a combination drill sergeant, cheerleader, and revival preacher was executive director Tom Dine. Named by *Washingtonian* magazine as one of the capital's most influential people in 1984, he was a thoroughly assimilated Jew from the Midwest—tall, thin, often described as having "boyish good looks," raised in Cincinnati, educated in California, married to a non-Jew, and ardently liberal.

As director of AIPAC, Dine brought the organization from the shadows into the spotlight. In speeches to AIPAC membership gatherings around the country, he openly boasted about the lobby's successful marshalling of "Jewish political power" and warned opponents that the Jewish community, led by AIPAC, "would not forget."

Publicity became a weapon for increasing AIPAC's clout. Before Dine, AIPAC had worked quietly behind the scenes, letting credit go to its masters in New York, or to its partners on Capitol Hill. Dine's AIPAC was not so shy. "The theory was, no one is scared of you if they don't know about you," said one former staffer.

AIPAC's biggest show of force was its annual policy conference, staged each spring in a Washington hotel. The conference brings together hundreds of activists from across the country for three days of speeches by Israeli and American politicians. Its climactic Congressional Dinner attracts hundreds of Congress members and dozens of foreign ambassadors every year, all of them eager to curry goodwill with AIPAC and the Jewish community. Lest the point be lost, the dinner chairperson always reads a "roll call" naming every senator, representative, and ambassador present in the hall. After dinner, delegates retire to receptions sponsored by AIPAC's regional divisions in the conference rooms around the ballroom, or to private receptions in hotel suites, sponsored by lawmakers courting Jewish campaign support.

"The AIPAC conference is like the Passover Haggadah," says attorney Jennifer Laszlo of Durham, North Carolina. "It's the same every year, but it never hurts to be reminded."

Laszlo first joined AIPAC in 1984, when she was recruited to AIPAC's student program on the campus of Emory University in Atlanta. Brought to national conferences, introduced to other young Jews, she was taught to mobilize her fellow students on Middle East issues, to organize meetings, and to collect petitions. She was united with other Jews her own age from around the country in a grand crusade. In 1994 she ran for Congress herself, turning to her AIPAC friends for campaign funding.

"What AIPAC shows young people like myself," Laszlo says, "is that everyone has a right to petition their own government and ask it to be accountable. It's a message that carries over to anything from health care to crime—that one person can make a difference. It's the most important message a young person can get."

And indeed, lobbying Congress on aid to Israel became just one small part of the AIPAC's work under Dine. Of 150 AIPAC staffers in the early 1990s, only a half-dozen were registered as lobbyists to meet with lawmakers and try to influence their voting. The rest operated a huge, diversified influence machine.

A large group of staffers worked in research, supplying the lobbyists with detailed information on issues ranging from Middle East water rights to new missile technology. Others wrote and published a series of booklets and a biweekly newsletter, *Near East Report,* a terse roundup of Israel-related news and policy analysis. Research and publication proved to be as useful as direct lobbying in shaping congressional opinion. "They quite simply have the best material of anybody dealing with foreign affairs," declared one House member, speaking on condition of anonymity, "and they give it to you in a form you can use. That's probably the key to their influence, in my opinion."

Several dozen staffers worked in administration and finance, raising the ever-growing sums needed to keep the machine running. As a lobbying organization, AIPAC's donations are not tax-deductible, unlike any other Jewish agency. Nonetheless, its revenues mushroomed during the 1980s, from $1.2 million in 1980 to $15 million in 1990. Regional AIPAC offices around the country worked hard to to keep the donations flowing into the Washington headquarters, through direct-mail appeals, fund-raising dinners and one-on-one solicitation.

Their success was testimony to AIPAC's appeal among Jewish activists in the 1980s and 1990s. AIPAC offered Jewish activists access to genuine power, rubbing shoulders with senators and representatives and bullying the White House. Members streamed in, quintupling the body's membership within a decade. And the more members joined, the more power AIPAC acquired, and the more members it attracted.

The real key to AIPAC's clout, according to current and former staffers and officers, is its ability to mobilize its members as a disciplined army of volunteer lobbyists across the country. A large part of the staff is assigned to work with members, helping them become involved in political campaigns—virtually every political campaign—as volunteers and donors.

With members active in the camp of nearly every candidate for every seat in Congress, AIPAC comes out of nearly every election a winner.

AIPAC staffers run regional training sessions for members, teaching them campaign skills and showing them how to leverage their money, thereby maximizing the political impact of each donation. Activists learn to "bundle" donations, extracting campaign contributions from friends, relatives, and coworkers, and delivering them to the candidate in a bundle so as to make a stronger impression.

None of this activity is secret. On the contrary, AIPAC members advertise their attachment to AIPAC and Israel. This practice is thought to help get their message across. No less important, it attracts new members.

During every congressional campaign, each candidate for every seat is asked to describe his or her views on the Middle East. Most office-seekers happily comply in writing. AIPAC then shares the results with its members, helping them to decide who is the most pro-Israel.

In a decade and a half of this political proselytizing, AIPAC has developed a huge network of contacts throughout the American political system. Members have entered politics themselves, some winning seats in state legislatures and running (so far unsuccessfully) for Congress. AIPAC staffers—many of them recruited from the congressional staffs of both parties—have gone on to a host of other positions on Capitol Hill, within the two parties and as freelance political consultants.

After the Republicans lost the White House in 1992, AIPAC's executive committee chose a Democratic president, Boston stationery executive Steven Grossman, continuing a tradition of staying in step with the political winds.

Grossman was in many ways an inspired choice. He had served as treasurer of Clinton's campaign in Massachusetts and had good entry to the Clinton White House. He quickly developed a positive rapport with Yitzhak Rabin, the Labor leader who had ousted Yitzhak Shamir's Likud bloc and taken charge in Jerusalem a few months before Clinton took over Washington.

Nevertheless, Grossman could not take charge of AIPAC. The four ex-presidents who led the officers' group—Weinberg, Asher, Levy, and Mitchell—refused to let go. Suspicious of both Clinton and Rabin, they kept AIPAC under tight rein and refused to allow it to plunge into the new era. They began to make decisions among themselves, sharing them with the other members of the officers' group only afterward.

In June 1993, the officers decided to fire Tom Dine. The reason given publicly was the publication of a book on Israeli politics that quoted Dine as saying that Orthodox Jews had a "smelly" image. Leaders of the Orthodox community demanded his head. The officers' group gave it to them.

The Israeli press corps promptly reported that the Dine ouster was Rabin's doing, that the Labor leader was settling accounts with the pro-Likud hawks who ran the American Jewish establishment. The truth was just the opposite. Dine was not the source of AIPAC's hawkish tilt; he himself was a liberal. The hawkish tilt had come from the officers' group, which had fired Dine, mainly because he was becoming too independent of them. His departure left them firmly in charge.

Dine's dismissal led to a fierce power struggle to name his replacement. The officers wanted to promote administrative director Howard Kohr, a conservative Republican who had been with the lobby for a decade. Grossman managed to mobilize a group of insurgent Democrats to block Kohr, arguing that it made no sense to move the lobby to the right when both Washington and Jerusalem had moved to the left. The lobby had always worked hard to stay in tune with both capitals.

The left eventually won the fight with the installation of Neal Sher, longtime chief of the Nazi-hunting Office of Special Investigations at the Justice Department. He was an attractive, articulate attorney with vast experience in the federal bureaucracy and a good deal of credibility in the Jewish community.

Unfortunately, Sher had no experience in Middle East diplomacy. The officers' group outmaneuvered him at every possible turn. After Rabin signed his peace accord with Yasser Arafat on the White House lawn in September of 1993, Robert Asher began working the halls of Congress himself, lobbying against Rabin's accord and the American initiatives that were meant to back it up. When Grossman convened the officers' group to discuss how AIPAC could block the obstructionists, the four simply overruled him. He may well have had a majority on the broader governing bodies, but Weinberg had created a tradition that kept decisions close to the center. Grossman could rarely break out of this inner circle. Neal Sher finally quit in 1996, and was succeeded by Howard Kohr.

One former top AIPAC staffer described the rule of the "Gang of Four" as essentially resulting from the acquiescence of the rest of the organization: "I can't imagine being on the board of an organization and allowing a situation where you get on a conference call and the decisions were made before you got on. It's amazing that no one ever stopped them."

Part III

THE CRISES OF JEWISH POWER

CHAPTER 9

"I Am Joseph Your Brother":
Jews and Public Office

*And Joseph said unto his brethren: 'Come near to me, I pray you.' And
they came near. And he said: 'I am Joseph your brother, whom ye sold
into Egypt. And now be not grieved, nor angry with yourselves, that ye
sold me hither; for God did send me before you to preserve life.'*
— Genesis 45:4–5

A BBA EBAN, Israel's elder statesman and foremost diplomat, argues
that only two American Jews have ever wielded real power as Jews.
For the most part, he says, American Jewry's vaunted "power" through
the years has not been true power, but merely influence. That is, Jews have
frequently been able to reach the decision-makers and convince them to
make favorable decisions. But only two individuals actually have found
themselves in a position where their own decisions and actions would
determine the fate of the Jewish people: Arthur J. Goldberg and Henry
Kissinger.

Goldberg was America's ambassador to the United Nations in 1967,
when the Security Council was debating ways to force an Israeli withdrawal
from the territories captured during the Six-Day War. Acting largely on his
own—the Johnson White House was distracted by the quagmire of
Vietnam—Goldberg maneuvered for months to protect Israel from losing
on New York's East River what it won on the battlefield. The result was
Resolution 242, adopted by the Security Council in November 1967.

"Two-four-two," as diplomats call it, required that Israel withdraw "from
territories" taken in the war. Missing, at Goldberg's insistence, was the word

"the." That left Israel free to withdraw from some or all of the territories, depending on what sort of deal it cut with its neighbors. The resolution also made Israeli withdrawal part of a package peace agreement, freeing Israel from Arab demands for a unilateral pullback. Resolution 242 has formed the legal basis for all Middle East diplomacy since then. Thanks to Goldberg, it allowed Israel to wait for Arab recognition before discussing withdrawal.

Kissinger, of course, was the national security adviser and secretary of state who guided American foreign policy for eight years during the Nixon and Ford administrations. These were years of nonstop Middle East crisis. They saw the rise of Palestinian terrorism; the Yom Kippur War of 1973; the Arab oil embargo; and the disengagement talks among Israel, Syria, and Egypt. According to Eban, Kissinger's management of the Yom Kippur War ceasefire, and of the disengagement talks that followed, set in motion the process leading to the historic Israel-Egypt peace treaty of 1978. During the Yom Kippur War, in particular, with President Nixon consumed by Watergate, Kissinger operated virtually autonomously.

In some senses, Eban's list is too short; it begins with a too-narrow definition of power. Public figures rarely enjoy the sort of absolute autonomy that lets them act without constraints. Even the president of the United States is constrained in his actions by Congress, the courts, and the public. To say that officials wield power only when they can do as they please, without asking permission or negotiating a bureaucracy, is to describe a power that exists nowhere.

Then, too, Eban's list begs a larger question: what does it mean for a Jew to act "as a Jew"? Hundreds of Jews have held important government jobs in the last quarter-century, many of them positions of considerable power and influence. More than a few of these people have acted at crucial moments to alter the flow of events in the Middle East, much as Goldberg and Kissinger did, if with less drama. Some clearly acted because they felt duty-bound as Jews. Others had motives that were much more ambiguous, even to themselves.

There are times, moreover, when a public official who is Jewish must make a decision "as a Jew" that has nothing to do with Israel. Occasionally, it concerns an issue of obvious Jewish interest, like the rescue of endangered Jewish communities in the Soviet Union, Syria, or Ethiopia. At other times, the Jewish interest is less obvious, yet an official may believe at the moment of crisis that Jewish interests or values are involved—trying to stop genocide in Bosnia, for example, or acting to ensure women access to abortion services.

Finally, there are times when a Jew in public office faces a decision "as a Jew" and opts to duck. Many Jewish government officials are simply not prepared to respond when Jewish duty calls, says Stuart Eizenstat, who served as chief of the White House domestic-policy staff under Jimmy Carter. "It depends on a couple of things. Are they Jews by birth, or do they have some strong Jewish community or pro-Israel contacts? Most don't. Most Jews who go into government tend to have strong public-service or political leanings, and they tend to be less strongly affiliated to the Jewish community. And second, Jews, like everyone else, represent the institutional interests of the institution for whom they work."

During George Bush's presidency, Secretary of State James Baker put together a team of Middle East experts whose full-time assignment was to advance the Israeli-Arab peace process. The head of the team was Baker's director of policy planning, Dennis B. Ross, who had headed the Middle East bureau at the National Security Council in the final Reagan years. Assisting Ross in his new duties were a deputy in the State Department's Near East bureau, Daniel Kurtzer, and one of Ross's own deputies in the policy-planning bureau, Aaron David Miller. Their liaison at the White House was Richard Haass, Middle East expert on the National Security Council staff.

All four—Ross, Haass, Kurtzer, and Miller—were Jews.

Baker's Jewish peace team infuriated Israeli prime minister Yitzhak Shamir and his American Jewish loyalists. Furious at Bush for pressuring Israel to freeze Jewish settlement of the occupied territories and trade land for peace, Shamir and his aides regularly referred to the foursome in private as "self-hating Jews" and "traitors." Some voices were even harsher. The *Jewish Press,* the mass-circulation Orthodox weekly in Brooklyn, regularly carried attacks on "Baker's apostates," comparing them to those baptised Jews who joined the Inquisition in the Middle Ages.

The four "peace processors" appeared quite differently in the eyes of moderate American Jewish leaders and Israeli career diplomats, at least to those with no ideological attachment to the Likud. For them, Ross and company were nothing less than allies on the inside, helping to steer the ship of U.S.-Israel relations between the Scylla and Charybdis of George Bush and Yitzhak Shamir. "All I can say about Dennis is that he's a friend," said the head of one key Jewish agency.

Some observers claimed to see two different groups at work among the peace processors. On one side was the State Department trio of Ross, Miller, and Kurtzer; they were often described as operating out of a deep commitment to Israeli security, which they believed could best be served by peace. On the other side was Haass, who was widely perceived as colder toward Israel, motivated more by his reading of U.S. interests than by any emotional commitment to the Jewish state.

In the words of one Washington journalist who covered Middle East politics, "the difference between Richie Haass and the three guys at State was like the difference between an Israeli leftist and one of those old Arabists at the State Department. Both want America to pressure Israel, but the Israeli leftist wants it because he loves Israel and the State Department Arabist wants it because he doesn't."

Coincidentally or not, the fault line between Haass at the White House and the trio at the State Department could be described in religious as well as diplomatic terms. Haass was educated in a Reform congregation and had little connection to organized Judaism after adolescence. Ross, Miller, and Kurtzer all were active synagogue-goers—Ross and Miller to Conservative congregations, Kurtzer to an Orthodox one. Miller and Kurtzer both maintained kosher homes and sent their children to Jewish parochial schools.

All three of the State Department peace processors were fastidiously insistent that they be seen professionally as American public servants serving U.S. foreign policy. Yet none made any bones about their personal feelings of attachment to Israel. "We act in America's interest, but through a prism," said one, speaking on condition of anonymity.

Indeed, both Kurtzer and Miller entered the foreign service as a result of their interest in Middle East affairs. Ross, trained in Soviet affairs, eased into Middle East work during the early 1980s, at the same time that his personal commitment to Judaism was growing. "The Soviet Union was always more an intellectual kind of preoccupation for me. The Middle East was more of an emotional commitment."

The peace processors unanimously insisted that by pushing Israel toward concessions, they were not acting against Israel. Rather, they were helping Israel to reach the peace with its neighbors that it had sought for so long. "I believe that peace is in Israel's interest," said Ross. "That is, peace with security. It's also in America's interest."

Even though the strategy brought them into bitter conflict with the Likud government of Yitzhak Shamir, it was well in line with the policies of Israel's opposition Labor Party. Indeed, some Washington insiders— including a pro-Likud administration official and an Arab-American leader with ties to the PLO—spoke of the peace processors in all seriousness as "Labor Zionists."

Administration insiders generally dismissed the notion, common among Jewish community activists, that there was any meaningful difference among the processors, either in broad policy or in their commitment to Israel. "In a sense, Richard [Haass] got a bad rap," said one Bush administration official who followed Middle East affairs. "He was identified with policies in the White House, and the general mood in the White House was less sympathetic to Israel's needs than was the case at the State Department. It was a function of [national security adviser General] Brent Scowcroft, of [White House chief of staff and longtime Arab-American activist] John Sununu, and to some extent of Bush himself. They fixated on the settlements as an ideological issue. Baker viewed the settlements from a tactical standpoint, and not something he was emotionally or ideologically attached to."

Most intriguing of all, some Jewish community officials who saw a difference between Haass and the State Department trio also claimed to see a change in Haass during the months following Bush's September 1991 "powerful forces" press conference. "The experience Judaized him," insisted the head of one major Jewish organization who was in regular contact with the administration.

The experience of "Judaization" is not uncommon when Jews enter public life. Dealing with public issues often intensifies their own personal awareness of being Jewish. More important, it opens their eyes to the political dimension of Judaism.

Most Jews who enter public service are mainstream American Jews, reared in the American Judaism of ethical values and personal sensibilities. Coming to Washington, they are thrust suddenly into a world where the Jews are a political entity with crucial interests to defend. No less important, Jewish officials find for the first time that much of the world—Jewish and non-Jewish alike—holds them responsible as Jews for the actions and the fate of other Jews.

This is particularly true in Congress. "I'm reminded of what my mother used to tell me—it doesn't matter whether you consider yourself a Jew, because other people will," says Senator Paul Wellstone, a Minnesota Democrat. "I've had a strong identity as a Jew for some time, particularly as my children have gotten older and I began to wonder about their identity. What's changed since I entered the Senate is this expectation that when issues come up around Israel, Jewish senators are *expected* to get involved."

In the executive branch, Jewish officials only rarely face issues of Jewish political interest. When they do, the weight of American law and tradition encourages them to do their jobs as professionals, to put American national interest first and last. If Jewish sentiment enters the picture, it is usually in private reflections.

Nonetheless, it can make a difference. Sherman Funk, inspector general of the State Department, issued a report in the spring of 1990 charging that Israel had illegally transferred U.S. arms technology to China and South Africa. Jerusalem was furious. The violation, its diplomats insisted, was at most a technicality of the sort long overlooked. Funk would not close his eyes; a devout Reform Jew and onetime pupil of the philosopher Martin Buber, he told the *Washington Jewish Week* that he was offended by such behavior in a Jewish state.

At the other extreme was Richard Schifter, head of the State Department's human rights bureau throughout the 1980s. He regularly issued human rights reports critical of Israel, particularly its practices in the occupied territories. But his critiques were milder than others', so much so that he was sometimes accused of a pro-Israel bias. Schifter shrugged it off. "As a Jew, some things that were being done by Israel upset me quite a bit," he said. "But when I put it in the context of what I had to do as assistant secretary for human rights, I had to ask myself at all times, compared to whom?"

In 1991, at the height of the Bush administration's confrontation with Israel, no fewer than seven of the nineteen assistant secretaries in the State Department were Jews. Some juggled Jewish issues on a daily basis, like

Dennis Ross in the policy-planning bureau, or Princeton Lyman in the refugee-affairs bureau, who oversaw the flow of Soviet Jewish émigrés. Others, like Bernard Aronson (son of NCRAC's Arnold Aronson) in the Latin American bureau, almost never faced them.

Still others ran headlong into Jewish crises at the most unexpected moments. Herman Cohen, an assimilated Jew from Brooklyn and career diplomat, was assistant secretary for African affairs in the Bush administration. In May 1991, at the height of the bloody civil war in Ethiopia, the administration arranged a one-day cease-fire so the Israeli air force could airlift the twenty thousand–member Jewish tribe known as the Falashas and bring them "home" to Israel. Cohen oversaw the delicate negotiations that made it possible.

"I have these conversations with myself all the time," Cohen says. "First of all, I thank God that I'm not working in Middle East affairs or at the U.N., where you might have to vote to condemn the Israelis."

Reflecting on his role in the Ethiopian Jewish exodus, he remains unsure whether being Jewish affected his behavior. "The United States government was interested in the Falashas, but it wasn't our highest priority. If our interests had dictated dropping the subject, I would have. So there you might have had a conflict between my Jewishness and my professional life. The question is, if I were not Jewish, would I have even put it on my list?"

The Falashas, once a quarter-million strong and Ethiopia's ruling tribe, had been decimated over the centuries by war, famine, and Christian missionizing. By the twentieth century, they were on the verge of collapse. Their cause was taken up in the 1960s by a tiny group of American Jewish militants, who demanded that Israel adopt the Falashas and bring them "home" as it had the Jews of Yemen, Morocco, and Romania in the 1950s.

Israel was reluctant, doubtful of the Falashas' Jewish roots and fearful of importing a domestic race problem. But the American militants, now calling themselves the American Association for Ethiopian Jews, waged an unrelenting pressure campaign. In 1977, under the newly elected Menachem Begin, Israel capitulated. Begin undertook secret talks with the Ethiopian regime. In 1984, a quiet exodus was arranged through neighboring Arab Sudan, whose aid was covertly enlisted by Vice President George Bush. It was cut short after just six weeks when word of it leaked to the press, blurted by Jewish Agency chairman Aryeh Dulzin at a fund-raising meeting.

Herman Cohen was introduced to the Falasha issue during his 1989 confirmation hearings, when he was questioned on the topic by Senator Rudy Boschwitz, a Jewish Republican from Minnesota. In follow-up conversations with NCRAC officials, he agreed to help if he could.

Cohen found his opening shortly afterward when Secretary of State Baker sent him to Geneva to meet with his Soviet counterpart, Kremlin Africa specialist Anatoly Adamishin. Cohen's instructions were to defuse the East-West confrontations in strife-torn Ethiopia and Angola.

In Geneva, the Soviets gave him a green light. Adamishin, it so happened, was Jewish too. In August, Cohen visited Addis Ababa, the Ethiopian capital, where dictator Mengistu Haile Mariam was eager for better American ties. Cohen gave him a list of conditions, including Jewish emigration. Shortly afterward, Mengistu invited Israel to open a consulate.

The Falashas, meanwhile, remained stuck in their isolated villages. Talks between Israel and the tottering regime were endlessly going nowhere. Exit visas were issued agonizingly slowly, while the civil war moved ever closer to the Falashas' home province.

In October 1990, enraged at Israeli foot-dragging, the militants of the American Association for Ethiopian Jews forced a showdown. They rented a fleet of trucks and carted the entire tribe down to the capital. The Falashas were deposited, twenty thousand strong, in a field opposite the Israeli consulate. "It was either the craziest stunt anyone ever pulled, or the most brilliant maneuver ever," said Michael Schneider, executive director of the Joint Distribution Committee, who flew into Addis Ababa with a team to erect a hasty tent camp.

At last Shamir gave a go-ahead for action. A secret task force was assembled, coordinated in Tel Aviv by government troubleshooter Uri Lubrani and in New York by Schneider. The Presidents Conference oversaw contacts with the administration.

At the State Department, Herman Cohen was not brought into the Jewish deliberations. His orders came from the secretary of state.

"Chaos was breaking out in Addis Ababa," he recalls. "The city was about to fall to the rebels. We had asked the rebels to stay out because we were trying to negotiate a peaceful solution to the war. The provisional government was desperately trying to have us save them. We said, 'Yes, but there's one precondition. You let the Israelis bring in planes and get the Falashas out.' "

The regime, wary of the U.S. embassy's promises, turned to the Israeli mission and asked for guarantees: a personal guarantee of safety for their leaders from President Bush, plus $35 million cash in a New York bank. The request went from Addis Ababa to Tel Aviv. Lubrani passed it to Schneider in New York, who got to work. A group of Jewish millionaires was assembled to raise the $35 million. At the same time, a group of Jewish lawmakers in Washington approached the House leadership and asked for $35 million to be set aside secretly as a contingency. Max Fisher and Rudy Boschwitz went to a dubious George Bush and asked him to personally guarantee the safety of the Ethiopian butchers. After some hesitation, Bush agreed.

Cohen now sent a deputy, Robert Houdek, to the rebels' headquarters in the Sudan to ask for a twenty-four-hour cease-fire while Israeli planes lifted out the Falashas. On Friday, May 24, just after noon, the first Israeli plane touched down at Addis Ababa, its markings painted over and its seats removed, and took off with one thousand refugees on board. Then another plane landed, and another. By Saturday afternoon, virtually every one of the black Jews of Ethiopia was an Israeli citizen.

"The question is," says Cohen, "if I were not Jewish, would I have put that on my list of things to do? Whoever it was, he would have heard from Boschwitz. And President Bush certainly had an interest in the issue. But how many times along the way would another guy have said, 'Look, we've got enough on our plates, maybe I'll leave the Falashas for next year'? I don't know the answer."

When Professor Henry Kissinger came from Harvard to Washington in 1969 to serve as Richard Nixon's national security adviser, he was given a strangely bifurcated job assignment. On one hand, his job was expanded beyond the responsibilities of previous national security advisers. The adviser originally had been conceived as a glorified traffic cop to manage the flow of foreign-policy ideas into the White House from State, Defense, and the intelligence agencies. Kissinger was invited to do more: to work with the president in directing foreign policy while reimagining America's role in the world. Nixon mistrusted the State Department's entrenched bureaucracy and intended to be his own secretary of state. Kissinger was to be his right hand.

In another sense, though, Kissinger's job was more limited than his predecessors'. His authority over U.S. foreign policy stopped at the borders of the Middle East. In that one region, management of foreign affairs remained in the hands of the State Department, headed by an old friend of Nixon's, William P. Rogers.

Not until the spring of 1971 did Nixon permit Kissinger to play a role in managing America's Middle East policy, after Rogers's approach had failed and Nixon had become convinced that Kissinger's approach might succeed. After that, Kissinger's influence over American policy in the region grew steadily. After August 1973, when he was named secretary of state as well as national security adviser, his control was nearly complete.

In his 1979 memoir *White House Years,* Kissinger suggested that the division of his duties during Nixon's first two years arose from a variety of motives. One was Nixon's "ambivalent relationship" with Rogers: having undercut the State Department by bringing foreign policy-making to the White House, Nixon wanted to give Rogers one region that was his alone to manage. "But what Nixon gave away with one hand he tended to take away with the other," Kissinger wrote; the president gave Rogers the region least open to diplomatic success. Then, too, dividing the world this way served Nixon's need to "enhance his own control" by pitting his advisers against each other.

Nixon's other motivation, which Kissinger dismissed in a stunningly brief, sixteen-word sentence: "He also suspected that my Jewish origin might cause me to lean too much toward Israel."

Those who were present at the time are less delicate in their evaluations. Says William Quandt, a National Security Council (NSC) staffer under Kissinger: "Kissinger didn't like to talk about his background. It made him uncomfortable. Nixon frequently told him his Jewish background made his views on the Arab-Israeli issue suspect. For a long time he wouldn't let him near it. Whenever Nixon would make those comments, you could see a lot of resentment on Kissinger's part that Nixon would raise this issue. But Nixon was the key to Kissinger's having power. And he had some kind of respect for the guy's native intellect, so he would swallow it."

Few actors in recent American history have seen their role more closely scrutinized than Henry Kissinger. Yet no actor in recent Jewish history has been more underexamined. No Jew in modern times has wielded greater power on the world stage than Kissinger. None has seen his loyalties more passionately debated.

Jewish community activists are frequently harsh in their assessment of Kissinger's Jewish loyalty. To many, he embodies the age-old truth that Jews in high places will serve their masters, not their brethren. "The judgment I would make is one that Golda Meir shared with me," says Morris Amitay, who became executive director of AIPAC in 1974 (and is now a Washington lawyer-lobbyist). "I visited her right after she left power, and we did a post-mortem on who did what. She said, 'I guess as an American secretary of state, he could have done more for us—aside from the fact that he was Jewish.' I think she was saying his Jewishness inhibited him from being as supportive of us as he could have been."

On the street, the Jewish community's judgment was harsher still, and became increasingly so as Kissinger's tenure continued. During his Middle East shuttle diplomacy of 1975 and 1976, when he was hammering out the second Israeli-Egyptian disengagement pact, Israeli protesters regularly greeted him with signs calling him a "traitor" for his efforts at Israeli concessions. Once demonstrators tried to tip over his car, while signs in front of him read, "Hitler spared you so you could finish the job." "It hurt him deeply," recalls Peter Rodman, a former Kissinger aide.

Even those Jewish leaders who are most inclined to be generous to Kissinger concede little except that his actions were understandable. "My premise is that these are people who are not working for the Jewish community," says Rabbi Israel Miller, who chaired the Presidents Confer-ence from 1974 to 1976, referring to Jews in public office. "Their constitu-ency is the whole American people. Many people feel Kissinger was unfriendly. I think they take it out on him because he was a Jew. I think he was doing his job as he saw his job."

Yet, to those outside the Jewish community, Kissinger looked very different. "There were people in the United States government who were absolutely sure he was a Zionist," says Rodman, a Jewish graduate student who accompanied Kissinger from Harvard to Washington as his personal aide (and is now foreign-policy director at the Nixon Center for World Peace). "That's why Nixon didn't let Henry get involved in Middle East stuff until much later, even though they shared a strategic viewpoint."

Much of the controversy over Kissinger's Jewish loyalty revolves around his role in the turbulent events that began with the outbreak of war in the Middle East on Saturday, October 6, 1973. Just before noon, the armies of Egypt and Syria launched the surprise attack against Israel that became the Yom Kippur War. Caught off guard on the holiest day in the Jewish calen-dar, Israel suffered devastating losses in personnel and territory as its standing army absorbed the onslaught, waiting for the civilian reserves to mobilize.

Overall, Israel lost some 2,600 soldiers in the three-week war, more than triple the 700 lives lost in the Six-Day War of 1967. The psychological toll was even greater. The Six-Day War had left Israel with a feeling of safety, verging on invincibility. In its wake, the occupied territories came to be seen as a safety margin, moving hostile armies away from Israel's population centers and reducing the vulnerability that Israelis felt inside their narrow pre-1967 borders.

The new territorial configuration turned out to be more complicated than most had expected. The territories may have given the army a tactical advantage in geographic depth, but it was offset by the strategic disadvantage of diplomatic isolation. Nevertheless, like so many peoples who thought themselves invincible but found themselves vulnerable, Israelis did not reevaluate their dearly held preconceptions of territory and safety. Instead, they looked for a traitor. They found one in the Jew, Kissinger.

Theories about Kissinger's betrayal of Jewish interests basically involve three issues. The first was a mysterious, four-day delay in the start of a U.S. weapons airlift to resupply Israel after its initial losses. Second was the October 22 cease-fire that stopped hostilities just before Israel completed its encirclement of the Egyptian Third Army. The third was Kissinger's overall conduct of the two-year disengagement talks between Israel, Egypt, and Syria, trading Israeli concessions on the ground for Arab commitments on paper.

The first of these, the airlift, should be the simplest question to resolve, yet it remains the most insoluble. In the wee hours of Tuesday morning, October 9, the fourth day of the war, as the extent of Israel's predicament was becoming clear, Ambassador Simcha Dinitz woke Kissinger at home to ask for an emergency arms airlift. The first resupply planes did not take off until Saturday, October 13. What caused the four-day delay has been probed and debated endlessly since then. Various researchers have found documents seeming to prove either that Kissinger worked to delay the airlift—because he was indifferent to Israel's agony, or worse—or that his efforts to move it along were stymied by the Defense Department. The culprits most often fingered at Defense are then-Secretary of Defense James Schlesinger or his deputy William Clements.

The truth appears to be much more complicated than either scenario. As Kissinger himself noted in his 1982 memoir *Years of Upheaval,* he called for a resupply on Sunday, October 7, the war's second day—over the objections of most of his colleagues—in order to send a firm message to the Soviet Union. At that point, however, no one in Washington expected Israel to suffer serious reverses. Once the crisis became evident and an emergency resupply was called for on Tuesday, there were countless technical obstacles to overcome. Israel was asked to send El Al planes to pick up the equipment, but could not muster the aircraft. Kissinger, fearing that a U.S. military operation would touch off a disastrous Arab oil boycott, ordered charter cargo planes. But no charter company was willing to send its equipment into the war zone. When a decision was finally reached to send the materiel in U.S. military planes, Portugal refused to let them fly over its airspace.

With all that, the obstacles could have been cleared had there been a determined push from above. Every narration of the incident paints a different picture of who was pushing and who was resisting. This is where the motives of the key players become essential.

In the most carefully documented account of the episode, Kissinger biographer Walter Isaacson suggests that a key culprit in the delay—other than circumstance—may have been Deputy Defense Secretary Clements, "a Texas oilman with pro-Arab sympathies." Isaacson portrays Schlesinger as leaning toward Clements, though Schlesinger's motives remain unclear.

Many Jewish community activists are convinced to this day that Schlesinger's feelings toward Israel were colored by his ambivalent relationship to Judaism. Born Jewish, he was baptised an Episcopalian as a young man. The act of conversion has historically been taken among Jews as a sign of disloyalty—particularly when the conversion is to Christianity, the faith that waged war against Judaism for so many centuries.

Medieval Jewish history is indeed filled with tales of baptised Jews who joined the persecutors. The modern record is more mixed. In the nineteenth century, British politician Benjamin Disraeli and German poet Heinrich Heine, both baptised as young men, were staunch defenders of Jewish rights at a time when it was not popular. Karl Marx, who was baptised with his parents when he was four, was deeply bigoted against Jews.

In contemporary America, the record is harder to read, partly because Jewish apostasy has radically declined as the social stigma against Jews has all but disappeared. Caspar Weinberger, Ronald Reagan's defense secretary, who had a Jewish grandfather, is commonly described by those who knew him as uncomfortable with his Jewish roots, to the point of volunteering to new acquaintances that he is not Jewish despite his name. Even close aides agree that Weinberger's apparent discomfort may have played a role in his occasional tilt against Israel in debates within the Reagan administration. Some observers believe it played a role in his harsh sentencing recommendation in the Jonathan Pollard spy case.

Whether a similar psychology operated on James Schlesinger during the second week of October 1973 cannot be finally resolved. Schlesinger himself has said publicly that his "feet were set in concrete" by the White House insistence—meaning Kissinger's insistence—on using chartered planes instead of U.S. aircraft. Kissinger and his defenders insist the charters could have been found if the Pentagon had tried harder.

Finally, there is the psychology of Henry Kissinger himself. Kissinger argues that the attempt to avoid using U.S. military aircraft was an honest attempt to prevent a total rupture with the Arab world, which could have led to an economically disastrous oil boycott. As it turned out, his prediction was correct.

His detractors suggest a more devious motive: by letting Israel squirm while the Arab armies advanced for several days, it is often claimed, he hoped to break the psychological deadlock in the Middle East and create a new atmosphere that might lead to a negotiated settlement after the war was over. The idea is not inconceivable, given Kissinger's generally acknowledged disposition toward cold-blooded deviousness. Tolerating a few thousand avoidable deaths in order to achieve a theoretical power balance is consistent with the Kissinger of Vietnam and Cambodia. Nonetheless, Kissinger and his defenders dismiss that scenario as pure fantasy.

Ironically, Kissinger's defenders advance much the same theory to explain the controversial timing of the October 22 cease-fire in the Sinai. Israel had turned the tide during the second week of the war, crossing over the Suez Canal into Egypt proper for the first time and surrounding the crack Third Army, which was on the canal's Israeli-occupied east bank. On October 19, Soviet leader Brezhnev summoned Kissinger to Moscow to negotiate a cease-fire. Kissinger went, partly because he thought he could bargain from a stronger position in Moscow rather than in Watergate-torn Washington. And he went partly because he thought the journey would allow him to stall the cease-fire and let the Israelis continue their advance.

Kissinger's cease-fire talks with the Soviets during the course of the Yom Kippur War bear a good deal of resemblance to Goldberg's during the Six-Day War: negotiations would rise and fall as each side put forward a formulation to protect its own client's shifting fortunes. But the similarity ended in Moscow on October 21, when Kissinger accepted a cease-fire that prevented Israel from completely cutting off the Third Army.

The cease-fire went into effect the next day. The Israelis were furious. Prime Minister Golda Meir accused Kissinger of joining with the Russians and Egyptians in ganging up against Israel. "It is impossible for us to accept," she said. In Washington, pro-Israel senators like Henry Jackson and Jacob Javits charged that he was sacrificing Israel to advance his U.S.-Soviet detente.

Kissinger himself argues that leaving the warring armies in a battlefield stalemate created a diplomatic opening that a total Israeli victory would have shut off. He had become aware during the war that Egypt's President Anwar Sadat wanted to break with his predecessor Nasser's radicalism and move toward the West, greater moderation, and an end to the confrontation with Israel. Leaving Egypt some dignity at the end of the war would strengthen Sadat, boost his country's optimism and allow him to move forward. Humiliation would return him to his Soviet protectors. "We did not think that turning an Arab setback into a debacle represented a vital interest," Kissinger wrote in his memoirs. This was the same point his detractors made about the delayed airlift.

Kissinger's tactic left the Israeli leadership feeling that victory had been snatched from their hands. Their rage only mounted over the next two years as Kissinger's plan bore fruit. On October 28, ranking Israeli and Egyptian commanders met at Kilometer 101 on the Trans-Sinai Highway for the first round of talks to "disengage" the two armies. The meeting marked the first formal, direct negotiations between Israel and an Arab state since the 1949 armistice. In December, the talks were civilianized when the foreign ministers of Israel, Egypt, and Jordan met in Geneva for a formal conference, chaired by Kissinger and Soviet foreign minister Andrei Gromyko.

Kissinger now entered a long cycle of shuttle diplomacy, traveling ceaselessly between Middle East capitals to broker agreements between Israel and its neighbors. The results were three historic agreements, one with Syria and two with Egypt.

The negotiations were often brutal. Kissinger's plan had been to freeze the Soviets out of Middle East diplomacy and give America exclusive influence over the region. His success meant that Washington was now the referee in the talks, and had to press both sides equally, or at least seem to. To the Israelis, it appeared as though they had been abandoned by their only friend. In March 1975, Kissinger arranged for the Ford administration to announce its "reassessment" of U.S.-Israel relations in order to pressure Israel. Popular sentiment against Kissinger exploded, both in Israel and among American Jews.

In the final analysis, however, Kissinger's strategy worked. Israel entered into the direct negotiations with its neighbors that it had sought for so long. It signed a series of durable agreements that increased its security. Ultimately, the process led directly to Sadat's 1977 trip to Israel, after Kissinger had left office. A year later, Israel and Egypt negotiated a peace treaty, removing Israel's largest and most dangerous enemy from the war. "The Geneva conference of 1973 opened the door to peace through which Egypt and Israel walked," he wrote in his memoirs.

It is difficult to exaggerate the effect of Kissinger's policies on Israeli security. If there had been no October 22 cease-fire saving the Third Army, there would have been no Kilometer 101 negotiations; no Geneva peace conference in December bringing Israeli, Egyptian, and Jordanian diplomats together for the first time; no Sinai disengagement agreements; and no Camp David accord. Israel would still be at war with Egypt, the only Arab country that can threaten Israel's existence.

The peacemaking process did not begin with the Yom Kippur War, however. Kissinger's strategy had begun years before he was even allowed to participate in Middle East policy. Almost from the moment Nixon entered office, when Secretary of State Rogers was given control of U.S. involvement the region, Kissinger began his now-infamous sniping and bureaucratic infighting to weaken Rogers. His argument against the secretary of state was substantive, however: he claimed that pursuing an evenhanded course between Israel and its radical, pro-Soviet enemies had the effect of punishing America's allies, rewarding its enemies, and strengthening the Soviets. Better, he argued, to abandon the peace process for now, stand firmly behind Israel and send a clear message to the Arabs that they would get nothing by opposing America.

Kissinger's argument was provocative. Up until then, America had remained formally neutral in the Middle East conflict. American administrations had shown sympathy toward Israel, both because of domestic pressures from the Jewish lobby and because of a widely held sense that Israel deserved sympathy for moral and humanitarian reasons. There was no formal alliance, however; American policy was consistently aimed at maintaining good relations with both Israel and its enemies.

Kissinger's argument was that Israel represented a strategic asset and not just a moral one. By backing Israel to the hilt, he said, Washington could weaken the Kremlin and ultimately strengthen its own influence in the Middle East. Events quickly seemed to prove him right.

In September 1970, Jordan went to war against Palestinian guerrillas. Syria threatened to intervene, but backed down under Israeli threats. Israel's defense of Jordan, a U.S. ally, impressed Nixon deeply.

"The September crisis in Jordan was run out of the White House, and it vindicated Henry's views," recalls Rodman, Kissinger's former aide. "It confirmed the strategic view that Kissinger had held all along. Then Henry started having a few discreet meetings, which Nixon knew about, breakfast meetings with King Hussein and Golda Meir and others. It wasn't until the spring of 1971 that Nixon gave Henry the ball." A year after that, Sadat sent home the fifteen thousand Soviet military advisers based in Egypt and broke his country's twenty-year alliance with Moscow.

Kissinger's arguments were couched entirely in the language of American national interest. Nonetheless, those around him remained convinced that his championing of Israel was at least partly emotional. "Henry was emotionally very sympathetic to Israel, and at the same time intellectually very sympathetic to Israel as an American national interest," Rodman says. "Nixon was not emotionally involved, but he bought into the strategic issue as Henry framed it."

"Egypt's switching sides was the most important event of the last twenty years, and it was a result of what Nixon and Henry had done," declares Rodman. "They had made it clear that any Arab who acted as a patsy of the Soviet Union would get nothing from us. Sadat's reversal was not an accident."

Kissinger and Nixon were slow to pick up Sadat's hints of a reversal. That was one reason he went to war in October 1973. "The Yom Kippur War came about because Sadat was not satisfied with what he was able to get us to do," Rodman explains. "We came back together after the Yom Kippur War."

Kissinger's view of Sadat finally caught up with reality during the first week of the war, as a result of signals received from Cairo. It was at that point that Kissinger took one of his most significant and least noticed steps as secretary of state: increasing U.S. aid to Israel to a level of $2.2 billion per year.

American aid to Israel had skyrocketed in the years after the Six-Day War from several tens of millions of dollars to $300 million annually. That made Israel one of the largest single U.S. aid recipients.

Kissinger's decision to send Israel's aid package into the stratosphere came on October 16, during a meeting of the Washington Strategic Action Group, the interagency working group that met in the White House to manage international crises. "For reasons that had a lot to do with U.S.-Soviet relations, Kissinger was arguing that we should come up with a number that was huge, to demonstrate that America was going to make a massive commitment of resources to ensure Israeli security after the war," says former NSC aide William Quandt. "In the end he sort of picked the number out of the air. I don't think anyone in the room had any doubt that there was a real, emotional concern for Israel."

The massive boost in aid to Israel was submitted to Congress by Nixon on October 19. Once approved, it would have the effect of casting in stone the special U.S.-Israel relationship that Kissinger had created. The aid continued even after the war when America began warming toward Sadat's Egypt and serving as neutral broker in the Middle East peace process.

In engineering a multibillion-dollar aid package to Israel, Kissinger had made Israeli security a top priority of U.S. foreign policy. He did this not by logic or sentiment, but by the simple power of the marketplace. Israel became America's largest individual foreign investment. This guaranteed that America would stand by Israel, if only to protect its huge and ever-growing investment. Before October 1973, America had regularly stated and restated its moral commitment to Israeli security, but the commitment consisted of just that: words. When the crunch came—as it did in the fall of 1956, in May 1967, and in the first week of the Yom Kippur War—American policy-makers responded by arguing, agonizing, weighing their moral commitment to Israel against various strategic and diplomatic objectives. Committing America to Israel to the tune of $2.2 billion per year put an end to the agonizing. America was now signaling to the world that it stood behind Israel's survival and security with the same full faith that it put behind the dollar itself.

The results did not take long to materialize. In December 1973,

Kissinger convened an Israeli-Arab peace conference in Geneva, cochaired by himself and Gromyko, with the foreign ministers of Israel, Egypt, and Jordan in attendance. The conference was a brief affair dominated by mutual name-calling, but it represented a turning point in history nonetheless: for the first time, representatives of Arab countries sat down formally and publicly with representatives of the Jewish state to discuss the future of the region.

Two months after Geneva, the PLO's Palestine National Council met in Algiers to adopt a "phased plan" for the liberation of Palestine. It called for the creation of a Palestinian state on any territory liberated through diplomatic activity. Days later, the Arab League endorsed the new PLO position at a summit meeting, also in Algiers. Israel scornfully greeted the Algiers plan as a restatement of the PLO's original program, destroying Israel in two stages rather than one. But Arab observers saw it for what it was: a step toward accepting Israel. In Algiers, the PLO abrogated no less than two clauses in the Palestine National Covenant: the "indivisibility of Palestine" and the sacredness of "armed struggle" as the "only path to liberate Palestine."

One hardline PLO leader, terrorist chieftain Sabri al-Banna, responded by declaring war on Yasser Arafat for betraying the Palestinian cause; under the name Abu Nidal he began a twenty-year campaign of terror against Arafat and the PLO. Another terrorist chief, Nayef Hawatmeh of the radical Democratic Front for the Liberation of Palestine, junior partner to Arafat's Fatah faction in the PLO governing coalition, claimed Algiers as a vindication of his 1970 call to recognize the "national rights" of Israeli Jews in Palestine. In his view, Algiers had brought Arafat, the PLO, and the Arab League into the peace process. Now it was just a matter of time before the Arab world finally gave formal endorsement to the 1947 U.N. decision that had divided Palestine and created the Jewish state of Israel. With the United States indissolubly standing behind it, Israel had won its long struggle for legitimacy.

Nixon's overall relationship with the Jewish community bears elaboration. Beyond his role in overseeing the greatest-ever escalation of U.S.-Israel ties, Nixon was pivotal in raising the Republican Party's standing among Jews. For a Republican, he had an extraordinary number of Jews in his inner circle, including White House counsel Leonard Garment, speechwriter William Safire, Federal Reserve chairman Arthur Burns, and Council of Economic Advisers chairman Herbert Stein, in addition to Kissinger. Nixon's friendship with megadonor Max Fisher encouraged dozens of other wealthy Jews to become Republican contributors, and led to the formation in 1972 of the GOP's influential Jewish arm, the National Jewish Coalition. All these factors—plus the Democrats' nomination of archdove George McGovern for president in 1972—helped boost the Republicans' share of the Jewish vote from 17 percent in 1968 to 35 percent in 1972.

And yet, no president since James Buchanan was more noisily at odds with American Jews as a group than Richard Nixon. The president keenly resented the fact that Jews were so vastly overrepresented among his opponents in the antiwar movement. Though he hid it from the public, his mistrust of Jews surfaced regularly in private. He once ordered an aide to make a list of Jewish staffers at the Labor Department, convinced that its gloomy economic forecasts were a conspiracy. The order was not an isolated incident. Jewish names surfaced repeatedly in Nixon's "enemies lists."

It is perhaps ironic, then, that Nixon was the one responsible, more than anyone else, for promoting the Jewish lobby to major-player status in Washington. In the manner of Washington, Israel's multibillion-dollar aid package quickly became an entitlement. Israel and its affairs became big business in Washington. Thanks to Nixon and his secretary of state, Jewish lobbyists, as Israel's most visible supporters, were suddenly very important people.

Did Kissinger foresee all those outcomes when he proposed a $2.2 billion aid package for Israel? No witnesses suggest such prescience. "He wasn't trying to be a hero in Jewish history," says Peter Rodman. "He was just trying to do something that was right."

"Henry would not deny that his first obligation was as an American secretary of state," adds Rodman. "But a lot of us would say that support for Israel is part of American national interest. There's a way of reconciling friendship with the Arabs and support for Israel. That's what the peace process is all about. One of the things that unlocked the peace process was Kissinger's and Nixon's perception that you had to unlock the Soviet-Arab connection."

Still, there is a good deal of evidence that simple fear as a Jew for Israel's safety was a major factor in Kissinger's thinking during the tense early days of the Yom Kippur War. "As Israel began to fall apart, Henry began to fall apart," Defense Secretary Schlesinger would say later.

Kissinger himself has said tantalizingly little over the years about the impact of his Jewish background on his thinking about the Middle East. In twenty-eight hundred pages of memoirs on his government service, he only offers one direct statement to that effect, writing that his arrival in Israel from Moscow on October 21, with the Yom Kippur War cease-fire in hand, "ranks high on the list" of the "most moving moments of my government service."

A more suggestive comment came during a speech to the Israel Bonds organization in 1992, when he accepted the organization's annual Elie Wiesel Holocaust Remembrance Award. "I have been in the position, as a Jew, of conducting the foreign policy of a superpower," he said. "I have never obscured the fact that twelve members of my family died in the Holocaust, and that therefore the fate of the Jewish people was always a matter of profound concern to me. At the same time, destiny put me in a position where I also had to look at other perspectives."

CHAPTER 10

Chosen People:
Jews and the Ballot Box

P AUL WELLSTONE first entered the U.S. Senate in 1990, defeating
Minnesota's incumbent Republican senator in a tight race that turned
at the last minute on the bizarre question of which candidate was a better
Jew.

The incumbent, Rudy Boschwitz, was a refugee from Hitler's Germany,
a genial conservative and self-made millionaire. He had a racked up a
mostly forgettable record in two terms as a Republican backbencher in
Reagan-era Washington. Other Jewish senators led the defense of Israel,
particularly Ohio's Howard Metzenbaum and Michigan's Carl Levin.
Boschwitz was best known for his Jewish holiday parties and his attempts to
play matchmaker among young Jewish congressional aides, which won him
the nickname "rabbi of the Senate." When Boschwitz did play a critical role
in policy, it was usually because of the access he enjoyed as a rare Jew
among the Republicans. (He was not so rare for one brief period in the
mid-1980s, when he was one of four Jewish GOP senators along with Arlen
Specter, Chic Hecht, and Warren Rudman. By 1993, Specter was the only
one left.)

Wellstone, the challenger, was a political science professor from Carle-
ton College, where he was known as an unreconstructed 1960s-era New
Leftist, a perpetual demonstrator and faculty adviser to campus radicals.
Outspent six to one, he ran a whimsical outsider's campaign, traveling the
state in a beaten-up campaign bus and refusing to take donations larger
than $100. His race seemed a long shot even for liberal Minnesota, the only
state to vote Democratic in the Reagan landslide of 1984.

Wellstone began closing in during the final weeks of the campaign with sharp attacks on Boschwitz for his dependence on PAC (political action committee) money. He also benefited from the last-minute collapse of the state Republican organization, when sexual allegations forced the GOP gubernatorial candidate to quit the race nine days before Election Day. The fiasco threw the entire Minnesota GOP into disarray, forcing Boschwitz to fly home and take personal charge of his reelection effort.

Less than a week before Election Day, a group of Boschwitz supporters sent out a mailing to Jewish voters, touting Boschwitz's support of Jewish causes. The letter noted that Wellstone was married to a non-Jew and had no record of Jewish affiliation. Wellstone counterattacked with full-page newspaper ads two days before Election Day, complaining that Boschwitz was attacking him "because my wife is a Christian." The ad gained Wellstone enough sympathy to squeak by with a 48,000-vote margin.

Had Wellstone lost, the race would have remained a footnote in political history as the first Senate race ever to pit two Jewish candidates against each other. But the Boschwitz letter and Wellstone's reply made Judaism more than a footnote. In a backwards kind of way, it became the decisive issue in the race.

Minnesota's Jewish voters, overwhelmingly Democratic, reacted coolly to the entire affair. Some, including Boschwitz's own rabbi, sided with Wellstone; others were turned off. More than a few groused, as one major Democratic fund-raiser put it, that "Wellstone's reference to his wife as a 'Christian' looked like an intentional appeal for a Christian backlash against Boschwitz."

In the final analysis, it is hard to imagine just what Boschwitz thought he would accomplish with the letter. In the whole state of Minnesota, population 4.4 million, there are barely thirty thousand Jews, or seven tenths of one percent.

In his *Jews and American Politics,* the pioneering 1974 study on the topic, journalist Stephen D. Isaacs devoted an entire chapter to explaining why Jews so seldom run for public office. "[W]hile Jews have become an ever larger and more potent force on the periphery of politics, few have held or, for that matter, will hold primary positions of power," Isaacs wrote.

After exploring the reasons offered by Jewish activists—that non-Jews would not vote for Jews, that Jews seeking office might incite anti-Semitism, that "Jews make better staff people"—Isaacs concluded that the problem was the Jews' own timidity. He called the syndrome a "ghetto mentality," a "feeling of limited expectations and vulnerability." By their timidity, he wrote, "in effect they censor themselves out of even trying for elective office."

At the time Isaacs's book came out, there were two Jews elected to the U.S. Senate: Jacob Javits of New York and Abraham Ribicoff of Connecticut (a third, Howard Metzenbaum of Ohio, had just been appointed to a vacant seat). There were a dozen Jewish members in the House of Representatives, down from a peak of eighteen in the late 1960s. The proportion of Jews in Congress was less than the proportion of Jews in the population at large. Nearly all the Jews in the House represented heavily Jewish districts. Two Jews served as state governors, in Pennsylvania and Maryland. Twenty-four states, mostly in the South and West, had never elected a Jew to high office at all.

Limited as the record was, it represented a huge advance over the 1930s and 1940s, when Jews made up 3.7 percent of the population but only 1.4 percent of the House, and no Jews served in the Senate.

A few months after Isaacs's book appeared, however, Jews entered electoral politics with a bang. The post-Watergate class of 1974 nearly doubled the number of Jews in the House of Representatives. Over the next decade, the number of Jewish members grew steadily on both sides of Capitol Hill. By 1991, there were thirty-three Jews in the House, or 7.5 percent. Following the 1992 elections, there were ten Jews in the Senate. Two states, California and Wisconsin, had two Jewish senators each. Thousands more Jews were serving in lower office around the country from the Maine state legislature to Louisville City Hall.

Within a generation, the place of the Jew in American politics had been utterly transformed. If a "ghetto mentality" had indeed inhibited Jews from running for office, it was gone now. Any anti-Semitism that might have restrained Americans from voting for Jews seemed equally gone.

By 1990, Jewish members of Congress had become one of the most important bases of organized Jewish political power in the United States. Working frequently as a solid bloc, they formed the core of pro-Israel activity in Washington. They led efforts to maintain and increase foreign aid, both for Israel and for every other country that received U.S. aid. They confronted administrations that tried to pressure Israel. They won passage

for legislative initiatives to extend American help to oppressed Jews in the
Soviet Union and Ethiopia. They crafted and fought for laws to guarantee
U.S. visas for Soviet Jewish refugees. They led the fight against school
prayer, year after year. Though few ever admitted it publicly, they were at
times a sort of legislature within the legislature.

In some ways, the Jews in Congress were more representative of American Jews than were the Jewish organizations whose job it was to represent
the Jewish community. To begin with, they were overwhelmingly Democratic, like their fellow Jews but unlike the organized Jewish leaders (only
six Jews in the House and two in the Senate were Republicans in 1992). For
another thing, they reflected a range of Jewish loyalties and affiliations that
was remarkably similar to American Jewry as a whole. There was Connecticut Senator Joseph Lieberman, former prosecutor and an Orthodox Jew
who refused to ride or write on Saturday. There was Vermont Representative Bernie Sanders, ex-mayor of "the people's republic of Burlington," a
freethinking, Brooklyn-born socialist whose antimilitary views often infuriated the other Jewish members.

There was California Senator Barbara Boxer, a suburban liberal from
affluent Marin County, one of the most influential feminists on Capitol Hill.
There was California's other senator, Dianne Feinstein, the half-Jewish,
tough-talking former mayor of San Francisco. There was Pennsylvania
Senator Arlen Specter, a lonely crusader for church-state separation in the
Republican party. And there was New York Representative Ben Gilman, a
Republican whose district stretched from the resort villages of the Catskills
to the booming Orthodox enclaves of semi-rural Rockland County.

As long as Democrats controlled Congress, the Jewish members formed
a relatively solid bloc that ably represented the needs, interests, and beliefs
of American Jews.

After the Republican revolution of 1994, a great deal depended on
Specter and Gilman.

The Senate and House are very different bodies, with very different political cultures. Senators are elected to represent a state, House members to
represent a neighborhood. Each of the one hundred members of the
Senate is expected to master the full range of public policy, from foreign aid
to health care. The 435 members of the House each are expected to bite off

a specialty and run with it. The Senate has a long and courtly tradition of etiquette and member privilege. The House is a rougher place, and members represent a much wider diversity of beliefs and sensibilities.

In effect, a senator who became known as a "Jewish lawmaker" would lose credibility and effectiveness. A House member could build a career on it.

The Jewish members of the Senate are careful to bear that in mind. "We consider ourselves to be senators from our states and United States senators, but I don't think we think of ourselves as Jewish senators," says Ohio Democrat Howard Metzenbaum, who retired in 1994 after twenty years in the upper house. "We're proud to be Jews, and we stand tall and fight for issues of concern to the American Jewish community. But we don't have any caucus in the sense of the Congressional Black Caucus. I opposed that. I'm one who doesn't believe American Jewry does best when there's an effort to separate us."

This is not to say that Jewish senators never get together. They do, but it is infrequent and informal. Meetings nearly always take place in the office of the senior Jewish member: Metzenbaum until his 1994 retirement, Carl Levin of Michigan thereafter.

"They really don't happen often, maybe three or four times a year," Connecticut's Joseph Lieberman says of the Jewish senators' meetings. "It usually has to do with Israel. When a prime minister of Israel comes, there tends to be a meeting with Jewish legislators. Sometimes the administration requests a meeting with Jewish legislators—for example, on a proposed arms sale to an Arab country."

Curiously, Lieberman says, "I don't think we have ever talked about more general domestic issues, except in passing. We talk about them with one another, one on one. But even when there's a domestic issue that's of great concern to the entire Jewish community, for example the Religious Freedom Restoration Act—the truth is, we never held a meeting on that."

Jewish members of the House are a different breed altogether. Like the Senate side, they have no formal Jewish caucus. But they meet more frequently than the Jewish senators, sometimes as often as once a month, usually over coffee and bagels in the office of the senior Jewish representative, Sidney Yates of Chicago, who was first elected to the House in 1948.

Their agenda is broader than the Jewish senators', too. In theory, they come together only to discuss Israel. In practice, the meetings often turn into free-floating bull sessions on matters of common interest to Jewish liberals. "It makes the Republicans at these meetings feel like outsiders," says New Mexico Republican Steven Schiff. "There are times when I'm invited for bagels at Sid's and I feel like I've accidentally wandered into a Democratic caucus meeting."

Periodically the Jewish members hold a joint meeting with the Congressional Black Caucus to discuss a matter of common interest. Most often it is civil rights legislation, though it has also involved Middle East and African policy. One crucial session was held in November 1988 with Prime Minister Yitzhak Shamir, to demand tougher Israeli sanctions against South Africa. Shamir took the position that Israel did not have to be stricter than the Reagan administration. The Congress members told him otherwise. He returned to Israel and ordered new measures.

About half the Jewish members in the House represent urban and suburban districts with large Jewish communities in New York, Miami, Los Angeles, San Francisco, Boston, Detroit, and Chicago. The other half represent districts with tiny Jewish populations: Norman Sisisky of Virginia, Martin Frost of Texas, Steven Schiff of New Mexico.

Those with small Jewish constituencies behave, for the most part, the way the Jewish senators do: as legislators who happen to be Jewish. The others, by contrast, could be called the "Jewish" Jewish representatives. These are the lawmakers who make careers out of defending Israel and attacking anti-Semites from the floor of the House, who openly taunt religious-right moralizing, like Boston's Barney Frank, or who spend days at a time chasing a $25 million grant for Russian Jews, like New York's Nita Lowey. They do it with the assurance that the voters at home will reward them as surely as if they had brought home a naval base.

The difference between the two types of constituencies is so extreme that it has become a running joke among Jewish House members. Larry Smith of South Florida and Dan Glickman of Kansas used to turn it into a veritable vaudeville routine when they appeared together at Jewish gatherings. "One time Larry and I appeared on a panel together in Israel," Glickman recalls, "and he was asked what's unique about American Jewish politics. He said, 'Look at it this way. Here I am, a congressman named

Smith representing South Florida with 200,000 Jews. And here's Dan Glickman with less than 1,000 Jews in his district. And boy, what we wouldn't do to trade names.' "

For some in Congress, fighting for Jewish causes is the passion that brought them to Washington to begin with. Representative Tom Lantos of suburban San Francisco, the only Holocaust survivor in either chamber, has spent most of his time in Congress on foreign policy, fighting with equal passion for Soviet Jews, Tibetan Buddhists, and trade unionists in right-wing El Salvador. Larry Smith of South Florida and Mel Levine of Los Angeles came to Washington in 1981 single-mindedly determined to make Israel their main business; after failing on arrival to win seats on the House Foreign Affairs Committee, they spent their first week in Congress lobbying (successfully) to have the committee enlarged. Throughout the 1980s, Smith was Israel's avenging angel on Capitol Hill, regularly savaging administration officials who dared to question Israeli policy. Republican policy-makers hated him passionately, and hated having to testify before the House because of him. His constituents in the retirement villages of South Florida loved him.

The most renowned member of the group, however, was Stephen Solarz of Brooklyn, who came to Congress in the post-Watergate class of 1974 and lost his seat in a race-based reapportionment in 1992.

Intensely cerebral, a published expert on foreign-policy issues from Turkey to India to the Philippines, Solarz was the House's most respected authority on international affairs for much of his career. He was the main architect of U.S. policies that eased Philippines dictator Ferdinand Marcos out of power in 1986 and ended the Cambodian civil war in 1991. He almost single-handedly mobilized House support for U.S. military action against Iraq in 1991, over the strong opposition of his fellow Democrats— including a majority (18 out of 33) of his fellow Jewish lawmakers. He also managed to block several popular House measures to commemorate the 1915 Turkish massacre of Armenians, arguing that they would offend Turkey, a key U.S. ally on Russia's southern flank (and Israel's closest friend in the Muslim world).

Much of the world viewed Solarz as the leading Jewish voice on Capitol Hill. Curiously, he was not a leader of the House Jewish caucus. His opinions were taken seriously, but he was not popular. Other lawmakers considered him aloof and arrogant. Jewish community leaders and Israeli diplomats found him uncooperative, unwilling to work as part of a team or follow another's lead. His secure base in Brooklyn's Borough Park section, a huge enclave of devoutly Orthodox Jews, made him seem invulnerable, an independent force in Washington. He was a loner, as distant from his fellow Jewish lawmakers as he was from his black-garbed constituents.

It was his aloofness, in fact, that ended his congressional career in 1992. When New York lost two House seats as a result of the 1990 census, other Congress members got busy lobbying the state legislature to save their districts. Solarz paid no attention, certain that the legislature would defer to his seniority and renown. It didn't work. When the new map was finalized, he found his seat eliminated.

Insiders in Albany, the state capital, say that Solarz's political demise was more complicated than he admitted. The legislature had not eliminated Solarz's seat, lawmakers explain, but reinforced it by combining his Ortho-dox stronghold in Brooklyn with the enormous Jewish population of Man-hattan's ultra-liberal Upper West Side. What they did not realize—but Solarz's polling revealed—was that the West Side liberals were unwilling to forgive him for backing Bush on the Gulf War. As a result, he had no chance of reelection. So he declined to run in his own district.

The New York legislature had handed Solarz the most solidly Jewish district in the country. The problem was, it was the wrong kind of Jews.

Solarz's downfall resulted in large measure from the collapse of the old-fashioned party machines that once ran politics in the big cities. Reviled as engines of corruption, the machines also served to mediate among politi-cians at various levels of government, and to impose order in the governing process. Their collapse in the post-Watergate era contributed mightily to making American politics what it is today: a chaotic universe of indepen-dent fund-raising machines, driven by ideological extremes and hostile to compromise.

Contemporary Jewish electoral politics is a product of the post-machine age. But it has spawned a few machines of its own here and there, in a handful of communities where Jewish voting power is sufficiently concen-trated.

The most successful is the so-called Berman-Waxman machine on the west side of Los Angeles. Not truly a product of the new era, it is actually one of the last of the old-time big-city machines still functioning in American politics. Its founders, House Democrats Henry Waxman and Howard Berman, do not fit the traditional image of the machine politician, though; both are brainy, liberal Jewish intellectuals with a passion for issues and causes. Still, their machine has dominated west-side politics for two decades by using much the same tools that political machines have favored for a century: handing out favors, controlling contracts, and most of all, ruling the local Democratic Party nominating process. Starting with just the two founding members, the machine has steadily moved young acolytes up through the ranks from city council to state legislature to Congress. In the process, it has has grown to encompass close to a dozen elected officials, both Jewish and non-Jewish, at the local, state, and federal level. Its heart, however, remains Waxman, Capitol Hill's most militant health-care crusader and scourge of the tobacco industry.

At the opposite end of the continent, an altogether different sort of political machine has been built in the last decade by New York State Assembly member Dov Hikind of Brooklyn. An Orthodox Jew and a militant Zionist, a onetime lieutenant to Rabbi Meir Kahane of the far-right Jewish Defense League, Hikind was first elected to the assembly in 1982 from the overwhelmingly Orthodox enclave of Borough Park. He has been reelected by comfortable majorities ever since.

Nominally a Democrat, Hikind's principal connections are not to his fellow Democrats, nor even to other Orthodox Jewish Democrats around Brooklyn, but to a network of talmudic academies and rabbinical associations peppered throughout his district and across the city. Over the years, Hikind's office has funneled hundreds of thousands of dollars in state discretionary funds to these institutions, much of it through the Hasidic-led Council of Jewish Organizations of Borough Park. In the process, he has welded his Orthodox allies into a potent force, fusing their social conservatism, their frictions with the black community, and their messianic views on Israel into an explosive presence in city and state politics.

Hikind's emergence as an independent force in New York politics began in 1988, when he broke with the party to endorse Republican presidential candidate George Bush. His stated reason was the influence in the Democratic Party of black preacher-politician Jesse Jackson, which he said represented a "danger" to Israel and American Jews. The following year, again

citing Jackson, he endorsed Republican New York City mayoral candidate
Rudolph Giuliani, who was running against black Democrat David Dinkins.
This time, Hikind spoke for an organization, the newly formed United
Jewish Coalition, a collection of several dozen community groups which he
introduced at a press conference as "a real mixture of what the Jewish
community of New York is all about."

Hikind's coalition was hardly a "real mixture" of New York Jews; it was
made up almost entirely of Orthodox Jews, who constitute less than 15
percent of New York Jewry. What the coalition did offer was a genuine
sample of the fears that would increasingly drive the Jewish far right in the
coming years: fear of Israel's enemies, fear of black militants, and an
unstated sense that the two were one and the same, combined with open
hostility toward the Jewish liberals who dominated mainstream Jewish
politics. One member of Hikind's coalition, Rabbi Abraham Hecht, spiritual
leader of Brooklyn's reclusive Syrian Jewish community, coupled his endorsement of Giuliani with the declaration that Jews should "vote as if your
life depended on the outcome. I assure you that it does." (In 1995, Hecht
would win notoriety for giving religious sanction to the assassination of
Israeli prime minister Yitzhak Rabin.)

Over the next four years, Hikind developed a close alliance with Republican U.S. Senator Alphonse D'Amato, who was emerging as the kingmaker
in New York's GOP. D'Amato became the Orthodox community's improb-
able tribune in Washington, speaking out on anything and everything from
local zoning variances to West Bank Jewish settlements. Hikind helped to
deliver cash and voters. D'Amato won reelection in 1992 by a narrow
108,000 votes, thanks in large part to his support among Orthodox Jews.
Hikind was standing next to him, hand in hand, on election night.

In 1993 and 1994, in what was now a regular ritual, Hikind endorsed
Republicans Rudolph Giuliani for mayor and George Pataki for governor.
Both candidates won, each with heavy support among Orthodox Jews. After
each election, Hikind promptly let it be known that he was to be the
principal liaison between the new administration and the Jewish community. The old Jewish establishment—the Jews who ran the Federation
of Jewish Philanthropies and the American Jewish Committee—were
finished.

The experience was an object lesson in the political limits of Jewish
extremism. It took Mayor Giuliani only a few weeks to learn that Dov
Hikind did not and could not represent the Jewish community. He certainly

represented an important segment of the Orthodox community, with a prodigious capacity for fund-raising and vote-getting. But he could hardly replace the Reform and Conservative Jews who dominated New York's real-estate, communications, and securities industries, the mainstream Jews without whose cooperation no one could govern New York. Giuliani took less than a month after his 1993 election to figure it out; by inauguration day in January, he was already a familiar visitor at UJA-Federation headquarters, the bastion of mainstream Jewish liberalism, and Hikind was on the outs.

Pataki, a small-town politician from rural upstate New York, took slightly longer to figure it out. Only after he had appointed Hikind's wife Shoshana as his state director of community relations, only to hear her call in May 1995 for the ouster of Prime Minister Yitzhak Rabin, did he begin to understand the nature of the Dov Hikind phenomenon. Within a month after that, Pataki too had jettisoned Hikind and made his pilgrimage to the Jewish mainstream, the true seat of Jewish power.

Hikind did not disappear, to be sure. Representing a distinct, highly opinionated voting bloc, his was a political voice that could not be ignored. But it could not easily be harnessed either, given his unbending, often messianic beliefs. When he sought a simple endorsement he could gather the very best of New York's political elite behind him, as he did in a May 1996 fund-raiser on the USS *Intrepid* that drew one thousand guests including the mayor and the governor. But when he tried to follow through on his outlandish agenda, he usually found himself standing virtually alone.

The election of 1992 marked a watershed in congressional Jewish politics. Along with Solarz, both Larry Smith and Mel Levine left Congress (Levine for an unsuccessful Senate race, Smith after a conviction for misusing campaign funds). In a single sweep, Israel lost its entire strategic command in the House.

Another group stepped forward quickly to replace them: Levine's Los Angeles neighbor and political ally, Howard Berman; Nita Lowey of suburban Westchester, New York, a second-term Democrat with good ties to the Democratic leadership; and Charles Schumer of Brooklyn, a protégé-turned-rival of Solarz, best known as the Democrats' leading voice on crime and banking. With varying degrees of enthusiasm, they took on extra staff, got themselves seats on the appropriate foreign-affairs subcommittees, and picked up the banner of Israel. Then they warily began feeling their way through the maze of spending bills, markups, and conferences that make up the pro-Israel cause in Congress.

The new team never had a chance to find its footing. In September 1993, Israel and the Palestine Liberation Organization signed a peace agreement on the White House lawn, committing Israel to hand over much of the West Bank to Palestinian self-rule under Yasser Arafat. Suddenly, a representative from a mostly Jewish district had a very difficult job. In some of the most heavily Jewish districts, the loudest Jewish voices were those of Orthodox rabbis who opposed the peace process. Suddenly, supporting Israel could be political suicide for a Jewish lawmaker. One by one, lawmakers with the most heavily Jewish districts began turning against Israel.

Three weeks after the signing of the Israeli-PLO accord, the White House sent Congress a bill lifting the ban on American contact with the PLO. The purpose of the bill was essentially to allow the Clinton administration to continue participating legally in the unfolding peace process that it was in effect sponsoring. More to the point, it authorized a half-billion dollars in U.S. aid to the Palestinians, which Israel had urgently requested in order to stabilize Arafat's authority and help him fight off Islamic radicals.

When the bill got to the House foreign-aid subcommittee, it ran into Charles Schumer. One of the House's most popular liberals, star of the Democrats' basketball team, Schumer was also the sole Jewish representative from Brooklyn, home of the largest Orthodox Jewish community in America. Schumer himself is not Orthodox, but he cannot be reelected without the support of the Orthodox community, the best organized and most vocal faction in his district.

When the Palestinian aid bill was introduced to the subcommittee, Schumer proposed an amendment that would make aid to the Palestinians conditional on an end to the Arab boycott of Israel. He was immediately invited to step into the hallway by Howard Berman of Los Angeles. In Berman's view, tying Palestinian aid to the Arab boycott was tantamount to killing it. The Arab League had made it clear that ending the boycott would come at the end of the Israel-Arab peace process, not the beginning. There was nothing Yasser Arafat or the PLO could do about it. Schumer knew that as well as Berman. Though he did not say so directly, both knew that was the whole point.

The two were joined in the hallway by two freshman Democrats from South Florida, Peter Deutsch, who had won Larry Smith's seat, and Alcee Hastings, a black representative from a heavily Jewish district just north of Deutsch's. Together the four representatives from the nation's three largest Jewish communities discussed the fate of aid to the Palestinians. Deutsch was in favor of linking it to the boycott. Hastings was against undermining the peace process in that manner. Berman suggested a substitute amendment that would let the aid go through, but required that Arafat try to convince his fellow Arabs to end the boycott. Schumer agreed to Berman's version, but said he would vote against the entire measure once it reached the House floor. He did not indicate whether he would demand a roll call on the bill when it came to the floor, as any House member is entitled to do, or let it go through on a voice vote.

In the coming days, panic spread among the Jewish members of the House, as they waited for Schumer to decide their fate. "I don't know what we're supposed to do now," said an aide to one leading Jewish lawmaker. "We can't let this fail and destroy the peace process. If we don't vote for it, the non-Jewish members certainly won't. They're waiting to see how we vote. But how are we going to explain to our constituents that our guys stood up and voted for aid to Yasser Arafat? They'll go crazy on us."

While Berman and Schumer were arguing, a pair of senators began their own effort to sabotage Palestinian aid. The two, Connecticut's Joe Lieberman and Florida Republican Connie Mack, had sponsored the original law prohibiting contact with the PLO. This time, in deference to Israel, they were not sponsoring a law to link aid with the boycott; they were merely circulating a letter to President Clinton, asking him to impose the linkage himself.

By the time the letter reached the White House at the end of October, it had been signed by fifty senators, including half the Senate's Jewish members: Lieberman, the Senate's only Orthodox Jew; Specter of Pennsylvania, the only Republican Jew; plus Boxer and Feinstein of California, and Herbert Kohl of Wisconsin, each of whom faced reelection.

Supporting Israeli peacemaking efforts has always been an act of courage for Jewish lawmakers in Washington. No Jewish lawmaker has taken greater risks to support Middle East peace than Senator Frank Lautenberg of New Jersey.

Elected to the Senate in 1982, Lautenberg was a self-made millionaire (founder of Automated Data Processing, the nation's largest processor of payrolls) and a leading Jewish philanthropist. He served in the early 1970s as national chairman of the United Jewish Appeal and a member of the international executive committee of the Jewish Agency for Israel. In the Senate, his office became the first address for Jewish community officials with problems to solve, from relations with the black community to details of charitable tax law.

He was also known among senators as a bellwether of Jewish commitment. When Likud supporters introduced a bill in 1995 to move America's Tel Aviv embassy to Jerusalem, despite (or because of) Arab threats to halt peace talks with Israel, confused senators were calling Jewish colleagues and asking how they ought to vote. "We've been getting calls all week," said an aide to a Jewish senator from the Midwest. "They all want to know, 'How are you guys handling this? How is Lautenberg voting?' "

Lautenberg won his place in Jewish history in 1990 by authoring the Lautenberg amendment, which ended a catch-22 that was keeping Soviet Jews out of America. The 1980 refugee law spearheaded by the Council of Jewish Federations had required would-be refugees to demonstrate a "well-founded fear" of persecution at home. But once Communism fell and Russia's desperate Jews were free to leave, U.S. immigration officers began ruling that their fears of persecution were no longer "well-founded." Given the long history of Jews in Russia, this view was at best shortsighted. To many Russian Jews, the collapse of Communism simply offered a window to escape before Russia's old anti-Semitic traditions were reborn.

Lautenberg, working with his old friends at the UJA and CJF, introduced an amendment that required immigration officers to consider whether "historical circumstances" might give refugees a "credible basis for concern," rather than the "well-founded fear" they had been required to prove. Emigration picked up at once.

To militants on the Jewish right, however, Lautenberg's Jewish bona fides ended in 1987, when he joined with Senator Carl Levin of Michigan to initiate a letter to Secretary of State George Shultz, commending him on his Middle East peace efforts and urging him to continue seeking Israeli-Arab compromise. The letter, which gathered thirty-seven signatures, infuriated the Shamir government in Jerusalem and prompted a furious outcry from Jewish hardliners in America.

The fiercest attacks were directed not at Levin, but at Lautenberg, who was facing reelection the next year. He was attacked by rabbis and Zionist activists the length and breadth of the state. One synagogue in the Orthodox enclave of Lakewood invited his opponent, Republican Pete Dawson, to address the congregation from the pulpit. Others fought with money. Lautenberg won reelection, but just barely. Six years later, another non-Jewish Republican, state assembly speaker Garabed "Chuck" Haytaian, used the 1987 letter yet again to undermine Lautenberg among Jewish voters. Again, Jewish rightists rallied strongly to the Republican challenger. Lautenberg narrowly won his third term, but the unforgiving hostility of Jewish rightists was beginning to rattle him.

"What I saw was almost a venomous response," he says. "Suddenly I was painted like a pariah.

"I was national chairman of the UJA, for God's sake. I'm on the board of Bank Leumi, the Hebrew University, the Diaspora Museum of Tel Aviv. But having taken an oath to protect the Constitution of the United States, with all my love and affection for Israel, my primary responsibilities begin with my country. And thank goodness I have not had to make decisions between my country and Israel. Because my allegiance to Israel is more than cultural, it's a contact with my past."

Lautenberg says that he takes it in stride when constituents question his views. "You make a decision, you can offend somebody. They can get even by taking away their vote, or taking away their financial help. It's not unusual in the world of politics."

Still, "I was shocked by the response from some segments of the Jewish community," Lautenberg recalls. "I was practically accused of being a traitor to the cause."

"In fact," he says, "the pain was more severe than the shock."

"There are various reasons why members support Israel," says Representative Major Owens of Brooklyn, former leader of the Congressional Black Caucus. "One of the most important is that there is a great deal of respect. People admire the fact that Israel is a democracy, that it takes care of itself in difficulty after difficulty, that it doesn't fall into chaos. For some guys it comes down to looking at the Israeli army as a fighting machine that they admire. For me it's the fact that they've held together a quality of life under siege and remained a democracy despite the siege."

"Most," adds Representative John Lewis of Georgia, "support Israel because they believe in it. Some are Southern Christian fundamentalists who support it for religious reasons. And there are a few members of Congress who support Israel for pragmatic reasons."

Well, at least a few. It is one of the worst-kept secrets in American Jewish politics that the campaign contribution is a major key to Jewish power.

Strikingly, almost none of those involved in the process of Jewish campaign funding—donors, fundraisers, candidates, monitors—are willing to talk about it on the record. The reluctance stems from a healthy fear of stirring old prejudices. Jews fear that discussing Jewish money will encourage anti-Semitic conspiracy theories. Non-Jews fear that talking about it will leave them open to charges of anti-Semitism.

But it is a fact. "One of the strengths of the American Jewish community is that they're very generous with their money," says a staff researcher with one of Washington's small anti-Israel lobbying groups. "They see money spent on political campaigns as money well spent. It's not that they do anything wrong. It's just that Arab-Americans apparently don't feel the same way. And that imbalance apparently has an effect on U.S. foreign policy in the Middle East."

Just how much of an effect is a subject of enormous controversy. One scholarly study published in 1990 compared senators' voting records on Israel-related issues with their campaign contributions from Jewish donors. The study found a strong correlation between donations and voting records. Looking at the voting records of 130 senators who served between 1970 to 1982, the study found that a senator's likelihood of voting in a "pro-Israel" manner—backing arms sales to Israel, opposing arms sales to Arab states, resisting administration efforts to pressure Israel—rose in direct relation to the amount of funding received from Jewish sources.

Of the 130 senators examined, ten received 15 percent or more of their total campaign funding from Jewish sources, meaning pro-Israel PACs and donors with Jewish surnames. These ten voted pro-Israel, on average, 95 percent of the time. By contrast, the fifty-three senators who received less than 2 percent of their funding from Jewish sources voted pro-Israel only 53 percent of the time (Table 4).

The numbers suggest that Jewish political donations do indeed play a critical role in dictating congressional support for Israel. And yet the author of the study, political scientist A. F. K. Organski of the University of Michigan, argues just the opposite.

While there is a clear tendency for Jewish donations to rise along with a

TABLE 4: JEWISH DONATIONS AND SENATE
VOTING RECORDS, 1970–1982

Jewish contributions as % of total	Number of senators	Pro-Israel voting record
<2%	53	53.0
2–5%	36	70.6
5–10%	23	85.1
10–15%	8	88.1
>15%	10	95.0
Overall	130	69

Source: A. F. K. Organski, *The $36 Billion Bargain*, p. 242.

senator's support for Israel, Organski notes, the trend is not absolute. Some of the Senate's most consistently pro-Israel members, such as Dale Bumpers of Arkansas, turn up among the lowest recipients of pro-Israel campaign donations. Some high-end receivers of Jewish campaign funding, such as Dennis DeConcini of Arizona, are found only in the middle ranks of pro-Israel voting. In any case, Organski notes, the overall voting record of the Senate is so solidly pro-Israel that targeted contributions from pro-Israel activists are not sufficient to explain it.

Organski argues that the strongest influence on pro-Israel voting in Congress is not Jewish lobbying or campaign giving, but ideology. The lawmakers who are the most pro-Israel tend to be the ones who are internationalist in their outlook, those who consistently back an activist U.S. role in supporting democracy around the world. For a variety of reasons, including Israel's democratic image, Arab unpopularity, and Christian sympathy for the Holy Land, most lawmakers need surprisingly little convincing to back Israel when it asks for help.

According to Organski, Jewish and pro-Israel campaign funding goes mainly to lawmakers who have already shown they are pro-Israel. "Money," he writes, "is not being used here to *change* a senator's mind; it reflects the fact that a senator's mind has already been favorably *made up*. Financial support is the *result*, not the cause of what senators do. [Emphasis in original.]"

He continues: "But why, one may ask, would pro-Israeli PACs and individuals make contributions to people already predisposed in their favor? Why carry coals to Newcastle? In order to insure that those who defend their interests *stay* in power. A loss of such a supporter is disastrous.

And if the senator who happens to be a strong supporter of a cause a potential contributor supports happens also to be a member, or, even better, the chairman of a committee or subcommittee critical to the success of that cause in Congress, then his or her price is indeed beyond that of rubies. [Emphasis in original.]"

Critics of America's Middle East policy insist the pro-Israel PACs play a more decisive role than Organski describes. "When I spoke at the Democratic convention in 1988," said Arab-American activist James Zogby, "I said we are trying to build friends, but people will vote against us, not because they're against us but because they're afraid. AIPAC will win because they have control over elected officials. These guys are not going to buck them."

According to Zogby, the power of the pro-Israel PACs lies in their ability to deliver a combined punch by colluding—illegally, he believes—to deliver large blocs of dollars to chosen candidates. Orchestrating the cash flow, he says, is AIPAC.

Despite its name, AIPAC is not a PAC. It is a registered congressional lobbying organization, and is barred from raising money for candidates. It is also barred by federal election law from advising PACs on how to distribute their campaign funds.

Nonetheless, Zogby is one of many Washington insiders who are convinced that AIPAC secretly coordinates the sixty-odd Jewish PACs, arranging their gifts so that candidates receive a share of the total in proportion to their importance to the pro-Israel lobby.

The accusation was made formally in 1989, in a suit filed before the Federal Election Commission. The plaintiffs were a group of former State Department officials involved in pro-Arab lobbying. The suit was eventually dismissed for lack of evidence in 1995.

Suit or no suit, many Washington insiders remain convinced that AIPAC and the Jewish PACs secretly collude. As evidence, they cite patterns of pro-Israel PAC giving that seem too elaborately hierarchical to be unplanned. In 1992, for example, pro-Israel PACs donated to nearly two thirds of the thirty-three Senate races. The totals donated to various candidates, as calculated by one anti-Israel lobbyist, formed a neat scale in which senators received pro-Israel PAC money in order of their importance to the pro-Israel lobby: Robert Kasten of Wisconsin, $177,000; Arlen Specter of Pennsylvania, $138,000; Robert Packwood of Oregon, $125,000; John

Glenn of Ohio, $113,000; and so on, down to a dozen or so who got $50,000 or less.

"If I've got ten marbles and you've got ten marbles and so on, and there's thirty of us and nobody's telling us what to do, how come somebody doesn't end up with 300 marbles at the end?" said one anti-Israel activist in Washington. "Why is it that three PACs maxed out [gave the maximum allowed] with this guy, and three other PACs maxed out with that guy, and there's almost no overlap? It doesn't just happen that way. Somebody decides. There has to be some level of coordination, or Kasten and Specter and Packwood would have gotten $400,000 each and not needed it."

Many Capitol Hill veterans scoff at the charge. "It's really a simple case of the marketplace at work," says a senior aide to one non-Jewish House member. "You're talking about maybe sixty Jewish PACs, each of which gives small donations to dozens of candidates. Everybody in that community knows exactly who's been a good friend of Israel and who hasn't. The better the friend, the more money they get. Of course it's going to show up in the numbers."

"There's much more cooperation between business PACs or labor PACs than between pro-Israel PACs," says a former AIPAC staffer turned freelance political consultant. "You never see pro-Israel PACs call a regular weekly meeting the way business PACs do.

"I once brought a friend to the AFL-CIO convention, a Jewish guy who heads up a pro-Israel PAC. We walked into a conference room where all these PAC directors were sitting and discussing the various races coming up. He was blown away. He said, 'Can you imagine what would happen if we tried to sit together in the same room like this? The press would scream conspiracy.' "

The most notorious use of Jewish campaign money is not to support candidates who have been friendly, but to oppose those who have been unfriendly. On several occasions in recent years, pro-Israel activists have mobilized from around the country to defeat a lawmaker who crossed some line regarding Israel. It has only happened a handful of times, mostly in the early and mid-1980s. But that was all that was needed to make the point.

The best-known victim was Senator Charles Percy of Illinois, a moderate Republican who had once been popular with Chicago Jewish voters. In his first reelection campaign in 1972, he won 70 percent of the local Jewish vote, a rare feat for a Republican. But in 1975, Percy took a trip to the Middle East and announced on his return that Israel ought to negotiate with the PLO. Later that year, he refused to sign the "Letter of Seventy-Six" to President Ford, demanding an end to the Kissinger "reassessment" of U.S.-Israel ties. He voted to uphold President Carter's F-15 sale to Saudi Arabia in 1978, and backed President Reagan's AWACS sale in 1981. When the Republicans took over the Senate in 1981, he became chair of the Foreign Relations Committee.

Defeating Percy for reelection in 1984 became virtually a national crusade among pro-Israel activists. His opponent, Representative Paul Simon, reputedly agreed to enter the race only after being promised by a Chicago Jewish businessperson that the Jewish community would give at least $1.5 million in campaign donations. In all, Simon raised $5.3 million to Percy's $6 million. Another $1.6 million was spent by a California Jewish activist, Michael Goland, who ran his own independent "dump Percy" campaign. Percy lost by a narrow 89,000 votes, many of them from conservative Republicans who saw him as a leader of the hated moderate wing. Jewish voters, in fact, gave Percy 35 percent, more than Ronald Reagan got that year.

Percy's Jewish supporters—including Senator Rudy Boschwitz of Minnesota, former Senator Jacob Javits of New York, and the founding chairman of the Presidents Conference, Philip Klutznik—indignantly pointed during the campaign to his record of support for Israel on numerous other occasions. They also noted the aid increases that Israel had received while Percy chaired the Foreign Relations Committee. Most accounts of the 1984 race, including one by the noted Jewish historian Howard Morley Sachar, imply that the dump-Percy campaign was an overreaction by an overzealous Jewish lobby.

If so, it is hard to imagine what a Jewish lobby *should* be doing.

Occasionally the targets are less obvious than Percy. Senator Roger Jepsen, an Iowa Republican, was truly one of Israel's best friends in the Senate until he let the lobby down by voting for the AWACS sale in 1981. In 1982, he lost his seat to Representative Tom Harkin, a left-leaning liberal who not been noticeably pro-Israel in the past. Pro-Israel PACs backed Harkin—to the tune of $108,000, far less than Paul Simon would get—for the simple reason that he was running against Jepsen.

Mostly, though, the targets have been lawmakers who made themselves into enemies of Israel. One was Representative Gus Savage, a black

Chicago Democrat known for his flamboyantly anti-Semitic rantings on and off the House floor. Another was Representative Paul Findley, an Illinois Republican who became an advocate of the PLO in the late 1970s. After Findley lost his seat in 1982, thanks to heavy Jewish support for his opponent, he wrote a book about the intimidating power of the Jewish lobby, *They Dare to Speak Out: People and Institutions Confront Israel's Lobby*. In it, he wonders aloud at the Jewish community's furious response to critics like him: "Surely they realized that I posed no serious threat. Could Israel's supporters not tolerate even one lonely voice of dissent?"

Findley went on to found his own lobbying organization, the Council for the National Interest, dedicated to countering the power of the Jewish lobby.

What *is* surprising about Jewish PACs is how much they give to Republicans. Given the Democratic leanings of American Jews, it is noteworthy that Senate Republicans were the three top recipients of Jewish PAC money during the 1992 Democratic landslide.

There are several reasons. One is that, as Organski points out, the PAC money flows most often to incumbents who have been supportive and are now in trouble. In 1992, with Democrats running strongly across the country, the pro-Israel PACs had their hands full protecting friendly Republicans who were endangered by Bush's unpopularity. Kasten of Wisconsin, who headed the list, was a Christian conservative with a deep emotional attachment to Israel. He was also the ranking Republican on the Senate's foreign-aid subcommittee. He had helped lead the Senate fight for the loan guarantees. His reelection bid became something of a minicrusade among pro-Israel activists across the country.

Kasten lost to a liberal Jewish Democrat, Russell Feingold, who was himself a staunch supporter of Israel. The son and brother of rabbis, Feingold got no pro-Israel PAC money. Yet he won handily. Jews in Wisconsin voted for him overwhelmingly.

The rallying of pro-Israel PACs behind Kasten and against Feingold was one more symptom of the ever-growing rift within the Jewish community between hardline Israel-firsters and the more liberal Jewish majority.

The same split between Jews and Jewish PACs was replicated in several other races across the country in 1992. In Missouri, Republican incumbent Senator Christopher Bond narrowly defeated Democratic challenger Geri

Rothman-Serot, a Jewish local politician. Bond got more than $50,000 from Jewish PACs across the country, while Rothman-Serot got nothing. She lost the race by a narrow 162,000 votes, though she won a convincing majority among local Jewish voters.

The split also appeared dramatically in the 1992 New York Senate race between Republican incumbent Alfonse D'Amato and his Democratic challenger, state attorney general Robert Abrams. Abrams, an Orthodox Jew, founding chairman of the New York Conference on Soviet Jewry, won 60 percent of the Jewish vote but received no significant Jewish PAC money. D'Amato, the Senate's most vocal defender of West Bank Jewish settlers, was one of the top ten recipients of Jewish PAC money that year.

(It could be argued that D'Amato's 40 percent share of the Jewish vote won him the election. The head of the Republican ticket, George Bush, won only 15 percent of the Jewish vote in New York. D'Amato's "Jewish differential" vote, therefore, was about 25 percent or 270,000 votes. D'Amato won reelection by just 108,000 votes.)

"The pro-Israel PACs," says one Washington political consultant, "are a good indication of how a given candidate votes on Israel. And that's their job. I think it serves a good purpose. But its limit is seeing the trees, not the forest. They do a job, but they are not what the Jewish community is about."

By 1996, Jewish PAC money was going to Republicans over Democrats by a six-to-four margin.

The current system of federal campaign financing was created by Congress in 1974, amid a national wave of revulsion over Watergate-related revelations about the 1972 presidential campaign. The Nixon reelection campaign had collected millions of dollars in six-figure gifts from well-connected individuals, who evidently expected favors in return from the administration. Some of the money was donated by corporations, which have been barred for a century from campaign finance. Some of it was donated in cash and used to finance illegal campaign activity, the notorious "dirty tricks" that drove Richard Nixon from office.

The post-Watergate campaign reforms limited individuals to a maximum $1,000 gift to a presidential candidate. Slightly larger amounts could be collected by so-called political action committees, or PACs, which could then donate up to $5,000 per PAC to a campaign. PACs were not new, but they gained a new status under the reforms. Now strictly regulated, they were required to register with the Federal Election Commission and to report their activities on an ongoing basis.

The organized Jewish community agonized over the campaign reform process. Though many agreed as civic-minded citizens that the Watergate revelations were shocking, quieter voices argued that a sweeping reform could undercut the Jewish community's considerable influence in Washington. For more than a decade, the most powerful voices for Israel in the capital had been large Jewish campaign donors like Abraham Feinberg, Arthur Krim, and Max Fisher. Reform could eliminate that access, and drastically reduce the influence of Jewish lobbyists.

As it turned out, there was nothing to worry about. The 1974 campaign-finance reforms had the unintended effect of increasing rather than decreasing the influence of money on campaigns. With donations limited to small amounts—even as the cost of campaigning skyrocketed in the television age—elected officials began to spend ever-greater portions of their time fund-raising instead of doing their jobs. The amount that could be raised in a single phone call had been drastically reduced, increasing the work needed to pay for a single ad. Any device that could reduce the bother became enormously valued. As a result, PACs proliferated by the thousands across the country, from 608 in 1974 to 4,681 in 1990. The total amount donated by PACs to congressional campaigns grew during that same period from $12.5 million in 1974 to $150.5 million in 1990.

Most PACs represented corporations, still at the core of campaign financing. Much smaller clusters represented specific interest groups such as organized labor, the women's movement, environmentalists, and the pro-Israel lobby. As the role of PACs in campaign funding increased, the role of these ideological PACS received enormous attention. Their role became shrouded in a vast cloak of mystery and intrigue.

Pro-Israel PACs are particularly mysterious because their names do not reflect their goals. A list of seventy-four pro-Israel PACs published by Organski includes names like Americans for Better Citizenship, Citizens Organized PAC, Flatbush Midwood Political Action Committee, and the largest of the pro-Israel PAC pack, National PAC. Not one name refers to Israel.

Philip M. Stern, author of the 1987 muckraker *The Best Congress Money Can Buy* and its 1992 sequel *Still the Best Congress Money Can Buy*, reports that during the 1990 election campaign some fifty pro-Israel PACs gave a total of just over $4 million to federal candidates. That, he notes, compares to $914,000 contributed by PACs opposed to gun control and a total of $747,000 from PACs "on both sides of the abortion issue." Moreover, he notes, the $4 million figure understates the magnitude of the pro-Israel PACs' influence, since another $3.5 million was given directly to candidates by individual donors who had given to the pro-Israel PACs "and could fairly, therefore, be assumed to have pro-Israel sympathies."

These large sums put the pro-Israel PACs in the big leagues of political giving—but only among ideologically motivated, single-issue PACs. The world of corporate-sponsored PACs is much larger. One corporation, AT&T, gave away nearly $1.4 million to congressional candidates through PACs it controlled between 1979 and 1986. In 1984 alone, three Mid-western dairy-industry cooperatives amassed more than $3.3 million in PAC money. Stern's list of the one hundred largest PACs operating in the 1990 campaign included only one pro-Israel PAC, National PAC, founded by New York entertainment lawyer Marvin Josephson. Known as NatPAC, it is the giant of the pro-Israel PACs, accounting for between one fourth and one third of all pro-Israel PAC money. It ranked number twenty-two among Stern's top one hundred.

As with every other aspect of Jewish politics, of course, the PAC fascination is misleading. "Jewish money is certainly the biggest chunk of money in the Democratic party," says a political consultant who specializes in fund-raising. "But when you talk about Jewish money, pro-Israel money is a relatively small piece of the puzzle."

In discussing Jewish campaign giving, political fund-raisers differentiate between what they call "disciplined" and "undisciplined" money. "Disci-plined" money comes from PACs and from individuals with close ties to the organized Jewish community who respond readily when community leaders ask them to. "Undisciplined" money comes from a much larger network of Jewish individuals who respond to any number of appeals. The secret of modern, post-Watergate Jewish political money is the ability of fund-raisers to deliver both kinds of money and make them look like parts of a larger whole.

"Because of the huge role of philanthropy in the Jewish community, Jews are trained to raise money from a very early age," notes a Democratic party activist. "They learn to raise it wherever they can find it. Most Jews who are good fund-raisers raise a lot of their money from non-Jews. And

Israel and the broader Jewish agenda is a central reason why they do it. It may not be the reason why the donor gives, but it's the reason why the fund-raiser went to him."

For this reason, the tiny world of Democratic political consulting and fund-raising is a world that is dominated by Jews. Many of them are former employees of AIPAC or the UJA.

Their targets range from the obvious to the unlikely. Wall Street and Hollywood provide the two best-known concentrations of wealthy Jews, and are closely watched as sources of Democratic fund-raising. But there are other worlds which are no less important to seekers of Jewish political money, less scrutinized only because they are less glamorous.

"You can't run a statewide Democratic campaign in Texas without trial lawyer support," declares a Democratic fund-raiser. "It's the dominant influence in statewide politics in Texas. And an awful lot of trial lawyers are Jewish. But in other states that's irrelevant. In New York, one of the big ones is generic drugs. The generic-drug folks are all Jewish. And they're all very pro-Israel. I doubt any of them would go for a candidate who's not good on Israel. You get them through the Jewish country club. You get them through the AIPAC network. Sometimes you get them through the generic-drug network. And once you bring them together in a room and tell them about the generic-drug situation, the first question they ask is, 'How is he on Israel?' "

In fact, says the fund-raiser, "If you asked around the room at one of these things, you'd find that about half belong to AIPAC at $1,000 a year. If you ask their politics they'll all say 'Democrat.' They're as pro-Israel as any AIPAC lunatic. They know when an AWACs or loan guarantee thing comes up, and they're willing to be somebody's silver bullet, but the rest of the time they have other interests. And that is the strength of the Jewish community."

The total amount of "Jewish money" in a campaign is calculated by combining the relatively small amount from pro-Israel PACs with "disciplined" and "undisciplined" donations from Jewish individuals, plus money raised by activist Jewish fund-raisers. The very process of counting the total is highly secretive and controversial, because of politicians' fears of stirring anti-Semitism. Yet campaigns do the counting, partly to help in future planning, partly to figure whom to thank—and reward—for a victory.

"The usual figure you hear passed around is fifty percent, meaning that the Democrats get half their campaign funding from Jewish sources," says the American Jewish Committee's emeritus Washington representative, Hyman Bookbinder. "I've never been able to find out where the figure comes from or whether it's apocryphal, but it keeps coming up."

Conversations with numerous Jewish and non-Jewish Democratic party figures suggest that the 50 percent figure represents a partial truth. "Jewish money" is widely believed to account for about half the funding of the Democratic National Committee, the national party organization that coordinates and supports individual races, and is exempt from donor limits. It also accounts for about half of Democratic presidential campaign funding—slightly more in the case of a candidate highly popular with Jews, like Bill Clinton, and slightly less in the case of a less popular candidate, like Jimmy Carter.

In state and local races, on the other hand, "Jewish money" is rarely a factor unless the local Jewish community is a political force in its own right. Jewish money does not often travel across state lines to assist local races, except in a rare case where a candidate has aroused nationwide interest among Jews, like Harold Washington, the successful black candidate for mayor of Chicago in 1983.

Between those two extremes lie congressional races, which vary widely in their ability to attract Jewish money. Jewish fund-raising efforts in the Senate and House tend to be targeted at individual legislators with the closest ties to the Jewish community. These may be Jewish lawmakers; sympathetic lawmakers in key decision-making positions, like Senator Claiborne Pell of Rhode Island, longtime head of the Senate Foreign Relations Committee; or simply good friends, like Senator Daniel Moynihan of New York, whose oratory in the Senate (and earlier at the U.N.) made him one of Israel's best allies, Jew or Gentile.

Given the outsized role that Jewish money plays in Democratic politics, much less attention has been paid over the years to its growing role in Republican Party finance.

As the party of lower taxes and less government regulation, Republicans have access to corporate funding on a scale that Democrats can rarely match. Even during the years when Democrats dominated Congress and tailored their policies to appeal to the business community, in the 1980s, corporate donations to the minority Republicans nearly matched those to the ruling Democrats. After the 1994 congressional election, when the Democrats lost control of Capitol Hill, the GOP's corporate donations almost immediately outstripped the Democrats' by more than two to one.

As a result, Republicans are far less dependent on Jews for their funding. The network of Jewish campaign consultants and fund-raisers that plays such a key role in national Democratic politics has no parallel on the Republican side. Nor does the Democratic practice of fishing for Jewish donors through heavily Jewish industries. Estimates of the role that Jewish money plays in GOP campaign funding, much less reliable than the Democratic estimates, never exceed 20 percent even in presidential campaigns, the national party, and favored congressional races.

The most visible source of Republican Jewish money is a small group of wealthy Jewish Republicans who have taken on a prominent role in both Jewish community life and GOP affairs since 1968. The unchallenged leader of the group is Max Fisher, the Detroit oil magnate and former UJA chairman. A fund-raiser of legendary prowess, Fisher regularly heads the major-donors effort in Republican presidential campaigns. He was the founding chair of the Republican National Committee's Team 100, made up of donors of $100,000 and more.

During the 1972 campaign, Fisher helped to found the National Jewish Coalition, an organization that speaks for Republican Jews both in the GOP and in the Jewish community. It gained enormous visibility during the Reagan and Bush administrations, when it was often invited to join with the Presidents Conference as cohost of Jewish delegations to the White House. Since Fisher stepped down as chair, its leaders—including New York realtor George Klein, New Jersey investor Cheryl Fox, and Cleveland investor Gordon Zachs—all have been major Republican donors and fund-raisers in their own right.

Jewish Democrats decided in 1988 to try emulating the success of the National Jewish Coalition by forming its opposite number, the National Jewish Democratic Council. The council has been far less successful. Unlike the Republican coalition, it does not fill a vacuum. As a liberal voice within the Jewish community, it competes with defense agencies such as the American Jewish Congress and the National Council of Jewish Women. As a Jewish voice to Democratic officeholders, it competes with AIPAC. As a focus for Jewish political fund-raising efforts, it is lost in the crowd of private Jewish Democratic campaign consultants.

The National Jewish Democratic Council has attracted some respected and generous lay leaders from the Jewish organizational world, such as former CJF president Morton Mandel of Cleveland, former NCRAC chair Jacqueline Levine of New Jersey, and longtime AIPAC vice president Monte Friedkin of Florida. It has occasionally staged public events that drew dozens of Jewish officeholders to one room and helped to highlight the outsized role of Jews in the Democratic Party, in case anyone needed reminding.

Yet, perhaps because it is in such a crowded field, or because it is so top-heavy with Jewish elected officials, or perhaps simply because it is Democratic, the council tends to recapitulate the very organizational style that differentiates Democrats from Republicans—the fact that, as one Washington insider puts it, "trying to organize Democrats is like trying to herd cats."

CHAPTER 11

We Have Met the Enemy, and It Is Us: Jews and the Media

Thou shalt not go up and down as a talebearer among thy people; neither shalt thou stand idly by the blood of thy neighbor: I am the Lord. Thou shalt not hate thy brother in thy heart; thou shalt surely rebuke thy neighbor, and not bear sin because of him.

—Leviticus 19:16–17

IN 1939, IT IS SAID, *New York Times* publisher Arthur Hays Sulzberger went to visit Franklin Roosevelt in the White House and urged him not to name Felix Frankfurter to the Supreme Court seat vacated by the death of Justice Benjamin Cardozo. Putting yet another Jew on the court—in addition to the already sitting Justice Louis Brandeis—might fuel public anti-Semitism, Sulzberger told the president.

As the incident is retold, perhaps apocryphally, Roosevelt replied that it might also fuel anti-Semitism to have a Jew running the *New York Times*, and then he threw Sulzberger out of his office.

No single element of American Jewish power is more tangled in myth and mystery than the relationship between Jews and the media. Nowhere is the gulf wider between the way Jews see themselves and the way their neighbors see them.

Put most starkly, the gap in perception is this: non-Jews commonly see the mass media as a key stronghold of Jewish power, a major source of whatever influence Jews wield in American society. Jews, by contrast—

especially affiliated, activist Jews—commonly describe the media as a major source of anti-Jewish bias.

The two views seem like polar opposites, either-or propositions, thesis and antithesis. They cannot both be true. And yet, to a great degree, they are.

It is true that Jews are represented in the media business in numbers far out of proportion to their share of the population. Studies have shown that while Jews make up little more than 5 percent of the working press nationwide—hardly more than their share of the population—they make up one fourth or more of the writers, editors, and producers in America's "elite media," including network news divisions, the top newsweeklies and the four leading daily papers (*New York Times, Los Angeles Times, Washington Post,* and *Wall Street Journal*).

In the fast-evolving world of media megacorporations, Jews are even more numerous. In an October 1994 *Vanity Fair* feature profiling the kingpins of the new media elite, titled "The New Establishment," just under half of the two dozen entrepreneurs profiled were Jews. In the view of the magazine's editors, these are America's true power elite, "men and women from the entertainment, communications and computer industries, whose ambitions and influence have made America the one true superpower of the Information Age."

And in a few key sectors of the media, notably among Hollywood studio executives, Jews are so numerically dominant that calling these businesses Jewish-controlled is little more than a statistical observation.

"If there is Jewish power, it's the power of the word, the power of Jewish columnists and Jewish opinion makers," says Eugene Fisher, director of Catholic-Jewish relations at the National Conference of Catholic Bishops, and one of the Jewish community's staunchest defenders in religious Christian circles. "The Jewish community is a very literate community, and it has a lot to say. And if you can shape opinion, you can shape events."

At the same time, it is common knowledge—to affiliated Jews, at least— that the media tends to be unfairly negative in its treatment of Israel and a few other hot-button Jewish causes. Jewish community activists have complained for a quarter-century that the press too often seems obsessed with exposing Israel's warts, that it holds the Jewish state to impossibly high standards of behavior for a small, embattled nation.

Some veteran news professionals have come to agree. "Since the Six-Day War in 1967, writers and editors have regarded the genuine threat to

Israel's existence as a chimera," says correspondent Morley Safer of CBS News' *60 Minutes*. "It's a powerful threat, which editorial writers here don't recognize."

"The problem that perhaps some writers have," Safer says, "is that in the atlas of their mind, Israel is somewhere up in Westchester, not in the Levant. So they're holding it to the standards of Westchester and not to the standards of the byzantine world of—well, Byzantium, which is literally where it is. The problem is, you end up calling for a kind of curious double standard."

A large segment of American Jewry concurs. In one 1994 survey of Jewish opinion, 54 percent agreed that the "American news media use a double standard in judging Israel more harshly than Arab countries." In 1989, when the West Bank Arab uprising was a focus of world attention, 79 percent felt that way.

How can both of these things be true? How can the media be both Jewish-dominated and anti-Jewish?

The answer is complicated, but it probably begins with this observation: while Jews are disproportionately represented in the media, those Jews who gravitate toward the media tend to come overwhelmingly from the most assimilated quarters of the Jewish community. They are Jews, all right, but most are not the sort of Jews who would make a high priority of Jewish concerns—at least not as the affiliated Jews understand Jewish concerns.

"Jews in the media tend disproportionately to be what I call apostate Jews," says veteran reporter Stephen D. Isaacs, former journalism dean at Columbia University and author of *Jews and American Politics*. "Apostate Jews are attracted to all sorts of businesses that allow them to cross over and not be Jewish. By being a journalist, a Jew *can't* be Jewish, because journalism per se requires a certain distance. You can't be tribal or racial and also be a hands-off journalist."

Nonetheless, in journalism, as in politics, some of the most outwardly assimilated Jews insist on proclaiming that they are guided by a sense of Jewish values, even if their work clashes with the agenda of the organized Jewish community.

Indeed, the Jewish-values claim seems to arise most often from journalists who clash most with the Jewish community, those Jews whose reporting on Israel has sparked the most furious indignation from pro-Israel activists.

Journalists such as Anthony Lewis and Thomas Friedman of the *New York Times* and Mike Wallace of CBS News make little secret of the fact that they feel an attachment to Israel, and that this attachment might make them focus more closely on Israel, warts and all. "If you love Israel, you want it to do right," says Lewis.

Wallace, whose reporting on *60 Minutes* has sparked repeated Jewish protests over the decades, insists that his coverage of stories is merely balanced and accurate. But he admits that he looks for stories that involve wrongdoing and injustice, and that he has sought over the years to make Israel and the Jewish community his beat. It would be inevitable, then, for some of his stories to be unflattering to Israel or the Jewish community, though he says the majority have not been.

"I'm inclined to believe that it has something to do with my background, if you will," Wallace says. "I never suffered excessively from anti-Semitism to my knowledge, but I think I probably identify to some degree with those who have felt the sting of discrimination. I really do like that kind of story. And that is why it used to burn me up when I was labeled a self-hating Jew when I did a story that the Jewish community didn't find 'acceptable,' in quotes."

Random interviews with a broad sample of Jewish journalists suggest that Wallace is in a minority. Most, it seems, see no direct connection between their Jewish background and the way they do their jobs. "I can't say it's something I think about," says CNN reporter Richard Roth, who covers the United Nations. "In television news, you barely have time to think about anything but doing your job."

On closer examination, Jewish media influence is actually several distinct phenomena. There are entertainment media and news media, which play vastly different roles in America and live by different sets of rules. Within each sphere, there are those who own or manage the media and those who write or edit the content. And then there is the unique case of the *New York Times*, America's "newspaper of record" and arguably the most Jewish of all major institutions in the world of American power—and the one that makes the greatest effort not to be.

Each sector of the sprawling communications industry—news and entertainment, management and editorial—has a distinctly different relationship to the Jewish community. Some are "Jewish" only in myth, others more so. In many ways, the various pieces have little to do with one another. Yet they form one story, if only because they are bound up in the popular imagination to become a whole that is greater than the sum of its parts.

In attempting to look at this larger story, the first question must be why Jews are drawn to the media in such numbers in the first place.

Most attempts at explaining it focus on the Jew's status as an outsider in Gentile society. Non-Jewish observers from Thorstein Veblen to Jean-Paul Sartre have pointed to the alienation of Jews who left the Jewish world without gaining full acceptance in the Gentile world; standing outside both, they gained an "exemption from hard-and-fast preconceptions," Veblen wrote.

The celebrated British-Jewish philosopher Sir Isaiah Berlin countered that the driving force was not Jewish alienation from the Gentile world, but rather "an over-intense admiration" for it. The Jews' urgent desire for acceptance drove them to learn the majority's ways, Berlin claimed, and that in turn gave rise to "their well-known genius for observation and classification, and explanation—above all for *reportage* in its sharpest and finest forms. [Emphasis in original.]"

Washington Post columnist Richard Cohen put it more succinctly: "Jews are foreign correspondents in their own country," he said in a 1983 interview.

Variations on the Jew-as-outsider theory dominate discussion of the topic. However, they do not stand up to scrutiny. Like the standard explanations for Jewish liberalism, they have been overtaken by events. If Jews were drawn to the media because they were outsiders, the attraction should have declined as Jews won greater acceptance in America over the past generation. What happened was the opposite. Jews have poured into the communications industry in ever-growing numbers in the last generation.

Other theories fare little better. One popular hypothesis holds that the cultural traditions of Jewish family life encourage a skill with words and images. But too many Jewish writers and artists come from families that have lost any noticeable contact with Jewish cultural traditions. What makes them excel in the communications business?

Many Jews are simply uncomfortable with the entire topic, since it lends itself so readily to unsavory speculation about conspiracies, or worse, racial stereotypes. "What I think is, Jews are just like anybody else," says Morley Safer. "They don't act in one way. They're contradictory, just like non-Jews. They have prejudices, just like non-Jews. They have loyalties, just like non-Jews. And they have a mixture of the above. That's my interpretation, that people are not predictable.

"I always get very, very edgy when people start doing these kinds of predictions. It's sort of the other side of the *Protocols of the Elders of Zion*."

It is a fact that Jewish control of the media is one of the most durable stereotypes in the lexicon of anti-Semitism. In its most extreme form, it suggests a conspiracy by Jews to manipulate Gentile society through control of media images. The *Protocols of the Learned Elders of Zion,* a fantasy of Jewish world conspiracy concocted in czarist Russia, alleges that the Jews' secret leadership uses the press to manipulate and dominate Gentile minds. "Through the Press we have gained the power to influence while remaining ourselves in the shade," the "elders" say in Protocol Number 2.

Henry Ford's *Dearborn Independent,* which popularized the *Protocols* in America in the early 1920s, extended the theory of Jewish press control to the theater and the movies. Both, he insisted, were "entirely Jew-controlled; with the natural consequence that the civilized world is increasingly antagonistic to the trivializing and demoralizing influence of that form of entertainment as at present managed."

"As soon as the Jew gained control of the 'movies' we had a movie problem, the consequences of which are visible," the *Dearborn Independent* wrote. "It is the peculiar genius of that race to create problems of a moral character in whatever business they achieve a majority."

In less delusional versions, the Jewish-conspiracy theory shows up frequently as a complaint that Jews are simply outside America's Christian mainstream, and their prominence in the media reflects that. During Hollywood's pre–Second World War Golden Age, it was commonly argued that Jews were insensitive or hostile to Christian values, and were shaping an American culture that offended America's Christian majority. "It is only because they are outside the moral sphere of American culture that they blunder so badly that they require periodic campaigns such as that of the Legion of Decency to set them right," one critic wrote in the 1930s. The Legion of Decency, a Catholic-led group, was the most powerful of several Christian groups that campaigned early in that decade for a film-industry production code.

The complaint largely went underground after the Second World War, when the Nazi ovens discredited overt anti-Semitism. Only in the past decade, with the shifting of American politics to the right, has the charge regained some of its respectability. When the controversial film *The Last Temptation of Christ* was released in 1988, angering conservative Christians by its portrayal of a too-imperfect, too-human Jesus, some protesters blamed Jewish film executives. The Reverend R. L. Hymers, pastor of the Fundamentalist Baptist Tabernacle in Los Angeles, warned in speeches and even airborne banners that the film would bring "hatred upon Jewish people" because the company that released it, MCA, was headed by two Jewish executives, chairman Lew Wasserman and president Sidney Sheinberg.

Hymers' anti-Jewish tone embarrassed the film's better-known opponents, who tried to distance themselves from the Jew-bashing extremists at their fringes. Yet some Jewish observers saw a covert anti-Semitism in the entire tone of the *Last Temptation* protest. By targeting the distributors, the protest campaign brought the spotlight back to the old bugbear of Hollywood's Jewish executives, obscuring the fact that the film was made by Gentiles: it was directed by Martin Scorsese, a Catholic, from a script by Paul Schrader, a Protestant, based on a novel by the celebrated Greek (Orthodox Christian) author Nikos Kazantzakis.

One of the protest leaders, the Reverend Donald Wildmon of the Mississippi-based American Family Association, took care to reject the explicit anti-Semitism of Hymers and his followers. He blamed the film's release on greed and on "a hostility toward Christians" that pervaded the "pagan" attitude common among "the Hollywood elite."

That covert hostility shows up frequently in the rhetoric and tactics of Christian conservatives who campaign against immorality in the entertainment industry. Senator Bob Dole, in a controversial 1995 attack on rap music, focused his anger on Time-Warner, not the biggest producer of the genre but the one most prominently identified with Jews because of its high-profile Jewish chairman, Gerald Levin. Patrick Buchanan, the conservative Republican gadfly and presidential candidate often accused of anti-Semitism, crept even closer to the heart of the matter in an ABC *Nightline* debate on Dole's broadside in May 1995. Pitted against the liberal Jewish television producer Norman Lear, Buchanan returned repeatedly to the charge that "you people in Hollywood" were undermining "America's Christian values."

Overt attacks on "Jewish Hollywood" also show up occasionally in the rhetoric of some secular extremists, especially at the fringes of the black community. The best known of these is Leonard Jeffries, former chairman of the black studies department at City College of New York. According to Jeffries, the poor image of blacks as depicted in films and television is due in the main to an entrenched racism among Jews who control Hollywood. "Powerful Jews in Hollywood conspired for the destruction of black people," Jeffries claimed in a controversial 1991 lecture.

For all of the rank anti-Semitism lurking in the Jewish-conspiracy theories, the notion of Jewish influence in the media is not *necessarily* anti-Semitic in and of itself. The awkward fact is that, indeed, "the Jews invented Hollywood," as historian Neal Gabler put it in the unfortunate subtitle of his 1988 historical study, *An Empire of Their Own*.

The movie camera was invented by non-Jews, but the Hollywood dream factory was created by a handful of immigrant Jewish entrepreneurs. They saw the motion picture's potential as a storytelling device, and they built the studios, distribution systems, and movie theaters to promote it nationwide. These few—Adolph Zukor, William Fox, Samuel Goldwyn, Louis B. Mayer, Carl Laemmle, Marcus Loew, the Warner Brothers, and a few others—turned a technological curiosity into a multibillion-dollar industry.

A generation later, a younger group of Jewish entrepreneurs did the same thing with the radio transmitter, the microphone, and the television camera. Three men—William Paley of CBS, David Sarnoff of NBC, and Leonard Goldenson of ABC—took a bundle of toys and turned it into the powerful network broadcasting industry.

As Gabler also noted in detail, the Jews of Hollywood were ambivalent about their Jewishness to a degree that is unusual even among assimilated American Jews. With very few exceptions—notably Barney Balaban at Paramount and Dore Schary at MGM—the Jewish moguls who created Hollywood gave a wide berth to Jewish organizations and their politics. Most dutifully joined a synagogue and wrote checks to Jewish charities. But they kept Judaism strictly out of their business.

For that matter, they also kept Jewish images largely off the screen. Though vaudeville rag-peddler stereotypes abounded during the Silent Twenties—along with the rare, authentic Jewish portrait like the 1927 classic *The Jazz Singer*—Jews essentially disappeared from the screen when sound appeared. They stayed off throughout Hollywood's Golden Age. When a rare Jewish story was told, it was frequently, like the 1947

Oscar-winning *Gentlemen's Agreement,* the work of non-Jews willing to fight the system.

As long as the founding Jewish moguls ruled Hollywood, the image that shone from the screen was of a homogenized America with the small-town virtues of love, patriotism, and piety. The Jews who "invented Hollywood" wanted to create, not a Jewish vision, but "a 'shadow' America, one which idealized every old glorifying bromide about the country," in Gabler's words.

Jews reappeared on the movie screen only in the 1960s. The civil rights movement and the celebration of American diversity made ethnic images acceptable, even popular. The cultural mainstream had taken overtly Jewish imagery to its heart in the work of artists like Philip Roth and Saul Bellow in literature, Barbara Streisand in popular music, Woody Allen and Mel Brooks in stand-up comedy.

The rise of the independent Hollywood auteur allowed directors like Allen, Brooks, and Paul Mazursky to tell any story they liked. Perhaps most important, the collapse of the studio system left the Jewish studio executives powerless to stop it.

What followed was a sort of Jewish culture war: a continuing clash between the organized Jews of New York and the assimilated Jews of Hollywood. The 1968 premiere of Mel Brooks' first feature film, *The Producers,* a burlesque about Jewish Broadway shysters in league with a Nazi, produced a massive outcry from offended Jewish activists. The 1972 debut of the popular CBS television sitcom *Bridget Loves Bernie,* the story of a happily intermarried couple, led to a national protest campaign against the network, spearheaded by the liberal American Jewish Congress.

The Hollywood intra-Jewish culture war has largely wound down, but only because the organized Jews gave up. Jewish characters have become commonplace in prime-time television. The latest twist is the *Seinfeld*-inspired wave of sitcoms that focus on young Jewish singles living in New York. Jewish commentators now mention the trend only to note how far American Jews have come in gaining acceptance. Hardly anyone bothers any longer to point out that almost every Jewish character in a prime-time series in the last quarter-century has been either single or intermarried.

Hollywood at the end of the twentieth century is still an industry with a pronounced ethnic tinge. Virtually all the senior executives at the major studios are Jews. Writers, producers, and to a lesser degree directors are disproportionately Jewish—one recent study showed the figure as high as 59 percent among top-grossing films.

The combined weight of so many Jews in one of America's most lucrative and important industries gives the Jews of Hollywood a great deal of political power. They are a major source of money for Democratic candidates. The industry's informal patriarch, MCA chairman Lew Wasserman, wields tremendous personal clout in state and national politics. So do Barbra Streisand, Norman Lear, and a handful of others. A few—very few—individual Jews in Hollywood have gotten involved directly in Jewish political issues: recording-industry executive Danny Goldberg in religious rights and civil liberties, actors Ron Silver and Richard Dreyfuss in Middle East politics.

But the same could be said, to a much greater degree, of other industries with significant concentrations of Jews: Wall Street, New York real estate, or the garment industry. In each of those industries, Jews make up a significant bloc—an important minority on Wall Street, near majorities in clothing and commercial real estate—and have translated their clout into a visible presence on the political scene.

The common impression of Jewish power in Hollywood—the ability of the group to create a desired image through control of the medium—simply never materialized. The Jews who went to Hollywood were not interested.

Legrand H. Clegg II is a deputy city attorney in the Los Angeles suburb of Compton and founder of the Coalition Against Black Exploitation, a pressure group that lobbies against negative screen images of African-Americans. In July 1990, during an NAACP panel discussion on black images in the media, Clegg proposed that the black community leadership arrange a "summit" with Jewish community leaders to discuss the role of Jewish film executives in Hollywood's degrading portrayal of blacks. "If Jewish leaders can complain of black anti-Semitism, our leaders should certainly raise the issue of the century-old problem of Jewish racism in Hollywood," he said. His speech was attacked bitterly in the mainstream press. It eventually won him a page of his own in a 1992 Anti-Defamation League booklet with the inflammatory title, *The Anti-Semitism of Black Extremists and Demagogues*.

Clegg was furious. In his view, a black-Jewish dialogue on Hollywood was no more bigoted than the continuing black-Jewish debate over the anti-Semitism of Louis Farrakhan. In fact, Clegg later said that he first raised the idea while participating in a black-Jewish dialogue at a Los Angeles Jewish community center. He was called an anti-Semite there, too, which continues to rankle.

"I have no stock in attacking Jewish people," Clegg said. "No Jewish people ever attacked or killed black people. But we're concerned with Jewish producers who degrade the black image. It's a genuine concern. And when we bring it up, our statements are distorted and we're dragged through the press as anti-Semites."

Some Jewish leaders insisted that Clegg got what he deserved. "His message was that they're bad because they're Jews," said David Lehrer, the Anti-Defamation League's Los Angeles regional director. "Not because the system is bad, or it's too commercial, or because they're aiming at middle America and reducing everything to the lowest common denominator. If that was the message, I wouldn't try to argue with him. I'm not in the business of defending Hollywood. But when he says 'Jewish producers' he's talking about 'the Jews' controlling Hollywood. It's just not true."

But Clegg's complaint was more focused than that: it was that certain Hollywood products were objectionable, and that many of the producers involved were members of a group, the Jewish community, that maintains ties to the black community.

"When Spike Lee produced the movie *Mo' Better Blues,* the ADL released a statement saying the movie was anti-Semitic," he noted. "When I attacked stereotypic sitcoms and complained, I was dragged through the mud."

"I don't like the fact that *Good Times* and *The Jeffersons* have degraded the black image," Clegg said. "We're being set up the way the Jews were set up in the 1930s. And just about every one of the producers is Jewish. If blacks had produced a Jewish *Good Times* or *Sanford and Son,* the world wouldn't tolerate it."

In the end, Clegg's argument failed because there was no one to talk to. The film industry is governed by people who are businesspeople first and everything else—Jews, Christians, Democrats, and the occasional Republican—a poor second. Film-industry executives rarely respond to appeals to their Jewish conscience; the organized Jewish community has tried that in the past and nearly always failed, even when it saw the image of Jews degraded.

"The truth is that most people in Hollywood who are Jews are not people who are involved in the organized Jewish community in any way," said Carol Plotkin of the American Jewish Congress' Los Angeles chapter. "They're not organized in any sense, so we don't have that much to say to them. Critics of the movie industry say it's a closed industry, and in fact it is. It's very hard to get in. It goes from father to son, from buddy to buddy. My kid would have as hard a time getting in as their kids did."

It is a peculiarity of the American private enterprise system that any legal economic activity can be justified by its profitability. Businesses are not generally considered responsible for bystanders who are left unemployed, homeless—or humiliated—as long as the activity was legal.

In the end, Hollywood's only consideration in deciding what images to project is what will draw the largest audience. It is in the business of making a profit, like every other industry in America.

The greater curiosity, then, is why so many Americans routinely expect the film industry, alone among American industries, to behave differently.

A much easier case for alleged Jewish bias—both pro- and anti-—can be made regarding the news business.

Unlike the entertainment media, the news media are widely considered to be a public trust. They are expected to operate, at least theoretically, according to inviolate principles. They are supposed to be *about* something.

The role and duty of the news media is to inform the public of the doings of those in power. This is the reason the press is traditionally called the "fourth estate of government," and is singled out for protection in the Constitution.

Whereas looking for a Jewish message in Hollywood might tax the skills of a cultural historian or a social psychologist, therefore, looking for a Jewish bias in the news media simply requires observation. Either it is there or it isn't.

And it is not hard to find. The hard part is interpreting the evidence: the visible bias is both pro-Jewish and anti-Jewish. Whether that indicates Jewish power in the media is not entirely clear.

The case for pro-Jewish bias rests largely on the work of a handful of influential writers who regularly take it upon themselves to defend Jews and Israel and to attack their enemies. The short list begins with a trio of columnists most often fingered as defenders of Israel and Jewish interests:

William Safire and A. M. Rosenthal of the *New York Times* and Richard Cohen of the *Washington Post*. Most versions of the list also include Charles Krauthammer of the *Washington Post* and Frank Rich of the *New York Times*, along with *New Republic* editor Martin Peretz and literary editor Leon Wieseltier.

There is also a small group of highly influential magazines edited by Jews, which devote a sizable proportion of their editorial space to matters of Jewish interest: in addition to the *New Republic*, they include the *New Yorker*, the *New York Review of Books*, and *Dissent*. These are not Jewish ethnic journals but magazines of general interest. Precisely for that reason, their frequent attention to Jewish concerns reaches a broad readership and helps keep the perspectives of the Jewish community in the public eye.

For many observers, especially non-Jews, the list of pro-Jewish voices in the media must also include commentators whose work mirrors thinking in the Jewish community, even if they do not toe the community line. This list includes writers like Anthony Lewis of the *New York Times* and Ellen Goodman of the *Boston Globe*, who consistently represent a liberal-Jewish sensibility even if they rarely identify themselves in that manner. "True, Anthony Lewis's views tend toward the liberal side on the Middle East," says Eugene Fisher of the Catholic bishops' conference. "But he spends a lot of time talking about it."

The cumulative effect of all this verbal firepower is to keep Jewish views and concerns at the center of America's national attention. It also serves to keep the Jews' opponents on their toes. Like the use of Jewish campaign donations to defeat an enemy by financing a challenger, media attacks by Jews on anti-Semites are not a daily event. Nevertheless, they are memorable enough to make others think twice before attacking Jewish interests.

No one wields this kind of power more effectively than William Safire. A former Nixon speechwriter, a *Times* columnist since 1973, he is one of the best connected and most feared members of the Washington press corps. One Safire column in December 1993 sank the nomination of Admiral Bobby Inman as director of the Central Intelligence Agency, largely by accusing Inman of being anti-Israel.

Inman's candidacy was already under fire because of unpaid taxes on a domestic employee and reports of poor business judgment. But when Inman announced in January that he was withdrawing his candidacy, he put the blame squarely on Safire, calling his attacks part of a "new McCarthyism."

Mainstream reaction to Inman's withdrawal focused on his oversensitivity to criticism. But on the gossip circuit, much of Washington saw the affair pretty much in the terms Inman hinted at: as an example of Jewish media power. Some Washington insiders called it the work of a "pro-Israel mafia." "That's a theme you hear quite often in this town, that there is a dedicated group of Israeli supporters who go after people they think are against them," *Newsweek* national security correspondent John Barry said in a radio interview the day Inman withdrew.

Safire typically does not devote a great deal of space to defending Jews or Israel. Neither do most of the other journalists commonly identified as part of the pro-Israel mafia. If they did dwell on such issues, their columns would have a narrow following and the writers would lack the platform and the clout they enjoy. Indeed, some black columnists have more freedom to devote themselves to black themes than Jewish writers have to devote themselves to Jewish themes. Because of America's racial history, the problems of the black community are widely considered an interest of the broader society. The Jews' problems, by and large, are not.

But all of the preceding are examples of Jewish *opinion,* not news. Because news is supposed to concern itself with objective fact, a Jewish bias in news coverage would be more remarkable. And in fact, for all the outsized representation of Jews in the newsrooms of the leading dailies and the network news divisions, a Jewish bias is extremely hard to find.

"Of all the people that I know in journalism, I can't think of almost any who are biased," says former CBS News White House correspondent Robert Pierpoint, who is not Jewish. "I could give you countless examples of reporters who are Jewish who are not biased toward Israel, who do not let whatever feelings of loyalty they have toward Israel get in the way of telling an honest story."

In Pierpoint's view, readers who detect a pro-Israel bias may be confusing the messenger with the message. "If you look at the last fifty years, you have to say the Democratic Party has been a major source of lack of balance in American policy in the Middle East. So if someone is saying the media are pro-Jewish, he may well be reading reports of what politicians are saying."

Where bias does show up, some say, is in the choice of stories to cover. During the frenetic Jewish political activity of the 1970s, activists say that their efforts on Soviet Jewish freedom and the Arab boycott were helped considerably by a handful of friendly editors—mostly but not all Jews—at the *New York Times* and the *Wall Street Journal* who were willing to hear stories pitched. The inclusion of the stories, mainly exposés of Soviet oppression or petrodollar power, nearly always reflected valid news decisions. Senior editors at the nation's two most influential newspapers do not have the liberty of slipping in stories that do not belong in the paper. It was in taking the calls from the Jewish community's publicists that these friendly journalists showed their bias.

On rare occasions, the slant of coverage is affected, too. "I'd like to say there's no influence, but I don't know," says Sanford Socolow, a former vice president of CBS News. "Speaking for myself, the answer is no. On the other hand, people will tell you that because of Jewish consciousness at the networks, the civil rights protesters got a better break. I would deny it, but people say it's true."

"The truest thing I can tell you," says David Gelber, executive producer of the ABC News documentary series *Peter Jennings Reporting,* "is that I've had a Bosnia obsession for the last two years, and it has everything to do with my being Jewish. I want to make that sound more dispassionate, but I can't. It is a passion. I was in a village in Bosnia where every building was damaged and all the people had been rounded up because they were Muslims, the men were in camps, the women had been raped, the children were starving. If that's not a Jewish issue, then what is?"

Gelber says that the kind of stories he picks are strongly affected by his Jewish background. As a child at a mostly Gentile school in New Jersey during the 1950s he was often singled out, "and I've always been aware of the connection between my sense of being an outsider then and my preoccupation with human rights issues."

That tendency of journalists—some call it a duty—to chase after stories about injustice has worked greatly to Israel's disadvantage in the quarter-century since the Six-Day War. The image of Israel as victor and Palestinians as victims has created a fertile atmosphere for negative coverage of Israel.

It could have worked the other way. Most Jews continued to see Israel as the victim of Arab aggression. Many Americans, particularly conservatives, agreed. And in fact, examinations of Israel coverage in the press show heavier coverage of Israeli wrongdoing in liberal publications like the *New York Times* or the *Washington Post* than in conservative papers like the *Wall Street Journal* or the *Washington Times*.

But coverage of Israel is complicated by several factors. One is the fact that the nation has been receiving upwards of $2 billion per year in U.S. aid since 1974. To many editors, covering Israel is simply a case of telling readers how their tax dollars are spent.

Second, the image of the Jewish state as a progressive Western country sometimes works against it. When twenty-nine Palestinians were killed by a militant Jewish gunman in a Hebron mosque in 1994, it was on the front page of many American papers for days. When ten thousand people were massacred in the African nation of Burundi in one week that same spring, the *New York Times* reported it briefly on an inside page. Editors consider a Jewish mass-murderer more surprising, and therefore it is news.

Finally, and most important according to many reporters, Israel offers journalists full access to cover its daily events and interview its citizens and officials. Most of the dictatorships with which it is at war do not offer that kind of access, so coverage of their affairs—including their warts—is inherently more limited.

"It's a question of access," says former CBS executive Socolow. "We used to get terrific complaints over the years from Arab countries about the lack of coverage. It was a question of access. Israel, very smartly or innocently, allowed much greater access to news institutions than the Arab countries. Access is the key. Israel is smart enough to know that without access they wouldn't be able to get the money they're getting. If the coverage is unfair and biased and unbalanced, how come Israel is still the biggest single recipient of American aid?"

Says CBS's Mike Wallace, "I've been going in and out of the Middle East for thirty-two years, and Israel was the only one that was open. They had a superb PR operation. They sponsored junkets for journalists, they welcomed American journalists with enthusiasm. At the same time it was almost impossible to get any access in the Arab world. For a long time it was very, very difficult. If you had an Israeli stamp on your passport they wouldn't even let you in.

"That period in the late sixties, there was a huge enthusiasm for Israel. It was a high point in the coverage of Israel in the Western press. And over a period of time the Arabs understood that they weren't getting better press in the United States because of this, and some had the wit to say, 'Hey, we're putting a thumb in our eye. We've got to get our story out too.' And when that happened, the coverage began to change."

Since coverage of Israel started to become more negative in the 1970s, scrutiny of the press has become a regular feature of pro-Israel activism. Frequent protests have helped to make journalists wary of offending Jewish readers. A few have backed away from Middle East topics to stay out of trouble, including *Times* columnist Anthony Lewis, who was frequently critical of Israeli policy in the 1970s and early 1980s but has steered clear of the topic since the mid-1980s.

The first public flareup between the Jewish leadership and a mainstream news organization was in 1973, when Robert Pierpoint delivered a commentary on CBS Radio about the power of the Jewish lobby. The broadcast came shortly after Israel mistakenly downed a Libyan airliner that had strayed over the Sinai, killing 106 civilians. Pierpoint compared the tepid U.S. response to the incident with the previous summer's outcry when Arab terrorists murdered eleven Israeli Olympic athletes in Munich. "What this seems to add up to is a double standard in this country toward terror and murder," he said. The reason for the imbalance, he went on, was "the political influence of six million American Jews."

The comment sparked nationwide protests. The ADL mobilized supporters to complain to local CBS affiliates. The Presidents Conference demanded a meeting with CBS News president Richard Salant, who ordered an internal inquiry. Pierpoint himself got some four hundred letters, the most he has ever received on a single broadcast. CBS backed him up, but he now admits he chose his words poorly. "I should have talked about the influence of some Jewish organizations, and not the whole Jewish community."

A year later, *National Geographic* magazine came under attack for an article on Syria that claimed the Jews there enjoyed "freedom of worship and freedom of opportunity," even though they suffered significant restrictions. The article got six hundred letters, some comparing the author to Hitler. The American Jewish Congress mounted a picket line outside the magazine's offices.

One year after that, Mike Wallace did a story about Syria on *60 Minutes* that committed the same sin, allegedly understating Syria's mistreatment of its Jewish minority. This time the Presidents Conference did not go to CBS, but made Wallace come to them for a meeting at Edgar Bronfman's office in the Seagram building.

"They went crazy, the Jewish community," Wallace says. "I've never seen anything like it before or since. I think it was early in the game, before the Arabs really started getting their message out. Israel's honeymoon hadn't begun to ebb. And the Jewish community was simply stunned to see this piece on the air."

Before long, negative coverage of Israel had become routine. The rise of Menachem Begin gave the press a field day, bringing out openly anti-Semitic stereotypes such as *Time* magazine's notorious "Begin (rhymes with Fagin)." When the Israeli army launched its ill-fated invasion of Lebanon in the summer of 1982, relations between the press and the Jewish community had deteriorated into something resembling a war. The American Jewish Committee commissioned a detailed study of network war coverage that documented what appeared to be a consistent anti-Israel bias. One group, the newly formed Committee for Accuracy in Middle East Reporting in America (CAMERA), produced a powerful documentary that simply re-viewed NBC's war coverage.

The most flagrant violation—though not the only one—was the report-ing of civilian deaths. Based mainly on PLO sources, most American news outlets reported casualties in the tens of thousands. Israel would later document a figure closer to one thousand.

But the Tel Aviv rally by four hundred thousand Israelis *against* their own government that September took some of the wind out of the Jewish press critics' sails, making it harder for them to occupy the moral high ground. It was no longer a simple case of Israel versus the anti-Semites; Israelis, too, were critical of their government's behavior.

The sniping continued through the 1980s, but mainstream groups like the American Jewish Committee and American Jewish Congress had largely dropped out of the fight. It was left to an increasingly shrill CAM-ERA to issue periodic reports counting the number of inches given to Israeli rioting on the *New York Times* front page.

The war between the Jews and the news flared up just once more, in October 1990, after what became known as the Temple Mount massacre. Israeli police opened fire on a crowd of Arab worshippers outside a Jerusa-lem mosque, killing seventeen. An Israeli commission reported two weeks later that the police fired because the crowd had begun throwing stones over a retaining wall onto a large crowd of Jewish worshippers standing below, at the Wailing Wall. Mike Wallace, in a *60 Minutes* report, claimed that there was no danger and the Israeli police had simply panicked.

The Temple Mount report touched off another national outcry, including a strong complaint from the ADL and—for the first time—from higher-ups at CBS. CBS chairman Laurence Tisch reportedly had a bitter exchange with *60 Minutes* executive producer Don Hewitt, one of the most respected figures in television journalism. Both Tisch and Hewitt are Jewish. By several accounts, Tisch accused Hewitt of "betraying your people."

Following a lengthy inquest, an Israeli court ruled the following July that the police had indeed panicked and fired unnecessarily, confirming most of the points in Wallace's report. ADL director Abe Foxman responded with a public letter of apology to Hewitt.

Perhaps the most intriguing fallout of the Temple Mount dispute was the impact on Tisch at CBS. There have been rumors in New York for years that Tisch took over CBS in 1986 at least partly out of a desire to do something about media bias against Israel. (Tisch has publicly denied it, saying the purchase was meant purely as an investment.)

Tisch was one of New York's most active Jewish philanthropic leaders, a former chairperson of the New York United Jewish Appeal and active in several other causes as well. With his brother Preston, he had built a small hotel business into a nationwide conglomerate that included hotels, a tobacco company, and numerous other holdings. He had never been involved in the media.

If defense of Israel was in his mind when he took over CBS, the choice was odd. Jewish media critics consistently singled out ABC as the worst offender, particularly anchor Peter Jennings of *World News Tonight*. NBC was considered second worst. CBS was criticized mainly for the occasional Mike Wallace reports on *60 Minutes* that put Israel in a bad light. (Wallace estimates they aired no more than once a year.) But CBS, the only one of three networks still owned by its Jewish founder, William Paley, was the one that was for sale.

It was also the network known as the "Tiffany network," the standard-setter in quality news and entertainment. A shift in coverage at CBS could well influence the rest of the industry.

If that was Tisch's plan, it was a failure. Except for a few arguments with Hewitt and Wallace, he never found a way to influence coverage. He quickly learned that journalists consider the "news process" sacred and do not easily accept outside interference. Wallace says that Tisch promised when he first acquired CBS not to interfere in coverage, except "to make sure it was accurate." And he "never, repeat never tried to put any pressure on me about a Jewish story before it was on the air."

Tisch's influence on the CBS news department was largely limited to much-criticized budget cuts, which reduced the reporting staff and arguably dropped the network from first to third place in viewership. Staff morale at CBS News dropped drastically.

"The difference between Tisch and Paley," says ABC's David Gelber, a former *60 Minutes* staffer, "is that Paley's idea of public service was to create the best news division in television. Tisch's idea of public service is to make a lot of money and then have a wing of a hospital at NYU named after him. And when the dust clears, what Larry Tisch will be remembered for is what he has done to CBS, because it is one of the tragedies of American journalism."

Tisch's experience at CBS proves one thing: Jewish ownership in the mass media does not represent any significant concentration of Jewish power, however much it may symbolize it in the popular imagination. Most media moguls have little control over the content of their properties. The larger their holdings, the less they can control their content. Nearly all of them are in the business for the same reason that most investors are in any business: to make money. An investor who wishes to make content decisions on the basis of ideology must be willing not to make them on the basis of profit. Not many investors are willing to lose money in that way.

Only two major American media forces have shown a willingness to risk loss for the sake of their vision in recent years. One is Rupert Murdoch's News Corporation, which has taken steady losses in the New York *Post* and invested a hefty sum in the newer *Weekly Standard* in order to promote Murdoch's archconservative views. The other is the Sulzberger family-owned New York Times Company, which has seen its stock lose value in recent years as it invested in expanded news coverage while everyone else was cutting back.

A few Jewish investors have managed to affect the direction of the media by making intelligent, targeted investments in *small* journals that can be subjected to hands-on control. One is real-estate investor Mortimer Zuckerman, who built a media mini-empire in the 1980s consisting of the *U.S. News and World Report*, the *Atlantic Monthly*, and the *New York Daily News*. His management of his news organs, *U.S. News*, and the *Daily News*, has been unremarkable. But his management of the *Atlantic* has demonstrated the power of a journal to launch new ideas into the culture. There are only a few influential journals in America that regularly run long essays and try out big ideas: *Harper's*, the *Atlantic Monthly*, *Foreign Affairs*, and a handful of others. Zuckerman has used his membership in that tiny club to Jewish advantage by publishing occasional pieces that manage, ever so slightly, to shift debate toward what might be called a Jewish way of seeing the world: articles, for example, on the changing nature of Islam, or on the continuing influence of Arabists in the State Department.

The best known of the Jewish-owned journals, though, is the *New Republic*. It has been one of America's most influential magazines for generations. Under current owner-editor Martin Peretz, it is also one of America's most militant defenders of Israel.

Peretz, a onetime leftist who underwent a highly public break with the left after the Six-Day War in 1967, prides himself on running a magazine that is not predictably of the left or right.

"I think we're the only small-circulation sheet that actually agitates and scares people in the opinion elites and the policy elites," says Peretz. "Why? Because we are a genuinely independent place. There is no party line. Well, there's a sort of party line on Israel."

Critics say that his magazine is merely cranky, that it delights in skewering sacred cows simply for the thrill of it, often trashing targets on the slimmest of evidence. Others call it a characteristic voice of neoliberalism: a sort of cuddly, borderline neoconservatism, listing perceptibly rightward without ever adopting the neoconservatives' venomous malice toward the left.

What is true of Peretz's *New Republic* is that its irreverence is selective. It is casually dismissive of most party lines that reflect America's balkanization into subgroups that base themselves on vulnerability and victimhood. But two sacred cows are spared the knife and kept on their pedestals: homosexuals and Israel. Their fears are nearly always endorsed, or at least understood. All others are laughed off. The *New Republic* has no patience for blacks who think whites inherently racist, nor for feminists who think males inherently sexist, nor populists who think government inherently dictatorial, nor Bible-thumpers who think humankind inherently sinful.

For all the influence that Jewish individuals wield in the American media, then, the media remains remarkably uninterested in exploring the Jewish community. This, in fact, is the biggest single reason why the power of the Jewish establishment remains such a mystery to Americans, both Jewish and non-Jewish: because its activities are so rarely written about.

The major exception to this rule is a tiny corner of the news business made up of Jewish ethnic and religious periodicals, and known collectively as the Jewish press. It includes about one hundred weekly newspapers, most of them published by local Jewish federations, and an equal number of monthly or quarterly magazines, most published by national Jewish organizations. Only a handful—notably the far-right weekly *Jewish Press* of Brooklyn, the apolitical monthly *Moment* magazine of Washington and a few others—are genuinely independent journals. Most of the others are tame affairs, filled with local synagogue news and worshipful accounts of Israeli prowess.

There are exceptions, to be sure. A few sponsored journals—such as the *Jewish Week* of New York, the *MetroWest Jewish News* of New Jersey, and the Jewish Telegraphic Agency, the federation-backed daily wire service— show a high level of intelligence and independence, thanks to smart editing and hands-off sponsorship. Most of the rest are held back by unimaginative writing and editing and by fear of the sponsors' anger (or the readers'). The result is that the public does not look to them as a main source of information on Jewish life and thought, and the Jewish leadership does not see them as its avenue to reach the public.

For that, most look to the *New York Times*.

Though it is not the largest-circulation newspaper in the country, not even in New York City, the *New York Times* is probably America's most influential news organ because it is read by the nation's most influential people as their primary source of information. It has maintained its reputation as the "newspaper of record" throughout the century, essentially by maintaining a standard of reliability that is generally respected. Because it is the newspaper of record, the paper read over morning coffee by journalists at other newspapers and television networks, it sets the news agenda for much of the rest of the media.

The *Times* is also the institution arguably most responsible for the image of Jewish media influence. In the eyes of much of the world, it is a Jewish newspaper. The reputation stems in large measure from the fact it was purchased in 1896 by a Jew, Adolph Ochs, and is still owned by his descendants.

The *Times*'s Jewish image has rankled the Ochs-Sulzberger clan since its beginning. "The idea of 'the Jewish media' is basically a bunch of nonsense," says New York Times Company chairman Arthur O. "Punch" Sulzberger Sr., Ochs's grandson. "There are a couple of important papers that were and are Jewish-owned, and people like to hold them up and somehow everything else follows from that. It's not true. And while the *New York Times* is owned by a Jewish family, it's not a Jewish newspaper, and I don't want it to be. We're Americans of Jewish descent, not Jews living in America."

Indeed the *Times*'s current publisher, Arthur Ochs Sulzberger Jr., is not even Jewish by traditional rabbinic standards. His mother is not Jewish, and he was baptised an Episcopalian.

Nonetheless, Sulzberger Jr. has acknowledged the power of his family's Jewish mystique. "Ninety-nine people out of one hundred consider me Jewish," he once told an interviewer. "How could a Sulzberger not be Jewish?" He has even made a point of taking his children to Passover observances because he does "not want them to be alienated from Judaism the way I was."

Within the *Times*, the efforts of the Sulzberger family to avoid letting theirs be seen as a Jewish newspaper are legend. The most discussed was the practice of forcing reporters with obviously Jewish names to use their initials. A. M. Rosenthal, whose first name is Abraham, often tells the story of how his name was "circumcised" when he got his first byline. Longtime reporter A. H. Raskin met the same fate. But another, Israel Shenker, did not. The myth is hardy, but it is only partially true.

Far more serious was the owners' refusal to promote Jews into senior editorial positions. It was a fixed rule until Punch Sulzberger became publisher in 1961. He scrapped it and opened the door for Jews to hold any position they could win on their merits.

Sulzberger took the final step to end the taboo in 1976 when he named

A. M. Rosenthal as executive editor, the first Jew to hold the paper's top editorial position. Every executive editor since then has been Jewish as well. Under Rosenthal and his successors Max Frankel and Joseph Lelyveld, the paper has gradually dropped its long history of Jewish self-consciousness. Author Gay Talese had written in his 1969 book *The Kingdom and the Power* that the *Times* "will bend over backwards to prove" it was not a Jewish paper. Now the issue is regarded as meaningless.

"A. M. Rosenthal, who is Jewish, runs a newspaper that had more news about Israel than other newspapers," says Rosenthal, referring to himself in third person. "But A. M. Rosenthal ran a paper that emphasized the arts, business, sports, and many other issues, including Jewish issues. I am a Jewish editor of the *New York Times*, which is the greatest newspaper in the world and covers every goddam topic."

Times executives acknowledge that the paper covers Israel and other Jewish issues more closely than other newspapers. They say this is not because the paper is a "Jewish newspaper" but because its readers are interested. Reader surveys have shown that Jews make up as much as one third of the *Times's* readership.

For organized Jews, the *Times* exudes an almost religious quality. It is looked upon as a sort of community bulletin board, the sole vehicle through which to reach the Jewish public. Advertisements in the *New York Times* are the standard way Jewish groups announce their existence and voice their protests.

Times executives are only vaguely unaware of the passions they arouse among organized Jews. To a degree, they shield themselves because of the intensity with which Jewish leaders fight to appear on the op-ed page.

One *Times* policy decision actually did have a devastating impact on the conduct of Jewish community affairs. It was a decision by A. M. Rosenthal, when he became metropolitan editor in 1963, to discontinue the *Times's* custom of reporting church doings and sermons. "I realized every Monday we were giving a page of coverage to handouts, and they were boring as hell and had nothing to do with religion."

Instead, Rosenthal started sending reporters out to cover the experiences of believers in their neighborhoods, and ended coverage of official church doings. Later, as assistant managing editor, he extended the same policy by ending coverage of the national Jewish organizations.

"When the organizations found out I was not going to cover their meetings they were furious," he recalls. "But they were not news. Looking back, perhaps we went from too much to too little immediately. It's possible that in not covering Jewish organizations we went too far in the other direction."

In fact, the refusal of the *Times* to cover the doings of the Jewish organizations as news during the 1970s and 1980s was of enormous significance. It meant that during the period when the organized Jewish community underwent meteoric growth in power and influence, most Jews had no way of finding out. It all happened in a vacuum. Only AIPAC, headquartered in Washington, survived the blackout.

The events were reported, after a fashion, in the weekly newspapers of the Jewish ethnic press. Most large cities have one Jewish weekly, usually published as an organ of the local Jewish federation. Total circulation nationwide is estimated at about just under 1 million—roughly the universe of federation donors—but since most receive free subscriptions, it is impossible to know whether these papers are read. Though there are exceptions, most are publicity sheets with little pretense of journalistic initiative. Investigative coverage of the Jewish organizational leadership is rare.

Nor are most Jewish ethnic journals open to the Jewish experiences of Jews outside the traditional community. Favorable articles about mixed marriage, or questioning of Jewish belief are nearly nil.

Under Max Frankel, who succeeded Rosenthal as executive editor in 1987, the *Times* began subtly stepping into the role of a voice for assimilated Jews. Articles began showing up frequently—essays in the travel section, confessions in the magazine section—by Jews struggling with the meaning of Jewishness. Frankel's successor Joseph Lelyveld, whose father was a rabbi and former American Jewish Congress president, appears to be taking the final step since taking over in 1994 by introducing news reporting on the Jewish community. News articles have appeared for the first time in living memory that cover internal political struggles within and among the Jewish organizations. For the first time, the Jews are visible in the *New York Times* as a community.

Times staffers unanimously insist that the Jewish atmosphere at the *New*

York Times is still not acknowledged openly, even when individual writers have to grapple with covering a sensitive story. "I guess you feel these things when the issues come up, but I've never heard it discussed," says one reporter.

"This is not a Jewish institution," declares an editor who is not Jewish. "It certainly isn't run that way day-to-day. But you feel the atmosphere in funny ways. For a long time I used to go home every year for the big family Christmas gathering and find that conversation would stop when I entered a room. For a while I thought it was me. Then I realized that it happened when people were talking about Jews. They would drop the subject when I came in, so as not to offend me. Because I worked for the *Times*, my relatives thought of me as some sort of honorary Jew."

On occasion, the *Times*'s unconscious Jewishness surfaces in almost hilarious ways. On January 7, 1996, the day after the Christian feast of Epiphany, the paper's Metro section marked the traditional end of the Christmas season with a whimsical feature in which "a diverse group of New Yorkers—all of whom might be considered wise—were asked what gifts they would give to a messiah born now." Five of the seven respondents were Jews. ("And why not?" said one Jewish ex-*Times* staffer. "We're the only ones still waiting for him.")

CHAPTER 12

Dueling Victims: The Mysterious Art of Intergroup Relations

O N   A   Q U I E T   M O N D A Y evening in late August of 1991, a car driven by a Hasidic Jew spun out of control and jumped a sidewalk in the Crown Heights section of Brooklyn, killing a seven-year-old black child, Gavin Cato, and wounding his nine-year-old cousin Angela. It was shortly after 8:15 P.M.

As the children's neighbors gathered at the accident scene, rumors began to spread through the crowd. It was reported that a private Jewish ambulance had arrived first on the scene, but departed with the driver and left the children behind. (This was true; the police ordered the ambulance crew to "take your guy and get out before they kill him.") It was said that the driver was a personal aide to the Grand Rabbi of Lubavitch, the powerful, reclusive religious leader of the neighborhood's Hasidic Jewish enclave. (Also true; the car was part of a police-escorted motorcade that sped the rabbi to and from a daily meditation at his father-in-law's grave.) It was said that the police would not charge the driver with homicide, because of police favoritism toward Jews. (Not quite true; a grand jury would rule the crash an accident and vote not to indict.)

In short order, the crowd set off on a protest march toward Lubavitch headquarters, a mile away on Eastern Parkway. En route the crowd swelled. By the time it reached the synagogue, it was an angry, rock-throwing mob, intermittently chanting, "No justice, no peace." Smaller groups peeled off to stone Jewish-owned stores and Jewish homes. At around 11:20 P.M., a group of teenagers attacked an Orthodox Jewish passerby coming from the subway, kicking, beating, and stabbing him amid shouts of "Get the Jew." The victim, Australian tourist Yankel Rosenbaum, died of his wounds three hours later at Kings County Hospital.

The rioting went on well into the night, then commenced again the next day, and the next. Every day for three days, a mob gathered in front of the Lubavitch synagogue, chanting "No justice, no peace," and "Jew, Jew," and "Heil Hitler," and then broke up into roaming groups of rock-throwing hoodlums. Jewish pedestrians were assaulted. Non-Jews who looked Jewish were attacked, one fatally. When David Dinkins, the city's black mayor, came to Crown Heights to appeal for calm, he was pelted with bottles and rocks.

By the time the rioting ended on Thursday, New York had suffered its worst civil disturbance in twenty years. American Jews had experienced the most prolonged, violent assault in their three-hundred-year history, the first organized anti-Semitic riot in American history.

To the Hasidic Jews of Crown Heights, the riots recalled nothing so much as the pogroms, the murderous anti-Jewish riots that periodically broke out in czarist Russia, often at police instigation. The image was at least partly false: the pogroms of Europe's past were government-sponsored, and the Crown Heights riot was not. Still, hundreds of the Hasidim were immigrants who had personally survived Nazi death camps; thousands more had parents or grandparents who had lived through the czarist pogroms. For them, the three days in August were a terrifying journey back in time. It seemed as though their black neighbors had turned against the Jews.

In the weeks ahead, this emotional reaction hardened into something resembling a political position. On September 20, the Hasidic community took out a full-page advertisement in the *New York Times* under the banner headline, "This year Kristallnacht took place on August 19th, right here in Crown Heights." (The reference was to the "Night of Broken Glass" in November 1938, an orgy of anti-Jewish rioting across Nazi Germany that historians regard as the opening salvo of the Holocaust.)

"The Jews of Crown Heights," the ad said, "will not be intimidated. Because we understand the simple truth—*if we run, you're next*. If we give in to the threats of the latter day Nazis and abandon *our neighborhood* and *our rights as American citizens,* the entire American Jewish community becomes vulnerable. [Emphasis in original.]"

The harshness of the Hasidic rhetoric alienated much of New York's mainstream Jewish community leadership. Most liberals did not consider the riots as the opening shot of a new Holocaust, but as an ethnic clash of the sort that has become all too familiar in urban America.

"We look at Crown Heights and we say it was an aberration in black-Jewish relations," says the Orthodox political scientist David Luchins, a senior aide to Senator Daniel Moynihan. "It was a tribal conflict, a turf battle between two groups. That's not Kristallnacht."

"Ten days after the Crown Heights riots," Luchins goes on, "Rabbi Shmuel Butman of the Lubavitch community was the honorary grand marshal of the annual Caribbean Day Parade. He marched down Eastern Parkway on Labor Day to standing ovation. It was on the front page of the *New York Times* the next morning.

"Now, American Jews can tell you there is rampant anti-Semitism today, which indeed there may or may not be. But I'm saying that a week and a half after Kristallnacht, the Germans didn't host a parade and have a Jew as the honorary grand marshal. A week after the Kishinev pogrom they didn't have a parade where the Jews marched through the city and a million goyim applauded."

In late September, the two opposing views of Crown Heights met head-on at the Jewish Community Relations Council (JCRC) of New York, which brings together the main Jewish organizations in the metropolitan area. Representatives of the Big Three defense agencies had come to propose that the council show solidarity with the Jews of Crown Heights by mounting a citywide rally against bigotry and hate. The Hasidic leadership wanted the rally narrowed to a single target: black anti-Semitism. As a compromise, the rally became a protest against anti-Semitism.

The liberals, seeking to ensure that the rally would not become a racial confrontation, demanded and won an agreement that no politicians be invited—especially not Ed Koch, the colorful, outspokenly Jewish ex-mayor whose rhetoric had made him a symbol of the city's racial divisions.

Koch came and spoke anyway, at the personal invitation of JCRC chairman Kenneth Bialkin.

A state investigation would report to the governor of New York in 1993 that the Crown Heights rioting was something almost unknown in the recent annals of civil unrest in New York: a deliberate, targeted attack against a specific segment of the community. "The aggression was systematic, intense, and injurious," said the report, authored by state criminal-justice director Richard Girgenti.

The rioting may have begun spontaneously, but it went on for three days because it was organized. Some of New York's most militant black activists, including Sonny Carson and the Reverend Al Sharpton, descended on Crown Heights the morning after the traffic accident to mount demonstrations and stoke the anger. Their ostensible purpose was to bring the Hasidic driver to justice. But their larger goal—made clear in speeches, leaflets, and comments to the press—was to make of Gavin Cato's death a metaphor for alleged Jewish oppression against people of color everywhere. Sharpton turned the Cato child's funeral into a veritable anti-Jewish rally, haranguing mourners with a litany of Jewish wrongdoing from the Middle East to South Africa.

"You don't want peace, you want quiet," Sharpton declared. "Don't just talk about the jewelry store on Utica [Avenue]. Talk about how Oppenheimer, in South Africa, sends diamonds straight to Tel Aviv and deals with the diamond merchants right here in Crown Heights. . . . The Bible says that which a man sows, that shall he also reap. Well, reverend, who sowed the violence? You sowed the violence. You took my brothers to the Persian Gulf and trained them how to kill. . . . Don't tell us about violence!"

In reply, New York's most militant Jewish conservatives launched a systematic campaign of their own. Their ostensible purpose was to bring Yankel Rosenbaum's killers to justice. Their larger goal was to turn the riots into a metaphor for alleged black hostility toward Jews nationwide. The campaign's leader was the dead man's brother, Norman Rosenbaum, a husky, bearded Melbourne attorney who would make New York a virtual second home in the months ahead.

In October 1992, a jury acquitted the sole suspect in the Rosenbaum murder, teenager Lemrick Nelson, even though he had been arrested moments after the crime a short distance away, hiding behind a hedge with a bloody knife in his pocket, and identified by the dying victim. The jury, composed of nine blacks, two Hispanics, and one white, joined Nelson afterward for a victory dinner.

The acquittal escalated the Jewish campaign into an angry groundswell. With Norman Rosenbaum as standard-bearer, a coalition of Orthodox separatists, hardline Likud Zionists, and conservative Republicans emerged to demand justice for the slain Australian. Yankel Rosenbaum became a symbol of the dangers that Jews faced, not only from militant black nationalism, but also from the moderate blacks of the Dinkins administration and their allies in the liberal Jewish establishment.

"The Crown Heights pogrom is the most disgusting example of anti-Semitism ever to confront us," Norman Rosenbaum told Yeshiva University students in a November 1992 speech, shortly after the verdict. "Remember that what is occurring here is occurring notwithstanding the so-called lessons of Adolf Hitler, and is occurring with the condoning of the so-called representatives of your people."

In early November, alarmed by the deteriorating situation, the National Jewish Community Relations Advisory Council convened an emergency consultation on the crisis in black-Jewish relations. More than one hundred people gathered at Anti-Defamation League headquarters in New York, representing all the major national Jewish agencies and close to one hundred local Jewish communities across the country. "The basic message we got from them," said Diana Aviv, then NCRAC's deputy director, "was, 'What crisis?' "

Except for Chicago, home of the notoriously anti-Semitic Black Muslim leader Louis Farrakhan, every community represented at the NCRAC consultation reported that relations with the local black community were unchanged. "We sympathize with what the New York Jewish community is going through," said one Midwestern participant. "But it's not what's going on in my town."

In fact, nothing remotely resembling the Crown Heights riot had ever happened before to American Jews. Most Jews and most blacks in America do not feel hostility toward one another. The riot represented a highly specific mix of circumstances: an outburst of ethnic anger in a troubled neighborhood, escalated by a small band of racial provocateurs into a deliberate assault against a small sect of urban mystics.

In the aftermath of the riot, however, an endless process was born of finger-pointing by militants on both sides. It created a dynamic of its own. Each side demanded justice for its dead, while belittling the other's grievances as posturing. Each new demand for justice on one side became evidence to the other of hostility, and fed the other's sense of grievance.

In the aftermath of the riot, there were few moderates willing to step forward from either group to suggest that their militant defenders were too vigilant in their defense. On both sides, the memory of past suffering had made it a sin to underestimate threats from the outside. Somehow, the very idea of defusing a conflict had become disloyal.

For much of the twentieth century, Jews and blacks shared the same enemy: white Christian racism. Sharing a common enemy had created a widespread sense of solidarity between the two groups. Moreover, it had made a sense of solidarity with the other into a moral value. Solidarity with other victimized groups became an expression of loyalty to one's own group.

Crown Heights was the end of a long process, begun two decades earlier, whereby Jews and blacks came in large numbers to abandon their common cause and identify each other as the enemy.

In some measure, the silencing of moderates was part of the militants' aim almost from the moment the rioting began.

On Monday evening, shortly after the start of the riot, representatives of the Jewish defense agencies contacted Lubavitch community leaders to see how they could help. One official, Rabbi Philip Abramowitz of the New York JCRC, was dispatched to Crown Heights that evening to assist in contacts between the Hasidic community and the city, police, and outside agencies. The other agencies—the ADL, the American Jewish Committee, and the American Jewish Congress—were asked not to send anyone to the neighborhood, a Hasidic official told a reporter later in the week. "It's clear to us that this is the work of agitators from outside the neighborhood," the Hasidic leader said. "We don't want to bring in our own people from outside and confuse things."

By Thursday, Hasidic leaders were making public statements condemning the major Jewish agencies for "abandoning" their community to its fate. The charge stuck.

On Friday, a joint American Jewish Committee–NAACP delegation went to Crown Heights to assess the situation and look for ways to heal the wounds. Not one of the daily newspapers reported the effort.

Community relations—the management of the Jewish community's external relations with other communities—is one of the oldest functions of Diaspora Jewish social structure. In premodern times, when Jewish communities were autonomous bodies, the importance of this work was obvious: the community mediated between the individual and the sovereign, negotiated over Jewish legal rights in every social and economic sphere, and even set the Jews' tax rates.

In modern-day America, the task of community relations is much less clear. Since each individual is directly answerable to the government, the mediating role of the ethnic community seems largely an anachronism. In the popular mind, the Jewish community's external role—the job of community relations—involves little more than defending Jews from anti-Semitic bigotry and discrimination. In a broader sense, it could include the defense of particular Jewish interests, such as the security of Israel and the legality of kosher slaughtering techniques, or advancing particular Jewish values, such as religious tolerance.

But to go from such a role to conducting relations with other communities—like a sort of quasi-foreign policy—is a leap that many Jews cannot make. In what sense do they share with other Jews in some collective relationship to the black, Hispanic, or any other "community"? And if there is such a collective relationship, who elected the ADL to manage it?

In fact, the process of community-relations management is inevitable. As political scientists often remark, American democracy is heavily dependent on the interplay of informal groups outside government. These informal groups are essential to mediate between the individual and society, and to speak up for minorities. Critics call them "special interests"; admirers call them voluntary associations, the building blocks of civil society.

These voluntary interest groups come in many shapes and sizes, from churches and chambers of commerce to bowling leagues, environmental groups, and gun clubs. Their role in the making of public policy is as old as the Republic.

When they work well, these civic groupings help to diffuse power broadly among various sectors of society. At its best, this diffusion reduces the unilateral power of government. In so doing, it protects the weak and prevents tyranny by the majority.

Unfortunately, this crucial function of democracy can seem extremely anti-democratic when a majority finds its wishes too often frustrated by assertive minorities.

Of the many contributions by organized Jewry to America's civil democracy, perhaps the most distinctive has been to establish the right of vulnerable minorities to legal protection from the majority. Through the courts and legislatures, the Jewish community has established a wide perimeter of protection for itself and other victims of prejudice. In the process, it has established itself as a legitimate partner in the democratic process, speaking out for the Jews as a vulnerable group and for other groups that are less able to speak for themselves.

This winning of legitimacy took place in the quarter-century between the Second World War and the Vietnam War. That was the period when the Jewish community, in alliance with the organized black community, established the legal and legislative framework of modern civil rights law. The Jewish and black civil rights organizations emerged from that period firmly established in the public mind as the nation's premier tribunes of conscience and voices of the downtrodden.

That image of victimhood became an essential weapon in the arsenal of Jewish political power—and, for that matter, of black political power. Both communities base their political programs on an assumption that, as powerless, vulnerable minorities, they can speak truth to power and demand accountability from others, without themselves being held accountable. Both communities take the reflexive position that the activities of the group they represent are inherently inoffensive because they are powerless.

The very suggestion that leaders of a victim group should take responsibility for offenses from within their group is taken to be an expression of bigotry.

Jewish defense organizations have used this power of victimhood to great effect in a host of arenas, from government to business to interfaith dialogue. One of the most effective manifestations is the thirty-year dialogue between Judaism and the Roman Catholic Church, begun in the wake of the historic Second Vatican Council of 1963–65. From the Vatican's point of view, the dialogue is largely an attempt to achieve understanding with a sister faith. From the Jewish community's point of view, it is largely a one-sided exercise in purging anti-Jewish teachings from Catholic theology. Indeed, some Jewish groups and individuals have approached Catholic-Jewish dialogue from a posture so one-sided that to Catholics it often seems grossly bigoted.

"There is some resentment among Catholics," says Eugene Fisher, director of the secretariat for Catholic-Jewish relations at the National Conference of Catholic Bishops. "But the bishops are by and large basically pastors, and they can understand and feel anguish when they see it, and that's what is going on here on the Jewish side. We know we are dealing with a people that has been deeply wounded."

That sort of forgiveness is essential to Jewish political strategy in dealing with outside groups.

The trouble with Jewish-black relations is that the blacks also see themselves as victims, no less than the Jews—and perhaps more so. In effect, once the two groups stopped focusing on the common enemy of white racism and began focusing on each other, they had no way to get along. Each one expected the other one to give and forgive.

The black-Jewish alliance is a staple in the mythology of American liberalism. Like many myths, its popular image took on a life of its own, divorced from the reality at its core. In the liberal imagination, it grew into a massive love affair among millions of blacks and Jews. More recently, it has become fashionable to suggest that the alliance never existed at all, except in the liberal imagination. Both extreme versions are wrong.

At its heart, the alliance was and is a formal, working relationship between two institutional communities. "There is a natural alliance," says veteran civil rights leader Eleanor Holmes Norton, the nonvoting congressional delegate of the District of Columbia. "It exists in a very strong way among the national black and Jewish leadership, including people in Congress and civil rights leaders. It is a very effective alliance at the national level, although those of us who operate at the national level have been less effective in taking alliance to the communities."

The formal alliance began in the waning days of the Second World War, when the main leadership bodies of the two communities, the NAACP and NCRAC, established a joint council to reconstitute the wartime President's Committee on Fair Employment Practices. In 1950, the council decided to expand its scope into a broad-based campaign against discrimination in housing, education, and jobs—all areas where blacks and Jews suffered equally. The new body, known as the Leadership Conference on Civil Rights, was chaired by NAACP director Roy Wilkins and staffed by NCRAC deputy director Arnold Aronson. Its headquarters were at the NCRAC office until 1963, when it moved to new quarters in the Washington office of the Reform movement.

It is easy to exaggerate the cooperation between Jews and blacks during this period. The two groups' agendas were not identical. Jewish advocacy in the postwar era worked hard to expand church-state separation, not an urgent matter for the black community. Much of the black effort was aimed at their problems in the rural South; most of these were irrelevant to Jews.

Even in the joint battle against legal discrimination, cooperation was not absolute. "The major strategic attack of the black organizations was school segregation," recalls Will Maslow, then head of the American Jewish Congress legal department. "We gave them moral support but not much help. In most places they were able to fight it on their own. They prepared the legal briefs; we would file briefs amicus. And they were rarely able to help us in our work."

In 1947, Maslow asked Roy Wilkins to join the steering committee of a new campaign to outlaw discrimination in New York State graduate school admissions. Wilkins agreed, Maslow recalls, "but he said this was not a major problem for them. He said they had very few people in colleges seeking admission to graduate school."

Still, in the broad context of American life, the strengths of the black-Jewish alliance far outweighed its weaknesses. It was quite simply unique. Nothing else like it existed. The very fact that the two most victimized groups in America had joined forces for reform gave their alliance a moral power. It became an important political presence at the federal, state, and local levels.

"In a period from 1945 to 1950," says NCRAC's Arnold Aronson, "maybe ten states enacted fair-employment statutes as a result of the work of coalitions we had operating at the state level. The financing was Jewish. The fight for state legislation in Michigan had an executive on loan from the Jewish Labor Committee. The Pennsylvania fight was run out of the Jewish community headquarters in Philadelphia. The same thing was true in New Jersey. The Ohio state fight was run out of the Jewish Community Council in Cleveland. When Ohio set up its state fair-employment practices commission, the local CRC executive became the director."

During the 1950s, the civil rights struggle moved from legislatures to courtrooms. The defining legal victory of the decade, the Supreme Court's 1954 decision to outlaw school segregation in *Brown v. Board of Education,* was decided in large part on the strength of research which convinced the justices that segregation hurt black children. The research, by black psychologist Kenneth Clark, was largely funded by the American Jewish Committee.

The decade's other defining court victory, the Supreme Court's so-called "One Man, One Vote" ruling in 1959, which guaranteed black voting rights, resulted from a ten-year legal crusade by a leader of the Georgia Jewish community and future president of the American Jewish Committee, attorney Morris B. Abram.

In an important sense, America's post–Second World War civil rights crusade was really two separate crusades.

The first was the legal struggle waged by the alliance of black and Jewish organizations. It began in 1945 and climaxed with the passage by Congress of the 1964 Civil Rights Act and the 1965 Voting Rights Act.

The second was the popular struggle waged across the South by students and civil rights activists under the leadership of the Reverend Martin Luther King Jr. It began with King's 1957 bus boycott in Montgomery, Alabama. With King's death in Memphis in 1968, just as black separatists were beginning to take over the civil rights movement, that second crusade too began to flag.

The two crusades, though related, were independent. One was largely a Northern effort aimed at changing laws; the other was largely a Southern effort aimed at changing attitudes.

Both involved vast levels of Jewish-black cooperation. But only one, the Northern crusade, was a formal alliance between two organized communities. The other, the Southern crusade, was a straightforward black campaign for black rights. Tens of thousands of whites joined the crusade as Freedom Riders, marchers, and voter registration workers. Thousands more volunteered as lawyers, helped organize demonstrations, and gave money to support the effort. But it was led by black leaders and organized by black institutions.

Of the white volunteers, it is often estimated, close to half were Jews. Thousands of Jewish students went South during the civil rights summers of the mid-1960s. Hundreds of Jewish lawyers volunteered to represent the civil rights workers who were jailed. One, New York attorney Stanley Levison, joined King in Montgomery and remained one of his closest and most trusted associates up to the end of his career.

In one of the most famous incidents of the Southern crusade, three young civil rights workers were murdered in Mississippi in the summer of

1964. They were two New York Jews and a Mississippi black: Michael Schwerner, Andrew Goodman, and James Chaney. Their deaths did much to galvanize broad national support for the civil rights struggle. The three became icons of the civil rights movement, recalled in speeches and essays to this day as symbols of black-Jewish cooperation.

The focus on Goodman and Schwerner, and on the wider struggle in the South, has had the effect of obscuring and distorting the nature of black-Jewish cooperation. Most of the Jews who went South—including Goodman and Schwerner—went without any clear notion of Jewish ethics as a motive. Their overwhelming numbers suggest that something about their being Jewish must have driven them to it. But few thought of it that way. "We felt we were going South as Americans," says Jewish religious educator Peter Geffen, who went in the summer of 1965 with a group of United Synagogue Youth members.

Individual Jews had been prominent among supporters of black civil rights throughout the century. The brothers Joel and Arthur Spingarn led the NAACP for decades. The presidents of both the American Jewish Committee and the American Jewish Congress, Louis Marshall and Stephen Wise, served on the board of the NAACP during the 1920s, beginning the NAACP's long tradition of semi-official "Jewish" board representation, which continues to this day. Chicago retailer Julius Rosenwald of Sears & Roebuck, one of American Jewry's leading philanthropists after the First World War, was the main supporter of Southern black education in this century, building over five thousand elementary schools across the region through a $30 million fund that he created in 1917. During the 1960s, some of America's most prominent rabbis went South to join the Reverend King in his civil rights marches. The most famous, the celebrated theologian Abraham Joshua Heschel, declared it a moral duty for Jews to fight for black rights.

In retrospect, the romantic image of these idealistic volunteers has largely obscured the very pragmatic nature of the black-Jewish alliance. "The black-Jewish alliance has been a marriage of convenience," says the Reverend Calvin Butts of the Abyssinian Baptist Church in Harlem. "From the beginning, both groups had a deep interest in civil rights legislation. Blacks were denied rights, but so were Jews."

And, Butts adds, "the movement of blacks in the streets was enhanced by the movement of blacks and Jews in the suites. It had a great deal to do with self-interest, and that's all right. We were both doing what we needed to do, to get what we desired."

Like everything else in black-Jewish relations, pinpointing the moment when the alliance began to unravel depends on where you stand.

Most Jews suggest that it happened in the late 1960s, though they disagree on the precise cause and timing. For many, the watershed moment was the New York City teachers' strike of 1968, which pitted the largely Jewish teachers' union against black community activists and gave rise to some vicious anti-Jewish rhetoric. Pro-Israel activists often date their feeling of betrayal to the previous year, 1967, when anti-Israel rhetoric became commonplace among black militants.

Conservatives place it even earlier, at the time that the black power movement emerged as a key force in the black community after 1965. "The transformation of the civil rights revolution into a race revolution is the central hook around which to understand the issue," says the neoconservative civil rights scholar Murray Friedman, Philadelphia regional director of the American Jewish Committee and author of the acclaimed 1995 study *What Went Wrong? The Creation and Collapse of the Black-Jewish Alliance*. "Blacks came along and pushed out the Jews, just as the Jews pushed out others before them. It's part of the game of ethnic succession."

A startlingly different view emerges from interviews with black activists, scholars, journalists, and politicians around the country. "My belief is that it really began with the *Bakke* case in 1978," says former NAACP national chair William Gibson. "That's when I started to see it escalate on a national basis with stories and accusations being traded back and forth in the media." This view is echoed frequently, though with slight variations, whenever black leaders discuss black-Jewish relations.

Bakke was a landmark civil rights case before the Supreme Court. In it, the justices ruled that some affirmative action programs to help minorities could result in reverse discrimination against whites.

The case involved Allan Bakke, a white Christian from Minnesota who was rejected by the medical school at the University of California at Davis in 1974. Bakke sued, charging that the school had admitted less qualified applicants under the university's minority admissions program, which set a minimum quota of 16 percent nonwhites each year. Bakke claimed that the program violated his Fourteenth Amendment right to equal protection under the law. The California Supreme Court ruled in his favor in 1976.

When the case went to the U.S. Supreme Court in 1978, all the major black civil rights organizations filed amicus briefs supporting the university's affirmative action program. The Big Three Jewish defense agencies all filed briefs supporting Bakke. It was the first direct, public, head-on confrontation between the black and Jewish communities over a basic civil rights issue. The blacks lost.

Reactions in the black community were furious. The Reverend Joseph Lowery, King's successor as head of the Southern Christian Leadership Conference, charged that Jews had led the forces that defeated affirmative action at the University of California. Louis Clayton Jones, a columnist with New York's *Amsterdam News,* blamed the defeat on the moderate black civil rights leader Bayard Rustin and "his friends from B'nai B'rith and the American Jewish Congress." Jesse Jackson compared the high court's ruling to a Nazi march earlier that year through Skokie, a mostly Jewish suburb of Chicago. These reactions, in turn, prompted Jewish counteraccusations of anti-Semitism.

Jewish community activists had been debating affirmative action since the late 1960s, when programs of racial preference became widespread under the Nixon administration. Jewish conservatives, led by the ADL and the Orthodox Union, argued that any government program favoring one group over another was a direct assault on the equal opportunity society that Jews had fought so long to achieve. It was only a quarter-century earlier that states had begun to outlaw the ethnic quotas used to exclude Jews from universities. Now quotas were returning through the back door.

Liberals, led by the Reform union and the National Council of Jewish Women, countered that quotas designed to bring minorities *into* the mainstream were a far cry from quotas designed to keep them *out.* The liberals argued that America's long history of racism had left blacks unequipped to compete on a level playing field, even after formal discrimination was outlawed. The only way to end racial injustice was a firm government effort to bring blacks up to the level of whites.

Speaking for the broad middle of American Jewry, the American Jewish Committee and the American Jewish Congress tried to split the difference. They proposed that the Jewish community support affirmative action to increase the numbers of blacks in key schools and professions, but reject timetables or quotas that measured the results in rigid group terms.

The debate gained urgency as affirmative action faced mounting court challenges from whites in the early 1970s. In January 1974, the three defense agencies filed briefs before the Supreme Court in the case of Marco De Funis, a white student denied admission to the University of Washington law school. The major black civil rights agencies filed opposing briefs. It threatened to become a major black-Jewish showdown.

De Funis was Jewish, though the Jewish agencies didn't know it when they filed briefs in his support. After his religion became known, the agencies continued to insist that their backing for De Funis was nothing more than a principled consistency. They had been fighting for a century for a color-blind society in which all were treated equally regardless of race or religion. To many blacks and their allies, it looked as though the Jews were simply sticking up for their own.

In a sense, argues former NAACP Legal Defense Fund chief Jack Greenberg, "it was the *De Funis* case where the opening shot was fired. It had a terrible impact. Blacks hated it. Here you're talking about a black community that, to the extent that it's achieved any success, it's because of affirmative action."

A head-on confrontation between the two communities was avoided when the U.S. Supreme Court decided in April 1974 not to hear the *De Funis* case. The decision left the law school's minority admissions program firmly intact, and the black-Jewish alliance barely so.

The NCRAC convention that year featured a heated debate over quotas and affirmative action. The majority voted to support the centrist AJC-AJC position, endorsing affirmative action but opposing fixed quotas. The Orthodox Union filed a formal dissent, arguing that any ethnic preference violated the constitutional right of equal protection to all. The other agencies, including a reluctant ADL, agreed to abide by the NCRAC ruling and support affirmative action.

Now began a round of intense efforts to patch things up between the black and Jewish communities. Heads of the major black and Jewish agencies met both publicly and secretly to search for ways to end the feuding. Black politicians held press conferences to demand freedom for Soviet Jewry. Jewish agencies joined with black groups to cosponsor forums on poverty and economic opportunity, and mounted furious Washington lobbying campaigns on behalf of civil rights programs. In the spring of 1975, after the U.N. Zionism-racism resolution, a group of leading black politicians and intellectuals (including David Dinkins, then New York city clerk) announced the creation of BASIC, the Black Americans in Support of Israel Committee.

For all the good will at the top, the relationship was undergoing a tectonic shift, which the leaders could not arrest. In each community, there was mounting grassroots sentiment that the other community had turned hostile.

Each community was watching with alarm and impatience as the other community produced an escalating series of noisy attacks against its most valued symbol of empowerment. Jews came in growing numbers to view the black community as a major source of anti-Israel agitation. Blacks saw the Jewish community as a leading center of opposition to affirmative action. Each new effort by one community to defend itself from the other's attacks appeared to the other side as just another assault.

At bottom, neither perception was accurate. Black opinion was overwhelmingly pro-Israel, both among leaders and at the grass roots. Only a minority of Third World–oriented radicals had turned anti-Israel. As for the Jewish community, while it opposed minority quotas, it was *in favor of* affirmative action as a broad principle. Only a minority of neoconservatives opposed all affirmative action as a remedy for racism.

Leaders in both communities understood this, and continued working together on a regular basis. But both leadership groups proved unable, or unwilling, to repudiate and isolate the radicals who were souring the relationship.

Thus it was that when the Supreme Court's 1978 *Bakke* decision touched off yet another round of accusations and counteraccusations, there was no room left for rapprochement. Too much bitterness had built up on both sides for any easy forgiveness.

Irving Levine, who was director of national affairs at the American Jewish Committee during the 1970s and 1980s, continues to reject the charge that Jews led the opposition to affirmative action. "The accusation is unfair," Levine says. "It simply isn't true that we were against affirmative action. Our position was much more nuanced. We were against quotas, but we were not opposed to affirmative action that did not include quotas. The notion that we were, was a parody of our position. I really don't know where people got it from. Maybe they were picking it up from some of the more extreme Jewish voices, like *Commentary*."

Levine is right up to a point. The problem is, *Commentary* was *published* by Levine's own American Jewish Committee. By the mid-1970s, it was the most widely quoted organ of Jewish opinion in America. And it was unabashedly, uncompromisingly opposed to any affirmative action to favor blacks, with or without formal quotas.

Nominally *Commentary* was in favor of ending racism and correcting injustice against black people. In practice, its coverage of black issues was generally limited to attacks, not on racism, but on programs to end it. Editor Norman Podhoretz's own essays, written in his signature sarcastic style, regularly savaged the very idea of government programs to help the disadvantaged. In one 1972 essay, "Is It Good for the Jews?," he argued that "discriminatory practices against Jews" were on the rise as efforts spread to boost the presence of women and nonwhites in civil service jobs and in university admissions and hiring. Over time, it would become clear that nothing of the sort had happened. That never stopped Podhoretz.

The American Jewish Committee took the position that *Commentary* did not represent the views of the organization. The magazine had complete editorial independence. But few outside the organization understood the nuance. To many blacks, the facts were straightforward: America's most prestigious Jewish publication, an organ of one of the leading Jewish organizations, was the nation's most important journal of opposition to black progress.

"If the mainstream Jewish community is supportive of the black community and *Commentary* represents only a minority, I never heard about it," says Shelton Waldon, a black journalist at the left-wing New York radio station WBAI. "It's too bad more people don't know about it. It would have made a difference."

But the American Jewish Committee, along with most of the rest of the national Jewish leadership, refused to recognize the damage that *Commentary* and its neoconservative allies were doing to black-Jewish relations. Occasionally, efforts were mounted by liberals on the Committee board to sever the magazine's relationship with the agency. But they were never successful. The magazine's supporters were stronger than its opponents.

No one—not in the American Jewish Committee, not in the broader

Jewish community—saw any obligation to repudiate the magazine, however damaging its influence might be in the eyes of much of the black leadership.

The inability of the Jewish leadership to repudiate the anti-civil rights crusade of *Commentary* and its coterie had a striking parallel in the inability of the black leadership to repudiate anti-Israel radicals in the black community.

Indeed, beginning shortly after the *Bakke* decision, Jewish efforts to isolate black radicals began to surface as one more sore point in the ever-deteriorating black-Jewish relationship.

In August 1979, the highest ranking black figure in the Carter administration, civil rights hero Andrew Young, was forced to resign as U.S. ambassador to the United Nations. Young stepped down after *Newsweek* disclosed that he had met secretly with a senior PLO official, in violation of a 1975 executive order against contact with terrorist groups.

Young's resignation caused a national uproar in the black community. In interviews and public statements, black leaders blamed the Jewish community. "The Jewish community and Israel don't realize how large a stake Andy had with us," said a pioneering black politician, Mayor Richard Hatcher of Gary, Indiana, in an interview with the *New York Times*.

One week after the resignation, on August 22, 1979, two hundred black leaders from across the political and social spectrum convened at NAACP headquarters in New York for an unprecedented national summit on black-Jewish relations. After a daylong meeting, the summit released a bristling series of statements on Jews, affirmative action, and Israel's alleged military links with South Africa. Without naming names, it sharply criticized Jewish organizations that had once supported civil rights but "abruptly became apologists for the racial status quo." This was actually an olive branch; earlier drafts had singled out the Big Three defense agencies by name.

Dr. Kenneth Clark, the distinguished black psychologist, called the meeting a "declaration of independence" by the black community.

Jewish leaders have insisted since the day Young resigned that they were not responsible. Within hours after the first report of Young's PLO contact appeared in *Newsweek,* the White House contacted nine national Jewish agency heads to sound them out. Only one, Rabbi Joseph Sternstein, president of the Zionist Organization of America, asked for Young's ouster.

Alexander Schindler, the Reform leader, says the decision to blame Young's dismissal on the Jews came directly from the Oval Office. "It was the first act of political anti-Semitism perpetrated by an American president," Schindler says. "Carter was facing a reelection challenge from the right. Andy Young was a problem for him. He kept saying outrageous things. The State Department didn't care for him. The CIA didn't care for him. But Carter didn't want to risk offending the black community."

The Jewish leadership, Schindler says, had purposely decided not to ask for Young's ouster so as to avoid a crisis with the black community. "Besides, there was a Jewish ambassador in Vienna, Milton Wolff, who was also meeting with the PLO, and there was no rumpus."

"I got a call from a reporter for the New York *Post,*" Schindler says. "He asked me if Young should be fired and I said no, and I gave him the names of five or six other Jewish leaders to talk to. They all said 'Don't fire,' except for one, Joe Sternstein. Sure enough, the next day the *Post* headline was 'Jews Say Fire Andy.' "

"[After that,] we begged, cajoled, demanded that Carter say that the Jews didn't do it. And he didn't do a damn thing. For forty days he didn't say anything. He was campaigning on some kind of riverboat down the Mississippi River. Finally, in November, when he appointed Young's successor, Don Henry, he said something."

The Jews' disavowal is heartfelt, but disingenuous. American Jewish leaders may not have asked for Young's resignation, but Israel did. It was Israeli intelligence that first discovered the Young-PLO contacts, through its ongoing surveillance of the PLO's New York mission. It was Prime Minister Menachem Begin who personally ordered a protest, overruling aides who feared a black-Jewish confrontation in America. Once Israel protested, the White House had little choice but to fire Young. The tension between the Carter White House and the Jewish community was uncomfortably high for any administration; for a Democratic administration heading into an election year it was intolerably so. Young threatened to become one sore spot too many.

It was, in effect, the flip side of congressional aide David Luchins's dictum: "Political power is when you don't have to ask for it."

❖   ❖   ❖

The national black summit of August 1979 marked a watershed in the formal relationship between the two communities. It was a defeat for moderate, Northern-based groups with close ties to the Jewish community, like the NAACP and the Urban League. It was a victory for the Southern Christian Leadership Conference, Dr. King's own organizational base, which had fewer ties to the Jewish community. The SCLC announced at the summit that it was opening its own dialogue with the PLO. It won the summit's unanimous endorsement.

The summit also marked an important stage in the emergence of another King disciple: the young, telegenic, and very militant Reverend Jesse Jackson, who headed an antipoverty organization in Chicago.

In the aftermath of Young's resignation, Jackson quickly surfaced as the most visible critic of Jewish influence in the black community. "Jews were willing to share decency, but not power," he said. In the fall, he departed for a highly publicized tour of the Middle East, where the press followed him like a head of state. In Israel he visited Yad Vashem, the national Holocaust memorial, emerging to speak of the Jews' "persecution complex." In Lebanon he attended a PLO rally and was photographed embracing Yasser Arafat.

A year later, addressing an Arab-American group in Birmingham, Jackson claimed that Zionism was a "poisonous weed" choking the religion of Judaism.

Over the next few years, Jackson became the senior figure in the American black leadership. He was a spellbinding orator with a strong appeal to groups that most black leaders could not reach, including white liberals and the disaffected, unorganizable blacks in the urban ghettoes of the North. He capped his rise in 1984 by running for president.

Neoconservative analyst Murray Friedman calls Jackson's 1984 bid for the Democratic nomination "one of the most extraordinary events in recent political history." "As the first black candidate to make a serious run for the presidency, he became a messenger of hope for many blacks," Friedman wrote.

Jackson was more than just a messenger of hope. He *embodied* hope. He had assumed heroic proportions in the black community as its dominant leader. His triumphant emergence on the national stage was the black community's triumph. And, to many blacks, any attack on Jackson was an attack on the black community.

In a way, Jackson had come to play the same role in the mind of black America that Israel played in the mind of Jewish America: a symbol of triumph over adversity, and the embodiment of ethnic pride.

For precisely that reason, Jesse Jackson now came to embody something else: the ongoing tension between blacks and Jews. He was no longer an indication of black-Jewish problems; he *was* the problem. His hostile record on Israel and Zionism made him anathema to the Jewish community. To many Jews, an attack on Israel was an attack on the Jewish community. And when Jews fought back, blacks in turn took it as an attack on the black community.

Jackson's threat to Jewish interests was more than symbolic. Jackson was running a credible campaign for president, emerging from primaries with blocs of delegates committed to him. While few believed he was White House–bound, he would be a force at the upcoming Democratic National Convention. No anti-Israel politician had achieved such influence in the Democratic party in a generation. It seemed to threaten everything the Jewish community had achieved in American politics.

In response, Jewish leaders began speaking out against Jackson at every opportunity, working to close off his access to Democratic clubs, pressuring black allies to repudiate him. To many blacks, it looked as though the Jewish community had declared all-out war on blacks.

As Jewish leaders pressured their black allies to repudiate Jackson because of his anti-Jewish past, the demand for repudiation itself became a point of friction. "It created a considerable backlash," says former Urban League official Clarence Wood, now president of the Human Rights Foundation of Chicago.

"Unfortunately," Wood notes, "the Jewish community has an expectation that the whole of the black community will repudiate an individual black leader when he says something wrong. What the Jewish community does not understand is that we in the black community are in a period where that sense of us needing to repudiate gets entangled in our need to develop a strong black community leadership."

And, Wood adds, when the black community hesitates to repudiate someone accused of anti-Semitism, "there is a sense in the Jewish community that the black community supports those views."

"The stress on the negative is putting pressure on the black community. You can repudiate the statement, but to repudiate the whole individual and his work is something the black community cannot afford to do."

When Jesse Jackson mounted his second presidential campaign in 1988, he was already showing signs of regret at what he had become. Early in the campaign, he appeared at a suburban Boston synagogue and sued for peace, saying that he had come to do *"teshuva,"* the Hebrew word for repentance. It did no good. When the primary campaign moved to New York in March, Mayor Ed Koch declared that Jews would "have to be crazy" to vote for Jackson.

The fact was that Jackson had become the third rail of the Democratic party. No one could go near him and live. His very presence as a player in party politics gave everyone else a Hobson's choice: embrace the reverend and lose the Jews, or snub him and lose the blacks.

One victim was Senator Al Gore, Jr. of Tennessee, who had been endorsed by Mayor Koch. He did so badly in the 1988 New York primary— thanks in large part to liberal outrage at Koch's overheated words—that the Tennessean quit the race soon after.

Another victim was California's ex-governor Jerry Brown. He came into the New York primary in April 1992 as the sole challenger to the badly wounded Bill Clinton. Brown had won the Connecticut primary in March, forcing third-place challenger Paul Tsongas to quit the race. But in New York, Brown announced that he might name Jesse Jackson as his running mate. His polling numbers among Jews promptly dropped from over 30 percent to less than 10 percent. Appearances at Jewish gatherings turned into screaming matches. On primary day, Brown came in third, behind ex-candidate Tsongas, and the field was left open to Clinton.

After the Crown Heights riot, Jackson began devoting a good deal of attention to the deteriorating black-Jewish relationship, for which his own earlier missteps were so largely responsible. He met publicly with ADL director Abe Foxman, who declared him a "friend." In May 1992, he flew to Brussels to deliver a keynote speech at an international conference on anti-Semitism, sponsored by the World Jewish Congress. That summer, at the Democratic National Convention, he offered a moving tribute to Israel's love of peace. Through the fall and into winter, he delivered dozens of speeches around the country, to black and white audiences alike, on the dangers of anti-Semitism and the need for black-Jewish cooperation.

"We must not underestimate our strength in unity nor underestimate our exposure when apart," Jackson declared in New York in December 1992. "We must not allow the cynics and the hatemongers to be dominant. In the heat of these tensions we must choose hope."

"We are not each others' enemies," he said. "We are allies."

The bitterness of the late 1970s and early 1980s has left lasting marks, however. Within each community extremist groups have sprouted that view the other community as their chief enemy. They are small groups, on both sides. But they wield enormous influence.

The affirmative action disputes in the mid-1970s set in motion a profound shift in attitudes toward Jews among many avant-garde black intellectuals who had looked to the Jews as allies and now sought an explanation for their betrayal. Some began to wonder out loud if there had ever been an alliance at all.

It was not a mass movement. Most of America's 30 million blacks remained untouched by the phenomenon for nearly a decade. It began where popular movements often begin: among those who shape ideas in the intellectual and political elite.

One of the leaders of the new wave was Leonard Jeffries, a professor of African and African-American studies at City College of New York. Raised in a largely Jewish neighborhood in Newark, New Jersey, he had been surrounded by Jewish friends in high school, served as president of a Jewish fraternity in college, and traveled through Europe after graduation with a Jewish buddy. In 1972, after receiving his Ph.D. in history and teaching briefly in California, he came to CCNY as chairman of the black-studies department, newly organized, he says, thanks largely to the efforts of the college's Jewish president.

In the late 1980s, after a decade of research, Jeffries emerged as a leading voice in a new school of black scholarship, which teaches that Jews have been among the chief tormentors of the black race for centuries: architects of the Atlantic slave trade, apologists for the Southern plantation system, demonizers of blacks through their control of Hollywood, then cynical manipulators of the civil rights movement. Today, Jeffries claims, "there is an alliance between conservative whites and conservative Jews to maintain control of black people."

Jeffries is blunt about the reasons for his souring on black-Jewish friendship: the fact that the Jews abandoned their black partners as soon as they no longer needed them, during the 1970s. "I was in college with Jews in 1955 when the society was closed to them," he said in an interview. "The civil rights struggle helped to open up American society to Jewish people. But the tragedy is that once they got in and won access to jobs and wealth, they closed the door behind them."

Jeffries and a handful of colleagues in black-studies departments across the country pioneered a school of black separatism during the 1980s, reminiscent of the Jewish separatism that spread after the Six-Day War. Jews played only a small part in the new black bitterness; for the most part, it was a frustrated reaction to the problems afflicting blacks in the major cities: the rise of chronic unemployment, the disintegration of the family, and the plagues of crime and drugs. "You've had twelve years of anti-black administrations that have starved the cities," District of Columbia congressional delegate Eleanor Holmes Norton would explain later. "They've created fertile ground for bigotry. And black people are not exempt."

By the mid-1980s, secular conspiracy theorists like Jeffries were beginning to make common cause with Minister Louis Farrakhan, leader of the Nation of Islam. Farrakhan was notorious for his flagrant use of antiwhite, antihomosexual, and anti-Jewish language in his speeches, which often drew crowds numbering in the thousands. In 1984, he called Judaism a "dirty religion," arguing that it had been turned into a political tool. He regularly railed against "the Jews" for attacking him and threatened retaliation.

Farrakhan's bigotry came under bitter media attack. And the more he was attacked, the greater following he won among angry black artists and intellectuals. Popular black musical groups like Public Enemy praised him in their concerts and quoted his bigoted views in interviews. Black leaders turned to him as a leader with credibility among black youth. His followers were credited with reintroducing law and decorum in decaying urban slums. By the early 1990s, he had become one of the most influential

leaders in the black community. In 1993, after a decade of relative ostracism, he was invited to the annual convention of the Congressional Black
Caucus, where caucus leader Kweisi Mfume announced a "covenant" between the caucus and Farrakhan. In October 1995, he organized a national
black men's march on Washington, the so-called Million Man March, which
drew an estimated eight hundred thousand participants, the largest black-
led gathering of black people in American history.

Mainstream black leaders have continued to insist that Farrakhan's
growing acceptance does not signal any growth in black anti-Semitism.
"Farrakhan gets a reception not because he's anti-Semitic, but because he
preaches a kind of middle-class black nationalism that is outside the mainstream of middle-class black politics," says black journalist Don Rojas, a
former managing editor of the *Amsterdam News*. "There is a young generation of blacks that is searching for a new kind of black leadership. They've
been disappointed by the mainstream black politicians and to a degree by
the Jesse Jacksons as well. They're looking for something different, and
Farrakhan fits the bill—not fully, but to a degree."

But Farrakhan was not merely a person with anti-Semitic attitudes, or
someone who had made unfortunate remarks in the past. Though it went
largely unreported in the mainstream press, he was waging a war against the
Jews.

His apparent goal was to promote the idea among young blacks that
Jews were their enemies. His organization's research department produced a thick volume in 1991, *The Secret Relationship Between Blacks
and Jews*, which purported to demonstrate through selective quotes and
shoddy logic that Jews were primarily responsible for the Atlantic slave
trade. (Numerous academic researchers have shown that the Jewish role
in the baleful enterprise was minuscule.) Farrakhan's followers sold copies
of the notorious *Protocols of the Learned Elders of Zion* at streetside
tables and promoted them to black-interest bookstores. Through his influence, the book's venomous fantasy of a worldwide Jewish conspiracy
gained new popularity among black activists and college students. Students cited it in research papers, and complained of censorship when it
was dismissed. In 1991, a university-funded black student newspaper at
the University of California at Los Angeles printed a favorable examination of the *Protocols,* then waged a war of words in its defense when
Jewish students protested. Campus authorities remained neutral in the
"exchange of ideas."

By the early 1990s, some leading figures in the black community were beginning to share the Jewish community's concerns about the spread of black anti-Semitism.

"Speaking as somebody who has not bought into the growing anti-Semitic movement in the black community," says black congressional aide Donna Brazile, "the fact is that the vast majority are not hostile. The few who are have the loudest voices. Having said that, I'm amazed myself at the number of young black kids on college campuses who are looking for Jews to protest."

How widespread was black anti-Semitism in the early 1990s? No one knew. "The truth is, we really don't know anything about black anti-Semitism," says NCRAC's Jerome Chanes. "There isn't very much data on the topic, and there is a great deal of myth that passes for information, even though it is not supported by any data. The classic example of this is the myth that anti-Semitism among blacks rises with increasing education. It came out of one local study in California, and has become conventional wisdom in many circles. In fact the cumulative weight of all other studies is that anti-Semitism falls as education rises among blacks, just as it does among whites."

Years of debunking the mythic black-Jewish alliance had left Jewish activists convinced that while sympathy for black rights was widespread among Jews, popular opinion in the black community was never sympathetic to Jews. The assumption was that while the leadership was friendly, the black populace was generally anti-Semitic. The assumption was wrong, but self-fulfilling.

Most research on anti-Semitic attitudes uses a measuring system developed by the Anti-Defamation League during the 1960s. It asks respondents for true-false responses to a list of stock anti-Jewish stereotypes, such as that Jews are greedy, clannish, and manipulative. ADL studies in the 1960s settled on a list of eleven stereotypes; those people agreeing with five or more were labeled "most anti-Semitic."

A 1969 survey found 47 percent of blacks scoring "most anti-Semitic," compared to 35 percent of whites. Another study in 1992, a quarter-century later, found that prejudice had dropped in both groups, but that blacks still scored higher than whites. This time, 37 percent of blacks showed a high rate of anti-Semitism, compared to 20 percent of whites.

However, the 1992 study turned up a startling flaw in the method. During follow-up interviews with respondents, researchers found that some—particularly blacks—considered some of the stereotypes to be *positive*. Some interviewees pointed to Jewish stereotypes such as "only help each other" and said they wished blacks could learn to be that way.

The finding so unnerved ADL staffers that they delayed the survey's publication for six months and polled extra samples of blacks, which confirmed the early findings. Some staffers urged scrapping the whole study. But ADL director Abe Foxman overruled them. Instead the study was released, but the threshold for "most anti-Semitic" was raised from five "yes" answers to six. The new threshold yielded the finding of 37 percent anti-Semitism among blacks and 20 percent among whites.

The trouble was, as some ADL staffers admitted privately, some unknown portion of those black anti-Semites were actually people who liked Jews and wished them well.

Though often overlooked, there is a substantial reserve of goodwill toward Jews within the black community. "As much as people try to pooh-pooh it," says Harlem's Reverend Calvin Butts, "there is a common value system, a Judaeo-Christian religious tradition that binds blacks and Jews in particular. Many of the same biblical phrases resonate for the two communities, like 'Let justice roll down like water.' We share a common value system. We are strong family people. We believe in community. It happens that Jewish people in this country were in a position where they could blend more easily because of the color of their skin. They have used that in many cases to try and help blacks and to help other people."

Says congressional aide Donna Brazile: "When you grow up in the South, you come to learn that the only white people you can count on in the struggle are Jewish people. As you get older you learn it's because your parents and their parents suffered in the same ways."

In time, the continuing anti-Jewish agitation from the radical fringe of the black community gave rise to a group in the Jewish community that was almost a mirror image of the black radicals: a militant, separatist Jewish movement, which saw the blacks as the Jews' main enemies. It closely overlapped the hard core of Jewish support for Israel's Likud and for the West Bank settler movement; its leadership included many of the same personalities and organizations. Their guiding premise was that Third

World radicalism was implacably committed to the destruction of the Jewish people throughout the world, from Jerusalem to Brooklyn.

This radical Jewish movement first appeared in 1968, during the New York City teachers' strike, in the form of Meir Kahane's far-right Jewish Defense League. The league's flamboyant rhetoric and occasional violence gave it notoriety far beyond its numbers. It virtually disappeared after Kahane settled in Israel in 1972. With that, many Jews congratulated themselves that the problem of Jewish extremism had been, if not eliminated, at least contained.

But while Kahane's influence may have been minuscule, Jewish anti-black sentiment was not. When it resurfaced as an organized movement in 1989, it had become a mass phenomenon that stretched across New York, with sympathizers in cities around the country.

It coalesced in response to the 1989 New York City mayoral campaign of David Dinkins. A coalition of Orthodox and pro-Likud Jews formed to oppose him, arguing that despite his long history of pro-Israel activism—he had raised funds for the UJA and traveled to Europe to demonstrate for Soviet Jewry—Dinkins's relationship with Jesse Jackson made him the Jews' enemy. "Every Jew should vote against David Dinkins, because we've already had one Auschwitz and we don't need another," real-estate developer Sam Domb, a Holocaust survivor and Likud contributor, told a reporter during the campaign. His comment, though wildly hyperbolic, was not unusual.

Much Jewish opposition to the Dinkins campaign was mere politics. Dinkins was running to unseat the city's three-term Mayor Ed Koch. Only the city's second Jewish mayor, Koch was hugely popular in middle-class Jewish neighborhoods for his defense of Israel and Soviet Jewry. He was just as unpopular in black neighborhoods for his overheated attacks on black militants and "welfare queens." In a sense, Dinkins's race for mayor was a political contest between the black and Jewish communities.

For the Jewish radicals, though, it was the beginning of a moral crusade.

On January 1, 1990, the city of New York came together as one to celebrate the inauguration of the city's first black mayor. It was a political coming of age for America's largest black community. Dignitaries were in attendance from around the world, including the Nobel laureate South African freedom fighter Bishop Desmond Tutu. Only one sour note marred the festive air: a protest demonstration across the street from City Hall by some four dozen Orthodox Jews. Their complaint: Bishop Tutu had spoken against Israeli policy during a recent Holy Land visit. Nobel Prize or no, he was an enemy of Israel. Dinkins, by honoring Tutu, was "excluding" the Jews.

The following June, the same group demonstrated again, this time when the city staged a ticker-tape parade down Broadway to honor Nelson Mandela, the iconic hero of South African liberation. Mandela's release from prison some weeks earlier, after a quarter-century behind bars, had occasioned worldwide rejoicing. He was coming to New York to address the United Nations, then continuing to Washington for a presidential reception at the White House. But for the Jewish radicals, only one fact counted: Mandela had shaken hands with Yasser Arafat and Libya's Moammar Qaddafi. For New York City to honor this friend of terrorists was an affront to the Jewish community.

As Mandela's arrival date neared, predictions of large-scale Jewish protest fueled a flurry of charges and countercharges between black and Jewish leaders, threatening to sour the hero's welcome. Finally it was arranged for a group of senior Jewish leaders to fly to Geneva, a day before the parade, to hear Mandela tell his side of the story. The meeting was set up by singer-activist Harry Belafonte, a respected civil rights leader with close ties to Jews through the music business and the Democratic Party. Jockeying continued almost until flight time to include at least one conservative in the mostly-liberal delegation, to lend the mission credibility with the militants; at the last minute ADL director Abe Foxman was persuaded to join. In Geneva, Mandela assured the group that he was a lifelong admirer of Israel, and that his embrace of Qaddafi was merely the act of a freedom fighter finding support wherever he could. The Jewish leaders declared themselves reassured, if not fully satisfied.

The radicals were not deterred, however. "If you embrace Arafat, you bring shame to the anti-apartheid struggle," wrote the group's leader, globe-trotting militant Rabbi Avi Weiss. In Weiss's view, the failure of mainstream Jewish leaders to join his many causes—his anti-Mandela protest, for example, or his support of Israeli spy Jonathan Pollard—was nothing more than "fear" of speaking out.

Certainly his courage was widely admired. In 1993 he was named "Rabbi of the Year" by the New York Board of Rabbis, an umbrella group representing over one thousand area rabbis from Reform to Orthodox.

✿ ✿ ✿

After the Crown Heights riots, a group of Orthodox Jews formed an organization called the Jewish Action Alliance to protest discrimination against Jews. One of their principal targets was a black-oriented radio station, WLIB, owned by a close ally of Dinkins's, that was known for its radical talk-show hosts and frequent anti-Jewish comments by callers. The Jewish Action Alliance undertook a two-year campaign to discredit the station and highlight its links to Dinkins, eventually forcing the management to curb on-air rhetoric. Flush with success, the Jewish Action Alliance threw itself a gala fund-raiser in November 1995, with some of the city's leading Jewish politicians in attendance. The evening's honoree: Jewish talk-show host Jay Diamond, known for his viciously antiblack on-air comments.

Another group, Response in Kind, was formed by Orthodox Jews in Brooklyn to press the legal aspects of the Crown Heights case. Among its main targets: Lee Patrick Brown, New York City police commissioner during the Crown Heights riots, believed by many Orthodox Jews to have conspired with Dinkins to prolong the riots. One of the nation's most respected black law-enforcement officers, Brown was named federal drug czar by the Clinton administration in 1992. Following that appointment, Response in Kind went after the Clinton administration.

Nowhere was Jewish antiblack rhetoric more persistent, nor more florid, than in the *Jewish Press,* a weekly newspaper published in Brooklyn with the widest circulation of any publication in the Orthodox community. Long associated with Meir Kahane—he and his followers had published no fewer than four weekly columns in the paper during the 1980s—the *Jewish Press* kept up a steady drumbeat against Dinkins, Tutu, Mandela, Lee Brown, and company. In 1992, the paper's managing editor, Arnold Fine, published a column attempting to prove that black slavery was exaggerated: in reality, he claimed, most blacks had come to America as indentured servants and later lost their liberty through financial incompetence.

It was, in a way, the Jewish equivalent of Holocaust denial. Unlike Holocaust denial, it evoked no protests.

Rabbi Avi Weiss was right that his fellow Jewish leaders lacked courage; his Rabbi of the Year award proved that. New York's Jewish leaders had the courage to speak out in favor of the things they believed in, as they did when they turned out to greet Mandela. Their courage failed them only when they needed it most: to confront the extremists within their own community who were fanning conflict where none existed. Like the leaders of the black community, the leaders of the Jewish community were unwilling or unable to take responsibility for their own community.

There was much that was solid in the black-Jewish alliance during the mid-1990s. Black and Jewish lawmakers in Washington continued to work together as closely as ever, supporting each others' causes more than 90 percent of the time, according to one study by the American Jewish Congress. The major black and Jewish civil rights agencies, after a brief chill in the early 1980s, continue to cooperate on a host of matters. In local communities across the country, there are thousands of ongoing dialogue groups that regularly bring together synagogues and black churches; black and Jewish clergy; black and Jewish business leaders, community organizers, and ordinary people.

"The conversation between blacks and Jews has moved past the leadership to the rank and file," says the Reverend Patricia Reeberg, executive director of the New York City Council of Churches and pastor of St. Paul Baptist Church in Harlem. "It's happening among women. It's happening in the religious area. There are congregations in dialogue together. There have been pulpit exchanges between black and Jewish clergy for years. The National Conference of Christians and Jews sponsors them. So do the African American Clergy Coalition, the National Council of Churches, and the local boards of rabbis. The Women's Interfaith Network brings together black and Jewish women. The Partnership of Faith brings together Muslims, Jews, Christians, African-Americans, and whites. These conversations have really been large-scale and across the board and throughout the country."

"The groups that are doing things together in coalition don't get the coverage, so their things are done in the dark, while the confrontations get publicized," Reeberg notes. "The truth is that there is a kinship between our two communities. It's based on past histories and a feeling that there is a gut understanding of what oppression is about. There is a feeling among black people that Jews understand what it means when those in power single out a particular group just because it is a group. There is a feeling that even if nobody else understands, that the Jews do."

"Focusing on the divisions skews the reality of black-Jewish relations," says Rabbi David Saperstein, influential head of the Washington-based Religious Action Center of Reform Judaism and a member of the NAACP governing board. "We vote more alike than any other groups. We vote for each others' candidates—blacks voting for Jews and Jews voting for blacks—at a far higher rate than anyone else does. Every day across this nation blacks and Jews are working together for social justice, addressing problems of hunger and racism and discrimination and the challenges to education and health care in America. We are clearly joined at the hip."

And yet, in a strange way, to recall what is strong and good in black-Jewish relations is to miss the point.

It may be true that the sniping is confined mainly to the fringes. Still, the fact remains that the relationship is troubled—if only because so many people think it is troubled. Extremists and fearmongers on each side have succeeded in frightening the rank and file on the other side. Fears have a way of overwhelming reality and becoming reality, as they did in Crown Heights in August 1991.

Within each community there is a mainstream leadership, speaking for the values of the great majority, which recognizes the extremist fear-mongers for what they are. But the mainstream leadership on each side hesitates to act against the extremists, fearing a backlash from the streets. The great majority is not mobilized. Normally, there is little that can mobilize them, except for their fears. How then can the leadership strive to ease their fears, and still retain its authority?

It is a dilemma that affects all Americans.

"The destiny of America depends on the great coalition of decency that has transformed this country for the better in the last seventy years, and that has been spearheaded by blacks and Jews," says Saperstein. "Only the enemies of social justice rejoice when blacks and Jews square off against each other.

"The fact is, we are the quintessential victims of Western civilization. If either one of us suffers discrimination in America, then neither one of us can make it, and all of us suffer."

CHAPTER 13

Separated by a Common Faith: American Jewry's One-Way Love Affair With Israel

IN THE FIVE DECADES since it began flexing its muscles on the world stage, the American Jewish community has known some dramatic successes and some embarrassing failures as it sought to defend its interests and advance its vision of justice.

Never, though, has there been a mightier display of naked Jewish power than in November 1988. In that month, the organized Jewish community's senior leadership led a protest that turned into a massive uprising involving thousands of ordinary American Jews. By the time they were done, they had brought down a government.

An Israeli government, that is.

The reason, oddly for American Jews, was religion. Following Israel's parliamentary elections on November 1, Likud leader Yitzhak Shamir signed a coalition agreement with a small group of Orthodox lawmakers whose votes he needed to form a government. He had just endured four years of power-sharing with the Labor Party in an ungainly government of national unity, "rotating" with Labor's Shimon Peres in the prime minister's seat. It was four years of backstabbing and intrigue, and Shamir was ready to pay a high price not to repeat it. The price that the Orthodox lawmakers named was an amendment of Israel's basic immigration law, the Law of Return.

The Law of Return gives every Jew in the world the right to immigrate to Israel and receive immediate citizenship. It is one of two sections relating to the Diaspora in Israel's quasi-constitutional Basic Law. An amendment, as the Orthodox parties demanded of Shamir, would amount

337

to a unilateral change in the constitutional structure of Israel-Diaspora relations.

In the law, a Jew is defined as someone born of a Jewish mother or converted to Judaism, and not practicing another religion. The Orthodox parties had been pushing for two decades to tighten the definition of conversion. They wanted the law to specify that conversion must be done "according to *halakha*," or rabbinic law.

The amendment, popularly known as the "Who is a Jew" bill, was aimed largely at Reform rabbis in America, and to a lesser degree at Conservative rabbis. Conversion is a difficult and infrequent process in traditional Judaism, but Reform rabbis have eased it by introducing procedures that the Orthodox rabbinate considers hopelessly lax. Tens of thousands of American Gentiles, most of them spouses of Jews, have been converted to Judaism through the Reform rite in the past generation. To Orthodoxy, they are still Gentiles. In effect, the "Who is a Jew" amendment was meant as an indictment of the Reform rabbis' radicalism.

From the standpoint of Israeli law, the "Who is a Jew" issue was much ado about nothing. Reform Judaism is practically nonexistent in Israel. Orthodox Judaism is the Jewish state's established religion, and four fifths of the population considers itself nonreligious. Almost no one in Israel would be affected by the amendment.

As for Reform Jews in America, they are largely untouched by Israel's immigration laws, since few Reform Jews—born or converted—ever emigrate to Israel. Only a half-dozen or so Reform converts actually move to Israel each year; most of these are the spouses of born Jews, and thus are entitled to immigrant rights in any case, because the Law of Return covers Jews' family members. The entire "Who is a Jew" dispute was almost purely symbolic.

Indeed, even most Orthodox leaders viewed the issue as a marginal annoyance. The issue had been on the front burner for two decades only because of the single-minded determination of Rabbi Menachem Schneerson, Brooklyn-based leader of Lubavitch Hasidism; his mystical theology attributed cosmic importance to such symbolic trivialities. Operating with a multimillion-dollar budget, much of it donated by liberal American Jews who admired his kindly image, Schneerson had built a powerful trans-Atlantic political machine to press his views on a reluctant Israeli Orthodox political establishment. They, in turn, had pressured Shamir. In effect, this was a dispute between two factions of American Jewry.

*   *   *

Shamir had patiently explained most of this back in July 1987, when Shoshana Cardin had led a lobbying mission to Jerusalem to fight an early version of the bill. The polite hearing she gave the prime minister may have lulled him into believing the following year that his coalition deal would bring little more than a few Reform protests.

Instead, he got a virtual declaration of war from the leadership of organized American Jewry. Even before the coalition pact was signed, leaders of nearly every non-Orthodox Jewish body in America began mobilizing. A meeting at Reform headquarters in New York brought a majority of the Presidents Conference member organizations together in a rump group to demand that the Law of Return be left alone. (The Presidents Conference itself refused to take a stand, citing "lack of consensus".) The normally docile Conservative movement called for a sweeping reform of the Israeli electoral system to eliminate the bargaining power of the Orthodox parties (as though another system—America's, for example—might eliminate minority blackmail). Even single-issue Zionist groups like Hadassah and AIPAC weighed in with outrage. "I've never seen this kind of reaction before," Ernest Michel, director of New York's local UJA-Federation, told a reporter. "This is the most difficult time between Israel and diaspora Jews since the establishment of the state of Israel."

The protests exploded at the General Assembly of the Council of Jewish Federations, which convened in New Orleans on November 16. The assembly, which was supposed to focus on the incipient Jewish exodus from the Soviet Union, instead turned into a four-day rally against Shamir. After hearing a string of fiery speeches and strategy debates, the assembly voted for a full-scale campaign to force Shamir's hand. Delegations would be sent to Israel to meet nonstop with every Israeli lawmaker. Letters would be written, petitions collected, ads taken in the Israeli press. Shoshana Cardin, CJF's immediate past president (and future Presidents Conference chief) was named to head the campaign. She left New Orleans for Jerusalem as soon as the assembly ended, with her first delegation in tow.

Over the next four weeks, planeload after planeload of American Jews flew to Israel, including the top leaders of the CJF, the UJA, NCRAC, AIPAC, the American Jewish Committee, the American Jewish Congress,

B'nai B'rith, Hadassah, the Reform and Conservative movements, and dozens of local federations and synagogues—perhaps three thousand people in all, though no one was keeping track. Some flew to Israel and back two or three times inside of a month. Hadassah president Bernice Tannenbaum made the trip four times.

For some Jews, even this was not enough. In Boston and Atlanta, the local federations voted to withhold their Israel-bound UJA contributions, some $16 million total, until Shamir killed the amendment.

What a decade of invasions, uprisings, and international pressure could not accomplish, a three-word amendment on rabbinic ritual had done: brought American Jewry to open revolt against Israel.

The protests found their mark. In mid-December, Shamir capitulated and tore up his coalition agreement. Instead, he reluctantly reentered the national unity coalition with an equally reluctant Peres.

"There are some who call that a defining moment in Jewish history," Cardin would say later. "It was the first time American Jewry had publicly challenged the Israeli government."

The "Who is a Jew" furor was not the only reason Shamir scrapped his coalition. "I would say it was one of two main factors," recalls Dan Meridor, Shamir's justice minister and one of his chief coalition negotiators. The other factor was a sudden shift on the diplomatic front that left Israel unexpectedly isolated. "Shamir wanted a national unity government because he wanted to work from a broad base in order to face the outside pressure," Meridor says.

The diplomatic crisis came on December 13. Yasser Arafat, addressing the U.N. General Assembly at a special session in Geneva (relocated from New York because the Reagan administration would not grant him a visa), announced that the Palestinians had given up their goal of destroying Israel and were now prepared to live in peace alongside the Jewish state. The next day at a press conference, he read a brief statement dictated to him by the State Department, saying he would "recognize Israel" and "renounce terrorism" (with his accented English, it sounded like he was renouncing "tourism"). In Washington, Secretary of State George Shultz promptly declared that Arafat had met American objections, and that the United States was ready to begin a dialogue with the PLO. Israel was now completely alone in its refusal to deal with the PLO.

✴ ✴ ✴

Meridor speculates that Shamir may never have intended to form a narrow coalition with the Orthodox parties at all. "The religious parties say he just used them to get a better coalition with Labor, and they may be right," Meridor says. "He was a good negotiator." In Meridor's view, Shamir wanted to renew his pact with Shimon Peres all along. The "Who is a Jew" flap put pressure not so much on Shamir to accept Labor, but on Peres to accept junior partner status. (Meridor's reading of Shamir may be colored wishfully by the fact that Meridor himself favored a unity coalition. This would not be unusual; reading the inscrutable Shamir was a favorite Israeli spectator sport for years, mastered by none.)

Whatever Shamir's original intention, Meridor says, "it was very clear to all of us that the American Jewish community in large percentage was very much opposed to this amendment and viewed it as very dangerous. I'm not sure that this delegation of Shoshana Cardin or that delegation headed by someone else made a difference."

Cardin concedes that the American protests may not have been the sole deal-breaker. In her mind, however, the protests were a watershed event—in the politics of American Jews, if not in the politics of Israel.

"I would not say we prevailed all alone," Cardin said. "But I will say we convinced the Israelis that this was a serious issue. They were aware that this was the most intense manifestation the American Jewish community had ever expressed, that it was intense, massive, painful, and personally felt. That people would look differently at a Jewish state that told them they were no longer members of the Jewish people. And the fact is, they did listen."

The "Who is a Jew" dispute was a high point in the political history of American Jewry: an awesome demonstration of the clout that the Jewish community can muster when leadership and grass roots join hands to confront a threat.

But it was also a warning signal. In facing down the government of Israel, the Jewish community confronted a threat unlike any it had faced before. This was not some band of anti-Semitic vandals attacking an isolated Jewish neighborhood. Nor was it a local school board staging Christmas pageants, nor yet a foreign power bullying its local Jews. This was the reborn Jewish state, the embodiment of Jewish identity and meaning in the modern age, and it was turning against American Judaism.

For two decades, Israel had been a unique source of inspiration and leadership to American Jewish community activists. It was in the name of Israeli security that the Jewish lobby had fought its most storied battles, from AWACS to the media wars. Israel had played a central role in other American Jewish struggles, too, whether for Soviet or Ethiopian Jewish freedom or to hunt down Nazi war criminals. Even in American Jewry's domestic campaigns, for immigration rights or religious freedom or against anti-Semitism, the American Jews' association with Israel had lent them an extra measure of credibility and clout.

More than any other single factor, the alliance between Israel and the American Jewish community had brought the community to the center of the world stage after 1967. Anything that threatened this alliance would threaten American Jewry's political future.

The "Who is a Jew" dispute suggested that the greatest threat was now coming from Israel itself. Put simply, Israel was becoming apathetic toward American Jewry.

"Israelis aren't sufficiently aware of the topic of American Jewry," says Uriel Palti, a respected Israeli career diplomat. "They don't understand it, not as an important Jewish power, not as a vibrant Jewish experience. They don't recognize the Jewish activity in the broad scope of American Jewish culture, in literature, in religion, in family life. If they are aware of anything about American Jewry, it's a vague awareness of its political influence. But because it's seen out of context of Jewish life, they don't have the tools to comprehend it."

" 'Who is a Jew' represented the first time since the state of Israel was born that the whole American Jewish community rose up in a united fashion," Palti argues. "It showed that the decisions of the Israeli government really matter to American Jewry. That's good news, but it hasn't sufficiently been understood that way in Israel.

"On no other issue has American Jewry risen up—so literally that they got up and went to the airport. And it's not a coincidence that it did not involve life and death, war and peace, or money. This was the issue that united American Jewry in such a fashion, the 'Who is a Jew' amendment to the Law of Return. The symbolism of this decision touched the very core of the American Jewish soul."

☼   ☼   ☼

When the "Who is a Jew" crisis erupted in 1988, Israelis generally found it bewildering. It was widely described around Israel as a tempest in a teapot, deliberately stirred up by self-serving American Jewish community apparatchiks. "The average Israeli didn't know what we were talking about and didn't care, because it didn't affect their lives," says Cardin. "We were not received with affection. The average Israeli felt it was only a matter of six or seven people and didn't affect the Jewish community as a whole."

There was some truth in the Israeli view. American Jews grossly misread the "Who is a Jew" amendment. Many protesters claimed it would have made Reform Jews into non-Jews in Israeli law, a blatant untruth. Orthodox doctrine considers Reform Jews to be Jews who practice Judaism incorrectly, not non-Jews. The only persons who would have been ruled non-Jewish were Gentiles converted to Judaism under non-Orthodox rites.

It is also true that the fury sweeping American Jewry in the fall of 1988 was partly the result of a deliberate campaign by Reform rabbis to present the bill in the worst possible light. Reform leaders had been trying without much success to mobilize their congregants against the bill since its introduction in 1971. But Reform congregants are not easily mobilized. New tactics were needed.

In September 1986, after a decade and a half of preaching to the unconverted, the Reform leadership tried a new tactic. In a well-coordinated campaign, Reform rabbis all across America rose to their pulpits on the Jewish New Year—the best-attended service of the year—and told congregants that Israel was seeking to delegitimize them as Jews. The rabbis suggested that congregants could show their distress by calling their local Jewish federation and threatening to withhold their UJA donations until the matter was resolved.

The campaign hit its mark. By the time the bill became a political issue in November 1988, the federations and the CJF had found a bracing measure of resolve.

On the other hand, it is equally true that the cool Israeli view of the crisis gravely misread the mood of American Jews. Even after discounting legal technicalities, the impact of the bill among grassroots American Jews would have been devastating. For the Jewish state, the embodiment of Judaism in the modern age, to tell 2 million American Jews that their Judaism was invalid could create an existential crisis.

But the Israeli leaders were convinced American Jews would simply gripe and move on. "Don't exaggerate the impact on American Jewish life," Shamir told Cardin in 1987. "If the law passes, you'll live with it." He was wrong.

The "Who is a Jew" issue had been simmering on the back burner of Israeli politics for decades. Periodically, the Orthodox parties brought an amendment to the parliament floor; each in turn was quashed by the nation's political leadership, which was loath to alienate American Jewry's non-Orthodox majority.

It was only during the 1980s that the dispute turned from an arcane theological debate into an international battle royale. Hostility between the Jewish right and left had grown into a vast, scarcely bridgeable gulf, thanks to the spread of fundamentalism among the Orthodox and the increasing liberalism of the liberals. Then, too, American Jews had generally become more aware of life in Israel, thanks to the Six-Day War and its aftermath. With growing awareness of Israel came growing resentment of its flaws.

As the gulf widened, the Israeli parliament became a battleground where the warring movements fought out their symbolic struggle for legitimacy.

A third factor in the explosion, ironically, was the declining importance of Diaspora Judaism in the mind of Israel. Earlier versions of the "Who is a Jew" amendment had been stopped early in the legislative process; Israel's senior leaders had refused to condone such an assault on their Jewish supporters abroad. By the late 1980s, however, Israeli leaders had more important things on their minds. The fight over the fate of the occupied territories was dwarfing every other item on the Israeli agenda. Both major parties were more than willing to use the "Who is a Jew" amendment, if needed, to woo Orthodox coalition partners, regardless of how it would affect the feelings of American Jews.

For that matter, a sizable proportion of Israelis, leadership and public alike, had by 1988 become positively apathetic toward American Jewry.

For most Diaspora Jews, the rebirth of the Jewish state is one of the central facts of modern Jewish history and a dominant presence in their lives as

Jews. For most Israeli Jews, the Jews of the Diaspora are an accident of history, and an irritating one at that.

The Zionist pioneers who created modern Israeli society at the turn of the century were a radical band who believed that Jewish life in exile was doomed. With anti-Semitism spreading in Eastern Europe and assimilation rampant in the West, they were convinced that a Jewish state was their people's last chance for survival in the modern world.

Many of them believed that the Diaspora was not only doomed, but deserved its fate. In a doctrine known as "negation of the Diaspora," Zionists taught that two thousand years of history in exile was a shameful interlude of impotence between periods of nationhood. They assumed that once Jews were offered "normalized" life as a free people on their own soil, they would flock to it from around the world "as naturally as a hat returning to a head," in the words of one early Zionist leader.

"When we first built this country, we wanted to get away from everything associated with the Jewish Diaspora," says Moshe Prywes, a pioneering educator from Israel's founding generation. "If they spoke Yiddish, we spoke Hebrew. If they excelled in finance and intellect, we returned to the land. We wanted to negate the Diaspora, and that determined our attitude."

Israeli nationhood did not have the expected result. Instead of ending Jewish life in the Diaspora, Israel strengthened it. Jews all over the world found renewed strength and meaning in Judaism because of Israel's existence. Celebrating Israel became a central theme in organized Jewish community life and culture, in synagogue ritual, and in religious education.

For Jews in America and around the world, all this was an inspiration. For Israelis, it was ironic.

Thanks to the Zionist revolution, generations of Israelis have been raised to view Jewish life as a normal process of waking up each morning in a Jewish country. In consequence, Jewish life in Diaspora has become utterly incomprehensible. If Jewishness consists of living in Israel, what can it possibly mean to live as a Jew in Cleveland?

"We speak a Jewish language, live by a Jewish calendar, serve in a Jewish army," says Israeli journalist Gideon Remez. "American Jews have to come up with all sorts of funny contraptions to identify themselves as Jewish, things like Reform temples, which strike the average Israeli as faintly ridiculous. If you're not religious, why go to *shul?*"

In a real sense, the "normalization" of Jewish life in Israel is simply the flip side of American Jewish assimilation. Except for the minority of Jews in both countries who are Orthodox—some 20 percent in Israel and 10 percent in America—both communities are now dominated by a new sort of Judaism, consisting essentially of modern world culture with an attitude.

In many ways, the two new Judaisms are strikingly similar. Both share a fascination with arts and learning. Both are dominated by a freethinking liberalism in politics and culture. Both share a culture of nostalgia for the old Judaism, coupled with a faint hostility toward its rules and rituals.

The differences between the new Judaisms are crucial, however. For one thing, the American version is a symbolic universe of voluntary acts and thoughts, while the Israeli version is a concrete world of daily life.

The other difference is this: the symbolic Jewish world of the American version requires firm leadership from that greatest of modern Jewish symbols, the state of Israel. But in the concrete world of modern Israel, most Israelis don't know what that means and don't much care.

"The Diaspora is not something the average Israeli thinks about a great deal," says American-born political scientist Charles Liebman of Bar-Ilan University, one of Israel's leading experts on American Jewry. "To be sure, there's a sense of dependence. In times of crisis, the Israeli expects the Diaspora to come to his assistance. But does he think about it on a regular basis? Of course not."

Today, nearly a decade later after Shamir's coalition fell, the "Who is a Jew" issue remains largely dormant. Yet the relationship between Israel and the Diaspora is in a state of full-blown crisis. "Who is a Jew" had revealed the larger storm brewing below the surface, for those willing to see it. But few noticed. Instead, the crisis remained invisible, suppressed by leaders on both sides. It boiled over in 1992.

For Israel's first quarter-century, its European-born founders were able to speak a ready common language with the European Jewish immigrants who dominated American Jewry. For fifteen years after that, beginning with the Begin revolution in 1977, Jerusalem was run by right-wing traditionalists with a traditional belief in worldwide Jewish solidarity. They found fellow traditionalists in the American community and elevated them to leadership, creating a new international bond. This served the political goals of Begin and Shamir no less than the cause of Jewish solidarity. If broad sections of the Jewish community's liberal majority were alienated by the conservative tone of Jewish leadership, few cared enough to protest.

The election of Yitzhak Rabin as prime minister in June 1992 could have restored a balance to American Jewish politics, by bringing back to center stage a liberal leadership that reflected the sensibilities of the Jewish majority. Rabin's daring policies of Israel-Arab reconciliation and regional peace, which so excited imaginations around the globe, might have ignited a new sense of purpose among mainstream American Jews. Perhaps decades of steady drift away from organized Jewish involvement might have been arrested or even reversed, if Israel's new leaders had stepped forward and taken up their inherited mantle as beacons to American Jewry.

That did not happen. Rabin's victory had brought to power an Israeli-born generation of secular liberals, Charles Liebman's "average Israelis." They simply could not take on a role of leadership for an American Jewish community that they fundamentally did not understand.

The result was a crisis in Israel-Diaspora relations that rapidly reached explosive levels.

Coming to America on his first official trip in August, Rabin held a series of stormy meetings with Jewish community leaders to tell them that they were no longer needed. In a Washington meeting with AIPAC staff, he lambasted them for propping up the Likud for so long, and dismissed as a fraud their claim that they supported whatever government Israel chose. From now on, he said, Israeli-U.S. ties would be conducted state-to-state without intermediaries. Moving on to New York, he told the Presidents Conference in a speech that the era of suppressing Jewish dissent was over. American Jews could say whatever they liked about Israeli policy, he said, since their views did not matter anyway.

The new government's point man for Diaspora affairs was Deputy Foreign Minister Yossi Beilin, a bespectacled intellectual known for his radically dovish views on foreign policy. Given the portfolio for Israel-Diaspora relations, he immediately began throwing verbal bombs. Speaking to the Presidents Conference in August 1992, he said that Israel would henceforth welcome a free and open debate with American Jewry. "We want you to disagree with us," he told them. ("We can't do that," shot back Hadassah ex-president Ruth Popkin. "Our job here is to defend you.")

The next year's CJF General Assembly, meeting in Montreal, was disrupted by pro-Likud activists complaining that Likud leaders were excluded from the assembly program (as Labor leaders had been excluded

during the Likud years). Beilin, in Montreal to represent the Labor government, took the protesters' side. To the dismay of CJF leaders who were
trying to swing their body behind his government, Beilin called for the
Jewish leadership to permit open debate on Israeli policy. "We can't do
that," a visibly angry CJF president Maynard Wishner told him.

In the winter, Beilin took on the most sacred institution in the entire
American Jewish communal machine: the UJA campaign. Fund-raisers,
Beilin complained in a series of speeches and interviews, were portraying
Israel as a pauper. In fact, it was now a high-tech regional superpower, and
had no need of charity. He suggested that American Jews keep their money
at home and look for ways to save themselves from assimilation.

Down below, at the staff level in Israeli diplomatic missions where
Israel-Diaspora relations are traditionally managed day-to-day, the problem
was not bomb-throwing but inertia. Rabin's choices to head the Israeli
diplomatic corps in America were two respected figures who shared his
indifference toward the Diaspora. By the time they realized that the Jewish
community mattered, it was out of control.

The ambassador in Washington, Itamar Rabinovich, one of Israel's
leading Arab affairs experts, was chosen to take charge of the fast-moving
Middle East peace negotiations. The consul general in New York, Colette
Avital, a well-regarded Israeli career diplomat, arrived with plans for outreach to the arts, media, and business worlds. Neither one had any real
plans for reaching out to the organized Jewish leadership.

Neither one had any experience working with the American Jewish
community. Like most Israelis of their generation, they had no real sense
that it mattered. Both assumed that the Jewish leadership would follow
Israel's lead more or less automatically. More important, both assumed that
American support for Israel in politics, the media, and especially in Congress resulted purely from admiration for Israel. Of Israel's role in nurturing
the Jewish lobby they knew little.

And suddenly, to everyone's great surprise, American Jewry's ship of state
found itself leaderless, rudderless, bobbing aimlessly on uncharted waters.

As Israel embarked on its daring, risky venture of peace with the Palestinians, lawmakers on Capitol Hill found themselves deluged with right-
wing Jewish activists lobbying to undercut the peace process. Efforts were
made to block aid to the Palestinians, to discredit Yasser Arafat as a negotiating partner, to disrupt Israeli-Syrian negotiations by barring in advance
any U.S. peacekeeping force on the Israeli-Syrian border. There even were

efforts to end U.S. aid to Egypt, Israel's original peace partner, after Egypt took the Arab side at several stages in the unfolding peace negotiations.

Each time one of these initiatives came close to inflicting real damage, the Israeli embassy or the Clinton administration stepped in with urgent appeals to lawmakers not to destroy the peace. The process continued to lurch forward, but no thanks to the Jewish leadership. The feared Jewish lobby, which for years had been the driving force behind American support for Israel, was now neutral at best, a hindrance at worst. In fact, the lobby was paralyzed, its governing councils divided between those who were bitterly opposed to Israeli compromise and those who were not.

Editors of Jewish community weeklies found their fax machines flooded each week with op-ed submissions attacking Israeli policy, while "getting a pro-government piece is like pulling teeth," as one editor complained. Central Jewish agencies such as AIPAC and the Presidents Conference, which traditionally had used pressure and threats to maintain the appearance of Jewish unity during the Likud years, suddenly found themselves singing the praises of diversity and free expression within the Jewish community. "People have a lot of concerns," said Presidents Conference chief Malcolm Hoenlein when pressed on the umbrella group's listlessness. Asked point-blank by Israeli government officials to mobilize in support of Israel, AIPAC launched a legislative initiative in the spring of 1995 to move the U.S. embassy from Tel Aviv to Jerusalem—embarrassing an Israeli government that claimed Jerusalem as its capital, but was about to enter delicate negotiations with its Arab partners over the fate of the disputed city.

There were efforts to mobilize Jewish liberals behind the Labor government during the Rabin years, but they were sporadic and half-hearted. NCRAC periodically brought groups of local leaders to Washington to lobby Congress on behalf of the peace process. The Israel Policy Forum, a new body organized in 1993 by Rabin supporters, managed to assemble a group of wealthy business leaders to fund periodic initiatives—now a newspaper advertisement, now an opinion poll—to demonstrate the overwhelming popular Jewish support for Rabin's policies.

None of these efforts managed to achieve any traction. Groups that had fought a lonely fight for Israeli liberalism during the Likud years, like Americans for Peace Now and the New Israel Fund, found no sudden growth in membership or fund-raising now that their friends ruled in Jerusalem. The Jewish right, which had enjoyed a burst of growth when the Likud came to power in 1977, enjoyed another burst now that Labor had returned. In the center, Jewish moderates were hesitant to offer Rabin the same whole-hearted support they had once given Begin and Shamir. Except for the stoutly independent Abe Foxman of the Anti-Defamation League, most centrists seemed afraid—afraid that outspoken rightists might tar them as pro-Arab, or that the Likud might return to power and punish them. Supporting Israeli liberalism continued to carry a price, even in an era of Labor rule.

There was a good deal of relief mixed with the dread, therefore, when the Likud did return to power, defeating Labor in May 1996 under the hardline leadership of Benjamin "Bibi" Netanyahu.

The dread received most of the attention in the first days after the Israeli election. It seemed that a Netanyahu government was planning a diplomatic retrenchment, which might set back the cause of Israel-Arab peacemaking. Renewed settlement seemed likely to reignite Israeli-Palestinian confrontations of the sort that had unsettled so many American consciences during the 1980s. Arab reactions to the new regime might consign Israel to the international isolation of the Shamir years and before. On top of all this, the electoral gains of Israel's Orthodox parties threatened to roll back the progress made by the Reform and Conservative movements since 1988 in advancing their agenda on the Israeli scene. There was much for American Jews to fear in a Likud restoration.

Balanced against all this, however, was the simple fact that a Likud government would restore the old, familiar patterns of Israel-Diaspora relations. An isolated, embattled Israel would be an Israel once again in need of its lonely, courageous Jewish defenders. A conservative Israeli government would provide traditional Jewish leadership, with old-fashioned views of Jewish solidarity. The Likud would reach out to the American Jewish establishment as it always had, bringing the fractious organizational heads into harness with a stern, sure hand. And the Jews would fall in line, some happily, others protesting, all comforted by the knowledge that someone was in charge.

In Israel's quasi-constitutional Basic Law, the formal liaison between the Jewish state and the Diaspora is the century-old World Zionist Organization and its operations arm, the Jewish Agency for Israel. Their officers represent the Diaspora at ceremonial events, state funerals, and the like. They report to the prime minister when a Jewish crisis occurs overseas. They are the main channel for mobilizing Diaspora support of the Jewish state.

The WZO, with its myriad membership divisions and youth clubs around the world, is the main vehicle through which Israel disseminates its message to Jews around the world. Through its elected councils and assemblies, it is also the vehicle through which Diaspora Jews are formally entitled to voice their views to Israel.

The Jewish Agency carries out nation-building tasks inside Israel, such as land reclamation and resettling Jewish immigrants, which are deemed to be the duty of Jews everywhere, not just of Israel's own citizens. The agency's half-billion-dollar annual budget comes mainly from federated Jewish fund-raising campaigns around the world, principally the UJA-federation campaign in the United States. The agency's governing board is evenly divided between WZO and federation representatives, though the WZO names its top officers and controls its day-to-day operations.

The WZO's role as a Diaspora voice in Israel is one of its least known but most potent functions. Because it is a confederation of groups with differing views on Israeli politics, it is one of the only Jewish organizations in the world that encourages debate instead of suppressing it. WZO debates become most heated—sometimes to the point of fisticuffs—at the World Zionist Congress, which meets in Jerusalem every four years to set policy and choose the WZO's executive officers.

The Israeli delegation usually dominates the proceedings, but not always. In 1983, congress delegates voted to bar the use of WZO funds for settlements in the West Bank. That move effectively ended the Likud government's settlements policy, since the WZO is the agency through which settlements are set up. (The disruption was brief; WZO chairman Aryeh Dulzin, a Likud politician, finessed the mutiny by ruling the vote out of order, adjourning the session, and convincing the American Hadassah delegation overnight to switch its vote.)

The election of delegates to the World Zionist Congress, conducted country-by-country and open to any dues-paying member of a Zionist organization, is the sole occasion in American Jewish life when Jews are permitted to vote en masse on issues that affect Jewish life. Close to 850,000 Americans registered to vote in the elections for the 1987 World Zionist Congress, or about one of every five Jews of voting age. Just over one fourth of those registered mailed in their ballots—a poor turnout by classic democratic standards, but a landmark in American Jewish life. With "Who is a Jew" in the background, the voting ended in a sweeping victory for groups linked to Reform and Conservative Judaism, and a drubbing for traditional Zionist groups associated with the Israeli political system. The results: a Reform-Labor coalition at the congress knocked Shamir's Likud out of the WZO–Jewish Agency executive offices, removing the powerful institutions from control by Israel's ruling party for the first time ever. A Reform rabbi was named to head the WZO's education department, and a Conservative rabbi to head its organization department, giving the liberal wings new leverage in their bid to win recognition in Israel. Perhaps most important, a Reform rabbi was named to chair the Zionist General Council, the third-ranking post in the WZO hierarchy, making him part of Israel's official state protocol at ceremonial occasions such as holidays and state funerals. For the first time in history, a Reform rabbi had entered Israel's constitutional hierarchy, thanks to the votes of American Jews.

One other important result of the 1987 elections was a decision by the heads of the American Zionist organizations to do away with elections in the future. In closed-door talks, with only the Reform movement objecting, the Zionist leaders concluded that elections were an expensive waste that bogged the WZO down in pointless squabbling rather than uniting Jews to support Israel. Henceforth, the American delegation was to be chosen in negotiations among the organizational heads.

As these words are being written, the WZO is in the process of negotiating its own demise. Israelis hold it in deep contempt, because whatever its achievements—from Jewish schools in Peru to summer camps in Pennsylvania—it has failed at the one task by which Israelis measure Zionism: inducing the Jews of America and the West to relocate to Israel. As for its fund-raising partners, the federations and the UJA, most of them have little use for the endless debates and political bargaining that make up Zionist politics. They live in a world of consensus. "I don't know how we ever got our Jewish Agency mixed up with the WZO in the first place, but I think we ought to separate the two of them once and for all," said accountant Irwin Hochberg, a top leader of New York UJA-Federation, on the eve of the annual Jewish Agency governing assembly meeting in June 1988.

For a half-century, the United Jewish Appeal has been the central engine driving all the other parts of the machine called the organized American

Jewish community. The billion-odd dollars raised in annual UJA-federation campaigns help to finance a prodigious network of federated institutions providing Jewish education, defense, and social services at a cost of more than $4 billion per year, counting user fees, foundation grants, and government aid.

Millions more are given out each year by federations in grants to Jewish agencies outside their own network. Through these grants, the federation system makes itself a partner in the management of a broad range of Jewish institutions, from the Anti-Defamation League, which gets about 5 percent of its budget from federations; to the Jewish Telegraphic Agency, which gets about half; to NCRAC, which is funded entirely by the federations. Through its sponsorship of NCRAC, the federation system effectively controls the central policy-making channel of the Jewish defense community.

Indeed, it is almost easier to name the few organizations that operate entirely outside the federated system—the Simon Wiesenthal Center of Los Angeles, Agudath Israel of America, the pro-Israel PACs, the right-wing Americans for a Safe Israel, the left-wing *Tikkun* magazine and its offshoots—than to try reciting every institution that is under the federation umbrella.

Overseas, the clout of the UJA-federation system is even more concentrated. The $300 million in federation revenues sent to Israel each year forms the budgetary core of the Jewish Agency for Israel, the Jewish state's largest private social-service provider. The Jewish Agency's half-billion-dollar annual budget makes it the largest single Jewish institution in the world, not counting the Israeli government itself. In addition to its rescue and rehabilitation work, the Agency operates programs of Diaspora Jewish education and culture that total more than $50 million per year.

The other beneficiary of the UJA, the Joint Distribution Committee, with an annual budget of about $60 million, remains the world's most effective Jewish relief agency, providing vital human services to Jews in trouble from Chechnya to Ethiopia to the slums of south Tel Aviv.

The UJA holds an awesome reputation among Americans, Jewish and non-Jewish, for its ability to separate Jews from their cash. Running a joint campaign with the federations in most cities, it has perfected a repertoire of techniques to inspire and embarrass Jews into giving, then giving more. Donors are organized by industry, increasing peer pressure and making the

UJA a useful place to be seen. A separate women's division often succeeds in yielding two checks from a single household. UJA dinners are lavish affairs where Jewish celebrities are feted, comics tell Yiddish jokes, and visiting Israeli politicians thunder on about the call of history. Most dinners end with the "calling of the cards," a devastating ritual in which each guest's pledge is read aloud, honoring the generous and humiliating the stingy. All told, the campaign receives just under nine hundred thousand gifts per year, representing about half of all American Jewish households.

The reality of the UJA does not match the image, however. Most of the money credited to the UJA-federation campaign is actually raised by local federations, which are only loosely affiliated to the United Jewish Appeal. From its New York headquarters, the UJA offers the federations its guidance and encouragement, and it helps to craft a unified image for each year's campaign; individual federations may follow the UJA's campaign theme or not, as they choose. The UJA also lobbies the individual federations to send in as large a share of their revenue as they can spare for the use of the two overseas relief agencies, the Joint and the Jewish Agency, which technically own the UJA. (A small share, amounting to about 5 percent of the UJA's income, goes to the New York Association for New Americans, a local agency that cares for Jewish immigrants in New York City.)

Despite its outsized image as a massive organization with tentacles spread to every corner of the Jewish world, the fact is that the UJA itself is primarily a speakers' bureau and cheering section for a diffuse, decentralized Jewish welfare process.

On April 16, 1991, the leaders of the nation's Jewish federations met in Washington for a special one-day midterm general assembly to discuss an extraordinary proposal.

In response to the snowballing Russian Jewish exodus to Israel, the Jewish Agency was planning to phase out its comprehensive welfare program for new immigrants and replace it with a sort of block-grant system. Instead of receiving the right to apply for a bewildering array of separate services, from housing to health insurance and language training, immigrants would receive cash—grants and loans—with which they could purchase individual services on the open market. With refugees arriving at a rate of nearly 150,000 per year, the Jewish Agency had asked the Council of Jewish Federations to help out by underwriting $900 million in personal loans to Russian newcomers.

The CJF, which oversees the local federations but has virtually no assets of its own, was passing the request along to its member agencies.

It was not a simple request. According to a plan developed by the heads of the CJF and UJA, each federation would become responsible for a "fair share" of the $900 million package, based on the population of its local Jewish community and the size of its annual fund-raising campaign. Communities would have to put up assets—Jewish community centers, old-age homes, and the like—as collateral against the loans which the Russian immigrants would draw on Israeli banks.

The proposal touched off a long, emotional debate at the Washington assembly. "We're putting our family businesses on the line," warned Cleveland federation president Henry Goodman. "We will lock up our credit for the future. We will hurt our ability to borrow the next time an emergency comes along. And the biggest loser, if we are not able to repay our debts, will be Israel."

Despite the misgivings of opponents, the proposal passed overwhelmingly, with only four nays and thirteen abstentions. Much of the opposition dissolved in the face of an emotional appeal by the senior statesman of the federation world, Max Fisher. "My father came to this country in 1904, and he told me about the problems the Jewish people faced," Fisher said. "It strikes me that we now have an opportunity to redress those wrongs."

No one said it out loud, but many of those present were aware of the historic nature of the proceedings. The United States and Israel had dickered for a year and a half before agreeing a few months earlier on a loan guarantee of $400 million. The Jewish community had just approved a loan guarantee twice that size in the course of an afternoon. "It's clearly a historic moment, not just for Jewish philanthropy but for American philanthropy," said Vince Stehle, a reporter covering the proceedings for the weekly *Chronicle of Philanthropy*. "Both in scope and in style, they're doing something here that's never been done."

The vote was historic for another reason, with longer-term implications for American Jewish life. For the first time in history, delegates representing the great bulk of organized American Jewry were coming together in a voting body and electing to tax themselves. The CJF was transforming itself from an advisory body, offering assistance to dozens of local charities, into a decision-making body that could control the lion's share of American Jewish community finances. "This thing is turning into a parliament," said the head of one national Jewish agency who was observing the proceedings.

A year earlier, the federations had met at a special assembly in Miami and adopted a fair-share taxation program. The problem to be addressed then was the continuing flow of Russian Jewish refugees to America, who were entering at a rate of close to forty thousand per year. Most were settling in just seven cities: half in New York, the rest in Miami, Philadelphia, Boston, Chicago, Los Angeles, and San Francisco. In each of these cities, the local federation alone bore the burden of caring for the newcomers. The CJF's 1980 refugee agreement with the U.S. government required the Jewish community to put up about one thousand dollars in social services for each refugee. The total, approaching $40 million annually, came from those seven federations.

At the 1990 Miami assembly, the federations voted to equalize the burden, by letting the CJF tax them for their "fair share" of the resettlement costs. Each community would be responsible for its share of the year's refugees, equivalent to its share of the total American Jewish population. Each community was bound either to take in that percentage of the year's refugees, or to pay the equivalent cost into a national fund to help those cities receiving more than their share.

It is difficult to exaggerate the meaning of the 1990 and 1991 fair-share agreements in the history of American Jewry. For the first time, a national Jewish organization won the power to tax local Jewish communities and make centralized decisions in their name. In much the same way, English democracy was born when taxpayers first assembled in what became Parliament. American Jews were taking a first tentative step toward giving their community a governing body.

There was much more to come. In 1992, the CJF set up a new committee to coordinate grants from local federations to national agencies like NCRAC and the Hebrew Immigrant Aid Society. Federations had been making these grants for years, after a CJF budgeting council reviewed the agencies' budgets and recommended how much they should receive. Once the budgeting council had made its recommendations, the agencies were invited to visit 187 local federations and ask for their grants. The new committee, approved in 1992, eliminated the last step; once it decided how much a national agency should receive, it sent each federation a bill.

The change sounded to many outsiders like a technicality, but insiders recognized it for what it was: a basic shift in the center of power. The CJF now controlled pieces of the budgets of a score of other national Jewish organizations. Some grantees recognized the new system for what it was and flatly refused to join; they preferred to go on begging from city to city, rather than submit their budgets for CJF approval. "You don't contribute a big enough share of our budget to tell us what to do," ADL director Abraham Foxman flatly told the CJF budgeting council at a 1992 meeting.

Also in 1992, the CJF began to study plans for a fair-share system to equalize the cost of Jewish campus chaplaincies around the country. The plan was approved in 1994. A committee now began examining the possibility of a fair-share system in care for the elderly. Bit by bit, it seemed, federations were surrendering their autonomy to an emerging national Jewish community. The CJF's board of directors was restructured and expanded. Each federation received a vote in proportion to the size of its local Jewish population. The new body was renamed the Board of Delegates, harking back to American Jewry's first national agency.

In late 1995, plans were tentatively approved for a merger between the CJF and the UJA. The merger, which still faces huge hurdles, would create a single national Jewish superagency.

The consolidation of the CJF may yet prove to be the most important event in the two-century history of American Jewish organizing efforts. The federations bring a resource to the organizing effort that no one before could muster: the power of the purse.

By sitting astride the cash flow that nourishes most of the Jewish institutional world, the CJF has become the closest thing there is to a central address in the organized Jewish community. If it learns how to control that flow, the CJF will have the power to make decisions for organized American Jewry. Its national board, representing the eight hundred thousand Jewish households that contribute to the federated campaign, will truly come to resemble a parliament-in-the-making. In a sense the Jewish community may recapitulate the experience of the English Parliament, which began as a taxpayers' assembly and went on from there.

One last step would be required, however, to make the new body into a truly representative council of American Jewry. The federations would have to bring the mass of donors into the decision-making processes that are now dominated by committees of the wealthiest donors.

This is not necessarily a pipe dream; other countries, including England and Canada, have central Jewish community councils with something resembling a democratic voting process. A few local federations, including Los Angeles and Chicago, offer mechanisms by which every donor has a chance to help choose the board.

All this could happen. But as the CJF-UJA consolidation process limps endlessly toward completion, all the signs point in the opposite direction.

"I think the push to merge has become the raison d'être for the current leadership," observes Milwaukee marketing consultant Bruce Arbit, a former officer of the UJA Young Leadership Cabinet. "People seem to be saying, 'We're having trouble raising more money? Let's find something else to do. Let's merge.'"

"Merger has been talked about as something that will reinvigorate the entire community," Arbit says. "Well, the entire community barely knows these institutions exist to begin with. Maybe the merger could have reinvigorated the leadership. But it's been bogged down in details and squabbling for the last two years and the participants are sick and tired of it. My biggest fear is that we're going to merge and end up with nothing."

Approaching the millenium, the entire UJA-federation system is a deeply troubled institution. Revenues have stagnated since 1990, when the campaign reached its peak at nearly $1 billion. The dip has led to widespread fears that the campaign has entered what will prove to be a long period of decline. For many UJA leaders, it is the first sign of the approaching endgame of assimilation, the disappearing cash of the disappearing Jews.

Added to this is a second crisis: a steady decline in the percentage of federation revenue that is sent to Israel. The "overseas" share of the total UJA-federation campaign has dropped from a high of about 66 percent in 1974, just after the Yom Kippur War, to a low of just over 40 percent in 1995. This decline in Israel's share of the campaign comes at a time when more and more Israelis actually insist, like Beilin, that they need less of the Diaspora's charity.

The crisis—hidden amid the good news—is that with Israel facing fewer dangers, Jews will feel less urgency to give. Thus the declining needs of Israel will contribute to the steady decline of Jewish giving, weakening American Jewish institutions and accelerating the rate of assimilation.

In effect, argues Samuel Norich, a consultant to several independent Jewish think tanks, "the balance of power in the Jewish world has shifted, and with it the focus of dread."

The doomsday scenario rests on several dubious statistical arguments, beginning with the infamous 52 percent intermarriage figure (see chapter 3) and ending with the equally dubious matter of the disappearing dollar.

UJA-federation campaign receipts have indeed dropped off in recent years. But this should have been expected: campaign receipts have dropped off sharply after every emergency since Israel was born. They dropped from $205 million in 1948 to $161 million in 1949, following Israel's war of independence. They dropped from $317 million in 1967 to $232 million in 1968, after the Six-Day War. They dropped from $686 million in 1974 to $491 million in 1975, after the Yom Kippur War.

The peak of close to $1 billion reached in the early 1990s was, like all the peaks before it, the result of an "emergency campaign." This one was an emergency drive to help Israel resettle its massive Russian immigration. Code-named Operation Exodus, the drive approached every UJA donor and asked for a second gift, earmarked directly for the Israeli immigration program. The five-year drive brought in an extra $884 million, or $176 million per year, on top of the "regular" campaign. Not surprisingly, the take was accompanied by a slight decline in giving to the regular campaign. When Operation Exodus ended, overall revenues dropped back to their usual level, causing a blow to morale within the UJA organizing network. The fact that regular-campaign revenues were in a slump—down to $706 million in 1993, from an all-time high of $737 million in 1990—only added to the shock.

Compounding the post-Exodus letdown was the fact that while the emergency campaign was finished, the emergency was not. Russian Jews were still streaming out of Russia at a rate of sixty thousand per year, well into the late 1990s. Israel was still spending thousands of dollars per immigrant, from plane fare and freight costs to initial housing and welfare.

But the American donors, mobilized on the basis of an emergency effort, could not keep up the peak giving. "We can't keep going back to them year after year and telling them it's an emergency," said one senior official. "It gets tired."

What *is* remarkable, perhaps, is the fact that UJA-federation revenues continue as high as they do, considering the harsh—and largely undiscussed—impact on Jews of the downsizing American economy of the early 1990s.

Cuts in executive and managerial jobs across the board, cuts in engineering positions in the aircraft and defense industries, and the continuing shakeout in the retail industry, all have had a disproportionate effect on the Jewish middle class. Beginning in the early 1990s, Jewish federations from Fort Lauderdale to St. Louis to Las Vegas began to find significant numbers of their donors showing up as social-service clients. New York's Federation Employment and Guidance Service saw the numbers of unemployed Jews seeking its help jump by hundreds of percentage points between 1989 and 1991.

Jewish federations today are squeezed between a host of conflicting forces. Economic hardship has created a growing demand for their social services while shrinking their donor base. Traditional sources of government assistance—Medicare and Medicaid for Jewish hospitals and old-age homes, antipoverty funds for Jewish family services—are drying up. At the same time, community leaders are desperately pressing the federations to redirect funds from social services to Jewish religious education.

This is the real crisis facing the UJA-federation system.

Israel's declining need for UJA assistance could not have come at a better time.

And yet, UJA leaders point to the declining share sent to Israel as a sign of sickness rather than health in the system. Even Israelis, for all their brave talk of their own increased confidence and declining need, habitually point to the falling contributions to Israel as a symptom of American Jewish decline.

To some extent, Israeli complaints about the declining level of American Jewish giving are simply a political football. Israelis tend to be intensely aware of the UJA campaign as a central feature of American Jewish life, but are generally ignorant of how it works. The fact that the money is raised by local federations, each of which decides how much to keep and how much to send abroad, is lost on the average Israeli. When news reports describe rising levels of UJA money being kept in the United States, therefore, Israel tends to resound with angry protests that American Jews are "stealing Israel's money," as Likud tourism minister Gideon Patt complained in a 1989 speech.

Still, the Israeli response is not entirely unjustified. The Zionist movement may have been the junior partner when it joined with the wealthier Joint Distribution Committee to form the original UJA in 1938. But the roles were long ago reversed. Since the birth of Israel in 1948, the drama and glamour of Jewish statehood have vastly overshadowed the pathos of Jewish rescue in Europe or at home. Israel itself long ago became the main motivator for Diaspora giving. In deference, the Jewish Agency's share of the yearly UJA take grew steadily through Israel's first three decades, peaking at two thirds of the total in 1975.

Since then, however, Israel's share of the revenues has dropped steadily, even though its role in raising the money has not. Local federation leaders insist that the needs of American Jews—educating the young, caring for the old and weak—have become more pressing than Israel's problems. National UJA leaders reply that the money would not be there if not for the heroic appeal of Israel.

The fact that the individuals involved in the fight are mostly the same people—UJA and CJF leaders are nearly all local federation activists who have moved up the ladder—gives the whole debate a certain comic tinge. But it does not change the urgency.

"The problem here is that if Israelis aren't suffering, American Jews don't seem to feel the need to be their partners," says Milwaukee activist Bruce Arbit. "The result is that federations are barely keeping even. People aren't writing checks, because nothing is exciting them. And among the leadership, there's a massive depression everywhere you look."

No less important, a deliberate cut in American Jewish donations to Israel would send a disastrous signal to the U.S. Congress, argues Akiva Eldar, Washington correspondent of Israel's respected daily newspaper *Ha'aretz*. "Whoever proposes chucking out the donations of the American Jews—as well as their opinions—has to know that he is at the same time discarding a sizeable segment of Israel's GNP," Eldar wrote in his newspaper in January 1996. "For what are you to do if the Jewish state does not need the money of America's Jews and where will those Jews find the [c]hutzpah to appropriate money from the Gentiles for that state?"

On the other hand, if Israel truly does not need the money, what sense does it make to continue sending it simply in order to maintain appearances?

Some mavericks in the UJA-federation system suggest that the answer is a simple one: send the money in a circle. American Jews could continue to raise money by pointing to Israel as the symbol of modern Jewish identity. Israel could spend that money on institutions that foster Jewish identity in the Diaspora. As the world's leading center of Jewish culture and learning, Israel is in a unique position to lead American Jewry's struggle for spiritual renewal. Its tourism facilities, religious academies, universities, and cadres of willing teachers could be mobilized to train a new generation of American Jewish religious teachers and cultural leaders. Already thousands of young and old American Jews travel to Israel each year for study, pilgrimage, or recreation. Most come back saying that they have found new meaning in Judaism.

The WZO and Jewish Agency have decades of experience in promoting Jewish education and culture by holding up Israel as a role model. Right now, most of the Agency's huge annual budget is devoted to bringing Jews out of Russia. But experts predict that the Russian Jewish exodus will end within a decade. When that happens, the Jewish Agency could begin turning its attention to the next crisis: the hunger of the American Jewish soul. American Jews hold a majority of seats on the Jewish Agency's governing board. They could begin to prepare for the millenium, if they had the will and the leadership.

Indeed, one top UJA leader has already proposed a first step in that direction. In 1993, Rabbi Brian Lurie, then UJA's executive vice president, proposed creating a $30 million-a-year program of marketing and subsidies to promote travel to Israel among American Jewish teens. His goal was to boost the number of teen visitors each year to fifty thousand from its current five thousand or more, in hopes of making an Israel visit part of the education of every American Jewish youngster. His $30 million fund was to come one third from the UJA, one third from the Jewish Agency, and one third from the Israeli government.

Israel vetoed the plan.

❖   ❖   ❖

In the winter of 1995, following the Republican victory in the 1994 congressional elections, CJF Washington representative Diana Aviv circulated a plan among the federations to mobilize the community against the proposed balanced-budget amendment. Aviv's argument was that the amendment, a key plank in the House GOP's Contract with America, would have the effect of sharply reducing federal aid to human services. This, she argued, would contradict a basic Jewish religious value. Equally important, it would strike at the heart of the federations' work.

Her mobilization stalled even before it started, vetoed by two of the largest federations. The two, New York and Miami, had solid majorities on their governing boards opposed to the balanced-budget amendment. But both had small groups of Republicans among their major donors who threatened to withhold their gifts if the federations mobilized against the amendment. Faced with losses in the millions of dollars, the two federations' executives decided to stay out of the balanced-budget fight. Several other cities followed suit, and Aviv's initiative collapsed.

The power of the major donor is not a new phenomenon in the Jewish organizational world. Big givers have played a key role in setting policy in every Jewish organization for as long as there have been organizations. In a voluntary community, funded by voluntary donations, this may be inevitable.

The phenomenon underwent a spectacular growth during the 1980s, however. The reason was economic: federations discovered that they could raise more money, at less cost per dollar, by seeking a few large gifts rather than reaching out to large numbers of small donors. The UJA's "major gifts" category—donations of $10,000 and more—ballooned. The New York federation alone saw major gifts grow from 48 percent of their total campaign income in 1980 to nearly 70 percent in 1987. Nationwide, UJA donors who gave $10,000 or more—less than 2 percent of all donors—contributed nearly 59 percent of all UJA-federation revenues in 1994. Twenty-four percent of the campaign that year came from a mere 906 individuals who gave $100,000 or more.

The rise in big gifts—not declining funds for Israel, not assimilation among young donors, and certainly not the declining UJA campaign total—is the most serious problem facing the organized Jewish community today, and it has brought this upon itself. There is little room left in the current system for the small donor. Most Jews are never approached by the UJA anymore.

The UJA is not alone in this development. AIPAC, which was once governed by the leadership of the Presidents Conference—however democratic that might have been—is now governed by a tiny group of its biggest donors. The result is that the most feared and respected pro-Israel lobbying organization can no longer be relied on to support the views of Israel, much less the views of American Jews. On the contrary, it lobbies for the views of its major donors, or it falls silent.

The American Jewish community faces a wrenching decision as it approaches the millenium.

The great battles of the last half-century are all but won. Israel's survival is largely assured, its legitimacy no longer even questioned except by a handful of outlaw states and their desperate minions. The Jews of Russia are free to practice their religion, or to leave, though no one knows for how long. Here at home, Jews have won acceptance as equal, even honored members of the American mosaic. Bill Clinton, the most pro-Jewish president in history, appointed no fewer than four Jews to his cabinet and two Jews to the Supreme Court. The American ambassador to Israel is a former AIPAC staffer. None of these appointments seems remarkable anymore— not even the sight of CIA director John Deutch visiting Israel with great fanfare to coordinate the two countries' joint efforts against terrorism, and taking an evening to visit his aunt in Tel Aviv.

Under the circumstances, it is tempting for some Jews to declare victory and walk away.

"There is a widespread sense that we've entered the post-rescue era of Jewish life," says David Twersky, the widely respected editor of the weekly *MetroWest Jewish News* in suburban New Jersey. "There's a sense that the central organizing principles of Jewish life outside the synagogue—rescue, defending Israel, creating an open society—have played themselves out."

In fact, much remains to be done. Jews are still fleeing the wreckage of the former Soviet Union at a rate of one hundred thousand per year, two thirds of them for Israel and one third for the United States, at an annual relocation cost of a quarter-billion dollars. Israel still faces powerful enemies; more important, its newfound partners have made peace only because they cannot destroy Israel as long as it is umbilically linked to Washington. The American Jewish lobby still has a great deal to do before its traditional civic tasks are complete.

At home, the Jewish community must begin to make sense of the new, post-liberal era that is emerging in American politics and society. For more than a quarter-century, Republicans have dominated the marketplace of ideas, while Democrats tried to hold together a fading coalition of yesterday's have-nots. The Jews' main ally for the last half-century—the New Deal coalition of labor, blacks, intellectuals, and Protestant church groups—has broken into a thousand pieces. The most vigorous force in national politics, the Republican right, symbolized by the House freshman class of 1994—isolationist on the international front, hostile to immigrants, championing Christian values—resembles nothing so much as a resurgence of the old Republican–Southern Democrat coalition that held shut America's gates in 1938.

No, there is no lack of work ahead for a strong, mobilized American Jewish community. What is lacking is domestic leadership. "For close to a half-century, in the absence of a strong, non-Orthodox religious leadership, everybody outside the Orthodox community has deferred to Israel," says journalist Twersky. "In the vacuum, we have a class of social workers and a group of rich people running our institutions. There's no arena for serious leaders to emerge."

During the Rabin years, when Israel refused to lead, the American Jews' institutional establishment stood still, frozen in time, unable to go back but unwilling to move forward. With the return of the Likud, the community leadership must make its choice. It can return to its old role as a mouthpiece for Jerusalem, silencing dissenters and ruling over a smaller, more cohesive Jewish community. Or the leaders can finally take the fate of American Judaism in their hands and reach out to the disaffected Jew with a message that makes sense, a traditional American Jewish message of compassion at home and hope abroad. This will require the courage to confront Israeli leaders head-on, to insist on an Israel-Diaspora partnership of equals.

For many of the Jewish community's senior officials, it is instead a time of great fear. "I'm afraid the days of Jewish power may be coming to an end," says the head of one major Jewish social-service agency. "If the

Republicans retain control of the House, it will mean a lot less influence for us. We simply don't have the same kinds of contacts with a Republican House dominated by guys from Indiana and Louisiana as we have in a Democratic House run by New Yorkers and Californians.

"We have good contacts among Republican moderates. But the hard-core leadership of the conservative wing, most of them come from areas where we just aren't a factor. They don't share our worldview. They're against government spending. They're against foreign aid. Where can it go but down?"

"It's a visionless time right now," says San Francisco real-estate developer Deborah Pell, former national chair of the UJA Young Leadership Cabinet. "Except for a few pieces, the system feels very broken right now. With the huge governmental cutbacks, people are going into a major slash mode. The social-service network that we've set up is going to get bashed. And this is at the same time that we're trying to launch a major effort for Jewish continuity. How do you expand Jewish education and cut social services? What kind of Jewish values are you teaching? And all this is at the same time that Israel is still calling for our help.

"I think people are very depressed. There is no real leadership. There isn't one person at the national level that people have faith in."

In fact, Jewish power could go up just as easily as down. The Jewish community retains enormous clout on the American scene. Jews are respected. Their concerns are taken seriously when they press them intelligently and respectfully. The community's institutions—especially the federations and the ADL, along with other defense agencies, the synagogue unions, and AIPAC—continue to command a loyal following and raise huge sums. The councils that unite them, NCRAC and the Presidents Conference, still meet regularly and are still capable of producing a strong, sensible consensus.

If those who lead these institutions can find it within themselves to step forward and speak for their public, the mainstream American Jews, they will find a ready following and a broader society that respects their courage. There is a solid, moderate center, willing and able to move forward and meet the next challenges. What is needed in the near term is mutual respect among Jews. The Jewish establishment and the Jewish public must start paying attention to each other, listening to each other, believing in each other. Each is able and willing to play the role required of it: leaders to lead, constituents to follow.

If Jews believed in themselves one half as much as non-Jews believe in them, they could continue to be a powerful force for their own good, and for America's.

EPILOGUE

Back to the Garden

S UNDAY, DECEMBER 10, 1995, was a freezing cold day in New York City. The temperature was barely fifteen degrees by eight o'clock that morning, when the Jews began gathering outside Madison Square Garden. They were coming to mourn the death of Israel's prime minister, Yitzhak Rabin, assassinated by an Orthodox Jewish zealot five weeks earlier.

They came by taxi and subway from all over New York City, by car and train from the suburbs, by chartered bus from as far away as Boston and Washington, D.C. Altogether, more than seventeen thousand people entered the arena, after waiting for hours in the bitter cold to pass one-by-one through ten malfunctioning metal detectors. Thousands more—no one knew how many—were turned away for lack of seats, including a busload that had left Washington before dawn.

Those who got in were treated to a moving tribute to the slain prime minister. There were speeches by his widow Leah Rabin, by his successor Shimon Peres, by the Orthodox chief rabbi of Israel, by Vice President Al Gore, World Jewish Congress president Edgar Bronfman, and others. Two Israeli pop stars sang, as did a choir of local Jewish parochial students under the direction of Marvin Hamlisch.

It was a powerful demonstration of Jewish solidarity, "something the kids should see at least once in their lifetime," said Philip Feuer, who had come with his wife and two small daughters from suburban Mamaroneck.

❖   ❖   ❖

In fact, the event itself was almost overshadowed by its logistics, which were historic in their ineptitude and would spark harsh recriminations in the days ahead. The Feuers had waited almost two hours in the cold before entering the Garden. Thousands of others had given up and gone home, daunted by the weather and the crush of the waiting, milling crowd. At least one former head of the Presidents Conference was kept out. So were the president-elect of the Reform movement and the editor of New Jersey's largest Jewish weekly.

The sponsors, including the Presidents Conference and New York UJA-Federation, had organized countless events many times this size in the past. They knew the drill. Yet something had gone very wrong this time.

Much of the morning's chaos was due to last-minute changes demanded by the Israeli and U.S. secret-service details assigned to protect Prime Minister Peres and Vice President Gore. They insisted on closing off an entire section of the auditorium a few hours before the event, reducing the number of available seats by 20 percent. They vetoed the organizers' plans to direct VIPs and the press through side entrances, instead forcing everyone through a single entryway.

But the Rabin memorial tribute suffered from a larger malaise: a malaise of the spirit. Almost from the moment that the event was conceived, the planning proceeded under a cloud of doubt and anxiety. The organizers were simply not sure they could fill Madison Square Garden.

For years, the community leadership had been rallying American Jews against external enemies. They had always drawn respectable crowds, often by relying on the cohesive, disciplined ranks of the Orthodox community. This time was different: they were trying to rally Jews in memory of a man who was widely reviled in the Orthodox community. Indeed, it was hostility among Orthodox Jews toward Rabin, carried to its extreme, that had killed him.

Would the Orthodox turn out to honor his memory? If they did not, who would? Was anybody else left out there?

Would the Jews come if they were called?

Rabin was killed on Saturday, November 4, 1995, while leaving a peace rally in Tel Aviv. His killer, apprehended on the scene, was Yigal Amir, a popular, successful law student at Orthodox-sponsored Bar Ilan University. Amir said that he had shot Rabin in order to stop his policy of giving away pieces of the land of Israel. He claimed that it was a religious imperative.

The leaders of Israel's religious right moved quickly to dissociate themselves from Amir. But news reports quickly revealed that his act had had theoretical grounding in the religious zealotry of the settler movement. Rabbis for months had been discussing the crime of giving away God's promised land, debating just how serious a crime it would be. An informant named three rabbis (one of them American-born) with close links to the settler movement, who reputedly judged the crime to be a capital offense. The three were called in for police questioning, to determine whether they might have influenced Amir. Others were called in as well, including some settler leaders.

While police began investigating whether the overheated rhetoric of the opposition right had helped create an atmosphere ripe for political violence, another probe focused on Rabin's own bodyguard detail. It found that the feared General Security Service, sometimes known by its Hebrew initials *Shin Bet*, had been overly concerned with threats from Arab terrorists and had paid too little attention to Jewish extremists.

By the end of December, the Israeli left was calling for a crackdown on the "ayatollahs" of the religious right, while rabbis, settler leaders, and opposition politicians were complaining of a witch-hunt. After a brief post-assassination lull, Israel's demolition derby–style political discourse was back to normal.

American Jewry, on the other hand, had no way of returning to normal. "Normal" meant rallying behind Israel in a wall-to-wall coalition. It meant papering over factional differences, insisting that what united Jews was more important than what divided them. It meant judging Jews by their commitment to the Jewish cause, their loyalty to Israel, and their opposition to its enemies.

This crisis was different, because it was entirely about the divisions among Israelis and Jews. There was no way to rally around the flag of Jewish unity and loyalty to Israel. It was loyalty to the land of Israel that had motivated Yigal Amir to shoot Yitzhak Rabin.

On the morning after the shooting, Israeli consul general Colette Avital met in her office with a group of local Jewish community leaders to plan a memorial service to mark the end of the traditional thirty-day mourning period. She wanted to fill Madison Square Garden with Jews rallying in memory of Rabin, in solidarity with Israel, and in support of the peace policies for which Rabin had died.

In midweek, the Presidents Conference offered to step in as the rally's chief sponsor. That would make it a national expression of Jewish sentiment instead of a local New York event. It would become a statement of complete American Jewish solidarity with Israel in its time of grief.

Almost as soon as the decision was made, problems began to surface. If the rally were to be an expression of the entire Jewish community, it could not adopt a theme that offended a whole sector of the community. Polls showed that most Orthodox Jews were opposed to the peace process that Rabin had launched, and for which he had been slain. Organize a rally "in support of the peace process," Orthodox leaders told the Presidents Conference, and the Orthodox community would stay away.

After several days of furious arguments back and forth between Israeli diplomats and Jewish leaders, a former Presidents Conference chair stepped in to suggest a compromise. The event would be advertised as a rally in support of "Israel and its pursuit of peace," but not of "the peace process." Speakers at the rally would be asked to avoid direct mention of "the peace process," in order not to offend Orthodox participants. The Orthodox organizations accepted the compromise and the rally proceeded as planned.

That was not the end of it, however. Planning meetings became a nonstop tug-of-war between the Israeli consulate and the Presidents Conference. From each side, there were others looking over the negotiators' shoulders, feeding in suggestions to infuriate the other side. At one meeting, it was suggested that Barbra Streisand be invited to perform. Orthodox groups said that her presence would keep them from the rally, since Orthodox rabbinic law forbids men from listening to the seductive sounds of a woman's singing voice. It turned out that Streisand was not available, in any case. But Miri Aloni was available; the popular Israeli chanteuse had led the singing of the Israeli left-wing anthem "Song of Peace" at the rally where Rabin was slain. Israeli officials insisted that she be permitted to sing. The argument had not yet been settled by the day before the rally.

On the other side, Mort Klein, president of the Zionist Organization of America, urged the organizers to invite a leader of Israel's Likud opposition to speak, to show a united Jewish opposition to political murder. Not inviting the opposition, Klein said, would make the rally a partisan demonstration of the left-wing. The consulate angrily rejected the idea. The lead speaker at the rally was to be Shimon Peres, and he, Avital noted, was "not the leader of the left but the prime minister of the state of Israel." Demanding equal time for the right-wing was, in effect, an attack on the government's legitimacy. The ZOA now announced that it would not participate. Shortly afterward, the National Council of Young Israel, a small congregational group to the right of the Orthodox Union, announced the same thing.

The *Jewish Press,* the mass-circulation voice of Brooklyn Orthodoxy, spoke for an unknown segment of traditionalist Jewry with a front-page editorial the week after Rabin's assassination, expressing "our grief over the death of the Prime Minister," but insisting that opposition to the peace process had nothing to do with the crime. In fact, asserted Rabbi Sholom Klass, the newspaper's publisher, it was the policies of the Rabin government that had fostered the violent atmosphere splitting Israeli politics. The "Peace Process violates the commandments of our Holy Torah," Klass wrote. "G-d promised our ancestors that the entire land of Biblical Israel was to be an inheritance for the Children of Israel in perpetuity." Supporters of the government peace policy were like the Pharaohs of Egypt in mocking God's will.

The tug-of-war over Orthodox participation had several implications. The larger one, perhaps, was philosophical: should the Jews pull together in this time of crisis, as they always had in crises past? Would they seek the lowest common denominator and make their stand there?

"I don't know how they did it," said the editor of one major Jewish weekly. "One month ago, Orthodox extremism killed Rabin, and now, somehow, they're the victims. They're geniuses."

But the more immediate question was the practical one: whether the Jewish community could fill Madison Square Garden without the Orthodox. Nobody had tried it in years. Discussion of non-Orthodox Jewry in recent years had focused mainly on assimilation and intermarriage. They were not giving to the UJA, not joining Jewish organizations, not marrying other Jews. How could one depend on them to show up en masse to fill the Garden on three weeks' notice?

And so the rally was watered down and watered down. A week before the event, the weekly *Jewish Forward* printed a report about the Barbra Streisand debate, fueling feminist anger across the city. There was talk of women boycotting the rally in protest. The turnout of the right was even more important. A few days before the rally, the ZOA and the National Council of Young Israel placed an ad in the *New York Times* to announce that they were boycotting and urging others to do the same.

And yet they came. On the morning of December 10, more than twenty thousand Jews gathered in the frigid cold outside Madison Square Garden and waited patiently to enter. Orthodox Jews were part of the crowd—up to 30 percent, by one estimate. The rest were non-Orthodox Jews, mainstream Jews from cities and suburbs up and down the East Coast.

The speakers, who had promised not to dwell on the peace process, spoke of it anyway, and the crowd applauded them for it. Leah Rabin, the slain leader's widow, got the second-warmest applause of the day when she said, "I see that in his death he bequested to us peace . . . peace which will come despite the opponents of peace."

The biggest applause was for Vice President Gore, who said, "Today we must show with conviction, with one steady voice, that the enemies of peace will not deter us from our causes. We will not be daunted. We will not be afraid." And they applauded Shimon Peres when he declared that Rabin "never tried to please you. He tried to lead you."

They sang along, haltingly, when Israeli pop star David Broza led them in a Hebrew song that most had never heard, *"Yihyeh Tov"*—"It will be all right." Swaying, clapping, singing softly, they reached out to the mainstream Jewish community of Israel, over the heads of the Jewish leaders who had tried to mold them in a way they never wanted to be molded.

They had come, perhaps, to reclaim their community, if only for a moment. Then they scattered again to the suburbs.

It remained to be seen whether their leaders saw them there, and realized that they were there to be led.

NOTES

PROLOGUE

Page xvii   Author interview with Shoshana Cardin, October 14, 1992.

Page xx   Quotes from Cardin's letter to Bush and Bush's reply are from texts released to the press by the Presidents Conference.

Page xxi   Author interview with James Carville, December 11, 1992.

Page xxii   Author interview with James Carville, December 11, 1992.

Page xxii   Author interview with Jacqueline Levine, July 26, 1993.

Page xxii   Author interview with Ed Ames, March 14, 1994.

Page xxii   Author interview (on condition of anonymity), March 13, 1994.

Page xxv   Author interview with Richard Thornburgh, December 5, 1991.

Page xxv   Author interview with James Carville, December 11, 1992.

Page xxvi   Author interview with Harris Wofford, March 14, 1994.

CHAPTER 1

Page 4   Author interview with David Luchins, September 2, 1992.

Page 5   Author interview with Mohamed al-Orabi, January 25, 1993.

Page 6   Biale, *Power and Powerlessness in Jewish History*, p. 199.

Page 6   A 1992 survey by the Anti-Defamation League found 20 percent of Americans holding what it called "strongly anti-Semitic" attitudes (more on this poll in chapter 12), down from 37 percent a decade earlier. Surveys by the National Opinion Research Center at the University of Chicago have suggested that 20 percent may be the baseline minimum of Americans who will express hostility toward almost any group.

Page 6   Statistics on Jewish fears of anti-Semitism are drawn from the American Jewish Committee's periodic National Survey of American Jews, 1983–1989, and from *Highlights of the CJF 1990 National Jewish Population Survey*.

In the National Survey of American Jews, respondents are asked to answer "yes" or "no" to the assertion: "Anti-Semitism is currently not a serious problem for American Jews." Answering "no," 1983: 45 percent; 1986: 54 percent; 1989: 73 percent (National Survey of American Jews 1989, p. 8.).

In the CJF 1990 National Jewish Population Survey, respondents were asked: "Do you agree or disagree that anti-Semitism is a serious problem in the U.S. today?" Among "core Jews," 82 percent agreed (*Highlights of the CJF 1990 National Jewish Population Survey*, p. 29).

Page 7   Kristol, "The Future of American Jewry," pp. 21–22.

Page 12   Hertzberg, *The Jews in America,* pp. 13–14.

Page 13   Jacobs, *Is Curly Jewish?,* p. 140ff.

Page 13   Findley, *They Dare to Speak Out,* p. 25.

Page 14   Ball and Ball, *The Passionate Attachment,* p. 207.

Page 16   Author interview with Abraham Foxman, September 2, 1992.

Page 16   Author interview with agency head, on condition of anonymity, November 2, 1992.

Page 18   Author interview with David Luchins, September 2, 1992.

CHAPTER 2

Page 22   Author interview with Michael Lieberman, February 5, 1995.

Page 22   Author interview with Oliver Thomas, February 7, 1995.

Page 23   Medding, "Towards a General Theory of Jewish Political Interests and Behaviour," p. 115.

Page 23   Liberal vs. conservative statistics reported by Robert Scheer, "Jews in U.S. Committed to Equality," *Los Angeles Times,* April 13, 1988.

Page 25   Family income data for all families is taken from U.S. Bureau of Census figures, March 1992. For Jewish families, the 1990 National Jewish Population Survey by the Council of Jewish Federations shows median annual household income at $39,000 (Highlights of NJPS, p. 19). The 1993 National Survey of American Jews by the American Jewish Committee shows just under $50,000 annually (p. 55).

Page 25   Richard Brookhiser quoted in book review by Elliot Abrams in *The American Spectator,* December 1994, p. 78.

Page 26   Steven M. Cohen, *The Dimensions of American Jewish Liberalism,* p. 17.

Page 26   Pogrebin, *Deborah, Golda and Me,* p. 113.

Page 26   Author interview with Letty Cottin Pogrebin, February 8, 1995.

Page 26   Lefkowitz, "Jewish Voters and the Democrats," p. 38ff.

Page 27   In Ruth Wisse, *If I Am Not for Myself: The Liberal Betrayal of the Jews,* p. 35.

Page 27   Author interview with the Reverend Calvin Butts, February 5, 1993.

Page 28   Author interview with Oliver Thomas, February 7, 1995.

Page 28   Author interview with Hyman Bookbinder, April 1993.

Page 28   Author interview with Hideo Sato, January 7, 1993.

Page 29   Benjamin Nones quoted in Schappes, *A Documentary History of the Jews,* p. 95.

Page 29   Nones's response to "Solomons" quoted in Borden, *Jews, Turks and Infidels,* p. 26. Emphasis in original.

Page 29   Republican overtures (1860 on) in Borden, p. 57f.

Page 30   Jewish voter registration and participation figures from author interviews with Morris Amitay, political consultant, and Irving Silverman, director of the

Jewish Voter Registration Campaign (sponsored by the Synagogue Council of America), June 1992.

Page 30   Jewish population figures from *The American Jewish Year Book,* 1995 ed. Jewish electorate figures from author interview with Morris Amitay, June 1992.

Page 32   Author interview with William Schneider, June 1992.

Page 33   Author interview with Maxwell Rabb, December 10, 1992.

Page 34   Jewish vote, 1916–72: data from Isaacs, *Jews and American Politics* pp. 152–4. General vote, 1916–60: data from *Encyclopedia of American Facts and Dates,* 3d ed., page entries by year. General vote, 1964–72: data from *The World Almanac,* 1989 ed., p. 103. All figures for 1976–92: data from *New York Times,* November 5, 1992, p. B9.

Page 35   The discussion of the Helms amendment is based on telephone interviews conducted by the author on February 7, 1995, with Jim Halpert of People for the American Way, Michael Lieberman of the ADL, Robert Peck of the ACLU, August Steinhilber of the National School Boards Association, and Oliver Thomas of the National Council of Churches.

Page 39   Community budget is author's calculation. To my knowledge, no scholarly estimate has ever been published.

Page 40   Author interview with Seymour Reich, March 1992.

Page 40   Author interview with David Harris, October 8, 1992.

Page 41   Incidents regarding the Louisiana abortion debate reconstructed from August 1990 author interviews with Robert Loewy, Leslie Gerwin, Madalyn Schenk, an aide to Senator Mike Cross, and New Orleans *Times-Picayune* political reporter John Pope, and from reports in the *Times-Picayune,* June 8, 1990. Biblical quote from *The Holy Scriptures According to the Masoretic Text,* vol. 1, p. 176.

Page 44   Author interview with Max Fisher, February 11, 1993.

Page 44   Robertson quotes taken from *The Collected Works of Pat Robertson,* (Inspirational Press, 1994) pp. 256–257, quoted by Michael Lind, "Rev. Robertson's Grand International Conspiracy Theory," p. 23.

Page 46   Author interview with David Zwiebel, December 1992; with Robert Peck, February 7, 1995; with Aryeh Neier, February 22, 1995.

CHAPTER 3

Page 48   Descriptions of events at White House, including quotes from briefing, are drawn from author's reporter notes.

Page 49   Author interview with Malcolm Hoenlein, December 7, 1994.

Page 50   Abraham Foxman quote from testimony before Large City Budgeting Conference of CJF, New York, November 11, 1992, from author's reporter notes.

Page 50   Lou Borman, Lawrence Rubin quotes: author interviews, May 3, 1993.

Page 51   The figure most often cited is the UJA-federation combined "general campaign" total of just over $700 million annually. It has stagnated in recent years, giving rise to much-publicized fears of disaster (more in chapter 13). But this figure does not include the local federations' capital campaigns, endowment campaigns, or "second-line" campaigns for Israeli urban renewal and Soviet refugee resettlement, bringing the annual total to more than $1 billion.

Page 55   Author interview with Israeli government source, on condition of anonymity, May 8, 1994.

Page 55   Author interview with congressional source, on condition of anonymity, August 18, 1994.

Page 57   ADL figures on estimates of American Jewish population by non-Jews from 1992 survey by Marttila and Kiley, master questionnaire, p. 10, question 75.

Page 57   Jewish population compared to other U.S. religious groups from *The World Almanac,* 1993 ed., p. 717.

Page 57   Author telephone interview with Sidney Goldstein, November 1990.

Page 58   The 1.8 percent figure came about as follows: the researchers who prepared the CJF's 1990 National Jewish Population Survey also published a broader survey of American religions for their cosponsor, the City University of New York, in 1991. The CJF's research had shown that of 5.5 million Jews in America (2.2 percent of the population), 4.3 million said they were Jewish "by religion." The rest identified themselves as Jewish by "ethnicity," "nationality," or "culture." The CUNY study gave the number of Americans claiming Jewish "religion" as 4.3 million, or 1.8 percent. The news media promptly reported a "new finding" that Jews had fallen below 2 percent of the U.S. population. The researchers declined to make any effort to correct the misinformation, contending in interviews with this author that it was "a matter of interpretation."

Page 58   The CJF's 1990 National Jewish Population Survey figures from in *The American Jewish Year Book,* 1992 ed., p. 172.

Page 58   The American Jewish Committee's 1989 survey figures from Steven M. Cohen, *Content or Continuity?,* p. 67.

Page 59   Steven M. Cohen, *American Modernity and Jewish Identity,* pp. 143–153.

Page 60   Author interview with journalist, on condition of anonymity, May 22, 1994.

Page 62   Author interview with rabbi, on condition of anonymity, April 6, 1995.

Page 62   Author interview with Eugene Fisher, December 21, 1992.

Page 62   Author interview with Ralph Reed, May 8, 1995.

Page 64   On Jewish involvement by denomination see Steven M. Cohen, *Content or Continuity?,* pp. 63, 75. See also Peter Medding et al., "Jewish Identity in Conversionary and Mixed Marriages," *American Jewish Year Book, 1992,* pp. 57–60. On "civic" leadership, see Steven M. Cohen, *Israel-Diaspora Relations: A Survey of American Jewish Leaders,* p. 23. See also Renae Cohen and Sherry Rosen, *Organizational Affiliation,* pp. 56–59.

Page 65   On membership and giving rates, see American Jewish Committee, *In the Aftermath of the Rabin Assassination: A Survey of American Jewish Opin-*

ion About Israel and the Peace Process (New York: American Jewish Committee, February 1996), p. 28. See also Steven M. Cohen, *Content or Continuity?*, p. 56; also *Los Angeles Times Poll Number 149: Israel and the Palestinians* (1988, no page numbers).

Page 66   Author interview with Pinchas Stolper, November 1992.

Page 66   Phil Krupp quote from author's reporter notes.

Page 68   Author interview with Steven M. Cohen, August 17, 1994.

Page 68   Author interviews with Barry Kosmin, Calvin Goldscheider, August 24, 1994.

Page 69   Richard Dreyfuss, Mortimer Zuckerman quotes from author's reporter notes, May 17, 1992. Elie Wiesel reply reported by columnist Tim Boxer in *New York Jewish Week,* May 29, 1992.

Page 70   All figures regarding Israel drawn from the American Jewish Committee, *The Israeli Peace Initiative and the Israel-PLO Accord: A Follow-Up Survey.* Conducted for the American Jewish Committee by Market Facts, Inc., August 11–18, 1994. One thousand respondents; estimated margin of error 3 percent.

Page 71   Rankings of Jewish symbols and activities from 1989 American Jewish Committee poll. See Steven M. Cohen, *Content or Continuity?*

Page 71   Data on most important quality to Jewish identity reported by Robert Scheer, "Jews in U.S. Committed to Equality," *Los Angeles Times,* April 13, 1988. In 1995 the American Jewish Committee added the "most important quality" question to its periodic surveys of American Jews, offering a fourth choice: "Being part of the Jewish people." "Being part" now took 51 percent, followed by religion and social justice at 17 percent each. "Support for Israel" was picked by 2 percent.

Page 71   Kristol, "The Future of American Jewry," pp. 21–26. "Conservative synagogue" quote from author interview, October 1991.

Page 72   Daniel Elazar column appeared in *Moment,* October 1995, p. 28f.

Page 72   For a fuller exploration of this three-way division, see *Content or Continuity?* by Steven M. Cohen, to whom I am indebted for the insight. See especially his comparison of three different surveys—his own AJC survey, the *Los Angeles Times* national survey, and the Brandeis University "seven-city" composite portraits—for confirmation of the relatively high figures cited here.

Page 72   Figures on observance and importance of rituals from *The Israeli Peace Initiative and the Israel-PLO Accord: A Follow-Up Survey.* See questions 30 to 34.

Page 73   Figures on loyalty to Judaism from 1989 American Jewish Committee poll. See Steven M. Cohen, *Content or Continuity?*

Page 74   Edgar Bronfman quotes from text supplied by CJF.

Page 76   Michael Lerner, "Who Speaks for American Jews?" *New York Times* oped page, February 24, 1989.

Page 76   Author interview with Jacqueline Levine, July 26, 1993.

Page 76   Author interview with Rabbi Israel Miller, January 24, 1994.

Page 77   Lookstein quotes from author's reporter notes, February 14, 1994.

Page 77   Morris Abram quoted in Robert Scheer, "Pollard Outrage," *Los Angeles Times,* June 11, 1987, p. 1.

Page 77   Nathan Perlmutter quoted in *Los Angeles Times* obituary of Perlmutter, July 14, 1987.

Page 77   Cohen column in *Washington Post,* March 10, 1987. Shamir quoted in Cohen column.

Page 78   Avraham Weiss quote from author's reporter notes.

Page 78   Author interview with official, March 1992.

Page 79   Survey figures on Pollard in Steven M. Cohen, *After the Gulf War: American Jews' Attitudes Toward Israel. The 1991 National Survey of American Jews,* (New York: American Jewish Committee, October 1991), p. 59.

CHAPTER 4

Page 84   For texts and chronology of Jewish correspondence with Washington, see Schappes, *A Documentary History of the Jews,* p. 77 ff. The Savannah letter is dated May 1789 in some sources, but all evidence suggests that this is an error. So much attention is given to the "delay" that it seems unlikely that the letter was actually sent just weeks after the inauguration.

Page 90   "Throughout their suffering . . .": Yirmiyahu Yovel, *Spinoza and Other Heretics,* p. 19.

Page 90   "[r]eligious skepticism . . .": Yovel, p. 26.

Page 90   Immolation dates in Cecil Roth, *A History of the Marranos,* p. 350. A Jesuit priest was burned in 1761, but not for "Judaizing." The Inquisition was formally abolished in 1825.

Page 91   On colonial-era Jewish schools, see Schappes, p. 113.

Page 92   De Tocqueville, *Democracy in America,* pp. 314, 317.

Page 92   Charleston synagogue petition quoted in Schappes, p. 171f.

Page 93   On Sunday-closing laws, see Naomi W. Cohen, *Jews in Christian America,* p. 63. On alliances with Catholics, see Schappes, pp. 126f, 139f.

Page 94   The 1832 petition is quoted from Schappes, p. 186.

Page 94   Mordecai M. Noah's letter to Robert Smith quoted in Jonathan Sarna, *Jacksonian Jew: The Two Worlds of Mordecai Manuel Noah,* p. 8. James Monroe's letter dismissing Noah is quoted in Sarna, p. 26.

Page 95   Abolitionist group quoted in Sloan, *The Jews in America, 1621–1970,* p. 74.

Page 95   For Leeser's view on slavery, see Schappes, p. 321. For Wise's opposition to abolition, see Grose, *Israel in the Mind of America,* p. 28.

Page 96   French Premier Louis Thiers is quoted in Howard M. Sachar, *The Course of Modern Jewish History,* p. 135.

Page 97   On the Mortara affair, Schappes, p. 674.

Page 98   Jewish fund-raising for overseas in Goldin *Why They Give,* p. 33.

Page 98   On Romanian pogroms, Sachar, *A History of the Jews in America,* pp. 83–84; also Schappes, pp. 545–546, 549–550.

Page 99   On the exaggerated riot death tolls, Schappes, p. 543 ff.

Page 101   Wise quote from Sachar, p. 125. *Tribune* quote from Goldin, p. 52. University Settlement and Bingham quotes in Fried, *Rise and Fall of the Jewish Gangster in America*, p. 54f.

Page 102   Theodore Roosevelt quoted in Rufus Learsi, *The Jews in America: A History*, p. 202.

CHAPTER 5

Page 109   Elliot Abrams and Ralph Reed quotes from author's reporter notes.

Page 111   Coolidge's views from Sachar, *A History of the Jews in America*, p. 324.

Page 111   The refugee bill of 1939 is discussed in Morse, *While Six Million Died*, p. 211.

Page 112   *Fortune* poll of 1939 from Morse, p. 213.

Page 112   Author interview with Arnold Aronson, December 1993.

Page 113   Wilson, "Thomas Jefferson and the Character Issue."

Page 113   Lookstein, *Were We Our Brothers' Keepers?*, p. 33.

Page 114   Wyman, *The Abandonment of the Jews*, p. 285.

Page 114   UJA luncheon invocation quote from author's reporter notes.

Page 115   Morse, p. 208.

Page 116   *Newsweek* report, November 30, 1942, quoted in Wyman, p. 57.

Page 117   Stember et al., *Jews in the Mind of America*, reports poll results for "menace," p. 128; "too much power," p. 121; "hiring a Jewish employee," p. 94; "Anti-Jewish feeling is rising," p. 79.

Page 118   Jews-Communism poll cited by Morton Keller, "Jews and the Character of American Life since 1930," in Stember, p. 268.

Page 118   Gabler's *An Empire of Their Own*, pp. 351–386, contains a concise, objective review of anti-Semitism in the 1944 HUAC Hollywood hearings; see especially the role of the ADL and the LA-CRC, p. 375f. Arnold Forster's own account of his activities for the ADL during McCarthy's anti-communist hearings appears in his autobiography, *Square One*, pp. 117–34 and 145–73.

Page 119   Stember, p. 83, shows polls from 1942 through 1946 asking reasons for the decline in anti-Semitism, but notes that only a minority believed that there had been a decline in the first place. Morton Keller (in Stember p. 268) dissects the polls and dismisses most of the reasons, including the role of Israel. He cites 1950s poll data revealing that most Americans do not associate American Jews with the Middle East crisis. (Keller's use of that poll seems weak, however.)

Page 119   Author interview with Arnold Forster, April 20, 1993.

Page 121   Author interview with Will Maslow, December 23, 1992.

Page 122   Pfeffer quotes taken from the NCRAC "Report of the Plenary Session," June 27–30, 1963, Atlantic City, New Jersey (from the NCRAC archive).

Page 123   Florida case in Naomi W. Cohen, *Jews in Christian America*, p. 192–197.

Page 124   U.S. Supreme Court, *Engel v. Vitale*, June 25, 1962; Justice Hugo Black for the majority. Quoted in Naomi W. Cohen, *Jews in Christian America*, p. 170.

Page 124   *Engel* reactions in Cohen, p. 172.

Page 124   William Brennan quote in Cohen, p. 203.

Page 124   "Social revolution" from 1964 CLSA report, quoted in Cohen, p. 203.

Page 126   Author interview with Irving Levine, March 7, 1995.

Page 126   Author interview with Israel Miller, January 24, 1994.

Page 127   Author interview with Irving Levine, March 7, 1995.

Page 129   The most important anti-Jewish refugee amendment was a technicality that required applicants to prove they had been living in a displaced-persons camp in the American zone since December 22, 1945. For complicated reasons, this rule effectively excluded most Jews, as its drafters knew would happen. Leonard Dinnerstein's *America and the Survivors of the Holocaust*, pp. 117–182, offers a thorough and masterly account of the American Jewish Committee's losing battle against the Senate isolationists, principally West Virginia Republican William Chapman Revercomb and Nevada Democrat Pat McCarran.

Page 129   On identities of DP act beneficiaries, see Dinnerstein, p. 251.

Page 130   Slawson quoted in Naomi W. Cohen, *Not Free To Desist*, p. 262. Slawson's role in the evolution of the Committee is based on Cohen's book and author interviews with Irving Levine, others.

Page 132   Oscar and Mary F. Handlin, "The Acquisition of Political and Social Rights by the Jews in the United States," p. 90f.

CHAPTER 6

Page 134   Eliezer Livneh, writing in *Ha'aretz*, May 31, 1967, quoted in Segev, *The Seventh Million*, p. 391.

Page 134   Eban quote taken from Laqueur, *The Israel-Arab Reader*, p. 221.

Page 134   Author interview with Jacqueline Levine, July 26, 1993.

Page 135   Author interview with Paul Berger, July 28, 1993.

Page 135   Author interview with Shoshana Cardin, October 14, 1992.

Page 136   Author interview with M. J. Rosenberg, August 6, 1993.

Page 136   Author interview with Richard Schifter, September 21, 1992.

Page 136   Author interview with Shoshana Cardin, October 14, 1992.

Page 136   Regarding intelligence analyses, see for example William Quandt, *Peace Process*, p. 28.

Page 137   "a sudden realization . . .": Milton Himmelfarb, "The 1967 War," originally published in *Commentary*, October 1967; reprinted in *The Jews of Modernity*, p. 344.

Page 137   "How then shall we . . .": Himmelfarb, p. 346.

Page 139   Cuba severed relations with Israel in October 1973, together with a group of states in sub-Saharan Africa that broke ties after Israeli troops crossed the Suez Canal in the Yom Kippur War.

Page 140   M. J. Rosenberg, "To Uncle Tom and Other Such Jews," originally published in *The Village Voice,* February 13, 1969; reprinted in Porter and Dreier, *Jewish Radicalism,* p. 10.

Page 141   Leaflet quoted in Jonathan Kaufman, *Broken Alliance,* p. 146.

Page 141   Shanker discussed in Kaufman, p. 147.

Page 142   "The sound heard . . .": Kaufman, p. 155.

Page 147   Marshall Sklare, "Lakeville and Israel: The Six-Day War and Its Aftermath," originally published in *Midstream,* October 1968; reprinted in Sklare, *Observing America's Jews,* p. 120ff.

Page 148   Sklare "sense of loss" data from Sklare and Greenblum, *Jewish Identity on the Suburban Frontier,* p. 215ff. Sklare "essential to being a good Jew," data, ibid., p. 322.

Page 148   Cohen "personal tragedy" data from Steven M. Cohen, *Ties and Tensions: The 1989 Survey of American Jewish Attitudes Toward Israel and Israelis* (New York: American Jewish Committee, July 1989), p. 8.

Page 149   Cohen "essential to being a good Jew" data from Steven M. Cohen, *Content or Continuity?,* p. 72.

Page 151   Brandeis speech in Symphony Hall, Boston, 1914 (no date given), quoted in Philippa Strum, *Louis D. Brandeis: Justice for the People,* p. 258.

Page 152   On Henry Byroade-Nahum Goldmann conversation, see Edward Tivnan, *The Lobby,* p. 40. See also Howard M. Sachar, *History of the Jews in America,* p. 725f.

Page 154   Author interview with Irving Levine, March 7, 1995.

Page 157   About Eisenhower's decision, see Peter Golden, *Quiet Diplomat,* pp. xviii–xix.

Page 159   Author interview with Irving Kristol, September 1991.

CHAPTER 7

Page 164   Senator Henry Jackson quote reconstructed from verbatim accounts given in author interviews with participants.

Page 166   Regarding the Liaison Bureau, see Max Kampelman, *Entering New Worlds,* pp. 194–195.

Page 167   Bertram Podell's role in the Jackson amendment is reconstructed from interviews with several sources, including Podell and the unidentified source quoted here.

Page 168   Author interview with Malcolm Hoenlein, August 31, 1992.

Page 169   Author interview with Mark Talisman, May 12, 1995.

Page 170   Author interview with Jack Stein, December 18, 1992; author interview with Max Fisher, February 11, 1993.

Page 170   Account of April 1973 Presidents Conference meeting from author interviews with participants.

Page 172   Tass quotes from William H. Korey, "The Struggle over the Jackson Amendment," *American Jewish Year Book, 1976,* vol. 76, p. 164.

Page 172   On the unraveling of the Kissinger-Jackson agreement, see Isaacson, *Kissinger: A Biography* (with which Kissinger cooperated), pp. 618–620.

Page 173   Author interview with Pete Lakeland, May 18, 1995.

Page 173   Author interview with Jerry Goodman, August 27, 1992.

Page 174   Author interview with Max Fisher, February 12, 1993.

Page 174   Author interview with Mark Talisman, May 18, 1995.

Page 176   Author interview with Jess Hordes, March 22, 1993.

Page 177   On Johnson's veto, see Bard, *The Water's Edge and Beyond,* p. 92.

Page 177   ADL activity from Forster, *An Oral Memoir,* p. 411.

Page 177   For Israeli reactions to boycott, see Bard, pp. 95–96.

Page 178   Sapir anecdote from Forster, *An Oral Memoir,* p. 426f.

Page 178   Boycott-related trade figures from Bard, p. 100.

Page 178   William Simon quote from Mitchell Bard, *The Water's Edge and Beyond,* p. 100.

Page 180   Author interview with Jess Hordes, March 22, 1993.

Page 182   Author interview with Philip Bernstein, May 12, 1995.

Page 183   Author interview with Mark Talisman, May 12, 1995.

Page 186   On the numbers of war criminals admitted under the Displaced Persons acts, see former OSI director Ryan, *Quiet Neighbors,* p. 27.

Page 187   Holtzman campaign in Ryan, p. 53ff.

Page 187   Assistant Secretary of State Linwood Holton (under Kissinger), quoted in Ryan, p. 54.

Page 188   ABC-TV broadcast March 25, 1995, cited in OSI press packet.

Page 188   Author interview with Neal Sher, May 8, 1995.

Page 189   Buchanan quoted in David Friedman, "But Can They Bury the Truth?," *Newsday,* February 22, 1995.

Page 190   From Sixth Circuit U.S. Court of Appeals ruling issued November 17, 1993, authored by Judge Gilbert Merritt. *Demjanjuk v Petrovsky,* 10 F3d 338, 355 (6th Cir. 1993). Cited in Lubet, "That's Funny, You Don't Look Like You Control the Government: The Sixth Circuit's Narrative on Jewish Power," p. 1530n.

Page 190   Lubet, p. 1528f. In a footnote, he explains that his reference to the last century was an allusion to Ulysses Grant's Order No. 11 of December 1862, expelling "Jews as a class" from military zones to prevent cross-border smuggling to the Confederacy.

Page 190   Author interview with Eli Rosenbaum.

Page 192   Holocaust memorial discussed in Judith Miller, *One, by One, by One,* p. 255ff.

Page 193   Author interview with Stuart Eizenstat, March 22, 1993.

Page 193   "Genocide" etymology from Gribetz et al., *The Timetables of Jewish History,* p. 453.

Page 193   Ted Turner quoted in the *Jerusalem Post,* August 18, 1995, p. 12, citing the New York *Post,* July 12, 1995. "Speaking to an audience of TV critics in Pasadena, California, the mogul lamented his inability to purchase a broadcast television network: 'I feel like those Jewish people in Germany in 1942,' he said. 'I know exactly what it is to be rounded up, herded out and sent to the east, somewhere, to be resettled.' "

Page 194   A good account of the efforts to include Armenians in the Holocaust museum appears in Judith Miller, p. 259.

Page 194   Author interview with Stuart Eizenstat, March 22, 1993.

Page 195   Author interview with Paul Berger, July 28, 1993.

Page 195   Author interview with Hyman Bookbinder, April 26, 1993.

CHAPTER 8

Page 197   Tivnan, *The Lobby,* p. 138.

Page 198   Spanier and Uslaner, *American Foreign Policy Making and the Democratic Dilemmas,* p. 244.

Page 201   Author interview with Thomas Dine, December 2, 1992.

Page 204   Author interview with Albert Chernin, January 6, 1994.

Page 205   Author interview with Israel Miller, January 24, 1994.

Page 205   "Complicity" quote from NJCRAC *Joint Program Plan 1977–78,* pp. 8–9.

Page 206   Author interview with Chernin.

Page 208   The most detailed history of Breira appears in "The Breira Story" by William Novak, a lengthy article published in *Genesis 2,* a Boston Jewish student monthly. A useful but less reliable account appears in Tivnan, *The Lobby,* pp. 90–96. The author was also given access to the files of Breira cofounder Peter Geffen.

Page 208   Irving Howe, "For Free Discussion in the Jewish Community," in *InterChange,* Breira monthly publication.

Page 208   Dinitz quoted in Howe, "For Free Discussion in the Jewish Community."

Page 209   Carter's Middle East goals cited in Tivnan, p. 101, based on his interview with Cyrus Vance.

Page 209   Carter's rapid loss of Jewish support in early 1977 is reviewed in detail by Tivnan, pp. 98–104.

Page 209   Author interview with Chernin.

Page 210   Author interview with Alexander Schindler, March 30, 1993.

Page 211   Sadat quote from Gribetz et al., *The Timetables of Jewish History,* p. 638.

Page 212   On Dayan's motives for quitting, see Gribetz et al., p. 648, and Quandt, *Decade of Decisions,* p. 328.

Page 212   Author interview with Chernin.

Page 212   The eight leaders who visited Israel in April 1978 were: Albert Chernin and Theodore Mann, executive director and president of NCRAC; Naomi Levine and Howard Squadron, executive director and president of the American Jewish Congress; Bertram Gold and Richard Wexler, executive vice president and president of the American Jewish Committee; and Benjamin Epstein and Burton Joseph, national director and chairman of the Anti-Defamation League.

Page 213   "might have difficulty . . .": Paul Findley, *They Dare to Speak Out*, p. 29.

Page 214   On Beirut resolution, see Findley, p. 28ff.

Page 215   Jewish vote figures from Sachar, *The Course of Modern Jewish History*, p. 824.

Page 216   Opinion poll data from Steven M. Cohen, "Attitudes of American Jews toward Israel and Israelis: The 1983 Survey of American Jews and Jewish Communal Leaders."

Page 217   Author interview with Peres advisor, May 17, 1988.

Page 221   Sportswriters quoted in "Portland Trail Blazers 1970–1995: From Dream to Business Empire," by Dwight Jaynes, Portland *Oregonian*, November 4, 1994.

Page 222   Author interview with William Quandt, June 23, 1993.

Page 223   Author interview with Jennifer Laszlo, March 13, 1994.

Page 226   Author interview with former AIPAC staffer, January 24, 1996.

CHAPTER 9

Page 229   Author interview with Abba Eban, September 23, 1993.

Page 231   Author interview with Stuart Eizenstat, March 22, 1993.

Page 232   ". . . through a prism" quote from author interview with State Department official, on condition of anonymity.

Page 232   Author interview with Dennis Ross, January 12, 1994.

Page 233   Author interview with administration official, on condition of anonymity.

Page 234   Author interview with Senator Paul Wellstone, September 21, 1992.

Page 234   Author interview with Richard Schifter, September 21, 1992.

Page 235   Author interview with Herman Cohen, January 23, 1993.

Page 236   Author interview with Michael Schneider, May 25, 1991.

Page 238   "He also suspected . . .": Kissinger, *White House Years*, p. 348.

Page 238   Author interview with William Quandt, June 23, 1993.

Page 239   Author interview with Morris Amitay, December 21, 1992.

Page 239   Author interview with Peter Rodman, June 21, 1995.

Page 239   Author interview with Israel Miller, January 24, 1994.

Page 241   "a Texas oilman . . .": Walter Isaacson, *Kissinger*, p. 513; on Schlesinger's sympathies, p. 519.

Page 243   Meir quote, Jackson-Javits references: Isaacson, pp. 528–529.

Page 243   "We did not think . . .": Kissinger, *Years of Upheaval*, p. 558.

Page 244   "The Geneva conference . . .": Kissinger, p. 798.

Page 245   Author interview with Rodman.

Page 246   Author interview with Quandt.

Page 247   Nayef Hawatmeh's views of Algiers conference were described to the author in an interview with a Hawatmeh deputy at U.N. headquarters in New York, November 1988.

Page 248   Jewish voting figures from Isaacs, *Jews and American Politics,* pp. 152–153.

Page 248   Author interview with Rodman.

Page 249   Schlesinger quoted in Isaacson, p. 521.

Page 249   "ranks high on the list . . . ": Kissinger, *Years of Upheaval,* p. 560.

Page 249   "I have been in the position . . .": quoted from the author's notes.

CHAPTER 10

Page 252   Author interview with Midwestern Democratic fund-raiser, on condition of anonymity, November 6, 1990.

Page 252   "[W]hile Jews have become . . .": Isaacs, *Jews and American Politics,* pp. 201–202.

Page 253   On "ghetto mentality," see Isaacs, pp. 214–215.

Page 253   On Jews serving as governors and in Congress, see Isaacs, p. 235 ff. On states never electing Jews, see Isaacs, p. 203.

Page 255   Author interview with Senator Howard Metzenbaum, July 28, 1993.

Page 255   Author interview with Senator Joseph Lieberman, October 27, 1992.

Page 257   Author interview with Dan Glickman, July 16, 1992.

Page 263   Author interview with House aide, on condition of anonymity, October 19, 1993.

Page 264   Author interview with Senate aide, on condition of anonymity, May 11, 1995.

Page 265   Author interview with Frank Lautenberg, May 30, 1995.

Page 265   Author interview with Major Owens, March 14, 1994.

Page 266   Author interview with John Lewis, March 13, 1994.

Page 266   Author interview with Washington researcher, on condition of anonymity, March 23, 1993.

Page 266   Israel-related voting study by Organski, *The $36 Billion Bargain,* pp. 219–242. Organski analyzed 130 senators who served during a 12-year period and voted on at least eight of the forty-four Middle East–related bills he used for reference.

Page 266   Organski's study of pro-Israel PACs was based on a list compiled by investigative reporter John Fialka of the *Wall Street Journal.* Organski studied individual Jewish donors by examining Federal Election Commission records and selecting Jewish surnames according to a statistical method developed by A.B. Data, a Milwaukee marketing firm.

Page 267   "Money . . . is not . . .": Organski, p. 73.

Page 268   "But why . . .": Organski, p. 73.

Page 268   Author interview with James Zogby, April 14, 1993.

Page 269   Author interview with anti-Israel activist, on condition of anonymity, December 1992.

Page 269   Author interview with senior House aide, on condition of anonymity, May 1993.

Page 269   Author interview with former AIPAC staffer, on condition of anonymity, March 15, 1994.

Page 270   Details on Percy in Findley, *They Dare to Speak Out,* p. 109f.; also in Sachar, *A History of the Jews in America,* p. 873.

Page 270   Iowa Senate race in Tivnan, *The Lobby,* p. 192f.

Page 271   "Surely they realized . . .": Findley, p. 23.

Page 272   Author interview with Washington political consultant, on condition of anonymity, January 21, 1993.

Page 273   PAC figures in Philip M. Stern, *Still the Best Congress Money Can Buy,* p. 45.

Page 273   Pro-Israel PACs listed in Organski, p. 222–223.

Page 274   Comparison of pro-Israel and other PACs in Stern, p. 14.

Page 274   PAC figures in Stern, p. 13 (AT&T); p. 41 (dairy industry); p. 313ff (hundred largest).

Page 275   Author interview with political consultant, on condition of anonymity, January 21, 1993.

Page 276   Author interview with Hyman Bookbinder, April 26, 1993.

CHAPTER 11

Page 279   Sulzberger anecdote from Will Maslow, then a reporter with the *New York Times* and later an official in the Roosevelt administration.

Page 280   Statistics on Jews in journalism from Silberman, *A Certain People,* p. 152. Silberman's notes (p. 394) cite academic studies in *Public Opinion, American Sociological Review,* and the Indiana University School of Journalism.

Page 280   "The New Establishment," *Vanity Fair,* October 1994, Of the twenty-three cited, eleven were Jews: Gerald Levin of Time-Warner, Michael Eisner of Disney, Sumner Redstone of Viacom, Barry Diller of QVC, Edgar Bronfman Jr. of Seagram (and now of MCA), Michael Ovitz of CAA (now of Disney), Herbert Allen of Allen & Company, David Geffen, Jeffrey Katzenberg, Steven Spielberg, and Barbra Streisand.

The non-Jewish kingpins were Ted Turner, Warren Buffett, Oprah Winfrey, Rupert Murdoch, Bill Gates of Microsoft, John Malone of TCI, Robert Allen of AT&T, Ray Smith of Bell Atlantic, H. Wayne Huizenga of Blockbuster, James C. Kennedy of Cox Enterprises, Scott Sassa of Turner Entertainment, and Craig McCaw of McCaw Cellular.

Page 280   "Information Age" quote from *Vanity Fair,* October 1994, p. 209.

Page 280   Author interview with Eugene Fisher, December 21, 1992.

Page 281   Author interview with Morley Safer, January 18, 1996.

Page 281   The question on media fairness is question no. 33 in the 1994 National Survey of American Jews, conducted by the Institute on American Jewish-Israeli Relations of the American Jewish Committee. The 1989 poll by the same organization asked about television coverage of Palestinian riots and Israeli response: agree or disagree "that the press treated Israelis unfairly" (p. 4).

Page 281   Author interview with Stephen D. Isaacs, June 17, 1992.

Page 282   Author interview with Anthony Lewis, January 1985.

Page 282   Author interview with Mike Wallace, February 4, 1994.

Page 282   Author interview with Richard Roth, January 16, 1996.

Page 283   Veblen, *Essays in Our Changing Order,* p. 221–226, quoted in Silberman, p. 146. Silberman's survey of explanations for the Jewish role in contemporary American culture is the most succinct roundup I have found.

Page 283   Berlin, "over-intense admiration," from *Against the Current: Essays in the History of Ideas,* p. 258, quoted in Gabler, *An Empire of Their Own,* p. 2.; "finest forms" from *Jewish Slavery and Emancipation* (Herzl Press pamphlet, 1961), quoted in Silberman, p. 147f.

Page 283   Richard Cohen quoted in Silberman, p. 154.

Page 284   Author interview with Safer.

Page 284   *The Protocols of the Learned Elders of Zion,* "Victor E. Marsden" (standard) translation of Russian original, first published 1934, p. 19.

Page 284   *The International Jew: The World's Foremost Problem,* (anthology of articles from the *Dearborn Independent*), p. 145. Abridged version published by Omni Publications, Hawthorne, California, no date.

Page 284   "It is only . . . blunder so badly," anonymous quote cited by Gabler, p. 2, citing a 1942 study of anti-Semitism.

Page 285   Hymers and Wildmon each quoted in "2 Step Back From Film Protest Over Anti-Jewish Tone," by John Dart, *Los Angeles Times,* July 23, 1988, Metro section, p. 1.

Page 286   Regarding Jewish images in film, see Lester D. Friedman, *Hollywood's Image of the Jew,* and the more recent works of *Village Voice* film critic J. Hoberman.

Page 286   Gabler, p. 6.

Page 288   Jewish "59 percent" figure cited by writer Philip Weiss in "Letting Go," *New York* magazine, January 29, 1996, p. 32, citing Seymour Martin Lipset and Earl Raab.

Page 288   Clegg's "If Jewish leaders" speech quoted in the *Los Angeles Times,* July 11, 1990.

Page 289   Author interview with Legrand H. Clegg II, February 3, 1993.

Page 289   Author interview with David Lehrer, February 5, 1993.

Page 290   Author interview with Carol Plotkin, February 5, 1993.

Page 291   Admiral Bobby Inman's reference to the Safire attack on him as "new McCarthyism" came in a press conference on January 18, 1994; the transcript appeared in the *Washington Post,* January 19, 1994.

Page 292   Barry interviewed on radio program *On the Line,* WNYC-AM, January 19, 1994.

Page 292   Author interview with Robert Pierpoint, May 2, 1995.

Page 293   Author interview with Sanford Socolow, April 28, 1995.

Page 293   Author interview with David Gelber, April 27, 1995.

Page 294   Author interview with Socolow.

Page 294   Author interview with Mike Wallace, February 4, 1994.

Page 295   Account of Pierpoint incident based on author interview with Robert Pierpoint, May 2, 1995, as well as account in Findley, *They Dare to Speak Out,* p. 307f. *National Geographic* incident described in Findley, p. 304ff.

Page 296   Author interview with Wallace.

Page 297   The Tisch rumor appears in part to have been spread by CBS chairman Tom Wyman in a bid to deflect a Tisch takeover. See Auletta, *Three Blind Mice,* p. 164. Wyman denied saying it, but other insiders claim to have heard it—and to have agreed.

Page 298   Author interview with Wallace.

Page 298   Author interview with Gelber.

Page 299   Author interview with Martin Peretz, February 25, 1993.

Page 301   Sulzberger, Jr. quoted in Goldman, *The Search for God at Harvard,* p. 155.

Page 302   Talese quoted in Goldman, p. 156.

Page 302   Author interview with A. M. Rosenthal, May 3, 1995.

Page 304   Author interview with *New York Times* staffers, on condition of anonymity, September 20, 1993, and August 15, 1993.

Page 304   Author interview with *New York Times* reporter, on condition of anonymity, January 11, 1996.

CHAPTER 12

Page 306   Hasidic ad in *New York Times,* September 20, 1991, p. A21.

Page 307   Author interview with David Luchins, September 2, 1992.

Page 308   Richard H. Girgenti, *A Report to the Governor on the Disturbances in Crown Heights,* vol. 1, pp. 341–342.

Page 308   Sharpton quoted in Kenneth S. Stern, *Crown Heights: A Case Study in Anti-Semitism and Community Relations,* pp. 4–5.

Page 313   Author interview with Eugene Fisher, December 21, 1992.

Page 313   Author interview with Eleanor Holmes Norton, February 5, 1993.

Page 314   Author interview with Will Maslow, December 23, 1992.

Page 315   On King and Levison, see Murray Friedman, *What Went Wrong?,* p. 163f. Friedman devotes much space to Levison's alleged (but still unproven) ties to the Communist Party, which were the object of extensive FBI surveillance. Levison was also an officer of the American Jewish Congress.

Page 316   One of the most comprehensive examinations of the paradox of Jewish ethical motivations for going South appears in Murray Friedman's *What Went Wrong?.*

Page 317   Author interview with Calvin Butts, February 5, 1993.

Page 317   Murray Friedman quoted from his lecture at American Jewish Committee headquarters, New York, March 7, 1995.

Page 317   Author interview with William Gibson, February 3, 1993.

Page 318   Black reactions to *Bakke,* including Jones quote, from Murray Friedman, *What Went Wrong?,* p. 314.

Page 319   Author interview with Jack Greenberg, July 14, 1993.

Page 321   Author interview with Irving Levine, March 8, 1995.

Page 321   Podhoretz, "Is It Good for the Jews?", p. 12.

Page 321   Author conversation with Sheldon Waldon, March 1993.

Page 322   Hatcher quoted in "Leaders Try to Avert Rift Between Blacks and Jews," *New York Times,* August 19, 1979, p. A1.

Page 322   Black summit quotes from reports in the *New York Times:* "Black Leaders Air Grievances on Jews," August 23, 1979; "Black Leaders' Meeting: 'Watershed' Effort for Unanimity," August 24, 1979, p. A11.

Page 323   Author interview with Alexander Schindler, March 30, 1993.

Page 324   Jackson's "Jews were willing to share" quote from "Leaders Try to Avert Rift Between Blacks and Jews," *New York Times,* August 19, 1979, p. A1.

Page 324   Murray Friedman, *What Went Wrong?,* p. 330.

Page 326   Author interview with Clarence Wood, February 7, 1993.

Page 327   Author interview with Jesse Jackson, December 10, 1992.

Page 328   Author interview with Leonard Jeffries, February 4, 1993.

Page 328   Author interview with Eleanor Holmes Norton, February 5, 1993.

Page 329   Author interview with Don Rojas, February 8, 1993.

Page 330   Author interview with Donna Brazile, February 3, 1993.

Page 330   Author interview with Jerome Chanes, February 4, 1993.

Page 330   The 1969 survey was *The Tenacity of Prejudice: Anti-Semitism in Contemporary America,* by Gertrude J. Selznick and Stephen Steinberg. It is cited in Quinley and Glock, p. 56. The 1992 survey was conducted for the Anti-Defamation League by Marttila & Kiley, Inc., Boston, April 28–May 1, 1992. It was published on November 16, 1992 as *Highlights from an Anti-Defamation League Survey on Anti-Semitism and Prejudice in America.*

Page 331   Author interview with Calvin Butts, February 5, 1993.

Page 332   Author interview with Sam Domb, September 28, 1989.

Page 333   Avi Weiss, "Sounding Off Against Fear," New York *Jewish Week,* September 9–15, 1994, p. 5.

Page 335   Author interview with Patricia Reeburg, February 5, 1993.

CHAPTER 13

Page 338   The status of Conservative-rite conversions under the bill was unclear. Conservative rabbis, devoted to *halakha,* observe canon law but do not require converts (or any other congregants) to live a traditionally observant life. Accordingly, Conservative rabbis were slow to join the protests against the bill, but the Conservative laity correctly interpreted the bill as an attack on its nonobservant lifestyle.

Page 339   Shamir's expectations reconstructed from author interviews with Shoshana Cardin, Israeli justice minister Dan Meridor, Israeli cabinet secretary Eliakim Rubinstein, and others.

Page 339   Michel comment from interview with Jewish Telegraphic Agency, quoted in David Landau, *Who Is A Jew?*, p. 23.

Page 340   Author interview with Shoshana Cardin, October 15, 1992.

Page 340   Author interview with Dan Meridor, May 21, 1993.

Page 341   Author interview with Cardin.

Page 342   Author interview with Uriel Palti, March 19, 1993.

Page 343   Author interview with Cardin.

Page 344   Shamir quoted by Cardin to author.

Page 345   Author interview with Moshe Prywes, November 1991.

Page 347   Author's reporting of Beilin's Presidents Conference visit, August 1992.

Page 348   Author's reporting of Beilin's CJF visit, 1993.

Page 348   Beilin's remarks about the UJA were made repeatedly and were widely reported in most Jewish community weeklies throughout the winter and spring of 1994.

Page 349   "... like pulling teeth" quoted from author interview with editor, on condition of anonymity, spring 1995. "People have a lot of concerns" quoted from author interview with Malcolm Hoenlein, December 1994.

Page 352   Author interview with Irwin Hochberg, June 1988.

Page 355   Goodman and Fisher quotes from author's notes of CJF meeting, April 16, 1991.

Page 355   Author interview with Vince Stehle, April 16, 1991.

Page 356   Author interview with agency head, on condition of anonymity, April 16, 1991.

Page 357   Foxman quote from author's notes of CJF meeting, 1992.

Page 358   Author interview with Bruce Arbit, March 12, 1996.

Page 359   Norich, *What Will Bind Us Now?: A Report on the Institutional Ties between Israel and American Jewry*, p. 1.

Page 359   Pre-1970 figures: *American Jewish Year Book, 1972*, p. 271. Post-1970 figures: Council of Jewish Federations.

Page 361   Author interview with Arbit.

Page 362   Akiva Eldar, "Standing Upright," *Ha'aretz*, January 15, 1996. Translation by Israel Government Press Office.

Page 364   Clinton's Jewish cabinet secretaries include Robert Reich (Labor), Robert Rubin (Treasury), Dan Glickman (Agriculture), Mickey Kantor (Commerce). Ambassador to Israel is Martin Indyk; CIA director is John Deutch.

Page 364   Author interview with David Twersky, March 28, 1996.

Page 366   Author interview with agency head, on condition of anonymity, April 24, 1996.

Page 366   Author interview with Deborah Pell, March 12, 1996.

BIBLIOGRAPHY

ARTICLES AND MONOGRAPHS

Highlights from an Anti-Defamation League Survey on Anti-Semitism and Prejudice in America. Conducted by Marttila & Kiley, Inc., Boston. New York: Anti-Defamation League, November 16, 1992.

Albright, Joseph. "The Pact of the Two Henrys: How the Deal to Buy Jews from Russia Grew from a Moral Impulse into the Unwanted Policy of Two Superpowers." *New York Times Magazine,* January 5, 1975.

Chanes, Jerome. "Affirmative Action: Jewish Ideals, Jewish Interests—The Evolution of a Jewish Communal Stance." In *Who's Driving Miss Daisy's Car? A History of Black-Jewish Relations,* edited by Jack Salzman and Cornel West. New York: Oxford University Press, forthcoming.

Cohen, Naomi W. "The Abrogation of the Russo-American Treaty of 1832." *Jewish Social Studies.*

Cohen, Renae, and Sherry Rosen. *Organizational Affiliation of American Jews: A Research Report.* New York: American Jewish Committee, 1992.

Cohen, Steven M. *Attitudes of American Jews toward Israel and Israelis: The 1983 Survey of American Jews and Jewish Communal Leaders.* New York: Institute on American Jewish-Israeli Relations of the American Jewish Committee, September 1983.

———. *Content or Continuity? Alternative Bases for Commitment.* New York: American Jewish Committee, 1991.

———. *The Dimensions of American Jewish Liberalism.* New York: American Jewish Committee, 1989.

———. *Israel-Diaspora Relations: A Survey of American Jewish Leaders.* Ramat Aviv, Israel: Israel-Diaspora Institute, January 1990.

———. *Ties and Tensions: The 1989 Survey of American Jewish Attitudes toward Israel and Israelis.* New York: American Jewish Committee, July 1989.

Elazar, Daniel J. "Israel and the Diaspora Must Unite to Struggle against Those Who Want a World That Is Good for Jews but Not Necessarily for Jewishness or Judaism." *Moment,* October 1995.

Finestein, Israel. "1939–1989: Assessing the Changes in Jewry." In *Survey of*

Jewish Affairs, 1990, edited by William Frankel. London: Institute of Jewish Affairs, 1990.

Goldstein, Sidney. "Profile of American Jewry: Insights from the 1990 National Jewish Population Survey." *American Jewish Year Book, 1992.* Vol. 92. New York: American Jewish Committee; Philadelphia: Jewish Publication Society, 1992.

Handlin, Mary F., and Oscar Handlin. "The Acquisition of Political and Social Rights by the Jews in the United States." *American Jewish Year Book, 1955.* Vol. 56.

Howe, Irving. "For Free Discussion in the Jewish Community." *InterChange,* June 1976.

Korey, William. "The Cacophony of Hate at the UN." *Midstream,* August–September 1967.

———. "The Struggle over Jackson-Mills-Vanik." *American Jewish Year Book, 1974–75.* Vol. 75.

———. "The Struggle Over the Jackson Amendment," *American Jewish Year Book, 1976.* Vol. 76.

Kosmin, Barry A., et al. *Highlights of the CJF 1990 National Jewish Population Survey.* New York: Council of Jewish Federations, 1991.

Kristol, Irving. "The Future of American Jewry." *Commentary,* August 1991.

Landau, David. *Who Is a Jew? A Case Study of American Jewish Influence on Israeli Policy.* New York: American Jewish Committee, 1996.

Lefkowitz, Jay P. "Jewish Voters and the Democrats." *Commentary,* April 1993.

Lind, Michael. "Rev. Robertson's Grand International Conspiracy Theory." *New York Review of Books,* February 2, 1995.

Lubet, Steven. "That's Funny, You Don't Look Like You Control the Government: The Sixth Circuit's Narrative on Jewish Power." *Hastings Law Journal,* August 1994.

Masaryk, Fred, and Alvin Chenkin. "United States National Jewish Population Study: A First Report." *American Jewish Year Book, 1973.* Vol. 74.

Medding, Peter. "Towards a General Theory of Jewish Political Interests and Behaviour." *Jewish Journal of Sociology,* December 1977.

——— et al. "Jewish Identity in Conversionary and Mixed Marriages." *American Jewish Year Book, 1992.*

Meier, Deborah. "The New York Teachers' Strike." *Midstream,* November 1967.

Norich, Samuel. *What Will Bind Us Now?: A Report on the Institutional Ties between Israel and American Jewry.* West Palm Beach, Fla.: Center for Middle East Peace and Economic Cooperation, 1994.

Novak, William. "The Breira Story." *Genesis 2,* March 16, 1977.

O'Shaughnessy, Elise, et al. "The New Establishment." *Vanity Fair,* October 1994.

Podhoretz, Norman. "Is It Good for the Jews?" *Commentary,* February 1972.

Smith, Tom W. *What Do Americans Think about Jews?* New York: American Jewish Committee, December 1991.

Stern, Kenneth S. *Crown Heights: A Case Study in Anti-Semitism and Com-*

munity Relations. New York: American Jewish Committee, September 1991.

Stern, Marc D. "Affirmative Action, the Law, and the Jews." In *Survey of Jewish Affairs, 1990,* edited by William Frankel. London: Institute of Jewish Affairs, 1990.

Tobin, Gary A., and Gabriel Berger. *Synagogue Affiliation: Implications for the 1990s.* Waltham, Mass.: Cohen Center for Modern Jewish Studies, 1993.

Weiss, Philip. "Letting Go," *New York,* January 29, 1996.

Wilson, Douglas. "Thomas Jefferson and the Character Issue." *The Atlantic,* November 1992.

BOOKS

Alexander, Edward, ed. *With Friends Like These: The Jewish Critics of Israel.* New York: Shapolsky, 1993.

Ambrose, Stephen A. *Nixon: The Triumph of a Politician, 1962–72.* New York: Simon & Schuster, 1989.

Auletta, Ken. *Three Blind Mice: How the TV Networks Lost Their Way.* New York: Random House, Vintage Books, 1991.

Ball, George W., and Douglas B. Ball, *The Passionate Attachment: America's Involvement with Israel, 1947 to the Present.* New York: Norton, 1992.

Bard, Mitchell Geoffrey. *The Water's Edge and Beyond: Defining the Limits to Domestic Influence on United States Middle East Policy.* New Brunswick, N.J.: Transaction, 1991.

Bauer, Yehuda. *My Brother's Keeper: A History of the American Jewish Joint Distribution Committee, 1929–1939.* Philadelphia: Jewish Publication Society of America, 1974.

———. *American Jewry and the Holocaust: The American Jewish Joint Distribution Committee, 1939–1945.* Detroit: Wayne State University Press, 1981.

Bernstein, Philip. *To Dwell in Unity: The Jewish Federation Movement in America since 1960.* Philadelphia: Jewish Publication Society of America, 1983.

Biale, David. *Power and Powerlessness in Jewish History.* New York: Schocken Books, 1986.

Birmingham, Stephen. *Our Crowd: The Great Jewish Families of New York.* New York: Harper & Row, 1967.

Bookbinder, Hyman. *Off the Wall: Memoirs of a Public Affairs Junkie.* Washington, D.C.: Seven Locks Press, 1991.

Borden, Morton. *Jews, Turks, and Infidels.* Chapel Hill: University of North Carolina Press, 1984.

Brownstein, Ronald. *The Power and the Glitter: The Hollywood-Washington Connection.* New York: Random House, Vintage Books, 1992.

Burt, Robert A. *Two Jewish Justices: Outcasts in the Promised Land.* Berkeley: University of California Press, 1988.

Carruth, Gorton, et al., eds. *The Encyclopedia of American Facts and Dates*. New York: Thomas Y. Crowell, 1962.

Chomsky, Noam. *The Fateful Triangle: The United States, Israel, and the Palestinians*. Boston: South End Press, 1983.

Cockburn, Alexander, and Leslie Cockburn. *Dangerous Liaison: The Inside Story of the U.S.-Israel Relationship*. New York: HarperCollins, 1991.

Cohen, Naomi W. *Jews in Christian America: The Pursuit of Religious Equality*. New York: Oxford University Press, 1992.

————. *Not Free to Desist: A History of the American Jewish Committee, 1906–1966*. Philadelphia: Jewish Publication Society of America, 1972.

Cohen, Steven M. *American Modernity and Jewish Identity*. New York: Tavistock Publications, 1983.

Comay, Joan. *The Diaspora Story*. Tel Aviv: Steimatzky's Agency; London: George Weidenfeld & Nicolson, 1981.

Davis, David Brion. *Slavery and Human Progress*. New York: Oxford University Press, 1984.

Dershowitz, Alan. *Chutzpah*. New York: Simon & Schuster, Touchstone Books, 1991.

Dinnerstein, Leonard. *America and the Survivors of the Holocaust*. New York: Columbia University Press, 1982.

Donovan, Robert J., and staff of *Los Angeles Times*. *Six Days in June: Israel's Fight for Survival*. New York: New American Library, Signet Books, 1967.

Dorrien, Gary. *The Neoconservative Mind: Politics, Culture, and the War of Ideology*. Philadelphia: Temple University Press, 1993.

Drachman, Edward. *Challenging the Kremlin: The Soviet Jewish Movement for Freedom, 1967–1990*. New York: Paragon House, 1991.

Elazar, Daniel J. *Community and Polity: The Organizational Dynamics of American Jewry*. Philadelphia: Jewish Publication Society of America, 1980.

Findley, Paul. *They Dare to Speak Out: People and Institutions Confront Israel's Lobby*. Chicago: Lawrence Hill Books, 1989.

Forster, Arnold. *Square One*. New York: Donald I. Fine, 1988.

————. *An Oral Memoir about the Anti-Defamation League of B'nai B'rith from 1938 to 1985*. Unpublished manuscript, December 1985.

Fried, Albert. *Rise and Fall of the Jewish Gangster in America*. New York: Holt, Rinehart & Winston, 1980.

Friedman, Lee M. *Jewish Pioneers and Patriots*. Philadelphia: Jewish Publication Society of America, 1942.

Friedman, Lester D. *Hollywood's Image of the Jew*. New York: Frederick Ungar, 1982.

Friedman, Murray. *What Went Wrong? The Creation and Collapse of the Black-Jewish Alliance*. New York: Free Press, 1995.

Gabler, Neal. *An Empire of Their Own: How the Jews Invented Hollywood*. New York: Crown Publishers, 1988; New York, Doubleday, Anchor Books, 1988.

Gerson, Allan. *The Kirkpatrick Mission: Diplomacy without Apology: America at the United Nations, 1981–1985.* New York: Free Press, 1991.

Gilman, Sander L. *Jewish Self-Hatred: Anti-Semitism and the Hidden Language of the Jews.* Baltimore: Johns Hopkins University Press, 1986.

Ginsberg, Benjamin. *The Fatal Embrace: Jews and the State.* Chicago: University of Chicago Press, 1993.

Girgenti, Richard H., New York State Director of Criminal Justice. *A Report to the Governor on the Disturbances in Crown Heights.* Vol. 1. Albany, July 1993.

Glazer, Nathan, and Daniel Patrick Moynihan. *Beyond the Melting Pot: The Negroes, Puerto Ricans, Jews, Italians, and Irish of New York City.* Cambridge, Mass.: MIT Press, 1963.

Golan, Mati. *With Friends Like You: What Israelis Really Think about American Jews.* New York: Free Press, 1992.

Golden, Peter. *Quiet Diplomat: A Biography of Max M. Fisher.* New York: Herzl Press, 1992.

Goldin, Milton. *Why They Give: American Jews and Their Philanthropies.* New York: Macmillan, 1976.

Goldman, Ari L. *The Search for God at Harvard.* New York: Times Books, 1991.

Goldmann, Nahum. *The Autobiography of Nahum Goldmann: Sixty Years of Jewish Life.* Translated by Helen Sebba. New York: Holt, Rinehart & Winston, 1969.

Goldscheider, Calvin, and Alan S. Zuckerman. *The Transformation of the Jews.* Chicago and London: University of Chicago Press, 1984.

Goulden, Joseph C. *Fit to Print: A. M. Rosenthal and His Times.* Secaucus, N.J.: Lyle Stuart, 1988.

Green, Stephen. *Taking Sides: America's Secret Relations with a Militant Israel.* New York: William Morrow, 1984.

Gribetz, Judah, with Edward L. Greenstein and Regina Stein. *The Timetables of Jewish History: A Chronology of the Most Important People and Events in Jewish History.* New York: Simon & Schuster, 1993.

Grose, Peter. *Israel in the Mind of America.* New York: Alfred A. Knopf, 1984.

Hacker, Andrew. *Two Nations: Black and White, Separate, Hostile, Unequal.* New York: Scribner's, 1992; New York: Ballantine Books, 1993.

Halberstam, David. *The Powers That Be.* New York: Alfred A. Knopf, 1979.

Hersh, Seymour M. *The Price of Power: Kissinger in the Nixon White House.* New York: Summit Books, 1983.

Hertzberg, Arthur. *The Jews in America: Four Centuries of an Uneasy Encounter: A History.* New York: Simon & Schuster, 1989.

Himmelfarb, Milton. *The Jews of Modernity.* New York: Basic Books, 1973.

Hoffman, Charles. *The Smokescreen: Israel, Philanthropy, and American Jews.* Silver Spring, Maryland: Eshel Books, 1989.

The Holy Scriptures According to the Masoretic Text. Vol. 1. Philadelphia: Jewish Publication Society of America, 1955.

Isaacs, Stephen D. *Jews and American Politics*. Garden City, N.Y.: Doubleday, 1974.

Isaacson, Walter. *Kissinger: A Biography*. New York: Simon & Schuster, 1992.

Jacobs, Paul. *Is Curly Jewish? A Political Self-Portrait Illuminating Three Turbulent Decades of Social Revolt, 1935–1965*. New York: Atheneum, 1965; New York: Random House, Vintage Books, 1973.

Kampelman, Max M. *Entering New Worlds: The Memoirs of a Private Man in Public Life*. New York: HarperCollins, 1991.

Karetzky, Stephen, and Peter E. Goldman, eds. *The Media's War Against Israel*. New York: Shapolsky, 1986.

Karpf, Maurice J. *Jewish Community Organization in the United States: An Outline of Types of Organizations, Activities, and Problems*. New York: Bloch, 1938.

Kaufman, Jonathan. *Broken Alliance: The Turbulent Times Between Blacks and Jews in America*. New York: Scribner's, 1988.

Kenen, I. L. *Israel's Defense Line: Her Friends and Foes in Washington*. Buffalo, N.Y.: Prometheus Books, 1981.

Kissinger, Henry. *Diplomacy*. New York: Simon & Schuster, 1994.

———. *White House Years*. Boston: Little, Brown, 1979.

———. *Years of Upheaval*. Boston: Little, Brown, 1982.

Klutznick, Philip M., with Sidney Hyman. *Angles of Vision: A Memoir of My Lives*. Chicago: Ivan R. Dee, 1991.

Laqueur, Walter, ed. *The Israel-Arab Reader: A Documentary History of the Middle East Conflict*. New York: Bantam Books, 1969.

Learsi, Rufus. *The Jews in America: A History*. New York: Ktav, 1972.

———. *Fulfillment: The Epic Story of Zionism*. Cleveland and New York: World, 1951.

Levin, Nora. *While Messiah Tarried: Jewish Socialist Movements, 1871–1917*. New York: Schocken Books, 1977.

Levine, Hillel. *Economic Origins of Anti-Semitism: Poland and Its Jews in the Early Modern Period*. New Haven: Yale University Press, 1991.

Levitan, Tina. *Jews in American Life*. New York: Hebrew Publishing, 1969.

Levkov, Ilya, ed. *Bitburg and Beyond: Encounters in American, German, and Jewish History*. New York: Shapolsky, 1987.

Lewis, David Levering. *W.E.B. Du Bois: Biography of a Race, 1868–1919*. New York: Henry Holt, 1993.

Liebman, Charles, and Steven M. Cohen. *The Two Worlds of Judaism*. New Haven: Yale University Press, 1990.

Lipstadt, Deborah E. *Denying the Holocaust: The Growing Assault on Truth and Memory*. New York: Free Press, 1993.

Lookstein, Haskell. *Were We Our Brothers' Keepers? The Public Response of American Jews to the Holocaust, 1938–1944*. New York: Hartmore House, 1985; New York: Random House, Vintage Books, 1988.

Miller, Judith. *One, by One, by One: Facing the Holocaust*. New York: Simon & Schuster, 1990.

Miller, Merle. *Lyndon: An Oral Biography*. New York: Ballantine Books, 1980.

Morris, Robert, and Michael Freund, eds. *Trends and Issues in Jewish Social Welfare in the United States, 1899–1952*. Philadelphia: Jewish Publication Society of America, 1966.

Morse, Arthur D. *While Six Million Died: A Chronicle of American Apathy*. New York: Random House, 1967; New York: Ace Books, 1968.

Organski, A. F. K. *The $36 Billion Bargain: Strategy and Politics in U.S. Assistance to Israel*. New York: Columbia University Press, 1990.

Persico, Joseph E. *Nuremberg: Infamy on Trial*. New York: Viking Penguin, 1994.

Pogrebin, Letty Cottin. *Deborah, Golda, and Me: Being Female and Jewish in America*. New York: Doubleday, Anchor Books, 1991.

Porter, Jack Nusan, and Peter Dreier, eds. *Jewish Radicalism: A Selected Anthology*. New York: Grove Press, 1973.

Quandt, William. *Decade of Decisions: American Policy Toward the Arab-Israeli Conflict, 1967–1976*. Berkeley: University of California Press, 1977.

———. *Peace Process: American Diplomacy and the Arab-Israeli Conflict since 1967*. Washington, D.C.: Brookings Institution and Berkeley: University of California Press, 1993.

Quinley, Harold E. and Charles Y. Glock. *Anti-Semitism in America*. New York: Free Press, 1979.

Raphael, Marc Lee. *Jews and Judaism in the United States: A Documentary History*. New York: Behrman House, 1983.

Redman, Eric. *The Dance of Legislation*. New York: Simon & Schuster, Touchstone Books, 1973.

Roberts, Sam. *Who We Are: A Portrait of America Based on the Latest U.S. Census*. New York: Random House, Times Books, 1993.

Roth, Cecil. *A History of the Marranos*. 5th ed. New York: Sepher-Hermon Press, 1992.

Ryan, Jr., Allan A. *Quiet Neighbors: Prosecuting Nazi War Criminals in America*. San Diego and New York: Harcourt Brace Jovanovich, 1984.

Sachar, Howard M. *The Course of Modern Jewish History*. New York: Dell, 1958.

———. *A History of the Jews in America*. New York: Alfred A. Knopf, 1992.

Safire, William. *Before the Fall: An Inside View of the Pre-Watergate Nixon White House*. Garden City, N.Y.: Doubleday, 1975.

Sarna, Jonathan D. *Jacksonian Jew: The Two Worlds of Mordecai Manuel Noah*. New York: Holmes & Meier, 1981.

Schappes, Morris U., ed. *A Documentary History of the Jews in the United States, 1654–1875*. 3d ed. New York: Schocken Books, 1971.

Segev, Tom. *The Seventh Million: The Israelis and the Holocaust*. Translated by Haim Watzman. New York: Hill & Wang, 1993.

Shevchenko, Arkady N. *Breaking with Moscow*. New York: Ballantine Books, 1985.

Shultz, George P. *Turmoil and Triumph: My Years as Secretary of State*. New York: Scribner's, 1993.

Silberman, Charles. *A Certain People: American Jews and Their Lives Today*. New York: Summit Books, 1985.

Simons, Howard. *Jewish Times: Voices of the American Jewish Experience*. Boston: Houghton Mifflin, 1988.

Sklare, Marshall. *Observing America's Jews*. Hanover, N.H.: University Press of New England, 1993.

Sklare, Marshall, and Joseph Greenblum. *Jewish Identity on the Suburban Frontier: A Study of Group Survival in the Open Society*. New York: Basic Books, 1967.

Slater, Robert. *Rabin of Israel*. New York: St. Martin's Press, 1993.

Sloan, Irving J. *The Jews in America, 1621–1970: A Chronology and Fact Book*. Dobbs Ferry, N.Y.: Oceana Publishers, 1971.

Smith, Hedrick. *The Power Game: How Washington Works*. New York: Random House, 1988; New York: Ballantine Books, 1989.

Smith, Sally Bedell. *In All His Glory: The Life of William S. Paley*. New York: Simon & Schuster, Touchstone Books, 1990.

Spanier, John, and Eric M. Uslaner. *American Foreign Policy Making and the Democratic Dilemmas*. Pacific Grove, Calif.: Brooks/Cole, 1989.

Spiegel, Steven L. *The Other Arab-Israeli Conflict: Making America's Middle East Policy, from Truman to Reagan*. Chicago and London: University of Chicago Press, 1985.

Stember, Charles Herbert, et al. *Jews in the Mind of America*. New York: Basic Books, 1966.

Stern, Philip M. *Still the Best Congress Money Can Buy*. Washington, D.C.: Regnery Gateway, 1992.

Stern, Selma. *The Court Jew: A Contribution to the History of the Period of Absolutism in Central Europe*. Philadelphia: Jewish Publication Society of America, 1950.

Strober, Gerald S., and Deborah H. Strober. *"Let Us Begin Anew": An Oral History of the Kennedy Presidency*. New York: HarperCollins, 1993.

Strum, Philippa. *Louis D. Brandeis: Justice for the People*. New York: Schocken Books, 1984.

Tivnan, Edward. *The Lobby: Jewish Political Power and American Foreign Policy*. New York: Simon & Schuster, 1987.

Tocqueville, Alexis de. *Democracy in America*. Vol. I. Translated by Henry Reeve, revised by Francis Bowen, corrected and edited by Phillips Bradley. New York: Alfred A. Knopf, 1945; New York: Random House, Vintage Books edition.

Urofsky, Melvin I. *American Zionism from Herzl to the Holocaust*. Garden City, N.Y.: Doubleday, Anchor Press, 1975.

van den Haag, Ernest. *The Jewish Mystique*. New York: Dell, 1969.

Vorspan, Albert, and David Saperstein. *Tough Choices: Jewish Perspectives on Social Justice*. New York: UAHC Press, 1992.

Voss, Carl Hermann, ed. *Stephen S. Wise: Servant of the People, Selected Letters*. Philadelphia: Jewish Publication Society of America, 1969.

Wallace, Mike, and Gary Paul Gates. *Close Encounters*. New York: William Morrow, 1984.

Watson, Denton L. *Lion in the Lobby: Clarence Mitchell, Jr.'s Struggle for the Passage of Civil Rights Laws*. New York: William Morrow, 1990.

Wertheimer, Jack. *A People Divided: Judaism in Contemporary America*. New York: HarperCollins, Basic Books, 1993.

Westin, Alan F., ed. *Freedom Now: The Civil-Rights Struggle in America*. New York: Basic Books, 1964.

Wiesel, Elie. *A Jew Today*. Translated from French by Marion Wiesel. New York: Random House, Vintage Books, 1978.

———. *The Jews of Silence*. New York: Holt, Rinehart & Winston, 1966.

Wisse, Ruth. *If I Am Not for Myself: The Liberal Betrayal of the Jews*. New York: Free Press, 1992.

Wistrich, Robert. *Antisemitism: The Longest Hatred*. New York: Pantheon Books, 1991.

Wolfe, Ann G., ed. *A Reader in Jewish Community Relations*. New York: Ktav, 1975.

Woocher, Jonathan S. *Sacred Survival: The Civil Religion of American Jews*. Bloomington, Ind.: Indiana University Press, 1986.

Wyman, David S. *The Abandonment of the Jews: America and the Holocaust, 1941–1945*. New York: Pantheon Books, 1984.

Young, James E. *The Texture of Memory: Holocaust Memorials and Meaning*. New Haven: Yale University Press, 1993.

Yovel, Yirmiyahu. *Spinoza and Other Heretics: The Marrano of Reason*. Princeton, N.J.: Princeton University Press, 1989.

INDEX

Abington Township School District v. Schempp, 124
Abortion rights, 25, 41–43, 61
Abram, Morris B., 77, 166, 218, 219–220, 315
Abramowitz, Rabbi Philip, 310
Abrams, Elliot, 109, 110
Abrams, Robert, 272
Ackerman, Nathan, 131
ACLU. *See* American Civil Liberties Union
Adamishin, Anatoly, 236
Addis Ababa, Ethiopia, 236–237
ADL. *See* Anti-Defamation League
Adorno, Theodor, 131
Affiliation. *See* Jewish identity
Affirmative action, 317–320
AFL-CIO, xxv, 269
African-Americans. *See* Black Americans
Agudath Israel of America, 45, 60, 67, 155, 210, 353
AIPAC. *See* American Israel Public Affairs Committee
AJC. *See* American Jewish Committee
Algiers plan (of PLO), 247, 386n
Allen, Woody, 287
Allied Jewish Appeal, 107
Allied Patriotic Societies, 111
Almanac of American Politics, 42
Aloni, Miri, 372
American Association for Ethiopian Jews, 235, 236
American Civil Liberties Union (ACLU), 22, 23, 38, 121, 123
American Enterprise Institute, 32
American Family Association, 285
American Federation of Labor, 23–24
American Foreign Policy Making and the Democratic Dilemmas (Spanier & Uslaner), 198

American Friends of the Israel Museum of the Diaspora, 69
American Israel Public Affairs Committee (AIPAC)
  functions of, xviii, 52, 54, 60, 153, 223–225
  growth of, 199–203, 220, 222–223
  organizational politics in, 225–226
  political action committees and, 268–269, 275
  political alliances of, 213–214, 215, 220–221, 224–225
  political clout of, 13, 15, 197–202
American Jewish Committee (AJC), 4, 12–13, 22, 28, 38, 39, 40, 49, 50, 52, 55, 75, 104, 106, 107, 111, 121, 124–125, 126, 127, 128–129, 137, 138, 154, 166, 167, 180, 195, 207, 259, 275, 296, 310, 314, 315, 317, 320, 339
  Middle-East policies of, 151, 219
  origins of, 101–103
  post-World War II evolution of, 128, 130–132
  publication of *Commentary* by, 45, 160–161, 214, 321–322
  social survey by, 25–26, 56, 58, 70, 73, 79, 216
American Jewish Conference on Soviet Jewry. *See* National Conference on Soviet Jewry
American Jewish Congress, xviii, 12–13, 22, 31, 38, 39, 49, 50, 52, 75, 76, 101, 107, 134, 142, 207, 276, 287, 290, 295, 296, 303, 318
  Middle-East policies of, 177, 217, 218, 219
  organizational growth of, 128
  origins of, 103
  post-World War II antidiscrimination campaign of, 120–124, 314